Income Inequality
and Social Stratification:
Causes and Consequences

Lynchburg College Symposium Readings

Third Edition

2008

Volume VII

Income Inequality and Social Stratification: Causes and Consequences

Edited by

Joseph Turek, PhD

To order additional copies of this book, contact:
Xlibris Corporation
1-888-795-4274
www.Xlibris.com
Orders@Xlibris.com
23032

CONTENTS

ACKNOWLEDGEMENTS

From ECONOMIC JUSTICE FOR ALL by U. S. Catholic Bishops © 1986 by USCCB Publishing. Used by permission of United States Conference of Catholic Bishops.

From THE JUNGLE by Upton Sinclair, copyright 1905, 1906 by Upton Sinclair. Used by permission of Viking Penguin, a division of Penguin Group (USA) Inc.

Friedman, M. (September 13, 1970). "The Social Responsibility of Business is to Increase its Profits." The New York Times Magazine. Used by permission of The New York Times New Service Division.

From CAPITALISM AND FREEDOM by Friedman, M. © 1962. Used by permission of The University of Chicago Press.

Reprinted with the permission of Scribner, an imprint of Simon & Schuster Adult Publishing Group, from TWO NATIONS: BLACK AND WHITE, SEPARATE, UNEQUAL by Andrew Hacker. Copyright © 1992 by Andrew Hacker.

EQUALITY AND EFFICIENCY by Arthur M. Okun. © 1975. Used by permission of the Brookings Institute, Washington. D. C.

From. ATLAS SHRUGGED by Ayn Rand © 1957. New York: Dutton (Penguin Group). Used by permission of the Estate of Ayn Rand.

THE FRAGMENTATION OF SOCIAL LIFE by D. Stanley Eitzen © 2000. Used by permission of D. Stanley Eitzen.

Marx, Karl & Engels, Fredrick. 1848. *Manifesto of the Communist Party.* In the *Collected Works.* Marxist Internet Archive http://www.marxists. org/archive/marx/works/1848/communist-manifesto/. Marx/Engels Internet Archive (marxists.org) 1987, 2000. Permission is granted to copy and/or distribute this document under the terms of the Creative Commons Attribution-ShareAlike License.

The editors further acknowledge with thanks the dedicated work of Rachel Moore ('08) for her editorial assistance.

Lynchburg College Symposium Readings Senior Symposium and the LCSR Program

The ten-volume series, Lynchburg College Symposium Readings, has been developed by Lynchburg College faculty for use in the Senior Symposium and the Lynchburg College Symposium Readings Program (SS/LCSR). Each volume presents primary source material organized around interdisciplinary, liberal arts themes.

In 1976, the College developed the Senior Symposium as a two-hour, interdisciplinary course, required of all graduating seniors. On Mondays, students in all sections of the course come together for public lectures, given by invited guest speakers. On Wednesdays, Symposium students meet in their sections for student-led discussions and presentations on associated readings from the LCSR series. The course requires students, who have spent their later college years in narrowing the scope of their studies, to expand their fields of vision within a discussion group composed of and led by their peers. Students can apply analytical and problem-solving capabilities learned in their major fields of study to issues raised by guest speakers and classical readings.

This approach works against convention in higher education, which typically emphasizes the gradual exclusion of subject areas outside of a student's major field. But Senior Symposium leads students, poised for graduation, into their post-college intellectual responsibilities. They gain experience in taking their liberal education into real world problems, using it to address contemporary problems thoughtfully and critically. In order to do this successfully, students must abandon their habitual posture as docile receptors of authoritative information for a much more skeptical attitude toward opinion, proof, reasoning, and authoritative experience. The effort to think constructively through a variety of conflicting opinions—on a weekly basis—prepares them well for the mature, independent, well-reasoned points of view expected of educated adults.

The LCSR Program's primary goals are to foster an appreciation of the connection between basic skills and interdisciplinary knowledge, and to promote greater cross-disciplinary communication among faculty and students. General education core courses or courses that serve other program requirements may be classified as "LCSR," as long as they fulfill certain speaking and writing activities connected to LCSR readings. The effect of the program has been to help create the atmosphere of a residential academic community; shared learning creates a climate in which teaching and learning take root more forcefully.

Since its inception, the SS/LCSR Program has helped create opportunities for faculty interaction across the disciplines in "pre-service" and "in-service" workshops. Each May, the LCSR Program sponsors a four-day pre-service workshop to which all new full-time and part-time faculty members are invited. Participants receive individual sets of the Lynchburg College Symposium Readings, which they make their own by using them during the workshop in exercises designed to promote familiarity with a wide variety of the readings. The goals of the workshop are several: for those unfamiliar with the program, to begin planning an LCSR course; for new faculty, to become acquainted with those they have not met and get to know their acquaintances better; for other faculty of various experiential levels, to share their pedagogical successes; for new teachers, to ask questions about teaching, about the College, and about the students in an informal setting; for experienced teachers to re-visit some of their assumptions, pedagogies, and strategies; to inspire strong scholarship, creative teaching, risk-taking, and confidence among all participants.

Another opportunity comes with the "in-service" workshops, which occur each month during the school year. The LCSR Program sponsors luncheons and dinners at which faculty teaching in the program give informal presentations on their use of specific teaching strategies or reading selections. Attendance is voluntary, but many try to be present for every session. For those involved in the LCSR program, teaching has become what Lee Schulman, President of the Carnegie Foundation, calls "community property."

On the Lynchburg College campus, there is evidence of a systematic change in teaching effectiveness as well as sustained faculty commitment to the program. By the 2002-2003 academic year, nearly two-thirds of all full-time faculty members and more than half of all part-time faculty members had completed the workshop at some time during their time at Lynchburg College. In any given semester, roughly ten to fifteen percent of the total class enrollments are in LCSR courses, not counting the required Senior Symposium. An important feature of this program is that participation is voluntary on the part of the faculty and, except for the required Senior Symposium, on the part of students. The program's influence quietly pervades the campus community, improving teaching and scholarship. Many see the LCSR Program as the College's premier academic program.

The Senior Symposium/LCSR program publishes *Agora*, an in-house journal that features the best of student writings responding to LCSR texts. The journal selections by students must integrate classical ideas and issues with contemporary ones. Faculty may also submit writings that address innovative teaching strategies. The journal takes its title from the marketplace at the heart of classical Athens, where much of Athenian public life was carried on: mercantile exchange, performance, political debate, athletic contests, and the public worship of deities all took place within the hustle and bustle of the Athenian agora. Similarly, the journal seeks to be a marketplace for compelling ideas and issues. Faculty members and students serve together on the editorial committee.

Since 1976, the Senior Symposium and the LCSR Program have affected the academic community both within and beyond the Lynchburg College campus. In 1991, Professor Richard Marius from Harvard University's writing center in reviewing the program favorably said, "I have seldom in my life been so impressed by an innovation in college education. I suppose the highest compliment that I could pay to the program was that I wished I could teach in it." Also in 1991, Professor Donald Boileau of George Mason University's Communication Studies department wrote, "what I discovered was a sound program that not only enriches the education of students at Lynchburg College, but what I hope can be a model for many other colleges and universities throughout our country." In spring 2003, in an article titled, "Whither the Great Books," Dr. William Casement described the LCSR program as the "most fully organized version" of the recent growth of great-books programs that employ an "across-the-disciplines structure." According to him, this approach perhaps encourages the use of the great books across the curriculum, which can be less isolating than even interdisciplinary programs. The Senior Symposium and LCSR Programs have received national acclaim in such publications as Loren Pope's *Colleges That Change Lives* and Charles Sykes and Brad Miner's *The National Review of College Guide, America's 50 Top Liberal Arts Schools.*

Income Inequality and Social Stratification: Causes and Consequences is the seventh volume of the third edition of the Lynchburg College Symposium Readings series. We gratefully acknowledge the work of the late Kendal North, PhD, Professor of Business and Finance who edited the *Poverty and Wealth* volume. In his honor, the editorial committee of the *Agora* selects the best written paper for the North Award annually. The Senior Symposium was the creation of Dr. James Huston, Dean of the College, *Emeritus* (1972-1984). With Dr. Michael Santos, professor of history, he co-founded the LCSR program. Dean Huston served as the first series editor, and with Dr. Julius Sigler, professor of physics, co-edited the second series. All three remain committed to the program today, and for this we are grateful.

Peggy Pittas, PhD
Series Managing Editor
Katherine Gray, PhD
Copy Editor

To my parents
Phyllis and Albert Turek
For a lifetime of encouragement and support

INTRODUCTION

This book is a complete revision of *Poverty and Wealth*, an earlier volume in the Lynchburg College Symposium Readings (LCSR) that covered essentially the same territory. The change in title represents a fundamental shift in the book's perspective. It reflects a growing realization that, in any society, the size of the gap between the "haves" and the "have-nots" has important social, political, and economic implications, and is at least as important as the number of "have-nots" in that society. It explicitly acknowledges that poverty and wealth are interdependent rather than independent phenomena, a fact that has important public policy implications. Finally, it emphasizes the need to think more broadly about the differences—race, class, and income—that separate us from one another.

The authors presented in this book are themselves a fascinating lot, aside from the many interesting and important things they had to say about the topic at hand. Almost to a person, they were integrative thinkers with intellectual histories that spanned multiple academic disciplines, philosophy being a common thread running through the entire group. They were a creative and courageous bunch, willing to challenge conventional wisdom and to take unpopular positions against overwhelming odds. Virtually all were intellectually gifted (almost frighteningly so), many were self-taught, and all were voracious readers. Most came from economically disadvantaged families and many were immigrants or the children of immigrants. They had an abiding faith in education, were fiercely opposed to injustice, cared deeply about human dignity, and were driven by a desire to make the world a better place in which to live. If you read closely and listen carefully to what they are saying, you will see that each, in his or her way, is searching for an answer to the question, "What is it that matters in life?"

As I reflect on all that I have learned in the process of preparing this book, I am more steadfast than ever in my belief that the analysis of inequality requires multiple disciplinary perspectives. This volume pulls together an eclectic set of readings—classical and contemporary, from economics, sociology, political science, philosophy, and business—on the subject of income inequality and social stratification. Considerable care was taken to ensure a balanced perspective. No one point of view is disproportionately represented by the authors included herein. The book is designed to stimulate discussion and spark debate, to raise questions but not necessarily to answer them. Some readers may be disappointed by the absence of essays advancing solutions to the problem being discussed. Unfortunately, space constraints precluded any examination beyond causes and consequences.

It may come as a surprise to learn that there is broad disagreement regarding the extent to which social and economic inequality is considered problematic. And there are not just two sides to this debate. People who consider inequality a problem, for example, may disagree with one another over the extent to which it is an individual problem versus a societal one. If not for people like Du Bois, Hacker, and Sinclair, we might easily forget that we are talking about people's lives when we talk about inequality and stratification. Regarding the social consequences of inequality, there is much that I wish could also have been included in this book. For example, Ted Gurr's (1970) argument, that inequality gives rise to a "frustration-aggression response"[1] which motivates individuals to violence, adds a fascinating dimension to the discussion of consequences and, perhaps, provides additional insight into the events described by the Kerner Commission. A similar argument in an international context opens the door to a discussion of the extent to which inequality contributes to transnational terrorism.

For people who believe that inequality is a problem, there is still the question of what to do about it. Here, the debate over the role of government in the marketplace assumes central importance. Friedman and Rand argue on both moral and economic grounds that government should not intervene, the Catholic bishops and Okun take the opposite position, and Bentham would weigh in with a decisive "it depends." Ultimately, however, the debate over policy turns back on itself, and we find ourselves once again talking about causes. Just as the questions we ask determine the kind of answers we get, so, too, the causes we identify influence the kind of solutions we adopt. The different policies adopted by liberals and conservatives, for example, reflect differences in the way the

---

[1]   Gurr, T. R. (1970). *Why Men Rebel*. Princeton University Press.

problem was defined rather than differences in the underlying economic, political, and social realities giving rise to the problem.

Banfield (1974) argues that individuals are poor because their decision making time horizon is too short. While everyone discounts future events, i.e., diminishes their importance, people with very short time horizons are more likely to ignore them altogether. Such individuals are less likely to invest in education, for example, because they perceive the costs of going to school, which are borne largely in the present, to exceed the benefits of going to school, the majority of which do not materialize for quite a while. These same individuals are more likely to engage in criminal activity since they "see" the benefits but not the costs. To the extent that one's time horizon is determined at an early age through the process of socialization—Banfield's contention—public policies to ameliorate poverty, and thus inequality, are unlikely to change attitudes and behaviors in any meaningful way. This theory, which would probably resonate with Rousseau, drew harsh criticism in the 1970s because (a) some people saw it as "blaming the victim," (b) it challenged Lyndon Johnson's War on Poverty, and (c) it led Banfield to suggest removing babies from their families and placing them in an environment where they would be more appropriately socialized.[2]

It is here, too, that the difference between inequality and poverty becomes crucial. If redistributive policies that transfer wealth from the "haves" to the "have-nots" give rise to disincentive effects that inhibit work effort, the size of the economic pie might actually shrink as a result, leaving less for everybody. Smith and Rand would think this likely, but Mill and Marx might not. Even if equality comes at the expense of efficiency, as Okun suggests, is that a reason to forego redistributive policies? If Eitzen is right and inequality does give rise to undesirable consequences, what price should we as a society be willing to pay to reduce the damage it causes? How do we put a price on human dignity? How do we measure the economic and social consequences of diminished human potential? Is this something that government should do and, equally important, is this something government is capable of doing? Friedman and Rand would take one side on both these questions, while Sinclair, Hacker, Du Bois and the Catholic Bishops would take the other. Veblen and Thoreau might smile sardonically and shake their heads in dismay.

This book lacks an international perspective, which might strike some readers as unforgivable in light of the growing interconnectedness

---

[2]   Banfield, E. C. (1974). *The Unheavenly City Revisited*. Boston: Little, Brown and Co.

between our way of life and the events taking place elsewhere in the world. Interestingly, the jury is still out on the impact that globalization has on the distribution of wealth and power. The standard party line in economics, that free trade benefits all trading partners, has been subjected to considerable scrutiny, and is beginning to show some signs of strain. The need to do business in an increasingly competitive global economy places significant constraints on the ability of both corporations and governments to pursue social goals at the expense of economic efficiency. Satellite broadcasts of American television shows and global distribution of American movies have raised international awareness of the disparity between living conditions in the U.S. and those enjoyed by people in other countries, shifting the focus from poverty in absolute terms to poverty in relative terms.

This book was two long years in the making. During this time, my wife and daughters graciously sacrificed precious family time, tolerating my protracted absences with remarkable equanimity. They cheered me on as each deadline approached and consoled me when deadlines went unmet. Thank you, Renee, Rebecca and Shoshana for making this project possible. I could not have done it without you. Thanks also to Peggy Pittas for her incredible patience and wise counsel—I could not have asked for a better partner in this enterprise.

Joseph Turek, PhD

SECTION I

GOVERNMENT VS. THE MARKET

Jeremy Bentham *The Principles of Morals and Legislation* (1823)
John Stuart Mill *Utilitarianism* (1910)
Adam Smith *The Wealth of Nations* (1776)
Milton Freidman *Capitalism and Freedom:* "The Role of Government" (1962)
Arthur M. Okun "Equality and Efficiency: The Big Tradeoff" (1975)

While the writings contained within this volume represent multiple academic disciplines and perspectives, the book's underlying orientation is strongly rooted in the economics tradition. The first two selections in this section focus on the principle of utility and the doctrine of utilitarianism. For readers who have never studied economics, it is useful to know that economists treat "utility" as being synonymous with "satisfaction" and that they define a "rational" person as one who attempts to maximize his or her utility. Economists seek to understand the choices people make in terms of the benefits and costs they derive therefrom, and—contrary to most other disciplines—attribute no normative significance to the notion of rationality. For the economist, rational individuals are utility-maximizing individuals and utility theory is a purely descriptive model. The assumption that people make choices that they believe—at the time and given the information at their disposal choice—are in their own best interest provides the foundation of an analytical framework that can be used to understand human behavior. The third reading describes the workings of a market economy when all behavior conforms to the assumption of economic rationality. One of the pivotal questions in economics has to do with the extent to which individuals should be able to exercise free choice. Another key question, not unrelated to the first, is whether—and to what degree—government should interfere with free markets. These are the issues addressed by Friedman in the fourth selection. There are, of course, no right answers to these questions. Most people will place themselves somewhere along a continuum, with the far right being pro-market and the far left being pro-government. Recognizing that ours is a mixed economy, characterized by a blending of both government and markets, Okun examines the implications of government-market interactions for efficiency and equity. This is an extremely important discussion because virtually all debates about ways to address social problems hinge on whether the solutions are to be found in the dynamics of a free market or in the halls of government.

JEREMY BENTHAM

1748-1832

THE PRINCIPLES OF MORALS AND LEGISLATION
1823

Born in London, England, Jeremy Bentham was a jurist, moral philosopher, economist, legal reformer, and political radical. Commonly regarded as the father of Utilitarianism, he is credited with adding the words "international," "maximize," "minimize," "utilitarian" (but not "utility," which Hume first used), and "codification" to our language. A stunning intellect, he taught himself to read and, at age three, he was devouring Rapin's *History of England* and studying Latin. Within two years, he was playing the violin and learning to speak French. At age twelve, he entered Queen's College, Oxford, where he obtained his Bachelor's and his Master's degrees.

Intending to follow in his father's footsteps, he studied law in Lincoln's Inn and then at Oxford under Sir William Blackstone, the leading legal theorist in England (Lekachman, 1959). As a student, he became profoundly disillusioned by the abuses he had witnessed in the courts and by the ambiguity, complexity, and lack of coherence in the law. Called to the bar in 1796, he chose instead to spend his life writing about the deficiencies in the legal system and advocating for legislative and judicial reform.

Bentham's first book (*A Fragment on Government*, 1776), published anonymously, was a scathing attack on Blackstone's *Commentaries on the Laws of England*. He criticized Blackstone's preoccupation with outdated laws, arguing that the law needed to evolve with changing social circumstances. He is best known for his *Introduction to Principles of Morals and Legislation* (1789), which advanced the proposition—called the "principle of utility"—that actions that promote the happiness of the greatest number of people are morally superior.

Bentham believed that people are motivated by their own self interest to maximize happiness (utility), defined as the presence of pleasure and the absence of pain. Coupled with the assumption that the utility of society is simply the aggregation of the utilities of the individuals comprising that society, he concluded that it is morally appropriate to evaluate institutions and actions according to the degree to which they increase or decrease overall happiness.[1] The principle of utility, in Bentham's mind, "was only his starting point for a radical critique of society, which aimed to test the usefulness of existing institutions, practices and beliefs against an objective evaluative standard" (Nicoll, 2007).

His position on relief for the poor is interesting in this regard. He believed that society had a moral obligation to reduce needless suffering and supported a minimum subsistence level of income. Noting that an extra dollar contributes less utility to a rich man than to a poor one, he believed that the reallocation of income was consistent with the good of the whole because the loss by the rich is more than offset by the gain for the poor. That said, he argued for carefully balancing the good of redistributive taxation against the harm associated with thwarting incentives and productivity, and thus abundance.

Bentham's belief that people made choices based on a "felicific (or hedonic) calculus" derived from his "philosophical view of humanity as so many living profit-and-loss calculators, each busily arranging his life to maximize the pleasure of his psychic adding machine" (Heilbroner, 1992, 174). This idea provided, among other things, the foundation for his approach to legal reform, which held that the punishment for breaking the law should be just sufficient to offset the pleasure thereby obtained. At a time when the death sentence was standard for even trivial offenses, his suggestion that the "penalty fit the crime" must have been quite revolutionary.

Bentham was strongly influenced by Joseph Priestly's *Essays on the First Principles of Government* (1768), Claude Adrien Helvétius's *On Mind* (1758), and David Hume's *A Treatises of Human Nature* (1740). Francis Hutcheson anticipated Bentham, writing in *An Inquiry Concerning Moral Good and Evil* (1725) that "that Action is best, which procures

---

[1] He assigned equal weights to each person's utility so that no individual counted more than any other.

the greatest Happiness for the greatest numbers."[2] What distinguished Bentham from his predecessors was his detailed discussion of the types of pain and pleasure (including the circumstances influencing the strength with which each is felt), his broad application of the principle of utility (for example, to religion and criminal behavior), and his attempts to numerically calculate the amount of pleasure and pain felt.

An inheritance in 1796 gave Bentham financial security and allowed him to spend the rest of his life writing, sometimes for as long as twelve hours a day. "Throughout life," says Lekachman (1959, 107), "it was always [his] habit to write, accumulate, never revise, and never publish." The Bentham Project at University College of London has posthumously produced 25 volumes of his collected works from tens of thousands of pages of manuscripts—more than 6 millions words unpublished at the time of his death.

Bentham's theories provide the foundation upon which much of modern economics is based. Given the difficulty of trying to make interpersonal comparisons of utility, the emphasis today (in economics, but not philosophy) focuses on how the quest for utility motivates individual behavior.

Consider how the "principle of utility" might help Okun balance the tradeoff between equality and efficiency and try to identify some of the obstacles that would have to be overcome in order to apply Bentham's Felicific Calculus.

SELECTION FROM:

Bentham, Jeremy. (1823). *The Principles of Morals and Legislation*. Oxford: Clarendon Press. 1-23.

CHAPTER I
OF THE PRINCIPLE OF UTILITY

I.   NATURE has placed mankind under the governance of two sovereign masters, *pain* and *pleasure*. It is for them alone to point out what we ought to do, as well as to determine what we shall do. On the one hand the standard of right and wrong, on the

---

2   Fieser, J. (2006). "David Hume (1711-1776) Moral Theory." *The Internet Encyclopedia of Philosophy*. Accessed at http://www.iep.utm. edu/h/humemora.htm.

other the chain of causes and effects, are fastened to their throne. They govern us in all we do, in all we say, in all we think: every effort we can make to throw off our subjection, will serve but to demonstrate and confirm it. In words a man may pretend to abjure their empire: but in reality he will remain subject to it all the while. The *principle of utility* recognises this subjection, and assumes it for the foundation of that system, the object of which is to rear the fabric of felicity by the hands of reason and of law. Systems which attempt to question it, deal in sounds instead of sense, in caprice instead of reason, in darkness instead of light.

But enough of metaphor and declamation: it is not by such means that moral science is to be improved.

II. The principle of utility is the foundation of the present work: it will be proper therefore at the outset to give an explicit and determinate account of what is meant by it. By the principle of utility is meant that principle which approves or disapproves of every action whatsoever, according to the tendency which it appears to have to augment or diminish the happiness of the party whose interest is in question: or, what is the same thing in other words, to promote or to oppose that happiness. I say of every action whatsoever; and therefore not only of every action of a private individual, but of every measure of government.

III. By utility is meant that property in any object, whereby it tends to produce benefit, advantage, pleasure, good, or happiness, (all this in the present case comes to the same thing) or (what comes again to the same thing) to prevent the happening of mischief, pain, evil, or unhappiness to the party whose interest is considered: if that party be the community in general, then the happiness of the community: if a particular individual, then the happiness of that individual.

IV. The interest of the community is one of the most general expressions that can occur in the phraseology of morals: no wonder that the meaning of it is often lost. When it has a meaning, it is this. The community is a fictitious *body*, composed of the individual persons who are considered as constituting as it were its *members*. The interest of the community then is, what?—the sum of the interests of the several members who compose it.

V. It is in vain to talk of the interest of the community, without understanding what is the interest of the individual. A thing is said to promote the interest, or to be *for* the interest, of an individual, when it tends to add to the sum total of his pleasures: or, what comes to the same thing, to diminish the sum total of his pains.

VI. An action then may be said to be conformable to the principle of utility, or, for shortness sake, to utility, (meaning with respect to the community at large) when the tendency it has to augment the happiness of the community is greater than any it has to diminish it.

VII. A measure of government (which is but a particular kind of action, performed by a particular person or persons) may be said to be conformable to or dictated by the principle of utility, when in like manner the tendency which it has to augment the happiness of the community is greater than any which it has to diminish it.

VIII. When an action, or in particular a measure of government, is supposed by a man to be conformable to the principle of utility, it may be convenient, for the purposes of discourse, to imagine a kind of law or dictate, called a law or dictate of utility: and to speak of the action in question, as being conformable to such law or dictate.

IX. A man may be said to be a partizan of the principle of utility, when the approbation or disapprobation he annexes to any action, or to any measure, is determined by and proportioned to the tendency which he conceives it to have to augment or to diminish the happiness of the community: or in other words, to its conformity or unconformity to the laws or dictates of utility.

X. Of an action that is conformable to the principle of utility one may always say either that it is one that ought to be done, or at least that it is not one that ought not to be done. One may say also, that it is right it should be done; at least that it is not wrong it should be done: that it is a right action; at least that it is not a wrong action. When thus interpreted, the words *ought*, and *right* and *wrong* and others of that stamp, have a meaning: when otherwise, they have none.

XI. Has the rectitude of this principle been ever formally contested? It should seem that it had, by those who have not known what they have been meaning. Is it susceptible of any direct proof? it should seem not: for that which is used to prove every thing else, cannot itself be proved: a chain of proofs must have their

commencement somewhere. To give such proof is as impossible
as it is needless.

XII. Not that there is or ever has been that human creature at
breathing, however stupid or perverse, who has not on many,
perhaps on most occasions of his life, deferred to it. By the natural
constitution of the human frame, on most occasions of their lives
men in general embrace this principle, without thinking of it: if
not for the ordering of their own actions, yet for the trying of their
own actions, as well as of those of other men. There have been, at
the same time, not many, perhaps, even of the most intelligent,
who have been disposed to embrace it purely and without reserve.
There are even few who have not taken some occasion or other
to quarrel with it, either on account of their not understanding
always how to apply it, or on account of some prejudice or other
which they were afraid to examine into, or could not bear to part
with. For such is the stuff that man is made of: in principle and
in practice, in a right track and in a wrong one, the rarest of all
human qualities is consistency.

XIII. When a man attempts to combat the principle of utility, it is
with reasons drawn, without his being aware of it, from that
very principle itself. His arguments, if they prove any thing,
prove not that the principle is *wrong*, but that, according to the
applications he supposes to be made of it, it is *misapplied*. Is it
possible for a man to move the earth? Yes; but he must first find
out another earth to stand upon.

XIV. To disprove the propriety of it by arguments is impossible;
but, from the causes that have been mentioned, or from some
confused or partial view of it, a man may happen to be disposed
not to relish it. Where this is the case, if he thinks the settling
of his opinions on such a subject worth the trouble, let him
take the following steps, and at length, perhaps, he may come
to reconcile himself to it.

1. Let him settle with himself, whether he would wish to
   discard this principle altogether; if so, let him consider what
   it is that all his reasonings (in matters of politics especially)
   can amount to?
2. If he would, let him settle with himself, whether he would
   judge and act without any principle, or whether there is any
   other he would judge an act by?

3. If there be, let him examine and satisfy himself whether the principle he thinks he has found is really any separate intelligible principle; or whether it be not a mere principle in words, a kind of phrase, which at bottom expresses neither more nor less than the mere averment of his own unfounded sentiments; that is, what in another person he might be apt to call caprice?

4. If he is inclined to think that his own approbation or disapprobation, annexed to the idea of an act, without any regard to its consequences, is a sufficient foundation for him to judge and act upon, let him ask himself whether his sentiment is to be a standard of right and wrong, with respect to every other man, or whether every man's sentiment has the same privilege of being a standard to itself?

5. In the first case, let him ask himself whether his principle is not despotical, and hostile to all the rest of human race?

6. In the second case, whether it is not anarchial, and whether at this rate there are not as many different standards of right and wrong as there are men? and whether even to the same man, the same thing, which is right to-day, may not (without the least change in its nature) be wrong to-morrow? and whether the same thing is not right and wrong in the same place at the same time? and in either case, whether all argument is not at an end? and whether, when two men have said, 'I like this,' and 'I don't like it,' they can (upon such a principle) have any thing more to say?

7. If he should have said to himself, No: for that the sentiment which he proposes as a standard must be grounded on reflection, let him say on what particulars the reflection is to turn? if on particulars having relation to the utility of the act, then let him say whether this is not deserting his own principle, and borrowing assistance from that very one in opposition to which he sets it up: or if not on those particulars, on what other particulars?

8. If he should be for compounding the matter, and adopting his own principle in part, and the principle of utility in part, let him say how far he will adopt it?

9. When he has settled with himself where he will stop, then let him ask himself how he justifies to himself the adopting it so far? and why he will not adopt it any farther?

10. Admitting any other principle than the principle of utility to be a right principle, a principle that it is right for a man to pursue; admitting (what is not true) that the word *right* can have a meaning without reference to utility, let him say whether there is any such thing as a *motive* that a man can have to pursue the dictates of it: if there is, let him say what that motive is, and how it is to be distinguished from those which enforce the dictates of utility: if not, then lastly let him say what it is this other principle can be good for?

CHAPTER II
OF PRINCIPLES ADVERSE TO THAT OF UTILITY

I. IF the principle of utility be a right principle to be governed by, and that in all cases, it follows from what has been just observed, that whatever principle differs from it in any case must necessarily be a wrong one. To prove any other principle, therefore, to be a wrong one, there needs no more than just to show it to be what it is, a principle of which the dictates are in some point or other different from those of the principle of utility: to state it is to confute it.

II. A principle may be different from that of utility in two ways: 1. By being constantly opposed to it: this is the case with a principle which may be termed the principle of *asceticism*. 2. By being sometimes opposed to it, and sometimes not, as it may happen: this is the case with another, which may be termed the principle of *sympathy* and *antipathy*.

III. By the principle of asceticism I mean that principle, which, like the principle of utility, approves or disapproves of any action, according to the tendency which it appears to have to augment or diminish the happiness of the party whose interest is in question; but in an inverse manner: approving of actions in as far as they tend to diminish his happiness; disapproving of them in as far as they tend to augment it.

IV. It is evident that any one who reprobates any the least particle of pleasure, as such, from whatever source derived, is *pro tanto* a partizan of the principle of asceticism. It is only upon that principle, and not from the principle of utility, that the most abominable pleasure which the vilest of malefactors ever reaped from his crime would be to be reprobated, if it stood alone. The case is, that it never does stand alone; but is necessarily followed by such a quantity of pain (or, what comes to the same thing, such a chance for a certain quantity of pain) that the pleasure in comparison of it, is as nothing: and this is the true and sole, but perfectly sufficient, reason for making it a ground for punishment.

V. There are two classes of men of very different complexions, by whom the principle of asceticism appears to have been embraced; the one a set of moralists, the other a set of religionists. Different accordingly have been the motives which appears to have recommended it to the notice of these different parties. Hope, that is the prospect of pleasure, seems to have animated the former: hope, the aliment of philosophic pride: the hope of honour and reputation at the hands of men. Fear, that is the prospect of pain, the latter: fear, the offspring of superstitious fancy: the fear of future punishment at the hands of a splenetic and revengeful Deity. I say in this case fear: for of the invisible future, fear is more powerful than hope. These circumstances characterize the two different parties among the partisans of the principle of asceticism; the parties and their motives different, the principle the same.

VI. The religious party, however, appear to have carried it farther than the philosophical: they have acted more consistently and less wisely. The philosophical party have scarcely gone farther than to reprobate pleasure: the religious party have frequently gone so far as to make it a matter of merit and of duty to court pain. The philosophical party have hardly gone farther than the making pain a matter of indifference. It is no evil, they have said: they have not said, it is a good. They have not so much as reprobated all pleasure in the lump. They have discarded only what they have called the gross; that is, such as are organical, or of which the origin is easily traced up to such as are organical: they have even cherished and magnified the refined. Yet this, however, not under the name of pleasure: to cleanse itself from the sordes[3] of its impure original, it was necessary it should change its name: the honourable, the glorious, the reputable, the becoming, the *honestum*, the *decorum*, it was to be called: in short, any thing but pleasure.

VII. From these two sources have flowed the doctrines from which the sentiments of the bulk of mankind have all along received

---

3   Unclean material on the lips and teeth.

a tincture of this principle; some from the philosophical, some from the religious, some from both. Men of education more frequently from the philosophical, as more suited to the elevation of their sentiments: the vulgar more frequently from the superstitious, as more suited to the narrowness of their intellect, undilated by knowledge: and to the abjectness of their condition, continually open to the attacks of fear. The tinctures, however, derived from the two sources, would naturally intermingle, insomuch that a man would not always know by which of them he was most influenced: and they would often serve to corroborate and enliven one another. It was this conformity that made a kind of alliance between parties of a complexion otherwise so dissimilar: and disposed them to unite upon various occasions against the common enemy, the partizan of the principle of utility, whom they joined in branding with the odious name of Epicurean.

VIII. The principle of asceticism, however, with whatever warmth it may have been embraced by its partizans as a rule of private conduct, seems not to have been carried to any considerable length, when applied to the business of government. In a few instances it has been carried a little way by the philosophical party: witness the Spartan regimen. Though then, perhaps, it may be considered as having been a measure of security: and an application, though a precipitate and perverse application, of the principle of utility. Scarcely in any instances, to any considerable length, by the religious: for the various monastic orders, and the societies of the Quakers, Dumplers, Moravians, and other religionists, have been free societies, whose regimen no man has been astricted to without the intervention of his own consent. Whatever merit a man may have thought there would be in making himself miserable, no such notion seems ever to have occurred to any of them, that it may be a merit, much less a duty, to make others miserable: although it should seem, that if a certain quantity of misery were a thing so desirable, it would not matter much whether it were brought by each man upon himself, or by one man upon another. It is true, that from the same source from whence, among the religionists, the attachment to the principle of asceticism took its rise, flowed other doctrines and practices, from which misery in abundance was produced in one man by the instrumentality of another: witness the holy wars, and the persecutions for religion. But the passion for producing misery in these cases proceeded upon some special ground: the exercise of it was confined to persons of particular descriptions: they were tormented, not as men, but as heretics and infidels. To have inflicted the same miseries on their fellow believers and fellow-sectaries, would have been as blameable in the eyes even of these religionists, as in those of a partizan of the principle of utility. For a man to give himself a certain number of stripes was indeed meritorious: but to give the same number of stripes to another man, not consenting, would have been a sin. We read of saints, who for the good of their souls, and the mortification of their bodies, have voluntarily yielded themselves a prey to vermin: but though many persons of this class have wielded the reins of empire, we read of none who have set themselves to work, and made laws on purpose, with a view of stocking the body politic with the breed of highwaymen, housebreakers, or incendiaries. If at any time they have suffered the nation to be preyed upon by swarms of idle pensioners, or useless placemen, it has rather been from negligence and imbecility, than from any settled plan for oppressing and plundering of the people. If at any time they have sapped the sources of national wealth, by cramping commerce, and driving the inhabitants into emigration, it has been with other views, and in pursuit of other ends. If they have declaimed against the pursuit of pleasure, and the use of wealth, they have commonly stopped at declamation: they have not, like Lycurgus,[4] made express ordinances for the purpose of banishing the precious metals. If they have established idleness by a law, it has been not because idleness, the mother of vice and misery, is itself a virtue, but because idleness (say they) is the road to holiness. If under the notion of fasting, they have joined in the plan of confining their subjects to a diet, thought by some to be of the most nourishing and prolific nature, it has been not for the sake of making them tributaries to the nations by whom that diet was to be supplied, but for the sake of manifesting their own power, and exercising the obedience of the people. If they have established, or suffered to be established, punishments for the breach of celibacy, they have done no more than comply with the petitions of those deluded rigorists, who,

---

[4]   A legendary law-giver of Sparta.

dupes to the ambitious and deep-laid policy of their rulers, first laid themselves under that idle obligation by a vow.

IX. The principle of asceticism seems originally to have been the reverie of certain hasty speculators, who having perceived, or fancied, that certain pleasures, when reaped in certain circumstances, have, at the long run, been attended with pains more than equivalent to them, took occasion to quarrel with every thing that offered itself under the name of pleasure. Having then got thus far, and having forgot the point which they set out from, they pushed on, and went so much further as to think it meritorious to fall in love with pain. Even this, we see, is at bottom but the principle of utility misapplied.

X. The principle of utility is capable of being consistently pursued; and it is but tautology to say, that the more consistently it is pursued, the better it must ever be for human-kind. The principle of asceticism never was, nor ever can be, consistently pursued by any living creature. Let but one tenth part of the inhabitants of this earth pursue it consistently, and in a day's time they will have turned it into a hell.

XI. Among principles adverse to that of utility, that which at this day seems to have most influence in matters of government, is what may be called the principle of sympathy and antipathy. By the principle of sympathy and antipathy, I mean that principle which approves or disapproves of certain actions, not on account of their tending to augment the happiness, nor yet on account of their tending to diminish the happiness of the party whose interest is in question, but merely because a man finds himself disposed to approve or disapprove of them: holding up that approbation or disapprobation as a sufficient reason for itself, and disclaiming the necessity of looking out for any extrinsic ground. Thus far in the general department of morals: and in the particular department of politics, measuring out the quantum (as well as determining the ground) of punishment, by the degree of the disapprobation.

XII. It is manifest, that this is rather a principle in name than in reality: it is not a positive principle of itself, so much as a term employed to signify the negation of all principle. What one expects to find in a principle is something that points out some external consideration, as a means of warranting and guiding the internal sentiments of approbation and disapprobation: this expectation is but ill fulfilled by a proposition, which does neither more nor less than hold up each of those sentiments as a ground and standard for itself.

XIII. In looking over the catalogue of human actions (says a partizan of this principle) in order to determine which of them are to be marked with the seal of disapprobation, you need but to take counsel of your own feelings: whatever you find in yourself a propensity to condemn, is wrong for that very reason. For the same reason it is also meet for punishment: in what proportion it is adverse to utility, or whether it be adverse to utility at all, is a matter that makes no difference. In that same *proportion* also is it meet for punishment: if you hate much, punish much: if you hate little, punish little: punish as you hate. If you hate not at all, punish not at all: the fine feelings of the soul are not to be overborne and tyrannized by the harsh and rugged dictates of political utility.

XIV. The various systems that have been formed concerning the standard of right and wrong, may all be reduced to the principle of sympathy and antipathy. One account may serve for all of them. They consist all of them in so many contrivances for avoiding the obligation of appealing to any external standard, and for prevailing upon the reader to accept of the author's sentiment or opinion as a reason for itself. The phrases different, but the principle the same.

XV. It is manifest, that the dictates of this principle will frequently coincide with those of utility, though perhaps without intending any such thing. Probably more frequently than not: and hence it is that the business of penal justice is carried on upon that tolerable sort of footing upon which we see it carried on in common at this day. For what more natural or more general ground of hatred to a practice can there be, than the mischievousness of such practice? What all men are exposed to suffer by, all men will be disposed to hate. It is far yet, however, from being a constant ground: for when a man suffers, it is not always that he knows what it is he suffers by. A man may suffer grievously, for instance, by a new tax, without being able to trace up the cause of his sufferings to the injustice of some neighbour, who has eluded the payment of an old one.

XVI. The principle of sympathy and antipathy is most apt to err on the side of severity. It is for applying punishment in many cases which deserve none: in many cases which deserve some, it is for applying more than they deserve. There is no incident imaginable, be it ever so trivial, and so remote from mischief, from which this principle may not extract a ground of punishment. Any difference in taste: any difference in opinion: upon one subject as well as upon another. No disagreement so trifling which perseverance and altercation will not render serious. Each becomes in the other's eyes an enemy, and, if laws permit, a criminal. This is one of the circumstances by which the human race is distinguished (not much indeed to its advantage) from the brute creation.

XVII. It is not, however, by any means unexampled for this principle to err on the side of lenity. A near and perceptible mischief moves antipathy. A remote and imperceptible mischief, though not less real, has no effect. Instances in proof of this will occur in numbers in the course of the work. It would be breaking in upon the order of it to give them here.

XVIII. It may be wondered, perhaps, that in all this while no mention has been made of the *theological* principle; meaning that principle which professes to recur for the standard of right and wrong to the will of God. But the case is, this is not in fact a distinct principle. It is never any thing more or less than one or other of the three before-mentioned principles presenting itself under another shape. The *will* of God here meant cannot be his revealed will, as contained in the sacred writings: for that is a system which nobody ever thinks of recurring to at this time of day, for the details of political administration: and even before it can be applied to the details of private conduct, it is universally allowed, by the most eminent divines of all persuasions, to stand in need of pretty ample interpretations; else to what use are the works of those divines? And for the guidance of these interpretations, it is also allowed, that some other standard must be assumed. The will then which is meant on this occasion, is that which may be called the *presumptive* will: that is to say, that which is presumed to be his will on account of the conformity of its dictates to those of some other principle. What then may be this other principle? it must be one or other of the three mentioned above: for there cannot, as we have seen, be any more. It is plain, therefore, that, setting revelation out of the question, no light can ever be thrown upon the standard of right and wrong, by any thing that can be said upon the question, what is God's will. We may be perfectly sure, indeed, that whatever is right is conformable to the will of God: but so far is that from answering the purpose of showing us what is right, that it is necessary to know first whether a thing is right, in order to know from thence whether it be conformable to the will of God.

XIX. There are two things which are very apt to be confounded, but which it imports us carefully to distinguish:—the motive or cause, which, by operating on the mind of an individual, is productive of any act: and the ground or reason which warrants a legislator, or other by-stander, in regarding that act with an eye of approbation. When the act happens, in the particular instance in question, to be productive of effects which we approve of, much more if we happen to observe that the same motive may frequently be productive, in other instances, of the like effects, we are apt to transfer our approbation to the motive itself, and to assume, as the just ground for the approbation we bestow on the act, the circumstance of its originating from that motive. It is in this way that the sentiment of antipathy has often been considered as a just ground of action. Antipathy, for instance, in such or such a case, is the cause of an action which is attended with good effects: but this does not make it a right ground of action in that case, any more than in any other. Still farther. Not only the effects are good, but the agent sees beforehand that they will be so. This may make the action indeed a perfectly right action: but it does not make antipathy a right ground of action. For the same sentiment of antipathy, if implicitly deferred to, may be, and very frequently is, productive of the very worst effects. Antipathy, therefore, can never be a right ground of action. No more, therefore, can resentment, which, as will be seen more particularly hereafter, is but a modification of antipathy. The only right ground of action, that can possibly subsist, is, after all, the consideration of utility, which, if it is a right principle of actions, and of approbation, any one case, is so in every other. Other principles in abundance, that is, other motives, may be the reasons why such and such an act *has* been done: that is, the reasons or causes of its being done: but it is this alone that can be the reason why it might or ought to have been done. Antipathy or resentment requires always to be regulated, to prevent it doing mischief: to be regulated by what? always by the principle of utility. The principle of utility neither requires nor admits of any another regulator than itself.

JOHN STUART MILL

1806-1873

UTILITARIANISM
1910

Born just outside London to a family of little means, John
Stuart Mill was to become one of the most influential thinkers of the
nineteenth century. He wrote on a vast array of subjects, including
logic, political economy, moral philosophy and even feminism. He is
best known for *On Liberty* (1859), *Utilitarianism* (1861), *System of
Logic* (1843), *The Subjection of Women* (1869), and his *Autobiography*
(1873). *The Principles of Political Economy* (1848) was the most
widely used textbook in Britain until Alfred Marshall's *Principles of
Economics* came along in 1890.

Mill's father, James, was a scholar in his own right, having written
The History of British India (1818) and *Elements of Political Economy*
(1821). A close friend of David Ricardo and a disciple of Jeremy Bentham,
James Mill organized a group of intellectuals known as the "Philosophic
Radicals" and rallied them around Utilitarianism's clarion call. They
advocated a variety of social and political reforms, including extending
voting rights to women, and founded the *Westminster Review*.

"The younger Mill," according to Heydt (2006), "was seen as the
crown prince of the Philosophic Radical movement and his famous
education reflected the hopes of his father and Bentham." John Stuart
Mill was home-schooled in the Benthamite tradition by his exceedingly
demanding and unforgiving father. He began learning Greek at the age
of 3 and Latin at the age of 8, by which time he had read the whole of
Herodotus and some Xenophon, Socrates, and Plato. Soon after, he began

the study of geometry and algebra and, between the ages of 8 and 12, he read the *Iliad* and the *Odyssey* in Greek and the *Aeneid* and *Metamorphoses* in Latin. He achieved fluency in French at 14 after having spent a year on the continent and is reputed to have been skilled in logic at 12 and in economics by 19.

One day, while reading Bentham's *Treatise on Legislation* in French translation, Mill experienced a turning point in his intellectual development. In his words,

> The feeling rushed upon me, that all previous moralists were superseded, and that here indeed was the commencement of a new era in thought . . . . When I laid down the last volume of the Traité, I had become a different being. The "principle of utility" understood as Bentham understood it, and applied in the manner in which he applied it through these three volumes, fell exactly into its place as the keystone which held together the detached and fragmentary component parts of my knowledge and beliefs. It gave unity to my conceptions of things. I now had opinions; a creed, a doctrine, a philosophy; in one among the best senses of the word, a religion; the inculcation and diffusion of which could be made the principal outward purpose of a life. And I had a grand conception laid before me of changes to be effected in the condition of mankind through that doctrine. (Mill, 1909, 44, 45-6)

Committed now to advancing the cause of utilitarianism, he was soon publishing articles and reviews in the *Westminster Review*. Within the year, he formed the Utilitarian Society, which met in Bentham's house and was comprised of like-minded young men who also wished to worship at the altar of Utility. A job with the East India Company allowed him to pay his bills while he devoted himself tirelessly to writing political articles for newspapers and editing his father's and Bentham's manuscripts for publication.

At the tender age of 20, Mill suffered an existential crisis and entered a deep depression, bringing all this activity to a standstill. He describes the precipitating event in his autobiography as follows:

> From the winter of 1821, when I first read Bentham, . . .
> I had what might truly be called an object in life; to be a

reformer of the world. My conception of my own happiness was entirely identified with this object . . . . But the time came when I awakened from this as from a dream. It was in the autumn of 1826. I was in a dull state of nerves . . . . In this frame of mind it occurred to me to put the question directly to myself: "Suppose that all your objects in life were realized; that all the changes in institutions and opinions which you are looking forward to, could be completely effected at this very instant: would this be a great joy and happiness to you?" And an irrepressible self-consciousness distinctly answered, "No!" At this my heart sank within me: the whole foundation on which my life was constructed fell down. All my happiness was to have been found in the continual pursuit of this end. The end had ceased to charm . . . I seemed to have nothing left to live for. (Mill, 1909, 85-6)

Mill concluded in retrospect that the single-minded emphasis on developing his analytical capabilities had left him unable to experience emotions. "I conceive," he admitted, "that the description so often given of a Benthamite, as a mere reasoning machine . . . was during two or three years of my life not altogether untrue of me" (Mill, 1909, 71). Finding comfort in reading poetry, especially Wordsworth, he gradually turned to Coleridge, Goethe, and other Romantic writers in order to nurture his aesthetic sensibilities. This also marked the beginning of his search for a way to reconcile his earlier views with his new-found emotional side.

While Mill never did abandon the principle of utility, through a subtle shift in reasoning he was able to expand utilitarian doctrine to accommodate feelings, imagination, and even compassion. He did this by distinguishing between higher pleasures (such as spirituality, morality, and aesthetics) and lower pleasures (such as monetary gain or material possessions). While some things (e.g., virtue, freedom, and beauty) appear to us to be intrinsically valuable, they are, according to Mill, actually valued because they make us happy, which gives us pleasure. We are motivated by things other than pleasure, he concludes, because we associate these things with pleasure. Since it turns out that higher pleasures are more satisfying than lower pleasures, i.e., they contribute more to happiness, they should carry more weight in identifying morally superior actions.

Having worked through the conflict, Mill was able to commit himself once more to improvement of the human condition. This time, however, individualism, self-development, and personal freedom took center stage. He supported freedom of expression, representative government, democracy, and women's rights, and expressed concerns over the impact of economic growth on the environment and the effect that industrialization had on worker morale.

After you have finished reading this selection, ask yourself whether Mill has, in fact, proved the principle of utility. Consider whether Smith and Mill would be able to agree on the definition of self-interest and ask yourself whether Veblen, Thoreau, and Mill would argue with one another about the source of happiness. To what extent do you think happiness and pleasure coincide?

SELECTION FROM:

Mill, J. S. (1910). *Philosophy and Theology: Utilitarianism, Liberty, and Representative Government*. London: J. M. Dent & Sons. 32-38.

CHAPTER 4
OF WHAT SORT OF PROOF THE
PRINCIPLE OF UTILITY IS SUSCEPTIBLE

It has already been remarked, that questions of ultimate ends do not admit of proof, in the ordinary acceptation of the term. To be incapable of proof by reasoning is common to all first principles; to the first premises of our knowledge, as well as to those of our conduct. But the former, being matters of fact, may be the subject of a direct appeal to the faculties which judge of fact—namely, our senses, and our internal consciousness. Can an appeal be made to the same faculties on questions of practical ends? Or by what other faculty is cognizance taken of them?

Questions about ends are, in other words, questions what things are desirable. The utilitarian doctrine is, that happiness is desirable, and the only thing desirable, as an end; all other things being only desirable as means to that end. What ought to be required of this doctrine—what conditions is it requisite that the doctrine should fulfil—to make good its claim to be believed?

The only proof capable of being given that an object is visible, is that people actually see it; the only proof that a sound is audible, is that people hear it: and so of the other sources of our experience. In like manner, I apprehend, the sole evidence it is possible to produce that any thing is desirable, is that people do actually desire it. If the end which the utilitarian doctrine proposes to itself were not, in theory and in practice, acknowledged to be an end, nothing could ever convince any person that it was so. No reason can be given why the general happiness is desirable, except that each person, so far as he believes it to be attainable, desires his own happiness. This, however, being a fact, we have not only all the proof which the case admits of, but all which it is possible to require, that happiness is a good; that each person's happiness is a good to that person; and the general happiness, therefore, a good to the aggregate of all persons. Happiness has made out its title as one of the ends of conduct, and consequently one of the criteria of morality.

But it has not, by this alone, proved itself to be the sole criterion. To do that, it would seem, by the same rule, necessary to show, not only that people desire happiness, but that they never desire any thing else. Now, it is palpable that they do desire things, which, in common language, are decidedly distinguished from happiness. They desire, for example, virtue and the absence of vice, no less really than pleasure and the absence of pain. The desire of virtue is not as universal, but it is as authentic a fact, as the desire of happiness; and hence the opponents of the utilitarian standard deem that they have a right to infer that there are other ends of human action besides happiness, and that happiness is not the standard of approbation and disapprobation.

But does the utilitarian doctrine deny that people desire virtue, or maintain that virtue is not a thing to be desired? The very reverse. It maintains not only that virtue is to be desired, but that it is to be desired disinterestedly, for itself. Whatever may be the opinion of utilitarian moralists as to the original conditions by which virtue is made virtue; however they may believe (as they do) that actions and dispositions are only virtuous because they promote another end than virtue; yet this being granted, and it having been decided, from considerations of this description, what is virtuous, they not only place virtue at the very head of the things which are good as means to the ultimate end, but they also recognise as a psychological fact the possibility of its being, to the individual, a good in itself, without looking to any end beyond it; and hold, that the mind is not in a right state, not in a state conformable to Utility, not in the state most conducive to the general happiness, unless it does love virtue in this manner—as a thing desirable in itself, even although, in the individual instance, it should not produce those other desirable consequences which it tends to produce, and on account of which it is held to be virtue. This opinion is not, in the smallest degree, a departure from the Happiness principle. The ingredients of happiness are very various, and each of them is desirable in itself, and not merely when considered as swelling an aggregate. The principle of utility does not mean that any given pleasure, as music, for instance, or any given exemption from pain, as for example health, is to be looked upon as means to a collective something termed happiness, and to be desired on that account. They are desired and desirable in and for themselves; besides being means, they are a part of the end. Virtue, according to the utilitarian doctrine, is not naturally and originally part of the end, but it is capable of becoming so; and in those who love it disinterestedly it has become so, and is desired and cherished, not as a means to happiness, but as a part of their happiness.

To illustrate this farther, we may remember that virtue is not the only thing, originally a means, and which if it were not a means to anything else, would be and remain indifferent, but which by association with what it is a means to, comes to be desired for itself, and that too with the utmost intensity. What, for example, shall we say of the love of money? There is nothing originally more desirable about money than about any heap of glittering pebbles. Its worth is solely that of the things which it will buy; the desires for other things than itself, which it is a means of gratifying. Yet the love of money is not only one of the strongest moving forces of human life, but money is, in many cases, desired in and for itself; the desire to possess it is often stronger than the desire to use it, and goes on increasing when all the desires which point to ends beyond it, to be compassed by it, are falling off. It may, then, be said truly, that money is desired not for the sake of an end, but as part of the end. From being a means to happiness, it has come to be itself a principal ingredient of the individual's conception of happiness. The same may be said of the majority of the great objects of human life—power, for example, or fame; except that to each of these there is a certain amount of immediate pleasure annexed, which has at least the semblance of being naturally inherent in them; a thing which cannot be said of money. Still, however, the strongest natural attraction, both of power and of fame, is the immense aid they give to the attainment of our other wishes; and it is the strong association thus generated between them and all our objects of desire, which gives to the direct desire of them the intensity it often assumes, so as in some characters to surpass in strength all other desires. In these cases the means have become a part of the end, and a more important part of it than any of the things which they are means to. What was once desired as an instrument for the attainment of happiness, has come to be desired for its own sake. In being desired for its own sake it is, however, desired as part of happiness. The person is made, or thinks he would be made, happy by its mere possession; and is made unhappy by failure to obtain it. The desire of it is not a different thing from the desire of happiness, any more than the love of music, or the desire of health. They are included in happiness. They are some of the elements of which the desire of happiness is made up. Happiness is not an abstract idea, but a concrete whole; and these are some of its parts. And the utilitarian standard sanctions and approves their being so. Life would be a poor thing, very ill provided with sources of happiness, if there were not this provision of nature, by which things originally indifferent, but conducive to, or otherwise associated with, the satisfaction of our primitives desires, become in themselves sources of pleasure more valuable than the primitive pleasures, both in permanency, in the space of human existence that they are capable of covering, and even in intensity.

Virtue, according to the utilitarian conception, is a good of this description. There was no original desire of it, or motive to it, save its conduciveness to pleasure, and especially to protection from pain. But through the association thus formed, it may be felt a good in itself, and desired as such with as great intensity as any other good; and with this difference between it and the love of money, of power, or of fame, that all of these may, and often do, render the individual noxious to the other members of the society to which he belongs, whereas there is nothing which makes him so much a blessing to them as the cultivation of the disinterested love of virtue. And consequently, the utilitarian standard, while it tolerates and approves those other acquired desires, up to the point beyond which they would be more injurious to the general happiness than promotive of it, enjoins and requires the cultivation of the love of virtue up to the greatest strength possible, as being above all things important to the general happiness.

It results from the preceding considerations, that there is in reality nothing desired except happiness. Whatever is desired otherwise than as a means to some end beyond itself, and ultimately to happiness, is desired as itself a part of happiness, and is not desired for itself until it has become so. Those who desire virtue for its own sake, desire it either because the consciousness of it is a pleasure, or because the consciousness of being without it is a pain, or for both reasons united; as in truth the pleasure and pain seldom exist separately, but almost always together, the same person feeling pleasure in the degree of virtue attained, and pain in not having attained more. If one of these gave him no pleasure, and the other no pain, he would not love or desire virtue, or would desire it only for the other benefits which it might produce to himself or to persons whom he cared for.

We have now, then, an answer to the question, of what sort of proof the principle of utility is susceptible. If the opinion which I have now stated is psychologically true—if human nature is so constituted as to desire nothing which is not either a part of happiness or a means of happiness, we can have no other proof, and we require no other, that these are the only things desirable. If so, happiness is the sole end of human action, and the promotion of it the test by which to judge of all human conduct; from whence it necessarily follows that it must be the criterion of morality, since a part is included in the whole.

And now to decide whether this is really so; whether mankind do desire nothing for itself but that which is a pleasure to them, or of which the absence is a pain; we have evidently arrived at a question of fact and experience, dependent, like all similar questions, upon evidence. It can only be determined by practiced self-consciousness and self-observation, assisted by observation of others. I believe that these sources of evidence, impartially consulted, will declare that desiring a thing and finding it pleasant, aversion to it and thinking of it as painful, are phenomena entirely inseparable, or rather two parts of the same phenomenon; in strictness of language, two different modes of naming the same psychological fact: that to think of an object as desirable (unless for the sake of its consequences), and to think of it as pleasant, are one and the same thing; and that to desire anything, except in proportion as the idea of it is pleasant, is a physical and metaphysical impossibility.

So obvious does this appear to me, that I expect it will hardly be disputed: and the objection made will be, not that desire can possibly be directed to anything ultimately except pleasure and exemption from pain, but that the will is a different thing from desire; that a person of confirmed virtue, or any other person whose purposes are fixed, carries out his purposes without any thought of the pleasure he has in contemplating them, or expects to derive from their fulfilment; and persists in acting on them, even though these pleasures are much diminished, by changes in his character or decay of his passive sensibilities, or are out weighed by the pains which the pursuit of the purposes may bring upon him. All this I fully admit, and have stated it elsewhere, as positively and emphatically as any one. Will, the active o the person's experience the pleasure naturally involved in the one or the pain in the other, that it is possible to call forth that will to be virtuous, which, when confirmed, acts without any thought of either pleasure or pain. Will is the child of desire, and passes out of the dominion of its parent only to come under that of habit. That which is the result of habit affords no presumption of being intrinsically good; and there would be no reason for wishing that the purpose of virtue should become independent of pleasure and pain, were it not that the influence of the pleasurable and painful associations which prompt to virtue is not sufficiently to be depended on for unerring constancy of action until it has acquired the support of habit. Both in feeling and in conduct, habit is the only thing which imparts and it is because of the importance to others of being able to rely absolutely on one's feelings and conduct, and to oneself of being able to rely on one's own, that the will to do right ought to be cultivated into this habitual independence. In other words, this state of the will is a means to good, not intrinsically a good; and does not contradict the doctrine that nothing is a good to human beings but in so far as it is either itself pleasurable, or a means of attaining pleasure or averting pain.

But if this doctrine be true, the principle of utility is proved. Whether it is so or not, must now be left to the consideration of the thoughtful reader.

ADAM SMITH

1723-1790

AN INQUIRY INTO THE NATURE AND CAUSES OF THE WEALTH OF NATIONS
1776

Adam Smith, born in Kirkcaldy, County Fife, Scotland, was a moral philosopher, a political economist, and an important figure in the Scottish Enlightenment. He attended the University of Glasgow, where he studied under Frances Hutcheson, and Balliol College at Oxford, where he read broadly in science, mathematics, literature, philosophy, and the classics. Ironically, the man reputed to be the father of modern-day economics never took an economics course himself. A professor of logic and then of moral philosophy at the University of Glasgow, his best known works are *The Theory of Moral Sentiments* (1759) and *An Inquiry Into the Nature and Causes of the Wealth of Nations* (1776), more commonly *The Wealth of Nations*.

Smith is probably one of the most widely quoted economists, and perhaps also one of the most misunderstood. The apparent contradiction between *The Theory of Moral Sentiments*, in which he analyzes the roots of altruism and benevolence, and *The Wealth of Nations*, in which he assumes that people are driven by self-interest, has given rise to what is sometimes called "The Adam Smith Problem."[1] And even though the

---

[1] It turns out that this contradiction is more apparent than real. Smith argues that people engage in benevolent behavior because of their ability to imagine what it would be like to be in someone else's shoes, which allows them to feel compassion when others are suffering and pleasure when others

expression "laissez faire" never appears anywhere in *The Wealth of Nations*, the term is invariably mentioned in association with his work.[2]

Smith's writings challenged many deeply held beliefs of the times, but especially the views that material wealth was a corrupting influence and that the pursuit of self-interest was contrary to virtue. Because the aggregate wealth of a society was considered to be fixed, it was thought that any attempt by one person to enrich himself necessarily implied a commensurate reduction in the wealth of others. The revolutionary nature of Smith's ideas is most easily seen against the backdrop of these beliefs. Not only did *The Wealth of Nations* explain the mechanism by which material wealth is created, it also described the institutions and conditions most conducive to that activity.

Trade, Smith argued, benefitted both parties involved in the transaction. It was not, as had been previously assumed, a zero-sum game in which one person's gains were another person's losses. Since both parties to any exchange emerge better off, the resulting gains from trade leave society as a whole more prosperous. The oil that greased the economic machinery? The pursuit of individual self-interest harnessed by the competitive forces of the marketplace! Unimpeded by government intervention, i.e., absent restraints on trade and the sheltering of industries from competition, the market itself would produce "universal opulence."

Contrary to popular opinion, Smith did not believe that the pursuit of self-interest was necessarily a good thing in and of itself. In fact, he strongly condemned the attempts of legislators and businessmen to advance their own interests by circumventing the market. His belief that people are motivated largely by self-interest led him to reject the idea of organizing a nation's economic affairs on the basis of benevolence alone. Always the moral philosopher, Smith observed that people might resort to morally demeaning ways of gaining the cooperation of others if unable to appeal to their self-interest.

---

are happy. Egoistic self-love is thus restrained by the benefit of behaving virtuously (the approbation of others and the satisfaction derived from feeling praiseworthy) and the cost of violating moral law (conscience).

[2] The expression, often translated as "hands off" but actually meaning "let do" or "allow to pass," was originally coined by Jean Claude Marie Vincent de Gournay (1712-1759), a wealthy French economist and businessman, an advocate of free trade, and co-founder (with François Quesnay) of the Physiocratic School of economics. The term was introduced into the English language in George Whatley's *Principles of Trade* (1774).

SELECTION FROM:

Smith, Adam. (1776). (1902). *An Inquiry into the Nature and Causes of the Wealth of Nations.* New York: P.F. Collier and Son. Vol. I: 39-40, 43-45, 52, 55-60, 60-61, 66-73, 75-76, 77-78, 98-99, 101, 104. Vol. II. 156-158, 159-166, 168-170, 172-173.

INTRODUCTION AND PLAN OF THE WORK.

THE annual labor of every nation is the fund which originally supplies it with all the necessaries and conveniences of life which it annually consumes, and which consist always either in the immediate produce of that labor, or in what is purchased with that produce from other nations.

According, therefore, as this produce, or what is purchased with it, bears a greater or smaller proportion to the number of those who are to consume it, the nation will be better or worse supplied with all the necessaries and conveniences for which it has occasion.

But this proportion must in every nation be regulated by two different circumstances; first, by the skill, dexterity, and judgment with which its labor is generally applied; and, secondly, by the proportion between the number of those who are employed in useful labor, and that of those who are not so employed. Whatever be the soil, climate, or extent of territory of any particular nation, the abundance or scantiness of its annual supply must, in that particular situation, depend upon those two circumstances.

The abundance or scantiness of this supply, too, seems to depend more upon the former of those two circumstances than upon the latter. Among the savage nations of hunters and fishers, every individual who is able to work is more or less employed in useful labor, and endeavors to provide, as well as he can, the necessaries and conveniences of life, for himself, and such of his family or tribe as are either too old, or too young, or too infirm, to go a-hunting and fishing. Such nations, however, are so miserably poor, that, from mere want, they are frequently reduced, or at least think themselves reduced, to the necessity sometimes of directly destroying, and sometimes of abandoning their infants, their old people, and those afflicted with lingering diseases, to perish with hunger, or to be devoured by wild beasts. Among civilized and thriving nations, on the. contrary, though a great number of people do not labor at all, many of whom consume the produce of ten times, frequently of a hundred times, more labor than the greater part of those who work; yet the produce of the whole labor of the society is so great, that all are often abundantly supplied; and a workman, even of the lowest and poorest order, if he is frugal and industrious, may enjoy a greater share of the necessaries and conveniences of life than it is possible for any savage to acquire . . . .

[***]

BOOK I

OF THE CAUSES OF IMPROVEMENT IN THE PRODUCTIVE POWERS OF LABOR, AND OF THE ORDER ACCORDING TO WHICH ITS PRODUCE IS NATURALLY DISTRIBUTED AMONG THE DIFFERENT RANKS OF THE PEOPLE.

CHAPTER I
OF THE DIVISION OF LABOR

THE greatest improvements in the productive powers of labor, and the greater part of the skill, dexterity, and judgment, with which it is anywhere directed, or applied, seem to have been the effects of the division of labor.

The effects of the division of labor, in the general business of society, will be more easily understood, by considering in what manner it operates in some particular manufactures . . . .

To take an example, therefore, from a very trifling manufacture, but one in which the division of labor has been very often taken notice of, the trade of a pin-maker; a workman not educated to this business (which the division of labor has rendered a distinct trade), nor acquainted with the use of the machinery employed in it (to the invention of which the same division of labor has probably given occasion), could scarce, perhaps, with his utmost industry, make one pin in a day, and certainly could not make twenty. But in the way in which this business is now carried on, not only the whole work is a peculiar trade, but it is divided into a number of branches, of which the greater part are likewise peculiar trades. One man draws out the wire, another straights it, a third cuts it, a fourth points it, a fifth grinds it at the top for receiving the head; to make the head requires two or three distinct operations; to put it on, is a peculiar business, to whiten the pins is another; it is even a trade by itself to put them into the paper;

and the important business of making a pin is, in this manner, divided into about eighteen distinct operations, which, in some manufactories, are all performed by distinct hands, though in others the same man will sometimes perform two or three of them. I have seen a small manufactory of this kind, where ten men only were employed, and where some of them consequently performed two or three distinct operations. But though they were very poor, and therefore but indifferently accommodated with the necessary machinery, they could, when they exerted themselves, make among them about twelve pounds of pins in a day. There are in a pound upwards of four thousand pins of a middling size. Those ten persons, therefore, could make among them upwards of forty-eight thousand pins in a day. Each person, therefore, making a tenth part of forty-eight thousand pins, might be considered as making four thousand eight hundred pins in a day. But if they had all wrought separately and independently, and without any of them having been educated to this peculiar business, they certainly could not each of them have made twenty, perhaps not one pin in a day; that is, certainly, not the two hundred and fortieth, perhaps not the four thousand eight hundredth, part of what they are at present capable of performing, in consequence of a proper division and combination of their different operations.[3]

[***]

This great increase in the quantity of work, which, in consequence of the division of labor, the same number of people are capable of performing, is owing to three different circumstances; first, to the increase of dexterity in every particular workman; secondly, to the saving of the time which is commonly lost in passing from one species of work to another; and, lastly, to the invention of a great number of machines which facilitate and abridge labor, and enable one man to do the work of many.

[***]

---

[3]   The "great industry" has produced results in pinmaking which reduce Adam Smith's illustration to insignificance. At the present time not more than 1000 persons are employed in all the processes of pinmaking These suffice to turn out, on an average, twenty-five tons of pins per week. In Adam Smith's time not less than 4,200 were required for the production of about one-seventh of that quantity.—ED.

It is the great multiplication of the productions of all the different arts, in consequence of the division of labor, which occasions, in a well-governed society, that universal opulence which extends itself to the lowest ranks of the people. Every workman has a great quantity of his own work to dispose of beyond what he himself has occasion for; and every other workman being exactly in the same situation, he is enabled to exchange a great quantity of his own goods for a great quantity or, what comes to the same thing, for the price of a great quantity of theirs. He supplies them abundantly with what they have occasion for, and they accommodate him as amply with what he has occasion for, and a general plenty diffuses itself through all the different ranks of the society.

[***]

CHAPTER II
OF THE PRINCIPLE WHICH GIVES OCCASION TO THE DIVISION OF LABOR.

THIS division of labor, from which so many advantages are derived, is not originally the effect of any human wisdom, which foresees and intends that general opulence to which it gives occasion. It is the necessary, though very slow and gradual, consequence of a certain propensity in human nature, which has in view no such extensive utility; the propensity to truck, barter, and exchange one thing for another.

[***]

. . . In civilized society he stands at all times in need of the co-operation and assistance of great multitudes, while his whole life is scarce sufficient to gain the friendship of a few persons. In almost every other race of animals, each individual, when it is grown up to maturity, is entirely independent, and in its natural state has occasion for the assistance of no other living creature. But man has almost constant occasion for the help of his brethren, and it is in vain for him to expect it from their benevolence only. He will be more likely to prevail if he can interest their self-love in his favor, and shew them that it is for their own advantage to do for him what he requires of them. Whoever offers to another a bargain of any kind, proposes to do this. Give me that which I want, and you shall have this which you want, is the meaning of every such offer; and it is in this manner that we obtain from one another the far greater part of those good offices which we stand in need of. It is not from the benevolence of the butcher the brewer, or the baker that we expect our dinner, but from their regard to their own interest. We address ourselves, not to their humanity, but to their self-love, and never talk to them of our own necessities, but of their advantages. Nobody but a beggar chooses to depend chiefly upon the benevolence of his fellow-citizens. Even a beggar does not depend upon it entirely. The charity of well-disposed people, indeed, supplies him with the whole fund of his subsistence. But though this principle ultimately provides him with all the necessaries of life which he has occasion for, it neither does nor can provide him with them as he has occasion for them. The greater part of his occasional wants are supplied in the same manner as those of other people, by treaty, by barter, and by purchase. With the money which one man gives him he purchases food. The old clothes which another bestows upon him he exchanges for other clothes which suit him better, or for lodging, or for food, or for money, with which he can buy either food, clothes, or lodging, as he has occasion.

As it is by treaty, by barter, and by purchase, that we obtain from one another the greater part of those mutual good offices which we stand in need of, so it is this same trucking disposition which originally gives occasion to the division of labor. In a tribe of hunters or shepherds, a particular person makes bows and arrows, for example, with more readiness and dexterity than any other. He frequently exchanges them for cattle or for venison, with his companions; and he finds at last that he can, in this manner, get more cattle and venison, than if he himself went to the field to catch them. From a regard to his own interest, therefore, the making of bows and arrows grows to be his chief business, and he becomes a sort of armorer. Another excels in making the frames and covers of their little huts or moveable houses. He is accustomed to be of use in this way to his neighbors, who reward him in the same manner with cattle and with venison, till at last he finds it his interest to dedicate himself entirely to this employment, and to become a sort of house-carpenter. In the same manner a third becomes a smith or a brazier; a fourth, a tanner or dresser of hides or skins, the principal part of the clothing of savages. And thus the certainty of being able to exchange all that surplus part of the produce of his own labor, which is over and above his own consumption, for such parts of the produce of other men's labor as he may have occasion for, encourages every man to apply himself to a particular occupation, and to cultivate and bring to perfection whatever talent of genius he may possess for that particular species of business.

The difference of natural talents in different men, is, in reality, much less than we are aware of; and the very different genius which appears to distinguish men of different professions, when grown up to maturity, is not upon many occasions so much the cause, as the effect of the division of labor. The difference between the most dissimilar characters, between a philosopher and a common street porter, for example, seems to arise not so much from nature, as from habit, custom, and education . . . . But without the disposition to truck, barter, and exchange, every man must have procured to himself every necessary and convenience of life which he wanted. All must have had the same duties to perform, and the same work to do, and there could have been no such difference of employment as could alone give occasion to any great difference of talents.

As it is this disposition which forms that difference of talents, so remarkable among men of different professions, so it is this same disposition which renders that difference useful . . . . The effects of those different geniuses and talents, for want of the power or disposition to barter and exchange, cannot be brought into a common stock, and do not in the least contribute to the better accommodation and convenience of the species. Each animal is still obliged to support and defend itself, separately and independently, and derives no sort of advantage from that variety of talents with which nature has distinguished its fellows. Among men, on the contrary, the most dissimilar geniuses are of use to one another; the different produces of their respective talents, by the general disposition to truck, barter, and exchange, being brought, as it were, into a common stock, where every man may purchase whatever part of the produce of other men's talents he has occasion for.

CHAPTER III
That The Division Of Labor Is Limited By The Extent Of The Market

As it is the power of exchanging that gives occasion to the division of labor, so the extent of this division must always be limited by the extent of that power, or, in other words, by the extent of the market. When the market is very small, no person can have any encouragement to dedicate himself entirely to one employment, for want of the power to exchange all that surplus part of the produce of his own labor, which is over and above his own consumption, for such parts of the produce of other men's labor as he has occasion for.

There are some sorts of industry, even of the lowest kind, which can be carried on nowhere but in a great town. A porter, for example, can find employment and subsistence in no other place. A village is by much too narrow a sphere for him; even an ordinary market-town is scarce large enough to afford him constant occupation. In the lone houses and very small villages which are scattered about in so desert a country as the highlands of Scotland, every farmer must be butcher, baker, and brewer, for his own family. In such situations we can scarce expect to find even a smith, a carpenter, or a mason, within less than twenty miles of another of the same trade. The scattered families that live at eight or ten miles distance from the nearest of them, must learn to perform themselves a great number of little pieces of work, for which, in more populous countries, they would call in the assistance of those workmen. Country workmen are almost everywhere obliged to apply themselves to all the different branches of industry that have so much affinity to one another as to be employed about the same sort of materials. A country carpenter deals in every sort of work that is made of wood: a country smith in every sort of work that is made of iron. The former is not only a carpenter, but a joiner, a cabinet-maker, and even a carver in wood, as well as a wheelwright, a ploughwright, a cart and waggon-maker. The employments of the latter are still more various . . . .

[***]

CHAPTER IV
OF THE ORIGIN AND USE OF MONEY

WHEN the division of labor has been once thoroughly established, it is but a very small part of a man's wants which the produce of his own labor can supply. He supplies the far greater part of them by exchanging that surplus part of the produce of his own labor, which is over and above his own consumption, for such parts of the produce of other men's labor as he has occasion for. Every man thus lives by exchanging, or becomes, in some measure, a merchant, and the society itself grows to be what is properly a commercial society.

But when the division of labor first began to take place, this power of exchanging must frequently have been very much clogged and embarrassed in its operations. One man, we shall suppose, has more of a certain commodity than he himself has occasion for, while another has less. The former, consequently, would be glad to dispose of; and the latter to purchase, a part of this superfluity. But if this latter should chance to have nothing that the former stands in need of, no exchange can be made between them. The butcher has more meat in his shop than he himself can consume, and the brewer and the baker would each of them be willing to purchase a part of it. But they have nothing to offer in exchange, except the different productions of their respective trades, and the butcher is already provided with all the bread and beer which he has immediate occasion for. No exchange can, in this case, be made between them. He cannot be their merchant, nor they his customers; and they are all of them thus mutually less serviceable to one another. In order to avoid the inconveniency of such situations, every prudent man in every period of society, after the first establishment of the division of labor, must naturally have endeavored to manage his affairs in such a manner, as to have at all times by him, besides the peculiar produce of his own industry, a certain quantity of some one commodity or other, such as he imagined few people would be likely to refuse in exchange for the produce of their industry.

Many different commodities, it is probable, were successively both thought of and employed for this purpose. In the rude ages of society, cattle are said to have been the common instrument of commerce; and, though they must have been a most inconvenient one, yet, in old times, we find things were frequently valued according to the number of cattle which had been given in exchange for them. The armor of Diomede, says Homer, cost only nine oxen; but that of Glaucus cost a hundred oxen. Salt is said to be the common instrument of commerce and exchanges in Abyssinia; a species of shells in some parts of the coast of India; dried cod at Newfoundland; tobacco in Virginia; sugar in some of our West India colonies; hides or dressed leather in some other countries; and there is at this day a village In Scotland, where it is not uncommon, I am told, for a workman to carry nails instead of money to the baker's shop or the ale-house.

In all countries, however, men seem at last to have been determined by irresistible reasons to give the preference, for this employment, to metals above every other commodity. Metals can not only be kept with as little loss as any other commodity, scarce any thing being less perishable than they are, but they can likewise, without any loss, be divided into any number of parts, as by fusion those parts can easily be re-united again; a quality which no other equally durable commodities possess, and which, more than any other quality, renders them fit to be the instruments of commerce and circulation. The man who wanted to buy salt, for example, and had nothing but cattle to give in exchange for it, must have been obliged to buy salt to the value of a whole ox, or a whole sheep, at a time. He could seldom buy less than this, because what he was to give for it could seldom be divided without loss; and if he had a mind to buy more, he must, for the same reasons, have been obliged to buy double or triple the quantity, the value, to wit, of two or three oxen, or of two or three sheep. If, on the contrary, instead of sheep or oxen, he had metals to give in exchange for it, he could easily proportion the quantity of the metal to the precise quantity of the commodity which he had immediate occasion for . . . .

[***]

It is in this manner that money has become, in all civilized nations, the universal instrument of commerce, by the intervention of which goods of all kinds are bought and sold, or exchanged for one another.

[***]

Chapter V
Of The Real And Nominal Price Of Commodities, Or Of Their Price In Labor, And Their Price In Money

Every man is rich or poor according to the degree in which he can afford to enjoy the necessaries, conveniences, and amusements of human life. But after the division of labor has once thoroughly taken place, it is but a very small part of these with which a man's own labor can supply him. The far greater part of them he must derive from the labor of other people, and he must be rich or poor according to the quantity of that labor which he can command, or which he can afford to purchase . . . .

The real price of every thing, what every thing really costs to the man who wants to acquire it, is the toil and trouble of acquiring it. What every thing is really worth to the man who has acquired it and who wants to dispose of it, or exchange it for something else, is the toil and trouble which it can save to himself, and which it can impose upon other people. What is bought with money, or with goods, is purchased by labor, as much as what we acquire by the toil of our own body . . . .

[***]

But when barter ceases, and money has become the common instrument of commerce, every particular commodity is more frequently exchanged for money than for any other commodity. The butcher seldom carries his beef or his mutton to the baker or the brewer, in order to exchange them for bread or for beer; but he carries them to the market, where he exchanges them for money, and afterwards exchanges that money for bread and for beer. The quantity of money which he gets for them regulates, too, the quantity of bread and beer which he can afterwards purchase. It is more natural and obvious to him, therefore, to estimate their value by the quantity of money, the commodity for which he immediately exchanges them, than by that of bread and beer, the commodities for which he can exchange them only by the intervention of another commodity; and rather to say that his butcher's meat is worth three-pence or fourpence a-pound, than that it is worth three or four pounds of bread, or three or four quarts of small beer. Hence it comes to pass, that the exchangeable value of every commodity is more frequently estimated by the quantity of money, than by the quantity either of labor or of any other commodity which can be had in exchange for it.

[***]

CHAPTER VI
OF THE COMPONENT PART OF THE PRICE OF COMMODITIES

IN THAT early and rude state of society which precedes both the accumulation of stock and the appropriation of land, the proportion between the quantities of labor necessary for acquiring different objects, seems to be the only circumstance which can afford any rule for exchanging them for one another. If among a nation of hunters, for example, it usually costs twice the labor to kill a beaver which it does to kill a deer, one beaver should naturally exchange for or be worth two deer. It is natural that what is usually the produce of two days or two hours labor, should be worth double of what is usually the produce of one day's or one hour's labor.

[***]

As soon as stock has accumulated in the hands of particular persons, some of them will naturally employ it in setting to work industrious people, whom they will supply with materials and subsistence, in order to make a profit by the sale of their work, or by what their labor adds to the value of the materials. In exchanging the complete manufacture either for money, for labor, or for other goods, over and above what may be sufficient to pay the price of the materials, and the wages of the workmen, something must be given for the profits of the undertaker of the work, who hazards his stock in this adventure. The value which the workmen add to the materials, therefore, resolves itself in this case into two parts, of which the one pays their wages, the other the profits of their employer upon the whole stock of materials and wages which he advanced. He could have no interest to employ them, unless he expected from the sale of their work something more than what was sufficient to replace his stock to him; and he could have no interest to employ a great stock rather than a small one, unless his profits were to bear some proportion to the extent of his stock.

[***]

In this state of things, the whole produce of labor does not always belong to the laborer. He must in most cases share it with the owner of the stock which employs him. Neither is the quantity of labor commonly employed in acquiring or producing any commodity, the only circumstance which can regulate the quantity which it ought commonly to purchase, command or exchange for. An additional quantity, it is evident, must be due for the profits of the stock which advanced the wages and furnished the materials of that labor . . . .

[***]

But the whole price of any commodity must still finally resolve itself into some one or other or all of those three parts; as whatever part of it remains after paying the rent of the land, and the price of the whole labor employed in raising, manufacturing, and bringing it to market, must necessarily be profit to somebody.

[***]

Book IV

Of Systems Of Political Economy

Chapter II
Of Restraints Upon Importation From Foreign Countries Of Such Goods As Can Be Produced At Home

By RESTRAINING, either by high duties, or by absolute prohibitions, the importation of such goods from foreign countries as can be produced at home, the monopoly of the home market is more or less secured to the domestic industry employed in producing them. Thus the prohibition of importing either live cattle or salt provisions from foreign countries, secures to the graziers of Great Britain the monopoly of the home market for butcher's meat. The high duties upon the importation of corn, which, in times of moderate plenty, amount to a prohibition, give a like advantage to the growers of that commodity. The prohibition of the importation of foreign woollen is equally favorable to the woollen manufacturers . . . .

That this monopoly of the home market frequently gives great encouragement to that particular species of industry which enjoys it, and frequently turns towards that employment a greater share of both the labor and stock of the society than would otherwise have gone to it, cannot be doubted. But whether it tends either to increase the general industry of the society, or to give it the most advantageous direction, is not, perhaps, altogether so evident.

The general industry of the society can never exceed what the capital of the society can employ. As the number of workmen that can be kept in employment by any particular person must bear a certain proportion to his capital, so the number of those that can be continually employed by all the members of a great society must bear a certain proportion to the whole capital of the society, and never can exceed that proportion. No regulation of commerce can increase the quantity of industry in any society beyond what its capital can maintain. It can only divert a part of it into a direction into which it might not otherwise have gone; and it is by no means certain that this artificial direction is likely to be more advantageous to the society, than that into which it would have gone of its own accord.

Every individual is continually exerting himself to find out the most advantageous employment for whatever capital he can command. It is his own advantage, indeed, and not that of the society, which he has in view. But the study of his own advantage naturally, or rather necessarily, leads him to prefer that employment which is most advantageous to the society.

First, every individual endeavors to employ his capital as near home as he can, and consequently as much as he can in the support of domestic industry, provided always that he can thereby obtain the ordinary, or not a great deal less than the ordinary profits of stock.

. . . Upon equal, or only nearly equal profits, therefore, every individual naturally inclines to employ his capital in the manner in which it is likely to afford the greatest support to domestic industry, and to give revenue and employment to the greatest number of people of his own country.

Secondly, every individual who employs his capital in the support of domestic industry, necessarily endeavors so to direct that industry, that its produce may be of the greatest possible value.

The produce of industry is what it adds to the subject or materials upon which it is employed. In proportion as the value of this produce is great or small, so will likewise be the profits of the employer. But it is only for the sake of profit that any man employs a capital in the support of industry; and he will always, therefore, endeavor to employ it in the support of that industry of which the produce is likely to be of the greatest value, or to exchange for the greatest quantity either of money or of other goods.

But the annual revenue of every society is always precisely equal to the exchangeable value of the whole annual produce of its industry, or rather is precisely the same thing with that exchangeable value. As every individual, therefore, endeavors as much as he can, both to employ his capital in the support of domestic industry, and so to direct that industry that its produce maybe of the greatest value; every individual necessarily labors to render the annual revenue of the society as great as he can. He generally, indeed, neither intends to promote the public interest, nor knows how much he is promoting it. By preferring the support of domestic to that of foreign industry, he intends only his own security; and by directing that industry in such a manner as its produce may be of the greatest value, he intends only his own gain; and he is in this, as in many other cases, led by an invisible hand to promote an end which was no part of his intention. Nor is it always the worse for the society that it was no part of it. By pursuing his own interest, he frequently promotes that of the society more effectually than when he really intends to promote it.

I have never known much good done by those who affected to trade for the public good. It is an affectation, indeed, not very common among merchants, and very few words need be employed in dissuading them from it.

What is the species of domestic industry which his capital can employ, and of which the produce is likely to be of the greatest value, every individual, it is evident, can in his local situation judge much better than any statesman or lawgiver can do for him. The statesman, who should attempt to direct private people in what manner they ought to employ their capitals, would not only load himself with a most unnecessary attention, but assume an authority which could safely be trusted, not only to no single person, but to no council or senate whatever, and which would nowhere be so dangerous as in the hands of a man who had folly and presumption enough to fancy himself fit to exercise it.

To give the monopoly of the home market to the produce of domestic industry, in any particular art or manufacture, is in some measure to direct private people in what manner they ought to employ their capitals, and must in almost all cases be either a useless or a hurtful regulation. If the produce of domestic can be brought there as cheap as that of foreign industry, the regulation is evidently useless. If it cannot, it must generally be hurtful. It is the maxim of every prudent master of a family, never to attempt to make at home what it will cost him more to make than to buy. The tailor does not attempt to make his own shoes, but buys them of the shoemaker. The shoemaker does not attempt to make his own clothes, but employs a tailor. The farmer attempts to make neither the one nor the other, but employs those different artificers. All of them find it for their interest to employ their whole industry in a way in which they have some advantage over their neighbors, and to purchase with a part of its produce, or, what is the same thing, with the price of a part of it, whatever else they have occasion for.

What is prudence in the conduct of every private family can scarce be folly in that of a great kingdom. If a foreign country can supply us with a commodity cheaper than we ourselves can make it, better buy it of them with some part of the produce of our own industry, employed in a way in which we have some advantage. The general industry of the country being always in proportion to the capital which employs it, will not thereby be diminished, no more than that of the abovementioned artificers; but only left to find out the way in which it can be employed with the greatest advantage. It is certainly not employed to the greatest advantage, when it is thus directed towards an object which it can buy cheaper than it can make. The value of its annual produce is certainly more or less diminished, when it is thus turned away from producing commodities evidently of more value than the commodity which it is directed to produce. According to the supposition, that commodity could be purchased from foreign countries cheaper than it can be made at home; it could therefore have been purchased with a part only of the commodities, or, what is the same thing, with a part only of the price of the commodities, which the industry employed by an equal capital would have produced at home, had it been left to follow its natural course. The industry of the country, therefore, is thus turned away from a more to a less advantageous employment; and the exchangeable value of its annual produce, instead of being increased, according to the intention of the lawgiver, must necessarily be diminished by every such regulation.

By means of such regulations, indeed, a particular manufacture may sometimes be acquired sooner than it could have been otherwise, and after a certain time may be made at home as cheap, or cheaper, than in the foreign country. But though the industry of the society may be thus carried with advantage into a particular channel sooner than it could have been otherwise, it will by no means follow that the sum-total, either of its industry, or of its revenue, can ever be augmented by any such regulation. The industry of the society can augment only in proportion as its capital augments, and its capital can augment only in proportion to what can be gradually saved out of its revenue. But the immediate effect of every such regulation is to diminish its revenue; and what diminishes its revenue is certainly not very likely to augment its capital faster than it would have augmented of its own accord, had both capital and industry been left to find out their natural employments.

Though for want of such regulations the society should never acquire the proposed manufacture, it would not, upon that account, necessarily be the poorer in anyone period of its duration. In every period of its duration its whole capital and industry might still have been employed, though upon different objects, in the manner that was most advantageous at the time. In every period its revenue might have been the greatest which its capital could afford, and both capital and revenue might have been augmented with the greatest possible rapidity.

The natural advantages which one country has over another in producing particular commodities are sometimes so great, that it is acknowledged by all the world to be in vain to struggle with them. By means of glasses, hotbeds and hot-walls, very good grapes can be raised in Scotland, and very good wine, too, can be made of them at about thirty times the expense for which at least equally good can be brought from foreign countries. Would it be a reasonable law to prohibit the importation of all foreign wines, merely to encourage the making of claret and burgundy in Scotland? But if there would be a manifest absurdity in turning toward any employment thirty times more of the capital and industry of the country than would be necessary to purchase from foreign countries an equal quantity of the commodities wanted, there must be an absurdity, though not altogether so glaring, yet exactly of the same kind, in turning toward any such employment a thirtieth, or even a three-hundredth part more of either. Whether the advantages which one country has over another be natural or acquired is in this respect of no consequence. As long as the one country has those advantages, and the other wants them, it will always be more advantageous for the latter rather to buy of the former than to make. It is an acquired advantage only, which one artificer has over his neighbor, who exercises another trade; and yet they both find it more advantageous to buy of one another, than to make what does not belong to their particular trades.

Merchants and manufacturers are the people who derive the greatest advantage from this monopoly of the home market. The prohibition of the importation of foreign cattle, and of salt provisions, together with the high duties upon foreign corn, which in times of moderate plenty amount to a prohibition, are not near so advantageous to the graziers and farmers of Great Britain, as other regulations of the same kind are to its merchants and manufacturers. Manufactures, those of the finer kind especially, are more easily transported from one country to another than corn or cattle. It is in the fetching and carrying manufactures, accordingly, that foreign trade is chiefly employed. In manufactures, a very small advantage will enable foreigners to undersell our own workmen, even in the home market. It will require a very great one to enable them to do so in the rude produce of the soil. If the free importation of foreign manufactures were permitted, several of the home manufactures would probably suffer, and some of them, perhaps, go to ruin altogether, and a considerable part of the stock and industry at present employed in them would be forced to find out some other employment. But the freest importation of the rude produce of the soil could have no such effect upon the agriculture of the country.

If the importation of foreign cattle, for example, were made ever so free, so few could be imported that the grazing trade of Great Britain could be little affected by it. Live cattle are, perhaps, the only commodity of which the transportation is more expensive by sea than by land. By land they carry themselves to market. By sea, not only the cattle, but their food and their water, too, must be carried at no small expense and inconvenience. The short sea between Ireland and Great Britain, indeed, renders the importation of Irish cattle more easy. But though the free importation of them, which was lately permitted only for a limited time, were rendered perpetual, it could have no considerable effect upon the interest of the graziers of Great Britain. Those parts of Great Britain which border upon the Irish Sea are all grazing countries. Irish cattle could never be imported for their use, but must be driven through those very extensive countries at no small expense and inconvenience, before they could arrive at their proper market. Fat cattle could not be driven so far. Lean cattle, therefore, only could be imported, and such importation could interfere, not with the interest of the feeding or fattening countries, to which, by reducing the price of lean cattle, it would rather be advantageous, but with that of the breeding countries only. The small number of Irish cattle imported since their importation was permitted, together with the good price at which lean cattle still continue to sell, seem to demonstrate that even the breeding countries of Great Britain are never likely to be much affected by the free importation of Irish cattle. The common people of Ireland, indeed, are said to have sometimes opposed with violence the exportation of their cattle. But if the exporters had found any great advantage in continuing the trade, they could easily, when the law was on their side, have conquered this mobbish opposition.

[***]

Country gentlemen and farmers are, to their great honor, of all people, the least subject to the wretched spirit of monopoly. The undertaker of a great manufactory is sometimes alarmed if another work of the same kind is established within twenty miles of him. The Dutch undertaker of the woollen manufacture at Abbeville stipulated that no work of the same kind should be established within thirty leagues of that city. Farmers and country gentlemen, on the contrary, are generally disposed rather to promote than to obstruct the cultivation and improvement of their neighbors' farms and estates. They have no secrets, such as those of the greater part of manufacturers, but are generally rather fond of communicating to their neighbors, and of extending as far as possible any new practice which they have found to be advantageous. "Pius Quaestus," says old Cato, "stabilissimusque, minimeque invidiosus; minimeque male cogitantes sunt, qui in eo studio occupati sunt."[4] Country gentlemen and farmers, dispersed in different parts of the country, cannot so easily combine as merchants and manufacturers, who being collected into towns, and accustomed to that exclusive corporation spirit which prevails in them, naturally endeavor to obtain against all their countrymen the same exclusive privilege which they generally possess against the inhabitants of their respective towns. They accordingly seem to have been the original inventors of those restraints upon the importation of foreign goods which secure to them the monopoly of the home market. It was probably in imitation of them, and to put themselves upon a level with those who, they found, were disposed to oppress them, that the country gentlemen and farmers of Great Britain so far forgot the generosity which is natural to their station as to demand the exclusive privilege of supplying their countrymen with corn and butcher's meat. They did not perhaps take time to consider how much less their interest could be affected by the freedom of trade than that of the people whose example they followed.

To prohibit by a perpetual law the importation of foreign corn and cattle, is in reality to enact that the population and industry of the country shall at no time exceed what the rude produce of its own soil can maintain.

There seem, however, to be two cases in which it will generally be advantageous to lay some burden upon foreign, for the encouragement of domestic industry.

The first is, when some particular sort of industry is necessary for the defence of the country. The defence of Great Britain, for example, depends very much upon the number of its sailors and shipping. The act of navigation, therefore, very properly endeavors to give the sailors and shipping of Great Britain the monopoly of the trade of their own country, in some cases by absolute prohibitions, and in others by heavy burdens upon the shipping of foreign countries . . . .

[***]

The second case, in which it will generally be advantageous to lay some burden upon foreign for the encouragement of domestic industry,

---

4   "A dutiful advantage," says old Cato, "and the most stable and scarcely causing of envy; and especially, those who have been occupied in that profession are hardly ill-esteemed." (Trans. Dr. Elza Tiner)

is, when some tax is imposed at home upon the produce of the latter. In this case, it seems reasonable that an equal tax should be imposed upon the like produce of the former. This would not give the monopoly of the home market to domestic industry, nor turn toward a particular employment a greater share of the stock and labor of the country than what would naturally go to it. It would only hinder any part of what would naturally go to it from being turned away by the tax, into a less natural direction, and would leave the competition between foreign and domestic industry, after the tax, as nearly as possible upon the same footing as before it. In Great Britain, when any such tax is laid upon the produce of domestic industry, it is usual at the same time, in order to stop the clamorous complaints of our merchants and manufacturers, that they will be undersold at home, to lay a much heavier duty upon the importation of all foreign goods of the same kind.

MILTON FRIEDMAN

1912-2006

CAPITALISM AND FREEDOM:
"THE ROLE OF GOVERNMENT"
1962

Born in Brooklyn, New York, Milton Friedman has been called the most influential economist of the twentieth Century. Winner of the 1976 Nobel Prize in Economic Science, he was a writer of both popular and scholarly articles and books, a television personality, and a public policy advisor. An impassioned defender of capitalism and free markets, Friedman believed that economic policy makers were generally inept and was strongly opposed to government intervention in the marketplace. The founder of Monetarism and the leader of the Chicago School of Monetary Economics, he argued that fluctuations in the money supply were the primary determinant of the business cycle and the ultimate cause of inflation in the economy.

The youngest of four children born to working-class Jewish immigrants, Friedman was raised in a warm and supportive family environment. A gifted mathematician, he graduated from high school just before his sixteenth birthday. While the family never went hungry, the income generated by their dry goods store was probably insufficient to raise them above the poverty level. An academic scholarship, supplemented by income made waiting tables and clerking in stores, enabled Friedman to attend Rutgers University, where he received his undergraduate degree in mathematics and economics.

Having graduated during the Great Depression, Friedman decided that "becoming an economist seemed more relevant to the burning issues of the day than becoming an applied mathematician or an actuary"

(Breit and Spencer, 1990, 83). He continued his study of economics in graduate school, earning his master's from the University of Chicago in 1933 and his doctorate from Columbia University in 1946. In 1938, he married Rose Director, a fellow graduate student in economics, who was to become a frequent collaborator on many of his projects.

Friedman was the Paul Snowden Russell Distinguished Service Professor Emeritus of Economics at the University of Chicago, where he taught for three decades. After he retired from teaching, he continued his scholarly work as a Senior Research Fellow at the Hoover Institution at Stanford University. A president of the American Economic Association, he was awarded nineteen honorary degrees from academic institutions in the US, Japan, Israel, Czech Republic, and Guatemala, and was a Fulbright Visiting Professor at Cambridge University.

Friedman's most significant contributions are *A Monetary History of the United States, 1867-1960* (1963), co-authored with Anna J. Schwartz, and *Capitalism and Freedom* (1962), co-authored with Rose D. Friedman. He is perhaps best known by the general public for his column in *Newsweek* magazine and for his ten-part television program *Free to Choose*, originally broadcast on PBS in 1980. A book of the same name, co-authored with his wife Rose, was translated into more than fourteen languages and became the best-selling nonfiction book of 1980.

During World War II, he helped the Treasury Department create the federal income tax withholding system to finance the war effort and used his statistical skills to help solve problems in weapons design and military tactics. Three decades later, his work on the Commission on an All-Volunteer Armed Force contributed to the abolition of the military draft in 1973.

After Friedman and Schwartz (1963) attributed the Great Depression to the Federal Reserve's misguided monetary policies, its Board of Governors discontinued their policy of making public the minutes from their meetings. The Milton and Rose D. Friedman Foundation for Educational Choice was established in 1996 to promote the use of school vouchers. Friedman, according to Bob Zimmer (2007), President of the University of Chicago, was a "brilliant analyst and fearless intellect . . . . He was a powerful thinker whose insights into his own discipline were profound, but whose work and approach had relevance far beyond his discipline's boundaries . . . . Milton Friedman was renowned for unrelenting argument, bringing out the best in himself and others through his insistence on rigor and relentless argument in search of clarity. Status counted for nothing, merit of argument counted for everything. He thereby changed economics through his argument-tested insights and his conviction and willingness to stand alone, if necessary, against . . . common belief."

As you read this selection, try to imagine how Friedman would respond to the arguments made by the Catholic bishops in their pastoral letter on the economy. To what extent do you think Friedman would support government regulations to address the kinds of abuses described by Sinclair in *The Jungle?*

SELECTION FROM:

Friedman, Milton. (1962). *Capitalism and Freedom*. Chicago: The University of Chicago Press. 22-36.

CHAPTER II
THE ROLE OF GOVERNMENT IN A FREE SOCIETY

A COMMON OBJECTION to totalitarian societies is that they regard the end as justifying the means. Taken literally, this objection is clearly illogical. If the end does not justify the means, what does? But this easy answer does not dispose of the objection; it simply shows that the objection is not well put. To deny that the end justifies the means is indirectly to assert that the end in question is not the ultimate end, that the ultimate end is itself the use of the proper means. Desirable or not, any end that can be attained only by the use of bad means must give way to the more basic end of the use of acceptable means.

To the liberal, the appropriate means are free discussion and voluntary co-operation, which implies that any form of coercion is inappropriate. The ideal is unanimity among responsible individuals achieved on the basis of free and full discussion. This is another way of expressing the goal of freedom emphasized in the preceding chapter.

From this standpoint, the role of the market, as already noted that it permits unanimity without conformity; that it is a system of effectively proportional representation. On the other hand, the characteristic feature of action through explicitly political channels is that it tends to require or to enforce substantial conformity. The typical issue must be decided "yes" or "no"; at most, provision can be made for a fairly limited number of alternatives. Even the use of proportional representation in its explicitly political form does not alter this conclusion. The number of separate groups that can in fact be represented is narrowly limited, enormously so by comparison with the proportional representation of the market. More important, the fact that the final outcome generally must be a law applicable to all groups, rather than separate legislative enactments for each "party" represented, means that proportional representation in its political version, far from permitting unanimity without conformity, tends toward ineffectiveness and fragmentation. It thereby operates to destroy any consensus on which unanimity with conformity can rest.

There are clearly some matters with respect to which effective proportional representation is impossible. I cannot get the amount of national defense I want and you, a different amount. With respect to such indivisible matters we can discuss, and argue, and vote. But having decided, we must conform. It is precisely the existence of such indivisible matters—protection of the individual and the nation from coercion are clearly the most basic—that prevents exclusive reliance on individual action through the market. If we are to use some of our resources for such indivisible items, we must employ political channels to reconcile differences.

The use of political channels, while inevitable, tends to strain the social cohesion essential for a stable society. The strain is least if agreement for joint action need be reached only on a limited range of issues on which people in any event have common views. Every extension of the range of issues for which explicit agreement is sought strains further the delicate threads that hold society together. If it goes so far as to touch an issue on which men feel deeply yet differently, it may well disrupt the society. Fundamental differences in basic values can seldom if ever be resolved at the ballot box; ultimately they can only be decided, though not resolved, by conflict. The religious and civil wars of history are a bloody testament to this judgment.

The widespread use of the market reduces the strain on the social fabric by rendering conformity unnecessary with respect to any activities it encompasses. The wider the range of activities covered by the market, the fewer are the issues on which explicitly political decisions are required and hence on which it is necessary to achieve agreement. In turn, the fewer the issues on which agreement is necessary, the greater is the likelihood of getting agreement while maintaining a free society.

Unanimity is, of course, an ideal. In practice, we can afford neither the time nor the effort that would be required to achieve complete unanimity on every issue. We must perforce accept something less. We are thus led to accept majority rule in one form or another as an expedient. That majority rule is an expedient rather than itself a basic principle is clearly shown by the fact that our willingness to resort to majority rule, and the size of the majority we require, themselves depend on the seriousness of the issue involved. If the matter is of little moment and the minority has no strong feelings about being overruled, a bare plurality will suffice. On the other hand, if the minority feels strongly about the issue involved, even a bare majority will not do. Few of us would be willing to have issues of free speech, for example, decided by a bare majority. Our legal structure is full of such distinctions among kinds of issues that require different kinds of majorities. At the extreme are those issues embodied in the Constitution. These are the principles that are so important that we are willing to make minimal concessions to expediency. Something like essential consensus was achieved initially in accepting them, and we require something like essential consensus for a change in them.

The self-denying ordinance to refrain from majority rule on certain kinds of issues that is embodied in our Constitution and in similar written or unwritten constitutions elsewhere, and the specific provisions in these constitutions or their equivalents prohibiting coercion of individuals, are themselves to be regarded as reached by free discussion and as reflecting essential unanimity about means.

I turn now to consider more specifically, though still in very broad terms, what the areas are that cannot be handled through the market at all, or can be handled only at so great a cost that the use of political channels may be preferable.

GOVERNMENT AS RULE-MAKER AND UMPIRE

It is important to distinguish the day-to-day activities of people from the general customary and legal framework within which these take place. The day-to-day activities are like the actions of the participants in a game when they are playing it; the frame work, like the rules of the game they play. And just as a good game requires acceptance by the players both of the rules and of the umpire to interpret and enforce them, so a good society requires that its members agree on the general conditions that will govern relations among them, on some means of arbitrating different interpretations of these conditions, and on some device for enforcing compliance with the generally accepted rules. As in games, so also in society, most of the general conditions are the unintended outcome of custom, accepted unthinkingly. At most, we consider explicitly only minor modifications in them, though the cumulative effect of a series of minor modifications may be a drastic alteration in the character of the game or of the society. In both games and society also, no set of rules can prevail unless most participants most of the time conform to them without external sanctions; unless that is, there is a broad underlying social consensus. But we cannot rely on custom or on this consensus alone to interpret and to enforce the rules; we need an umpire. These then are the basic roles of government in a free society: to provide a means whereby we can modify the rules, to mediate differences among us on the meaning of the rules, and to enforce compliance with the rules on the part of those few who would otherwise not play the game.

The need for government in these respects arises because absolute freedom is impossible. However attractive anarchy may be as a philosophy, it is not feasible in a world of imperfect men. Men's freedoms can conflict, and when they do, one man's freedom must be limited to preserve another's—as a Supreme Court Justice once put it, "My freedom to move my fist must be limited by the proximity of your chin."

The major problem in deciding the appropriate activities of government is how to resolve such conflicts among the freedoms of different individuals. In some cases, the answer is easy. There is little difficulty in attaining near unanimity to the proposition that one man's freedom to murder his neighbor must be sacrificed to preserve the freedom of the other man to live. In other cases, the answer is difficult. In the economic area, a major problem arises in respect of the conflict between freedom to combine and freedom to compete. What meaning is to be attributed to "free" as modifying "enterprise"? In the United States, "free" has been understood to mean that anyone is free to set up an enterprise, which means that existing enterprises are not free to keep out competitors except by selling a better product at the same price or the same product at a lower price. In the continental tradition, on the other hand, the meaning has generally been that enterprises are free to do what they want, including the fixing of prices, division of markets, and the adoption of other techniques to keep out potential competitors. Perhaps the most difficult specific problem in this area arises with respect to combinations among laborers, where the problem of freedom to combine and freedom to compete is particularly acute.

A still more basic economic area in which the answer is both difficult and important is the definition of property rights. The notion of property, as it has developed over centuries and as it is embodied in our legal codes, has become so much a part of us that we tend to take it for granted, and fail to recognize the extent to which just what constitutes property and what rights the ownership of property confers are complex social creations rather than self-evident propositions. Does my having title to land, for example, and my freedom to use my property as I wish, permit me to deny to someone else the right to fly over my land in his airplane? Or does his right to use his airplane take precedence? Or does this depend on how high he flies? Or how much noise he makes? Does voluntary exchange require that he pay me for the privilege of flying over my land? Or that I must pay him to refrain from flying over it? The mere mention of royalties, copyrights, patents; shares of stock in corporations; riparian rights, and the like, may perhaps emphasize the role of generally accepted social rules in the very definition of property. It may suggest also that, in many cases, the existence of a well specified and generally accepted definition of property is far more important than just what the definition is.

Another economic area that raises particularly difficult problems is the monetary system. Government responsibility for the monetary system has long been recognized. It is explicitly provided for in the constitutional provision which gives Congress the power "to coin money, regulate the value thereof, and of foreign coin." There is probably no other area of economic activity with respect to which government action has been so uniformly accepted. This habitual and by now almost unthinking acceptance of governmental responsibility makes thorough understanding of the grounds for such responsibility all the more necessary, since it enhances the danger that the scope of government will spread from activities that are, to those that are not, appropriate in a free society, from providing a monetary frame work to determining the allocation of resources among individuals. We shall discuss this problem in detail in chapter iii.

In summary, the organization of economic activity through voluntary exchange presumes that we have provided, through government, for the maintenance of law and order to prevent coercion of one individual by another, the enforcement of contracts voluntarily entered into, the definition of the meaning of property rights, the interpretation and enforcement of such rights, and the provision of a monetary framework.

ACTION THROUGH GOVERNMENT ON GROUNDS OF TECHNICAL MONOPOLY AND NEIGHBORHOOD EFFECTS

The role of government just considered is to do something that the market cannot do for itself, namely, to determine, arbitrate, and enforce the rules of the game. We may also want to do through government some things that might conceivably be done through the market but that technical or similar conditions render it difficult to do in that way. These all reduce to cases in which strictly voluntary exchange is either exceedingly costly or practically impossible. There are two general classes of such cases: monopoly and similar market imperfections, and neighborhood effects.

Exchange is truly voluntary only when nearly equivalent alternatives exist. Monopoly implies the absence of alternatives and thereby inhibits effective freedom of exchange. In practice, monopoly frequently, if not generally, arises from government support or from collusive agreements among individuals. With respect to these, the problem is either to avoid governmental fostering of monopoly or to stimulate the effective enforcement of rules such as those embodied in our anti-trust laws. However, monopoly may also arise because it is technically efficient to have a single producer or enterprise. I venture to suggest that such cases are more limited than is supposed but they unquestionably do arise. A simple example is perhaps the provision of telephone services within a community. I shall refer to such cases as "technical" monopoly.

When technical conditions make a monopoly the natural out come of competitive market forces, there are only three alternatives that seem available: private monopoly, public monopoly, or public regulation. All three are bad so we must choose among evils. Henry Simons, observing public regulation of monopoly in the United States, found the results so distasteful that he concluded public monopoly would be a lesser evil. Walter Eucken, a noted German liberal, observing public monopoly in German railroads, found the results so distasteful that he concluded public regulation would be a lesser evil. Having learned from both, I reluctantly conclude that, if tolerable, private monopoly may be the least of the evils.

If society were static so that the conditions which give rise to a technical monopoly were sure to remain, I would have little confidence in this solution. In a rapidly changing society, how ever, the conditions making for technical monopoly frequently change and I suspect that both public regulation and public monopoly are likely to be less responsive to such changes in conditions, to be less readily capable of elimination, than private monopoly.

Railroads in the United States are an excellent example. A large degree of monopoly in railroads was perhaps inevitable on technical grounds in the nineteenth century. This was the justification for the Interstate

Commerce Commission. But conditions have changed. The emergence of road and air transport has reduced the monopoly element in railroads to negligible proportions. Yet we have not eliminated the ICC. On the contrary, the ICC, which started out as an agency to protect the public from exploitation by the railroads, has become an agency to protect railroads from competition by trucks and other means of transport, and more recently even to protect existing truck companies from competition by new entrants. Similarly, in England, when the railroads were nationalized, trucking was at first brought into the state monopoly. If railroads had never been subjected to regulation in the United States, it is nearly certain that by now transportation, including railroads, would be a highly competitive industry with little or no remaining monopoly elements.

The choice between the evils of private monopoly, public monopoly, and public regulation cannot, however, be made once and for all, independently of the factual circumstances. If the technical monopoly is of a service or commodity that is regarded as essential and if its monopoly power is sizable, even the short-run effects of private unregulated monopoly may not be tolerable, and either public regulation or ownership may be a lesser evil.

Technical monopoly may on occasion justify a *de facto* public monopoly. It cannot by itself justify a public monopoly achieved by making it illegal for anyone else to compete. For example, there is no way to justify our present public monopoly of the post office. It may be argued that the carrying of mail is a technical monopoly and that a government monopoly is the least of evils. Along these lines, one could perhaps justify a government post office but not the present law, which makes it illegal for anybody else to carry mail. If the delivery of mail is a technical monopoly, no one will be able to succeed in competition with the government. If it is not, there is no reason why the government should be engaged in it. The only way to find out is to leave other people free to enter.

The historical reason why we have a post office monopoly is because the Pony Express did such a good job of carrying the mail across the continent that, when the government introduced transcontinental service, it couldn't compete effectively and lost money. The result was a law making it illegal for anybody else to carry the mail. That is why the Adams Express Company is an investment trust today instead of an operating company. I conjecture that if entry into the mail-carrying business were open to all, there would be a large number of firms entering it and this archaic industry would become revolutionized in short order.

A second general class of cases in which strictly voluntary exchange is impossible arises when actions of individuals have effects on other individuals for which it is not feasible to charge or recompense them. This is the problem of "neighborhood effects" An obvious example is the pollution of a stream. The man who pollutes a stream is in effect forcing others to exchange good water for bad. These others might be willing to make the exchange at a price. But it is not feasible for them, acting individually, to avoid the exchange or to enforce appropriate compensation.

A less obvious example is the provision of highways. In this case, it is technically possible to identify and hence charge individuals for their use of the roads and so to have private operation. However, for general access roads, involving many points of entry and exit, the costs of collection would be extremely high if a charge were to be made for the specific services received by each individual, because of the necessity of establishing toll booths or the equivalent at all entrances. The gasoline tax is a much cheaper method of charging individuals roughly in proportion to their use of the roads. This method, however, is one in which the particular payment cannot be identified closely with the particular use. Hence, it is hardly feasible to have private enterprise provide the service and collect the charge without establishing extensive private monopoly.

These considerations do not apply to long-distance turnpikes with high density of traffic and limited access. For these, the costs of collection are small and in many cases are now being paid, and there are often numerous alternatives, so that there is no serious monopoly problem. Hence, there is every reason why these should be privately owned and operated. If so owned and operated, the enterprise running the highway should receive the gasoline taxes paid on account of travel on it.

Parks are an interesting example because they illustrate the difference between cases that can and cases that cannot he justified by neighborhood effects, and because almost everyone at first sight regards the conduct of National Parks as obviously a valid function of government. In fact, however, neighborhood effects may justify a city park; they do not justify a national park, like Yellowstone National Park or the Grand Canyon. What is the fundamental difference between the two? For the city park, it is extremely difficult to identify the people who benefit from it and to charge them for the benefits which they receive. If there is a park in the middle of the city, the houses on all sides get the benefit of the open space, and people who walk through it or by it also benefit. To maintain toll collectors at the gates or to impose annual charges per window overlooking the park would be very expensive and difficult. The entrances to a national park, like Yellowstone, on the other hand, are few; most of the people who come stay for a considerable period of time and it is perfectly feasible to set up toll gates and collect admission charges. This is indeed now done, though the charges do not cover the whole costs. If the public wants this kind of an activity enough to pay for it, private enterprises will have every incentive to provide such parks. And, of course, there are many private enterprises of this nature now in existence. I cannot myself conjure up any neighborhood effects or important monopoly effects that would justify governmental activity in this area.

Considerations like those I have treated under the heading of neighborhood effects have been used to rationalize almost every conceivable intervention. In many instances, however, this rationalization is special pleading rather than a legitimate application of the concept of neighborhood effects. Neighborhood effects cut both ways. They can be a reason for limiting the activities of government as well as for expanding them. Neighborhood effects impede voluntary exchange because it is difficult to identify the effects on third parties and to measure their magnitude; but this difficulty is present in governmental activity as well. It is hard to know when neighborhood effects are sufficiently large to justify particular costs in overcoming them and even harder to distribute the costs in an appropriate fashion. Consequently, when government engages in activities to overcome neighborhood effects, it will in part introduce an additional set of neighborhood effects by failing to charge or to compensate individuals properly. Whether the original or the new neighborhood effects are the more serious can only be judged by the facts of the individual case, and even then, only very approximately. Furthermore, the use of government to overcome neighborhood effects itself has an extremely important neighborhood effect which is unrelated to the particular occasion for government action. Every act of government intervention limits the area of individual freedom directly and threatens the preservation of freedom indirectly for reasons elaborated in the first chapter.

Our principles offer no hard and fast line how far it is appropriate to use government to accomplish jointly what it is difficult or impossible for us to accomplish separately through strictly voluntary exchange. In any particular case of proposed intervention, we must make up a balance sheet, listing separately the advantages and disadvantages. Our principles tell us what items to put on the one side and what items on the other and they give us some basis for attaching importance to the different items. In particular, we shall always want to enter on the liability side of any proposed government intervention, its neighborhood effect in threatening freedom, and give this effect considerable weight. Just how much weight to give to it, as to other items, depends upon the circumstances. If, for example, existing government intervention is minor, we shall attach a smaller weight to the negative effects of additional government intervention. This is an important reason why many earlier liberals, like Henry Simons, writing at a time when government was small by today's standards, were willing to have government under take activities that today's liberals would not accept now that government has become so overgrown.

Freedom is a tenable objective only for responsible individuals. We do not believe in freedom for madmen or children. The necessity of drawing a line between responsible individuals and others is inescapable, yet it means that there is an essential ambiguity in our ultimate objective of freedom. Paternalism is inescapable for those whom we designate as not responsible.

The clearest case, perhaps, is that of madmen. We are willing neither to permit them freedom nor to shoot them. It would be nice if we could rely on voluntary activities of individuals to house and care for the madmen. But I think we cannot rule out the possibility that such charitable activities will be inadequate, if only because of the neighborhood effect involved in the fact that I benefit if another man contributes to the care of the insane. For this reason, we may be willing to arrange for their care through government.

Children offer a more difficult case. The ultimate operative unit in our society is the family, not the individual. Yet the acceptance of the family as the unit rests in considerable part on expediency rather than principle. We believe that parents are generally best able to protect their children and to provide for their development into responsible individuals for whom freedom is appropriate. But we do not believe in the freedom of parents to do what they will with other people. The children are responsible individuals in embryo, and a believer in freedom believes in protecting their ultimate rights.

To put this in a different and what may seem a more callous way, children are at one and the same time consumer goods and potentially responsible members of society. The freedom of individuals to use their economic resources as they want includes the freedom to use them to have children—to buy, as it were, the services of children as a particular form of consumption. But once this choice is exercised, the children have a value in and of themselves and have a freedom of their own that is not simply an extension of the freedom of the parents.

The paternalistic ground for governmental activity is in many ways the most troublesome to a liberal; for it involves the acceptance of a principle—that some shall decide for others—which he finds objectionable in most applications and which he rightly regards as a hallmark of his chief intellectual opponents, the proponents of collectivism in one or another of its guises, whether it be communism, socialism, or a welfare state. Yet there is no use pretending that problems are simpler than in fact they are. There is no avoiding the need for some measure of paternalism. As Dicey wrote in 1914 about an act for the protection of mental defectives, "The Mental Deficiency Act is the first step along a path on which no sane man can decline to enter, but which, if too far pursued, will bring statesmen across difficulties hard to meet without considerable interference with individual liberty."[1] There is no formula that can tell us where to stop. We must rely on our fallible judgment and, having reached a judgment, on our ability to persuade our fellow men that it is a correct judgment, or their ability to persuade us to modify our views. We must put our faith, here as elsewhere, in a consensus reached by imperfect and biased men through free discussion and trial and error.

CONCLUSION

A government which maintained law and order, defined property rights, served as a means whereby we could modify property rights and other rules of the economic game, adjudicated disputes about the interpretation of the rules, enforced contracts, promoted competition, provided a monetary frame work, engaged in activities to counter technical monopolies and to overcome neighborhood effects widely regarded as sufficiently important to justify government intervention, and which supplemented private charity and the private family in protecting the irresponsible, whether madman or child—such a government would clearly have important functions to perform. The consistent liberal is not an anarchist.

Yet it is also true that such a government would have clearly limited functions and would refrain from a host of activities that are now undertaken by federal and state governments in the United States, and their counterparts

---

[1]   A. V. Dicey, *Lectures on the Relation between law and Public Opinion in England during the Nineteenth Century* (2d. ed.; London: Macmillan & Co., 1914), p. li.

in other Western countries. Succeeding chapters will deal in some detail with some of these activities, and a few have been discussed above, but it may help to give a sense of proportion about the role that a liberal would assign government simply to list, in closing this chapter, some activities currently undertaken by government in the U.S., that cannot, so far as I can see, validly be justified in terms of the principles outlined above:

1. Parity price support programs for agriculture.
2. Tariffs on imports or restrictions on exports, such as current oil import quotas, sugar quotas, etc.
3. Governmental control of output, such as through the farm program, or through prorationing of oil as is done by the Texas Railroad Commission.
4. Rent control, such as is still practiced in New York, or more general price and wage controls such as were imposed during and just after World War II.
5. Legal minimum wage rates, or legal maximum prices, such as the legal maximum of zero on the rate of interest that can be paid on demand deposits by commercial banks, or the legally fixed maximum rates that can be paid on savings and time deposits.
6. Detailed regulation of industries, such as the regulation of transportation by the Interstate Commerce Commission. This had some justification on technical monopoly grounds when initially introduced for railroads it has none now for any means of transport. Another example is detailed regulation of banking.
7. A similar example, but one which deserves special mention because of its implicit censorship and violation of free speech, is the control of radio and television by the Federal Communications Commission.
8. Present social security programs, especially the old-age and retirement programs compelling people in effect (a) to spend a specified fraction of their income on the purchase of retirement annuity, (b) to buy the annuity from a publicly operated enterprise.
9. Licensure provisions in various cities and states which restrict particular enterprises or occupations or professions to people who have a license, where the license is more than a receipt for a tax which anyone who wishes to enter the activity may pay.
10. So-called "public-housing" and the host of other subsidy programs directed at fostering residential construction such as F.H.A. and V.A. guarantee of mortgage, and the like.

11. Conscription to man the military services in peacetime. The appropriate free market arrangement is volunteer military forces; which is to say, hiring men to serve. There is no justification for not paying whatever price is necessary to attract the required number of men. Present arrangements are inequitable and arbitrary, seriously interfere with the freedom of young men to shape their lives, and probably are even more costly than the market alternative. (Universal military training to provide a reserve for war time is a different problem and may be justified on liberal grounds.)
12. National parks, as noted above.
13. The legal prohibition on the carrying of mail for profit.
14. Publicly owned and operated toll roads, as noted above.

This list is far from comprehensive.

ARTHUR M. OKUN

1928-1980

EQUALITY AND EFFICIENCY: THE BIG TRADEOFF
1975

Arthur Melvin Okun, a liberal Democrat born in Jersey City, New Jersey, was an American economist and economic policy advisor to U.S. presidents. He is best for quantifying the relationship between unemployment and economic activity,[1] known as "Okun's Law," and as the originator of the "Misery Index," the sum of the unemployment and the inflation rates, which has since become a standard measure of economic performance.

Okun graduated from Columbia University in 1956 with his PhD in Economics and went on to teach at Yale University, where he attained the rank of Professor in 1963. A consultant to the Council of Economic Advisors during the Kennedy Administration, he was appointed to the Council by President Lyndon Johnson in 1964 and served as its chairman from 1968 to 1969. When the Nixon Administration came into power, Okun joined the Brookings Institution in Washington, D.C. as a Senior Fellow.

As President Johnson's chief economic advisor, Okun had a hand in shaping the War on Poverty, which, along with civil rights reform,

---

[1]   Specifically, he found that each percentage point decrease in the unemployment rate was associated with a three percent increase in real gross national product (GNP), which is the most comprehensive measure of economic activity available. As a result of changes in the way the Bureau of Economic Analysis measures economic activity, we now focus, instead, on gross domestic product (GDP).

occupied center stage in the administration's Great Society Program. Ironically, according to Pizzigati (2004, 198), conservatives undermined this initiative by turning his "carefully argued case for thoughtful tradeoffs into an admission, by liberals, that any attempts to make America more equal . . . would inevitably backfire on everyone, the poor included, by slowing economic growth."

Okun placed heavy emphasis on bridging the gap between theory and practice, and was widely respected by both academics and politicians. The evolution of his views illustrates, according to one essayist, "that rare combination of an open mind and the willingness to admit errors publicly."[2] Another observes that "he combined great analytical powers with lucid exposition, . . . and a compassionate concern for ordinary men and women, especially 'for those who start the competitive race from behind.'"[3]

The willingness to trade equality for efficiency, or vice versa, will vary from person to person and will depend upon many things, including one's social and political values and whether he or she anticipates gaining or losing from such a redistribution. Whether and to what extent we should engage in this tradeoff will be determined by the collective preferences of the society. Nonetheless, it is an important question for each of us to ponder. The point in reading Okun is not to learn the "correct" answer to this question or to become familiar with his position so you can agree or disagree with it. We read him because his analysis, and especially his "leaky bucket" metaphor, so effectively illustrates the economic approach to thinking about such issues.

The dangers of generalizing notwithstanding, liberals are more likely to come down on the equality side of the debate, conservatives on the efficiency side. Okun, you'll notice, is not so easy to pin down. In considering the problem he poses, try not to gravitate immediately to the position most compatible with your (or your family's) political orientation. Evaluate the arguments on each side of the issue, keeping in mind that there is no "correct" way to manage the equality-efficiency tradeoff.

Imagine the equality-efficiency tradeoff as a continuum, with complete equality on the left and complete efficiency on the right. Where

---

[2]   See Murray Weidenbaum's review of *Economics for Policymaking: Selected Essays of Arthur M. Okun*, edited by Joseph A. Pechman, in *The Journal of Economic Literature*, Vol. 22, No. 2, June 1984.

[3]   See G. C. Harcourt's review of *Economics Without Equilibrium: The Okun Memorial Lectures at Yale University*, by Nicholas Kaldor, in *The Economic Journal*, Vol. 96, No. 382, June 1986.

along this continuum would you place Friedman, Rand, More and the Catholic Bishops? To what extent can the arguments made by each of these writers be couched in terms of Okun's analytical framework? How might Hacker's essay contribute to our understanding of the problem and influence where along the continuum we choose to locate?

This selection is drawn from *Equality and Efficiency*, a collection of lectures delivered by Okun at Harvard's John F. Kennedy School of Government in 1974.

SELECTION FROM:

Okun, A.M. (1975). *Equality and Efficiency: The Big Tradeoff.* Washington, D.C.: The Brookings Institute. 1-5, 32-34, 88-95, 116-120.

CHAPTER ONE
RIGHTS AND DOLLARS

AMERICAN SOCIETY proclaims the worth of every human being. All citizens are guaranteed equal justice and equal political rights. Everyone has a pledge of speedy response from the fire department and access to national monuments. As American citizens, we are all members of the same club.

Yet at the same time, our institutions say "find a job or go hungry," "succeed or suffer." They prod us to get ahead of our neighbors economically after telling us to stay in line socially. They award prizes that allow the big winners to feed their pets better than the losers can feed their children.

Such is the double standard of a capitalist democracy, professing and pursuing an egalitarian political and social system and simultaneously generating gaping disparities in economic well-being. This mixture of equality and inequality sometimes smacks of inconsistency and even insincerity. Yet I believe that, in many cases, the institutional arrangements represent uneasy compromises rather than fundamental inconsistencies. The contrasts among American families in living standards and in material wealth reflect a system of rewards and penalties that is intended to encourage effort and channel it into socially productive activity. To the extent that the system succeeds, it generates an efficient economy. But that pursuit of efficiency necessarily creates inequalities. And hence society faces a tradeoff between equality and efficiency.

Tradeoffs are the central study of the economist. "You can't have your cake and eat it too" is a good candidate for the fundamental theorem of economic analysis. Producing more of one thing means using labor and capital that could be devoted to more output of something else. Consuming more now means saving less for the future. Working longer impinges on leisure. The crusade against inflation demands the sacrifice of output and employment—posing the tradeoff that now concerns the nation most seriously.

[***]

To the economist, as to the engineer, efficiency means getting the most out of a given input. The inputs applied in production are human effort, the services of physical capital such as machines and buildings, and the endowments of nature like land and mineral resources. The outputs are thousands of different types of goods and services. If society finds a way, with the same inputs, to turn out more of some products (and no less of the others), it has scored an increase in efficiency.

This concept of efficiency implies that more is better, insofar as the "more" consists of items that people want to buy. In relying on the verdicts of consumers as indications of what they want, I, like other economists, accept people's choices as reasonably rational expressions of what makes them better off. To be sure, by a different set of criteria, it is appropriate to ask skeptically whether people are made better off (and thus whether society really becomes more efficient) through the production of more whiskey, more cigarettes, and more big cars. That inquiry raises several intriguing further questions. Why do people want the things they buy? How are their choices influenced by education, advertising, and the like? Are there criteria by which welfare can be appraised that are superior to the observation of the choices people make? Without defense and without apology, let me simply state that I will not explore those issues despite their importance . . . .

. . . Impressionistically, I shall speak of more or less equality as implying smaller or greater disparities among families in their maintainable standards of living, which in turn implies lesser or greater disparities in the distribution of income and wealth, relative to the needs of families of different sizes . . .

The presence of a tradeoff between efficiency and equality does not mean that everything that is good for one is necessarily bad for the other. Measures that might soak the rich so much as to destroy investment and hence impair the quality and quantity of jobs for the poor could worsen both efficiency and equality. On the other hand, techniques that improve the productivity and earnings potential of unskilled workers might benefit society with greater efficiency *and* greater equality. Nonetheless, there are places where the two goals conflict, and those pose the problems . . . .

In this chapter, I will examine the ways in which American society promotes equality (and pays some costs in terms of efficiency) by establishing social and political rights that are distributed equally and universally and that are intended to be kept out of the marketplace. Those rights affect the functioning of the economy and, at the same time, their operation is affected by the market. They lie basically in the territory of the political scientist, which is rarely invaded by the economist. But at times the economist cannot afford to ignore them. The interrelationships between market institutions and inequality are clarified when set against the background of the entire social structure, including the areas where equality is given high priority.

A society that is both democratic and capitalistic has a split-level institutional structure, and both levels need to be surveyed. When only the capitalistic level is inspected, issues concerning the distribution of material welfare are out of focus. In an economy that is based primarily on private enterprise, public efforts to promote equality represent a deliberate interference with the results generated by the marketplace, and they are rarely costless. When the question is posed as: "Should the government tamper with the market?" The self-evident answer is a resounding "No." Not surprisingly, this is a common approach among anti-egalitarian writers. Forget that the Declaration of Independence proclaims the equality of human beings, ignore the Bill of Rights, and one can write that only intellectuals—as distinguished sharply from people—care much about equality.[4] With these blinders firmly in place, egalitarianism in economics can be investigated as though it were an idiosyncrasy, perhaps even a type of neurosis.[5]

It is just as one-sided to view enormous wealth or huge incomes as symptoms of vicious or evil behavior by their owners, or as an oversight of an egalitarian society. The institutions of a market economy promote such inequality, and they are as much a part of our social framework as the civil and political institutions that pursue egalitarian goals. To some, "profits" and "rich" may be dirty words, but their views have not prevailed in the rules of the economic game.

To get a proper perspective, even an economist with no training in other social sciences had better tread—or at least tiptoe—into social and

---

[4]   Irving Kristol, "About Equality," *Commentary*, Vol. 54 (November 1972), pp. 41-47.

[5]   Harry G. Johnson, "Some Micro-Economic Reflections on Income and Wealth Inequalities,": *Annals of the American Academy* of *Political and Social Science*, Vol. 409 (September 1973), p. 54. Johnson attributes the concern with inequality, in part, to "a naive and basically infantile anthropomorphism."

political territory. And that is where I shall begin. I shall travel through the places where society deliberately opts for equality, noting the ways these choices compromise efficiency and curb the role of the market, and examining the reasons why society may choose to distribute some of its entitlements equally. I shall focus particularly on some of the difficulties in establishing and implementing the principle that the equally distributed rights ought not to be bought and sold for money.

[***]

CHAPTER TWO
THE CASE FOR THE MARKET

UNLIKE the equal rights discussed in chapter 1, the economic institutions of the United States rest on voluntary exchange and on private ownership of productive assets; and they involve money rewards and penalties that generate an unequal distribution of income and wealth. Thus the anatomy of the American economy contrasts sharply with the egalitarian structure of its polity. At the same time, the functioning—indeed, the very life—of the market depends on the coercive powers of political institutions. The state uses these powers to establish and ensure rights in the marketplace, directly supply some essential services, and indirectly generate the environment of trust, understanding, and security that is vital to the daily conduct of business.

WHY CAPITALISM?

Our economic institutions are precariously perched on the will—or the whim—of the body politic. Neither rights to ownership of any class of physical assets nor rights to after-tax income are given constitutional safeguards; in principle, they could be curbed drastically by a vote of 51 percent of the elected representatives of the public. And a majority could easily wish to curb them drastically. The bottom half of all American families has only about one-twentieth of all wealth and roughly a quarter of all income.[6] How then does capitalism survive in a democracy? What makes the not-so-affluent majority so charitable toward the rich

---

6   Sources and concepts for data on income and wealth distribution are
discussed in footnotes to chapter 3.

minority? For one thing, those on the low end of the economic totem pole do not have identical interests on many issues; elderly white rural ex-sharecroppers, young black urban welfare mothers, and middle-aged low-wage janitorial workers would find it hard to unite behind a particular program of redistribution. Nonetheless, the tolerance of the masses for economic inequality is puzzling.

At least, it is to me. It does not puzzle some radicals, who see the basic explanation in the transgressions of dollars on rights. According to that argument, because money buys votes, democracy is a sham. Because money controls the media, people are misinformed; hence, their votes fail to express their true economic interests. Thus, both economic and political power remain concentrated in the same minority, which perpetuates oppression and inequality.[7]

Nor does the question puzzle some of the most ardent enthusiasts for the marketplace. They have a ready package of reasons why a rational citizen—rich or poor—*should* support capitalism. That package highlights the contribution of a decentralized market economy to personal freedom. It may also include an ethical defense for wide income differentials that reflect differences in productive contribution. It features the superior efficiency of a market economy. Compared with any alternative system, American capitalism provides higher standards of living for most families, even though some live better than others. Fortunately, it is argued, most voters recognize their true interests and do not behave like the dog in the manger.

The limited evidence available from surveys of public opinion and attitudes suggests that Archie Bunker's preference for capitalism rests on grounds similar to those of the intellectual protagonists for the market. (I will not try to infer who is influencing whom.) In one recent survey, a 28-year-old lower-class woman from Boston offered a rather typical declaration of attitudes toward an equal distribution of income: "It's communism—everybody is the same and they all share. I wouldn't want it. If I work harder than somebody else, why should I share or . . . why shouldn't

---

7   See, for example, Arthur Lothstein (ed.), *"All We Are Saying . . ." The Philosophy of the New Left* (Putnam, 1970): ". . . established forms of representative and parliamentary democracy . . . serve only to legitimize the economic hegemony of the ruling class, and to perpetuate class politics . . . . power which has been usurped by the ruling class . . . is wielded by [the ruling class] for the twin purposes of economic self-aggrandizement and political domination" (p. 15).

I be able to . . . live better . . . ?"[8] In particular, people show surprisingly little resentment toward the extremely wealthy.[9] While they express some concern about inequalities of opportunity and discriminatory treatment, most view those aspects as flaws rather than fundamental defects of the system.

More generally, the public displays deep-seated conservatism toward any major economic reform. People fear the unknown; they know what they have; and they have much to lose besides their alleged chains. Moreover, public criticism or even discussion of income inequality is rare, perhaps because differences in incomes arise so naturally. In the process of producing goods and services, the market also grinds out a set of wage, interest, and profit rates that determine the incomes of the participants. The production and distribution aspects are separated in economic analysis, but not in economic life. Production and income come out of the same machine, much as light and heat emanate from the sun. Except for the occasions when people reach for sunglasses or the air conditioning switch, they do not perceive the two separate aspects of sunshine either.

[***]

CHAPTER FOUR
INCREASING EQUALITY IN AN EFFICIENT ECONOMY

THIS ESSAY began with a visit to the domain of social and political rights in which society gives priority, at least in principle, to equality over economic efficiency. It moved into the marketplace and other economic institutions, in which efficiency gets priority and a large degree of inequality is accepted. It then inspected a few bright prospects for increasing economic efficiency and equality simultaneously. Those prospects are important, but they are limited. Frequently, society is obliged to trade between efficiency and equality. Those trades pose the difficult choices and they are the subject of this final chapter.

THE AREA OF COMPROMISE

If both equality and efficiency are valued, and neither takes absolute priority over the other, then, in places where they conflict, compromises

---

8   Lee Rainwater, *What Money Buys: Inequality and the Social Meanings of Income* (Basic Books, 1974), p. 168.

9   Ibid., pp. 170-74.

ought to be struck. In such cases, some equality will be sacrificed for the sake of efficiency, and some efficiency for the sake of equality. But any sacrifice of either has to be justified as a necessary means of obtaining more of the other (or possibly of some other valued social end). In particular, social decisions that permit economic inequality must be justified as promoting economic efficiency. That proposition is not original,[10] but it is important and apparently remains controversial. Efficiency alone is the criterion for anyone who opposes progressive taxes because he detects *some* adverse effects on incentives. Equality gets no weight in the verdict of an economist who recommends the same formula for any and every shortage: let the price rise to its own level without government interference. At the other extreme, anyone who views high profits anywhere as a prima facie case for public action must be judging by equality alone.

The cartelization of the world oil market engendered a display of such pure no-tradeoff views. Free-market exponents argued the efficiency case: at a new, high, market-clearing price within the United States, curtailment of consumption and expansion of domestic production would both be encouraged. No disruptive shortages would emerge, and the limited supplies would flow to those users who needed oil most, as evidenced by their willingness to pay the most. And this argument may well have been correct, in terms of efficiency alone. But at least during the embargo, the market-clearing solution might have transferred as much as $60 billion of income (at annual rates)—a toll of $20 a week, for the average American family—from oil consumers to domestic oil producers. Wasn't some queuing at gas stations a lesser evil of inefficiency compared to that huge additional inequality?

On the other hand, the antiprofiteering hawks focused on eliminating the windfalls enjoyed by the producers rather than the shortages endured by the consumers. Although the embargo was instituted and the cartel price set by foreign potentates and not by American businessmen, the gains of a few corporations were resented, particularly because they accompanied the losses to most Americans. In this case, what was bad for the country was unquestionably good for Exxon. Still, some of the measures espoused (like hefty excess-profits taxes or inflexible price

---

10   See Lester Thurow, "Toward a Definition of Economic Justice," *Public Interest*, No. 31 (Spring 1973), p. 63. The germ of the idea can be found in Pigou; I suspect that it goes back a lot farther, but I can't trace it. This is a much weaker condition than Rawls' difference principle, discussed below.

freezes) would have made things less good for Exxon only by making them worse for the country.

The actual policies adopted in 1974 lay somewhere between the promarket and antiprofit positions. The price of crude oil for that part of U.S. production that had been geared up by 1972 was controlled at a ceiling of $5.25 per barrel. Since the capability for producing such "old oil" was established and expected to be profitable when the price was $3.50, the ceiling limited the size of windfall profits. Similarly, ceilings were set on refinery and distribution margins. On the other hand, the price of incremental crude production—"new oil"—was not controlled and soared above $10 to the world price fixed by the cartel. In effect, the price of U.S. new oil was allowed to be set by OPEC, the organization of petroleum-exporting countries, while that of old oil was fixed by the U.S. government; neither reflected competitive forces, since the cartel had strangled competition. The case for letting new-oil prices soar rested on efficiency; the policy sought to generate enormous profit incentives for expanded domestic production. Considerations of efficiency and equality were thus blended into an imperfect compromise.

In critical areas, such compromises tend to emerge from the political process. The real question is usually one of degree. On what terms is the nation willing to trade equality for efficiency? Anyone who has passed a course in elementary economics can spout the right formal rule: promote equality up to the point where the added benefits of more equality are just matched by the added costs of greater inefficiency. As is so often the case with the rules that are taught in basic courses, this one provides insight but is hard to apply to the real world. The consequences of most redistributive measures on both equality and efficiency are uncertain and debatable. Confronted with a proposed tax or welfare equalization, no legislator or voter can assess how much the program would add to equality or subtract from efficiency. Thus decision-makers do not get opportunities in the real world to test neatly their priorities between the two competing objectives. But the author of a book can create a hypothetical world that suits him. And so I can propose an experiment by which you can test your attitudes toward the tradeoff.

The Leaky-Bucket Experiment

First, consider the American families who make up the bottom 20 percent of the income distribution. Their after-tax incomes in 1974 were less than $7,000 averaging about $5,000. Now consider the top 5 percent of families in the income pyramid; they had after-tax incomes ranging upward from about $28,000, and averaging about $45,000. A proposal is made to levy an added tax averaging $4,000 (about 9 percent) on the income of the affluent families in an effort to aid the low-income families.[11] Since the low-income group I selected has four times as many families as the affluent group, that should, in principle, finance a $1,000 grant for the average low-income family. However, the program has an unsolved technological problem: the money must be carried from the rich to the poor in a leaky bucket. Some of it will simply disappear in transit, so the poor will not receive all the money that is taken from the rich. The average poor family will get less than $1,000, while the average rich family gives up $4,000.

I shall not try to measure the leak now, because I want you to decide how much leakage you would accept and still support the Tax-and-Transfer Equalization Act. Suppose 10 percent leaks out; that would leave $900 for the average poor family instead of the potential $1,000. Should society still make the switch? If 50 percent leaks out? 75 percent? Even if 99 percent leaks out, the poor get a little benefit; the $4,000 taken from the rich family will yield $10 for each poor family. Where would you draw the line? Your answer cannot be right or wrong—any more than your favorite flavor of ice cream is right or wrong.

Of course, the leak represents an inefficiency. The inefficiencies of real-world redistribution include the adverse effects on the economic incentives of the rich and the poor, and the administrative costs of tax-collection and transfer programs. The opponent of redistribution might argue that my experiment obscures the dynamics of the incentive effects. He might contend that any success in equalization today is likely to be transitory, as the adverse impact on work and investment incentives mounts over time and ultimately harms even the poor. What leaks out, he might insist, is the water needed to irrigate the next crop. In addition, anyone who views market-determined incomes as ethically ideal rewards for contribution would oppose the switch, regardless of the size of the leak.

On the other hand, some would keep switching from rich to poor as long as anything at all remains in the bucket. That is the import of

---

[11]   As the redistribution is described here, the abrupt termination of the tax just below the top 5 percent of the distribution as well as of the transfer just above the bottom 20 percent would imply inequitable "notches." Any real-world proposal would have to smooth these out, and also to determine the proper sharing of the tax burden and transfer benefits.

John Rawls' difference principle, which insists that "all social values . . . are to be distributed equally unless an unequal distribution of any . . . is to everyone's advantage"—in particular, to the advantage of the typical person in the least-advantaged group. [12]

Rawls has a clear, crisp answer: Give priority to equality. And, as he always does, Milton Friedman has a clear, crisp answer: Give priority to efficiency.[13] My answer isn't neat. My answers rarely are, and that is one trouble I generally encounter in such ideological debates. Here, as elsewhere, I compromise. I cannot accept Rawls' egalitarian difference principle. It is supposed to emerge as a consensus of people in the "original position," when they develop social rules without knowing where their own future incomes will lie on the pyramid. But, as other economists have noted,[14] that difference principle would appeal only to people who hate to take any risk whatsoever. That is the implication of the view that no inequality is tolerable unless it raises the lowest income of the society. According to this "maximin" criterion, society is worse off if the lowest-income family loses one dollar, no matter how much everybody else in the society gains. For example, a framer of the social constitution would embrace the difference principle only if he preferred a society that guaranteed every family $14,000 a year—no more and no less—over one that provided 99 percent of all families with $20,000 and 1 percent with $13,000. Put the American people in an "original position," and I certainly would not expect them to act that way.[15]

If I were in Rawls' original position, I would argue that the social Constitution should not seek to settle forever the precise weighting of inequality. It should instruct the society to weight equality heavily, but it should rely on the democratic political process it establishes to select reasonable weights on specific issues as they arise.

[12]   John Rawls, *A Theory of Justice* (Harvard University Press, 1971), p. 62.

[13]   This position is clearly implied by Friedman's discussion in *Capitalism and Freedom* (University of Chicago Press, 1962), pp. 161-66, although it obviously is not addressed to my particular experiment.

[14]   See Kenneth J. Arrow, "Some Ordinalist-Utilitarian Notes on Rawls's *Theory of Justice," Journal of Philosophy,* Vol. 70 (May 10, 1973), pp. 245-63; and Sidney S. Alexander, "Social Evaluation Through National Choice," *Quarterly Journal of Economics,* Vol. 88 (November 1974), pp. 597-624.

[15]   I do believe that risk aversion encourages preferences for equality. In my view, Rawls' original position provides a better framework for a

Unlike Friedman, I would make the switch in the leaky-bucket experiment with enthusiasm if the leakage were 10 or 20 percent. Unlike Rawls, I would stop short of the 99 percent leak. Since I feel obliged to play the far-fetched games that I make up, I will report that I would stop at a leakage of 60 percent in this particular example.

If your answer, like mine, lay somewhere between 1 and 99 percent, presumably the exact figure reflected some judgment of how much the poor needed the extra income and how much the rich would be pinched by the extra taxes. If the proposed tax were to be imposed only on the handful of wealthiest American families with annual incomes above $1 million, you might well support the equalization up to a much bigger leakage. In fact, some people would wish to take money away from the super-rich even if not one cent reached the poor. And those avid redistributors are not necessarily either mean or radical. Some think such a levy might help to curb the political and social power of the Hugheses and Gettys—an argument about which I expressed my skepticism in chapter 1. Others see it as a symbolic kind of environmental program; they feel that the villas, yachts, and jets of the super-rich poison our land, water, and air. Still others are frankly envious. For any of these reasons, many would go even farther than would John Rawls.

I shall now carry that leaky bucket on one final trip, in an effort to determine attitudes about various income levels. Consider two groups of families, one with after-tax incomes of $10,000 and the other with $18,000—figures that bracket the $14,000 national mean in 1974. Suppose the proposal is to raise taxes on the $18,000 group and aid the $10,000 families by reducing the taxes they now pay. How much of a leak would you accept and still support that transfer? These families are quite far apart on the totem pole: the $10,000 family is only about

---

behavioral interpretation of egalitarian preferences than previous attempts to derive them from interpersonal comparisons. Anyone who dislikes gambling to some degree and who doesn't know where he will land on the income pyramid would tend to prefer less inequality in the distribution of income. Moreover, I would expect civilized human beings to display some degree of risk aversion (although not an absolute aversion). I'm not convinced, however, that egalitarian social preferences must rest on personal risk aversion. Suppose a bunch of gamblers were forming a society from an original position; would they necessarily prefer a world in which the winner takes all or might they see some justice in a degree of equality?

three-eighths of the way up, while the $18,000 family stands four-fifths of the way to the top. I see some value in that redistribution, but my enthusiasm is limited; a leakage of 15 percent would stop me.

Somehow, everyone seems to develop a sense of where deprivation and hardship begin along the income scale. Among economists and laymen alike, the subjective threshold of deprivation most often mentioned is half of the average income of American families.[16] If the average is taken as the mean, that would run about $7,000 in 1974 (half the median would be $6,000). Filling that gap seems far more important to many reformers than narrowing disparities above that level. That attitude has very important implications for policy. Additional doses of the old tax-and-transfer compound can essentially cure the deficiency below half of average income, as I shall argue below. But they would have only limited effects on the differentials between the $10,000 and $18,000 groups. To shrink those differentials significantly would call for alternative prescriptions. In particular, society would need to find ways for more people to climb the ladder from fair jobs to good jobs by choosing some combination of various proposals for expanded formal education, enhanced vocational and manpower training programs, subsidies to employers for promoting workers within their own ranks, or an induced narrowing of wage differentials between higher and lower job classifications. These issues intrigue me. But because the bottom end of the income scale is the top of my priority list, I shall concentrate largely on the tax-transfer options.

[***]

To capitalize on such opportunities, those who would raise the banner of equalization should also enroll in a crash course, one that studies the mistakes of their predecessors. The case made in behalf of taxing the rich and aiding the poor during the election campaign of 1972 provided an object lesson in how *not* to present a program of equalization to the American people. Ironically, the cause of reform received a serious setback from those who sought to advance it. With friends like that, it needed no enemies.

---

[16]   The criterion of half of average income is used in Victor R. Fuchs, "Toward a Theory of Poverty," in Task Force on Economic Growth and Opportunity, *The Concept of Poverty* (Chamber of Commerce of the United States, 1965). Lee Rainwater finds that the public's subjective attitudes correspond to this criterion. See *What Money Buys: Inequality and the Social Meanings of Income* (Basic Books, 1974), pp. 41-63, 110-17.

A new effort should display more concern for the preservation of market incentives and more respect for genuine skepticism; and it should eschew divisive rhetoric. My fellow reformers should want to design programs of aid to the poor that will not spawn laziness, as they can, guided by a solid body of factual—even scientific—evidence.[17] Given their importance in the values of many middle-class Americans, opportunities for jackpot prizes should be preserved. Reformers should explore wider use of the principles of cooperation and contribution that have kept social security untainted by the suspicion of freeloading. And they should respect wealthy Americans who have won their prizes playing by the rules of the game—even as they work to raise their taxes. Equalization should have a unifying theme: this can be a better nation for rich and poor alike by fulfilling the right to a reasonable standard of decent living for all citizens.

[***]

. . . The political climate has been chilled by disappointments about the housing, manpower, urban, and education programs of the 1960s. I believe that the main fault of those programs lay in "overpromising" rather than "underperforming." The initial prophecies of their enthusiasts set unrealistic standards by which they have been condemned. In this case, the dog got kicked because he was given such an exalted name. Those who write off all the federal efforts of the sixties leave an unsolved mystery. How do they explain the major social and economic gains made in some areas? For example, economic growth and prosperity cannot nearly account in full for the decline in the number of poor people from 40 million in 1961 to 24 million in 1969—a number that incidentally was still 24 million in 1972 before dipping to 23 million in 1973. Lyndon Johnson's domestic programs must have been doing something right!

CONCLUSION

The fulfillment of the right to survival and the eradication of poverty are within the grasp of this affluent nation. And within our vision is the target of half of average income as the basic minimum for all who

---

[17]   For some important experimental results that show little or no adverse work incentives on primary earners from cash grants, see Joseph A. Pechman and P. Michael Timpane (eds.), *Work Incentives and Income Guarantees: The New Jersey Negative Income Tax Experiment* (Brookings Institution, 1975).

choose to participate in the community's economic life. The ability of industrial capitalism to end deprivation for all has been proclaimed for generations by conservative thinkers. Just before the Great Crash, Herbert Hoover stated his goal to "remove poverty still further from our borders."[18] John Stuart Mill insisted that he would be a communist if he believed that economic misery and deprivation were inherent in a capitalistic economy.[19]

And Mill was right; they are not inherent and they can be eliminated. Indeed, in a democratic capitalism, they must be eliminated. The society that stresses equality and mutual respect in the domain of rights must face up to the implications of these principles in the domain of dollars.

I have stressed particularly the urgency of assisting the bottom fifth on the income scale and helping them into the mainstream of our affluent society. I believe that programs to help them rise would generate momentum through time and into wider ranges of the income scale. If those at the bottom receive the contents of the leaky bucket and are granted greater equality of opportunity, most will get on their own two feet. As I noted in chapter 3, some other social scientists are less optimistic than I am, partly because they believe that only a small part of the existing inequality of income reflects family advantages or other inequalities of opportunity. That debate cannot be settled unless and until an effort is made to equalize opportunity.

In part, my optimism reflects my standards of successful equalization. I personally would not be greatly exercised about unequal prizes won in the marketplace if they merely determined who could buy beachfront condominiums, second cars, and college slots for children in the bottom quarter of academic talent. It is the economic deprivation that blocks access to first homes, first cars, and college slots for solid students that troubles me deeply. And through the kinds of reforms I have urged, these can become available to all who want them. As Tawney stated the goal, "Differences of remuneration between different individuals might remain; contrasts between the civilization of different classes would vanish."[20]

18   Herbert Hoover, in his inaugural address, March 4, 1929. See William Starr Myers (ed.), *The State Papers and Other Public Writings of Herbert Hoover*, Vol. 1 (Doubleday, Doran, 1934), p. 7.

19   John Stuart Mill, *Principles of Political Economy*, Vol. 1 (5th ed., Appleton, 1877), book 2, chap. 1. ∫ 3, pp. 262-71.

20   R. H. Tawney, *Equality* (5th ed., London: Allen & Unwin, 1964), 150.

Throughout this essay, I have sounded a recurrent two-part theme: the market needs a place, and the market needs to be kept in its place. It must be given enough scope to accomplish the many things it does well. It limits the power of the bureaucracy and helps to protect our freedoms against transgression by the state. So long as a reasonable degree of competition is ensured, it responds reliably to the signals transmitted by consumers and producers. It permits decentralized management and encourages experiment and innovation.

Most important, the prizes in the marketplace provide the incentives for work effort and productive contribution. In their absence, society would thrash about for alternative incentives—some unreliable, like altruism; some perilous, like collective loyalty; some intolerable, like coercion or oppression. Conceivably, the nation might instead stop caring about achievement itself and hence about incentives for effort; in that event, the living standards of the lowly would fall along with those of the mighty.

For such reasons, I cheered the market; but I could not give it more than two cheers. The tyranny of the dollar yardstick restrained my enthusiasm. Given the chance, it would sweep away all other values, and establish a vending-machine society. The rights and powers that money should not buy must be protected with detailed regulations and sanctions, and with countervailing aids to those with low incomes. Once those rights are protected and economic deprivation is ended, I believe that our society would be more willing to let the competitive market have its place. Legislators might even enact effluent fees and repeal usury laws if they saw progress toward greater economic equality.

A democratic capitalist society will keep searching for better ways of drawing the boundary lines between the domain of rights and the domain of dollars. And it can make progress. To be sure, it will never solve the problem, for the conflict between equality and economic efficiency is inescapable. In that sense, capitalism and democracy are really a most improbable mixture. Maybe that is why they need each other—to put some rationality into equality and some humanity into efficiency.

Section II

Moral and Cultural Dimensions of Inequality

Catholic Bishops
> "Economic Justice for All, Pastoral Letter on Catholic Social Teaching and the U.S. Economy" (1986)

Thomas More
> *Utopia* (1516)

Ayn Rand
> *Atlas Shrugged* (1957)

Milton Friedman
> "The Social Responsibility of Business is to Increase Its Profits" (1970)

Henry David Thoreau
> *Walden*: "Economy" (1854)

Inequality is as much a moral issue as it is an economic or political one, and it would be naïve to suggest that we could reasonably treat the subject without explicitly considering its moral dimension. Okun's "leaky bucket" experiment (see the last reading in Section I) described a delicate and complex balancing act between efficiency and equality, and made the point that societal values are critical in determining the degree to which we are willing to trade one for the other. The first reading in Section II addresses this issue head-on. The Catholic bishops discuss inequality in terms of economic justice, arguing that our economic system should be evaluated according to the degree to which it promotes human dignity and solidarity of community. Thomas More, saint and martyr, provides us with a richly detailed picture of Utopia, an island paradise built on many of the same principles put forth by the bishops almost five hundred years later. It is not clear, however, that life in Utopia will necessarily proceed as smoothly as More suggests. The realities of the marketplace aside, there is always human nature—and Rand's version of the "Utopian ideal" produces results that deviate dramatically from More's. The demise of the Twentieth Century Motor Company dramatizes Rand's conviction that sacrificing for the good of others can lead to unfortunate outcomes, a position that is quite consistent with Friedman's belief that social responsibility is a subversive doctrine that undermines freedom. Thoreau turns a jaundiced eye upon our entire economic system in this section's last reading. Questioning the value we place upon material possessions, he allows up to profitably rethink the meaning of economic inequality and demonstrates that both poverty and wealth are culturally determined variables.

NATIONAL CONFERENCE OF CATHOLIC BISHOPS

ECONOMIC JUSTICE FOR ALL: PASTORAL LETTER ON CATHOLIC SOCIAL TEACHING AND THE U.S. ECONOMY
1986

The roots of the Conference go back to 1917, when the bishops of the United States formed an organization to provide support for American servicemen during World War I. Following the war, Pope Benedict XV suggested broadening the scope of the Council's interests to include working for social justice. The bishops responded by setting up the National Catholic Welfare Council in 1919. Three years later, the organization—renamed the National Catholic Welfare Conference—was focusing its efforts on education, immigration, and social action. In 1966, the National Conference of Catholic Bishops (NCCB) and the United States Catholic Conference (USCC) were established, the former to attend to the Church's domestic affairs and the latter to address issues that concern the Church as part of the larger society. The NCCB and the USCC were combined in 2001 to form the United States Conference of Catholic Bishops (USCCB).

This selection, which contains excerpts from the bishop's pastoral letter on the U.S. economy, is part of the literature known as Catholic Social Teaching (CST). Despite a lack of agreement on exactly which documents constitute CST, there appears to be a consensus that the tradition of social teaching originates with the 1891 encyclical written by Pope Leo XIII, entitled *Rerum Novarum* (translated as *On the Condition of Labor*), which discussed the conditions under which workers labored during the Industrial Revolution.

The inclusion of this selection in a book on social and economic inequality may seen curious to some readers. It is thus worth noting that, when asked why the Church should get caught up in political and economic affairs rather than focusing its efforts solely on the spiritual dimension of life, the bishops responded by pointing out that their religious mission spills over into social concerns, specifically, their concern for human dignity, human rights, unity among all peoples, and the deeper significance of human work.

An alternative perspective is offered by Wogaman, who argues that "economics is too important to the human enterprise to leave in the hands of economists alone" (1986, 3-4). While economists can use their knowledge and skills to help clarify technical matters and to inform public debate, which Wogaman readily acknowledges, he is quick to point out that economic policy decisions involve nontechnical value judgments as well. In fact, according to Wogaman (1986, 6), the relationship between economics and ethics is a two-way street:

> Ethics can help us understand the good and clarify the things that can be done in the real world to enhance its possibilities. In that sense, ethics is concerned about ends (the goods we seek) and means to ends (the steps required to achieve the ends). Ethics can help us see the relationship between the ultimate source of good . . . and the lesser goods or values that gain their meaning from that ultimate source or center. Since economic life involves a host of such "lesser goods," ethics can best serve economics by clarifying how these economic values are related to the ultimate good.

It is interesting to note that the first draft of the pastoral letter was released to the public only days before the 1984 presidential election. Democrat Walter Mondale was then trying to wrest the White House from Republican incumbent Ronald Reagan, whose administration had reduced federal spending on social welfare programs and advocated lowering tax rates for businesses and relatively wealthy individuals. These targeted reductions in tax rates, referred to as supply-side tax cuts, were supposed to stimulate production by eliminating the disincentive to work created by high taxes. The contention of Reagan economists that lower tax rates would actually generate increased tax revenues and that the benefit of supply-side tax cuts would "trickle down" to the less advantaged in the form of jobs was, at the time, dubbed "voodoo economics."

As you read the pastoral letter, consider how treating "human dignity" as an outcome of the economic system might alter the way we think about Okun's equality-efficiency tradeoff. Ask yourself, also, how much weight we as a society should place on values as opposed to technical considerations when we allocate scarce resources.

SELECTION FROM:

U.S. Catholic Bishops. (1986). *Economic Justice for All: Pastoral Letter on Catholic Social Teaching and the U.S. Economy.* Retrieved February 13, 2006, from http://www.osjspm.org/economic_justice_for_all. aspx.

ECONOMIC JUSTICE FOR ALL

1   . . . . Our faith calls us to measure this economy, not by what it produces but also by how it touches human life and whether it protects or undermines the dignity of the human person. Economic decisions have human consequences and moral content; they help or hurt people, strengthen or weaken family life, advance or diminish the quality of justice in our land.

15. All people have a right to participate in the economic life of society. Basic justice demands that people be assured a minimum level of participation in the economy. It is wrong for a person or a group to be excluded unfairly or to be unable to participate or contribute to the economy. For example, people who are both able and willing, but cannot get a job are deprived of the participation that is so vital to human development. For, it is through employment that most individuals and families meet their material needs, exercise their talents, and have an opportunity to contribute to the larger community . . . .

17. . . . In Catholic teaching, human rights include not only civil and political rights but also economic rights. As Pope John XXIII declared, "all people have a right to life, food, clothing, shelter, rest, medical care, education, and employment." This means that when people are without a chance to earn a living, and must go hungry and homeless, they are being denied basic rights. Society, must ensure that these rights are protected. In this

way, we will ensure that the minimum conditions of economic justice are met for all our sisters and brothers.

CHAPTER I

5. ... People shape the economy and in turn are shaped by it. Economic arrangements can be sources of fulfillment, of hope, of community—or of frustration, isolation, and even despair. They teach values—or vices—and day by day help mold our characters. They affect the quality of people's lives; at the extreme even determining whether people live or die. Serious economic choices go beyond purely technical issues to fundamental questions of value and human purpose.

URGENT PROBLEMS OF TODAY

16. Harsh poverty plagues our country despite its great wealth. More than 33 million Americans are poor; by any reasonable standard another 20-30 million are needy. Poverty is increasing in the United States, not decreasing. For a people who believe in "progress," this should be cause for alarm. These burdens fall most heavily on blacks, Hispanics, and Native Americans. Even more disturbing is the large increase in the number of women and children living in poverty. Today children are the largest single group among the nation's poor. This tragic fact seriously threatens the nation's future. That so many people are poor in a nation as rich as ours is a social and moral scandal that we cannot ignore.

17. Many working people and middle-class Americans live dangerously close to poverty. A rising number of families must rely on the wages of two or even three members just to get by. From 1968 to 1978 nearly a quarter of the U.S. population was in poverty part of the time and received welfare benefits in at least one year. The loss of a job, illness, or the breakup of a marriage may be all it takes to push people into poverty.

C. THE NEED FOR MORAL VISION

22. Sustaining a common culture and a common commitment to moral values is not easy in our world. Modern economic life is

based on a division of labor into specialized jobs and professions. Since the industrial revolution, people have had to define themselves and their work ever more narrowly to find a niche in the economy. The benefits of this are evident in the satisfaction many people derive from contributing their specialized skills to society. But the costs are social fragmentation, a decline in seeing how one's work serves the whole community, and an increased emphasis on personal goals and private interests. This is vividly clear in discussions of economic justice. Here it is often difficult to find a common ground among people with different backgrounds and concerns . . . .

CHAPTER II
ETHICAL NORMS FOR ECONOMIC LIFE

70. Distributive justice requires that the allocation of income, wealth, and power in society be evaluated in light of its effects on persons whose basic material needs are unmet. The Second Vatican Council stated: "The right to have a share of earthly goods sufficient for oneself and one's family belongs to everyone. The fathers and doctors of the Church held this view, teaching that we are obliged to come to the relief of the poor and to do so not merely out of our superfluous goods." Minimum material resources are an absolute necessity for human life. If persons are to be recognized as members of the human community, then the community has an obligation to help fulfill these basic needs unless an absolute scarcity of resources makes this strictly impossible. No such scarcity exists in the United States today.

71. . . . In the words of Pius XI, "It is of the very essence of social justice to demand from each individual all that is necessary for the common good."

74. Basic justice also calls for the establishment of a floor of material well-being on which all can stand. This is a duty of the whole of society and it creates particular obligations for those with greater resources. This duty calls into question extreme inequalities of income and consumption when so many lack basic necessities. Catholic social teaching does not maintain that a flat, arithmetical equality of income and wealth is a demand of justice, but it does challenge economic arrangements that leave large numbers of people impoverished. Further, it sees extreme

inequality as a threat to the solidarity of the human community, for great disparities lead to deep social divisions and conflict.

75. This means that all of us must examine our way of living in the light of the needs of the poor. Christian faith and the norms of justice impose distinct limits on what we consume and how we view material goods. The great wealth of the United States can easily blind us to the poverty that exists in this nation and the destitution of hundreds of millions of people in other parts of the world. Americans are challenged today as never before to develop the inner freedom to resist the temptation constantly to seek more. Only in this way will the nation avoid what Paul VI called "the most evident form of moral underdevelopment," namely greed.

76. These duties call not only for individual charitable giving but also for a more systematic approach by businesses, labor unions, and the many other groups that shape economic life—as well as government. The concentration of privilege that exists today results far more from institutional relationships that distribute power and wealth inequitably than from differences in talent or lack of desire to work. These institutional patterns must be examined and revised if we are to meet the demands of basic justice. For example, a system of taxation based on assessment according to ability to pay is a prime necessity for the fulfillment of these social obligations.

79. . . . Vatican II described the common good as "the sum of those conditions of social life which allow social groups and their individual members relatively thorough and ready access to their own fulfillment." These conditions include the right to fulfillment of material needs, a guarantee of fundamental freedoms, and the protection of relationships that are essential to participation in the life of society. These rights are bestowed on human beings by God and grounded in the nature and dignity of human persons. They are not created by society. Indeed society has a duty to secure and protect them.

80. . . . A number of human rights also concern human welfare and are of a specifically economic nature. First among these are the rights to life, food, clothing, shelter, rest, medical care, and basic education. These are indispensable to the protection of human dignity. In order to ensure these necessities, all persons have a right to earn a living, which for most people in our economy

is through remunerative employment. All persons also have a right to security in the event of sickness, unemployment, and old age . . . .

85. . . . Everyone has special duties toward the poor and marginalized. Living up to these responsibilities, however, is often made difficult by the social and economic patterns of society. Schools and educational policies both public and private often serve the privileged exceedingly well, while the children of the poor are effectively abandoned as second-class citizens. Great stresses are created in family life by the way work is organized and scheduled, and by the social and cultural values communicated on TV. Many in the lower middle class are barely getting by and fear becoming victims of economic forces over which they have no control.

86. The obligation to provide justice for all means that the poor have the single most urgent economic claim on the conscience of the nation . . . . To see a loved one sick is bad enough, but to have no possibility of obtaining health care is worse. To face family problems, such as death of a spouse or a divorce, can be devastating, but to have these lead to the loss of one's home and end with living on the streets is something no one should have to endure in a country as rich as ours. In developing countries these human problems are even more greatly intensified by extreme material deprivation. This form of human suffering can be reduced if our own country, so rich in resources, chooses to increase its assistance.

90. The fulfillment of the basic needs of the poor is of the highest priority. Personal decisions, policies of private and public bodies, and power relationships must be all evaluated by their effects on those who lack the minimum necessities of nutrition, housing, education, and health care. In particular, this principle recognizes that meeting fundamental human needs must come before the fulfillment of desires for luxury consumer goods, for profits not conducive to the common good, and for unnecessary military hardware.

91. Increasing active participation in economic life by those who are presently excluded or vulnerable is a high social priority. The human dignity of all is realized when people gain the power to work together to improve their lives, strengthen their families, and contribute to society. Basic justice calls for more than

providing help to the poor and other vulnerable members of society. It recognizes the priority of policies and programs that support family life and enhance economic participation through employment and widespread ownership of property . . . .

92. The investment of wealth, talent, and human energy should be specially directed to benefit those who are poor or economically insecure . . . . Investment and management decisions have crucial moral dimensions: they create jobs or eliminate them; they can push vulnerable families over the edge into poverty or give them new hope for the future; they help or hinder the building of a more equitable society. They can have either positive or negative influence on the fairness of the global economy. Therefore, this priority presents a strong moral challenge to policies that put large amounts of talent and capital into the production of luxury consumer goods and military technology while failing to invest sufficiently in education, health, the basic infrastructure of our society and economic sectors that produce urgently needed jobs, goods and services.

94. . . . "The needs of the poor take priority over the desires of the rich; the rights of workers over the maximization of profits; the preservation of the environment over uncontrolled industrial expansion; the production to meet social needs over production for military purposes." . . .

C. WORKING FOR GREATER JUSTICE: PERSONS AND INSTITUTIONS

102. . . . Labor has a great dignity, so great that all who are able to work are obligated to do so. The duty to work derives both from God's command and from a responsibility to one's own humanity and to the common good. The virtue of industriousness is also an expression of a person's dignity and solidarity with others. All working people are called to contribute to the common good by seeking excellence in production and service.

103. Because work is this important, people have a right to employment. In return for their labor, workers have a right to wages and other benefits sufficient to sustain life in dignity. As Pope Leo XIII stated, every working person has "the right of securing things to sustain life." The way power is distributed in a free market economy frequently gives employers greater

bargaining power than employees in the negotiation of labor contracts. Such unequal power may press workers into a choice between an inadequate wage or no wage at all. But justice, not charity, demands certain minimum wage guarantees. The provision of wages and other benefits sufficient to support a family in dignity is a basic necessity to prevent this exploitation of workers. The dignity of workers also requires adequate health care, security for old age or disability, unemployment compensation, healthful working conditions, weekly rest, periodic holidays for recreation and leisure, and reasonable security against arbitrary dismissal. These provisions are all essential if workers are to be treated as persons rather than simply a "factor of production."

115. The common good may sometimes demand that the right to own be limited by public involvement in the planning or ownership of certain sectors of the economy. Support of private ownership does not mean that anyone has the right to unlimited accumulation of wealth. "Private property does not constitute for anyone an absolute or unconditional right. No one is justified in keeping for his exclusive use what he does not need, when others lack necessities." . . . The Church's teaching opposes collectivist and statist economic approaches. But it also rejects the notion that a free market automatically produces justice . . . .

119 . . . . All who have more than they need must come to the aid of the poor. People with professional or technical skills needed to enhance the lives of others have a duty to share them. And the poor have similar obligations: to work together as individuals and families to build up their communities by acts of social solidarity and justice . . . .

123. More specifically, it is the responsibility of all citizens, acting through their government, to assist and empower the poor, the disadvantaged, the handicapped, and the unemployed. Government should assume a positive role in generating employment and establishing fair labor practices, in guaranteeing the provision and maintenance of the economy's infrastructure, such as roads, bridges, harbors, public means of communication, and transport. It should regulate trade and commerce in the interest of fairness . . . . The political debate about these policies is the indispensable forum for dealing with the conflicts and tradeoffs that will always be present in the pursuit of a more just economy.

CHAPTER III
SELECTED ECONOMIC POLICY ISSUES

128. Such an assessment of economic practices, structures, and outcomes leads to a variety of conclusions. Some people argue that an unfettered free-market economy, where owners, workers, and consumers pursue their enlightened self-interest, provides the greatest possible liberty, material welfare, and equity. The policy implication of this view is to intervene in the economy as little as possible because it is such a delicate mechanism that any attempt to improve it is likely to have the opposite effect. Others argue that the capitalist system is inherently inequitable and therefore contradictory to the demands of Christian morality, for it is based on acquisitiveness, competitiveness, and self-centered individualism. They assert that capitalism is fatally flawed and must be replaced by a radically different system that abolishes private property, the profit motive, and the free market.

132. Although we have chosen in this chapter to focus primarily on some aspects of the economy where we think reforms are realistically possible, we also emphasize that Catholic social teaching bears directly on larger questions concerning the economic system itself and the values it expresses—questions that can not be ignored in the Catholic vision of economic justice. For example, does our economic system place more emphasis on maximizing profits than on meeting human needs and fostering human dignity? Does our economy distribute its benefits equitably or does it concentrate power and resources in the hands of a few? Does it promote excessive materialism and individualism? Does it adequately protect the environment and the nation's natural resources? Does it direct too many scarce resources to military purposes? These and other basic questions about the economy need to be scrutinized in light of the ethical norms we have outlined . . . .

141. The severe human costs of high unemployment levels become vividly clear when we examine the impact of joblessness on human lives and human dignity. It is a deep conviction of American culture that work is central to the freedom and well-being of people. The unemployed often come to feel they are worthless and without a productive role in society. Each day they are unemployed our society tells them: We don't

need your talent. We don't need your initiative. We don't need you. Unemployment takes a terrible toll on the health and stability of both individuals and families. It gives rise to family quarrels, greater consumption of alcohol, child abuse, spouse abuse, divorce, and higher rates of infant mortality. People who are unemployed often feel that society blames them for being unemployed. Very few people survive long periods of unemployment without some psychological damage even if they have sufficient funds to meet their needs. At the extreme, the strains of job loss may drive individuals to suicide.

142. In addition to the terrible waste of individual talent and creativity, unemployment also harms society at large . . . . The costs to society are also evident in the rise in crime associated with joblessness. The Federal Bureau of Prisons reports that increases in unemployment have been followed by increases in the prison population. Other studies have shown links between the rate of joblessness and the frequency of homicides, robberies, larcenies, narcotics arrests, and youth crimes.

146. Increased competition in world markets is another factor influencing the rate of joblessness in our nation. Many other exporting nations have acquired and developed up-to-the-minute technology, enabling them to increase productivity dramatically. Combined with very low wages in many nations, this has allowed them to gain a larger share of the U.S. market to cut into U.S. export markets. At the same time many corporations have closed plants in the United States and moved their capital, technology and jobs to foreign affiliates.

3. GUIDELINES FOR ACTION

153. We must first establish a consensus that everyone has a right to employment. Then the burden of securing full employment falls on all of us—policy makers, business, labor, and the general public—to create and implement the mechanisms to protect that right. We must work for the formation of a new national consensus and mobilize the necessary political will at all levels to make the goal of full employment a reality.

154. Expanding employment in our nation will require significant steps in both the private and public sectors, as well as joint action between them . . . . The market alone will not automatically

produce full employment. Therefore, the government must act to ensure that this goal is achieved by coordinating general economic policies, by job creation programs and by other appropriate policy measures.

165. Jobs that are created should produce goods and services needed and values [valued] by society. It is both good common sense and sound economics to create jobs directly for the purpose of meeting society's unmet needs. Access [Across] the nation, in every state and locality, there is ample evidence of social needs that are going unmet. Many of our parks and recreation facilities are in need of maintenance and repair. Many of the nation's bridges and highways are in disrepair. We have a desperate need for more low-income housing. Our educational systems, day-care services, senior citizen services, and other community programs need to be expanded. These and many other elements of our national life are areas of unmet need. At the same time, there are more than 8 million Americans looking for productive and useful work. Surely we have the capacity to match these needs by giving Americans who are anxious to work a change of productive employment in jobs that are waiting to be done. The overriding moral value of enabling jobless persons to achieve a new sense of dignity and personal worth through employment also strongly recommends these programs.

B. POVERTY

170 . . . . Dealing with poverty is not a luxury to which our nation can attend when it finds the time and resources. Rather, it is a moral imperative of the highest priority.

172 . . . . Homeless people roam city streets in tattered clothing and sleep in doorways or on subway grates at night. Many of these are former mental patients released from state hospitals. Thousands stand in line at soup kitchens because they have no other way of feeding themselves. Millions of children are so poorly nourished that their physical and mental development are seriously harmed. We have also seen the growing economic hardship and insecurity experienced by moderate-income Americans when they lose their jobs and their income due to forces beyond their control. These are alarming signs and trends. They pose for our nation an urgent moral and human challenge: to fashion a society where

no one goes without the basic material necessities required for human dignity and growth.

176. Poverty strikes some groups more severely than others. Perhaps most distressing is the growing number of children who are poor. Today one in very four children under the age of six, and one in every two black children under six, are poor. The number of children in poverty rose by four million over the decade between 1973 and 1983, with the result that there are now more poor children in the United States than at any time since 1965. The problem is particularly severe among female-headed families, where more than half of all children are poor. Two-thirds of black children and nearly three-quarters of Hispanic children in such families are poor.

177. Very many poor families with children receive no government assistance, have no health insurance, and cannot pay medical bills. Less than half are immunized against preventable diseases such as diphtheria and polio. Poor children are disadvantaged even before birth; their mothers' lack of access to high quality prenatal care leaves them at much greater risk of premature birth, low-birth weight, physical and mental impairment, and death before their first birthday.

178. The past twenty years have witnessed a dramatic increase in the number of women in poverty. This includes women raising children alone as well as women with inadequate income following divorce, widowhood, or retirement. More than one-third of all female-headed families are poor. Among minority families headed by women the poverty rate is over 50 percent.

179. Wage discrimination against women is a major factor behind these high rates of poverty. Many women are employed but remain poor because their wages are too low. Women who work outside their homes full-time and year-round earn only 61 percent of what men earn. Thus, being employed full-time is not by itself a remedy for poverty among women. Hundreds of thousands of women hold full-time jobs but are still poor. Sixty percent of all women work in only ten occupations, and most new jobs for women are in areas with low pay and limited chances of advancement. Many women suffer discrimination in wages, salaries, job classifications, promotions, and other areas. As a result, they find themselves in jobs that have low status, little security, weak unionization, and few fringe benefits. Such

discrimination is immoral and efforts must be made to overcome the effects of sexism in our society.

181. Most poor people in our nation are white, but the rates of poverty in our nation are highest among those who have borne the brunt of racial prejudice and discrimination. For example, blacks are about three times more likely to be poor than whites. While one out of nine white Americans is poor, one of every three blacks and Native Americans and more than one of every four Hispanics are poor. While some members of minority communities have successfully moved up the economic ladder, the overall picture indicates that black family income is only 55 percent of white family income, reflecting an income gap that is wider now than at any time in the last fifteen years.

182. Despite the gains which have been made toward racial equality, prejudice and discrimination in our own time as well as the effects of past discrimination continue to exclude many members of racial minorities from the mainstream of American life.

183. Important to our discussion of poverty in America is an understanding of the degree of economic inequality in our nation. Our economy is marked by very uneven distribution of wealth and income. For example, it is estimated that 28 percent of the total net wealth is held by the richest 2 percent of families in the Untied States. The top ten percent holds 57 of the net wealth . . . .

184. Although disparities in the distribution of income are less extreme, they are still striking. In 1984 the bottom 20 percent of American families received only 4.7 percent of the total income in the nation and the bottom 40 percent received only 15.7 percent, the lowest share on record in U.S. history. In contrast, the top one-fifth received 42.9 percent of the total income, and the highest share since 1948. These figures are only partial and very imperfect measures of the inequality in our society, however, they do suggest that the degree of inequality is quite large. In comparison with other industrialized nations, the United States is among the more unequal in terms of income distribution. Moreover, the gap between rich and poor in our nation has increased during the last decade. These inequities are of particular concern because they reflect the uneven distribution of power in our society. They suggest that the level of participation in the political and social spheres is also very uneven.

185. Catholic social teaching does not require absolute equality in the distribution of income and wealth. Some degree of inequality not only is acceptable, but also may be considered desirable for economic and social reasons, such as the need for incentives and provision of greater rewards for greater risks. However, unequal distribution should be evaluated in terms of several moral principles we have enunciated: the priority of meeting the basic needs of the poor and the importance of increasing the level of participation by all members of society in the economic life of the nation. These norms establish a strong presumption against extreme inequality of income and wealth as long as there are poor, hungry, and homeless people in our midst. They also suggest that extreme inequalities are detrimental to the development of social solidarity and community. In view of these norms we find the disparities of income and wealth in the United States to be unacceptable. Justice requires that all members of our society work for economic, political and social reforms that will decrease these inequities.

188. The principle of participation leads us to the conviction that the most appropriate and fundamental solutions to poverty will be those that enable people to take control of their own lives . . . . Therefore, we should seek solutions that enable the poor to help themselves through such means as employment. Paternalistic programs which do too much for and too little with the poor are to be avoided.

189. The responsibility for alleviating the plight of the poor falls upon all members of society. As individuals, all citizens have a duty to assist the poor through acts of charity and personal commitment. But private charity and voluntary action are not sufficient. We also carry out our moral responsibility to assist and empower the poor by working collectively through government to establish just and effective public policies.

193. Before discussing directions for reform in public policy, we must speak frankly about misunderstandings and stereotypes of the poor. For example, a common misconception is that most of the poor are racial minorities. In fact, about two-thirds of the poor are white. It is also frequently suggested that people stay on welfare for many years, do not work, could work if they wanted to, and have children who will be on welfare. In fact, reliable data show that these are not accurate descriptions of most people

who are poor and on welfare. Over a decade people move on and off welfare, and less than 1 percent obtain these benefits for all ten years. Nor is it true that the rolls of Aid to Families with Dependent Children (AFDC) are filled with able-bodied adults who could but will not work. The majority of AFDC recipients are young children and their mothers who must remain at home. These mothers are also accused of having more children so that they can raise their allowances. The truth is that 70 percent of AFDC families have only one or two children and that there is little financial advantage in having another. In a given year, almost half of all families who receive AFDC include an adult who has worked full or part-time. Research has consistently demonstrated that people who are poor have the same strong desire to work that characterizes the rest of the population.

194 . . . . The belief persists in this country that the poor are poor by choice or through laziness, that anyone can escape poverty by hard work, and that welfare programs make it easier for people to avoid work. Thus, public attitudes toward programs for the poor tend to differ sharply from attitudes about other benefits and programs. Some of the most generous subsidies for individuals and corporations are taken for granted and are not even called benefits but entitlements. In contrast, programs for the poor are called handouts and receive a great deal of critical attention, even though they account for less than 10 percent of the federal budget.

201. Poor people must be empowered to take charge of their own futures and become responsible for their own economic advancement. Personal motivation and initiative, combined with social reform, are necessary elements to assist individuals in escaping poverty. By taking advantage of opportunities for education, employment, and training, and by working together for change, the poor can help themselves to be full participants in our economic, social, and political life.

203. All of society should make a much stronger commitment to education for the poor. Any long-term solution to poverty in this country must pay serious attention to education, public and private, in school and out of school. Lack of adequate education, especially in the inner city setting, prevents many poor people from escaping poverty. In addition, illiteracy, a problem that affects tens of millions of Americans, condemns many to joblessness or chronically low wages.

D. The U.S. Economy and the Developing Nations: Complexity, Challenge, and Choices

252. . . . our emphasis on the preferential option for the poor moves us to focus our attention mainly on U.S. relations with the Third World. Unless conscious steps are taken toward protecting human dignity and fostering human solidarity in these relationships, we can look forward to increased conflict and inequity, threatening the fragile economies of these relatively poor nations far more than our own relatively strong one . . . .

253. Developing countries, moreover, often perceive themselves as more dependent on the industrialized countries, especially the United States, because the international system itself, as well as the way the United States acts in it, subordinates them. The prices at which they must sell their commodity exports and purchase their food and manufactured imports, the rates of interest they must pay and the terms they must meet to borrow money, the standards of economic behavior of foreign investors, the amounts and conditions of external aid, etc, are essentially determined by the industrialized world. Moreover, their traditional cultures are increasingly susceptible to the aggressive cultural penetration of the Northern (especially U.S.) advertising and media programming. The developing countries are junior partners at best.

254. The basic tenets of church teaching take on a new moral urgency as we deepen our understanding of how disadvantaged large numbers of people and nations are in this interdependent world . . . . No aggregate of individual examples could portray adequately the appalling inequities within those desperately poor countries and between them and our own. And their misery is not the inevitable result of the march of history or the intrinsic nature of particular cultures, but of human decisions and human institutions.

256. In this arena, where fact and ethical challenges intersect, the moral task is to devise rules for the major actors that will remove [move] them toward a just international order. One of the most vexing problems is that of reconciling the transnational corporations' profit orientation with the common good that they, along with governments and their multilateral agencies, are supposed to serve.

260. Here, as elsewhere, the preferential option for the poor is the central priority for policy choice. It offers a unique perspective on foreign policy in whose light U.S. relationships, especially with developing countries, can be reassessed. Standard foreign policy analysis deals with calculations of power and definitions of national interest; but the poor are, by definition, not powerful. If we are to give appropriate weight to their concerns, their needs, and their interests, we have to [go] beyond economic gain or national security as a starting point for the policy dialogue. We want to stand with the poor everywhere, and we believe that relations between the U.S. and developing nations should be determined in the first place by a concern for basic human needs and respect for cultural traditions.

292. We share his [the Pope's] conviction that most of the policy issues generally called economic, are at root, moral and therefore require application of moral principles derived from the Scriptures and from the evolving social teaching of the Church and other traditions. We also recognize that we are dealing with sensitive international issues that cross national boundaries. Nevertheless, in order to pursue justice and peace on a global scale, we call for a U.S. international economic policy designed to empower people everywhere and enable them to continue to develop a sense of their own worth, improve the quality of their lives, and ensure that the benefits of economic growth are shared equitably.

294. Many of the reforms we have suggested in this chapter would be expensive. At a time when the United States has large annual deficits some might consider these costs too high. But this discussion must be set in the context of how our resources are allocated and the immense human and social costs of failure to act on these pressing problems. We believe that the question of providing adequate revenues to meet the needs of our nation must be faced squarely and realistically. Reforms in the tax code which close loopholes and generate new revenues, for example, are among the steps that need to be examined in order to develop a federal budget that is both fiscally sound and socially responsible. The cost of meeting our social needs must also be weighted against the $300 billion a year allocated for military purposes. Although some of these expenditures are necessary for the defense of the nation, some elements of

the military budget are both wasteful and dangerous for world peace. Careful reduction should be made in these areas in order to free up funds for social and economic reforms. In the end, the question is not whether the United States can provide the necessary funds to meet our social needs, but whether we have the political will to do so.

CHAPTER IV

305. The parts played by managers and shareholders in U.S. corporations also need careful examination. In U.S. law, the primary responsibility of managers is to exercise prudent business judgment in the interest of a profitable return to investors. But morally this legal responsibility may be exercised only within the bounds of justice to employees, customers, suppliers, and the local community . . . .

306. Most shareholders today exercise relatively little power in corporate governance. Although shareholders can and should vote on the selection of corporate directors and on investment questions and other policy matters, it appears that return on investment is the governing criterion in the relation between them and management. We do not believe this is an adequate rationale for shareholder decisions . . . .

324. Locked together in a world of limited material resources and a growing array of common problems, we help or hurt one another by the economic policies we choose. All the economic agents in our society, therefore, must consciously and deliberately attend to the good of the whole human family . . . . But whatever the difficulty, the need to give priority to alleviating poverty in developing countries is undeniable; and the cost of continued inaction can be counted in human lives lost or stunted, talents wasted, opportunities foregone, misery and suffering prolonged, and injustice condoned.

363. Confronted by this economic complexity and seeking clarity for the future, we can rightly ask ourselves one single question: How does our economic system affect the lives of people—all people? Part of the American dream has been to make this world a better place for people to live in; at this moment of history that dream must include everyone on this globe. Since we profess to be members of a "catholic" or universal Church,

we all must raise our sights to a concern for the well-being of everyone in the world. Third World debt becomes our problem. Famine and starvation in sub-Saharan Africa become our concern. Rising military expenditures everywhere in the world become part of our fears for the future of this planet. We cannot be content if we see ecological neglect or the squandering of natural resources. In this letter we bishops have spoken often of economic interdependence; now is the moment when all of us must confront the reality of such economic bonding . . . . We commit ourselves to this global vision.

THOMAS MORE

1478-1535

UTOPIA
1516

The son of an influential judge, Thomas More was born in the city of London at a time of great political ferment[1]. An important figure in both the English Renaissance and the Protestant Reformation, he distinguished himself as a lawyer, humanist scholar, political philosopher, and statesman. A man of strong principle, More rapidly rose to prominence as the right-hand man of King Henry VIII and just as quickly fell into disfavor with the King over matters of conscience. He is best known for his masterpiece *Utopia*, which was originally written in Latin, published in Belgium, and never printed in England during his lifetime.

At twelve, More entered as a page into the household of Cardinal John Morton, Archbishop of Canterbury and Lord Chancellor of England. Two years later, Morton sent him to Canterbury College (subsequently, Christ Church), Oxford, where he mastered the classical languages. In 1494, he returned to London to study law, first at New Inn and then at Lincoln's Inn.

A deeply pious man, More found himself torn between the priesthood and the practice of law. He went so far as to move into the London Charterhouse (a Carthusian monastery), where he spent four years (1499-1503) in prayer, fasting, and doing penance. During this time, he

---

[1]   Tudor England was characterized by vast disparities in wealth, a complete absence of freedom of speech and thought, and monstrous social injustice (Turner, 2003, xx).

wore a sharp hair shirt (a practice he was to maintain throughout his life), used a log as a pillow, flogged himself, and slept only four or five hours a night. Desirous of married life and unsure of his ability to maintain the harsh discipline of the monastery, he abandoned the idea of becoming a monk and, in 1504, entered Parliament.

In 1510, More accepted an appointment as Under-Sheriff of London. He helped negotiate a trade settlement in Flanders in 1515, was knighted in 1521 and elected Speaker of the House of Commons in 1523, and became High Steward of Oxford University in 1524 and of Cambridge University in 1525. Despite the intimate relationship he enjoyed with the King Henry VIII (as his secretary and most trusted personal advisor), More told his son-in-law, "If my head should win him a castle in France . . . it should not fail to go" (Roper, 173).

In 1509, Henry VIII had married his brother's widow, Catherine of Aragon, daughter of Ferdinand and Isabella of Spain. When it became obvious that Catherine would not provide him with a male heir to the throne, his affections began to wander and he eventually fell in love with Anne Boleyn, one of Catherine's attendants and the sister of one of his mistresses. In 1527, Henry unsuccessfully petitioned Pope Clement VII for an annulment of his marriage so that he and Anne could wed. In 1530, More, who had recently been appointed Lord Chancellor, refused to sign a letter asking the Pope to annul Henry's marriage to Catherine. Growing increasingly uneasy over the widening rift between king and pope, More resigned the Chancellorship in 1532.

Matters came to a boil in 1533 when Anne became pregnant. Henry challenged the Pope's authority to regulate the affairs of the Church outside the Holy See and moved forward with his plans to remarry. Thomas Cranmer, the newly appointed Archbishop of Canterbury, declared Henry's marriage void and blessed the union between Henry and Anne. More, who was a close friend of Catherine, refused to attend Anne's ensuing coronation as Queen of England. One year later, Parliament passed the Act of Succession, which stipulated that subjects, when commanded to do so, must take an oath recognizing the offspring of Henry and Anne as legitimate heirs to the throne. A man of conscience, More would not publicly take the oath. Adding insult to injury, he also refused to acknowledge Henry as the "Supreme Head of the Church," a title granted him in the 1534 Act of Supremacy.

Charged with treason, More was imprisoned in the Tower of London, where he wrote his "Dialogue of Comfort Against Tribulation." He was eventually found guilty—albeit on the basis of false testimony offered by the Solicitor General—and beheaded, uttering these famous last words: "I die the King's good servant and God's first."

The story of Utopia[2] is told by Raphael Hythloday[3], who ostensibly discovered the island while traveling with Amerigo Vespucci to the New World in 1504. In More's prefatory letter to fellow humanist Peter Gilles, he lends credence to this farce, stating, "I didn't have the problem of finding my own subject-matter . . . all I had to do was repeat what Raphael told us" (Turner, 2003, 7). Gilles, in turn, writes, "[More] sets it all so vividly before one's eyes that by reading his words I seem to get an even clearer picture of it than I did while Raphael['s] . . . voice was actually sounding in my ears—for I was with More when the conversation took place" (Turner, 2003, 10).

The blending of real people and events into the story, observed Hudleston (1996), "leaves the reader sadly puzzled to detect where truth ends and fiction begins, and has led not a few to take the book seriously." But this, of course, was quite intentional. Turner (2003, xiv) suggests that

> The form, then, of *Utopia* was designed not only to entertain, but also to create a context in which More could say what he liked, without laying himself open to too much criticism. It enabled him, in an age when rash expressions of opinion were apt to land one in the Tower, to disclaim responsibility for any view that might be considered subversive.

As you read the following excerpt, ask yourself how the social and economic organization of Utopia differs from that of Rand's Twentieth Century Motor Company. Consider the extent to which the dramatically different outcomes of these "social experiments" can be attributed to differences in cultural values. Do you think that the Catholic Bishops would be willing to accept the loss in personal freedom that accompanies the reduction in economic inequality in Utopia? Do you think Marx and Engels would be willing to sacrifice individuality for the good of the community?

---

2   Utopia translates from the Greek as "no place" or "good place." The terms "syphogrants" and "tranibors" refer to Utopian city officials, the former being the equivalent of magistrates elected by households and the latter, the overseers of the syphogrants. It is likely that Amaurot, the preeminent city and the site of the annual congress, is intended to symbolize London.

3   Hythloday translates as "speaker of nonsense."

Selection from:

More, Thomas. (1516). *Utopia*. In *Ideal Commonwealths*. Reissued New York: Kennikat Press. Originally published by P.F. Collier & Son. The Colonial Press. 1901. 30-32, 40-52, 54, 56, 57-59, 59-60, 70-71, 95-99.

BOOK I

[***]

"Though to speak plainly my real sentiments, I must freely own that as long as there is any property, and while money is the standard of all other things, I cannot think that a nation can be governed either justly or happily: not justly, because the best things will fall to the share of the worst men; nor happily, because all things will be divided among a few (and even these are not in all respects happy), the rest being left to be absolutely miserable. Therefore when I reflect on the wise and good constitution of the Utopians—among whom all things are so well governed, and with so few laws; where virtue hath its due reward, and yet there is such an equality, that every man lives in plenty—when I compare with them so many other nations that are still making new laws, and yet can never bring their constitution to a right regulation, where notwithstanding everyone has his property; yet all the laws that they can invent have not the power either to obtain or preserve it, or even to enable men certainly to distinguish what is their own from what is another's; of which the many lawsuits that every day break out, and are eternally depending, give too plain a demonstration; when, I say, I balance all these things in my thoughts, I grow more favorable to Plato, and do not wonder that he resolved not to make any laws for such as would not submit to a community of all things: for so wise a man could not but foresee that the setting all upon a level was the only way to make a nation happy, which cannot be obtained so long as there is property: for when every man draws to himself all that he can compass, by one title or another, it must needs follow, that how plentiful soever a nation may be, yet a few dividing the wealth of it among themselves, the rest must fall into indigence.

"So that there will be two sorts of people among them, who deserve that their fortunes should be interchanged; the former useless, but wicked and ravenous; and the latter, who by their constant industry serve the public more than themselves, sincere and modest men. From whence I am persuaded, that till property is taken away there can be no equitable or just distribution of things, nor can the world be happily governed: for as long as that is maintained, the greatest and the far best part of mankind will be still oppressed with a load of cares and anxieties. I confess without taking it quite away, those pressures that lie on a great part of mankind may be made lighter; but they can never be quite removed. For if laws were made to determine at how great an extent in soil, and at how much money every man must stop, to limit the prince that he might not grow too great, and to restrain the people that they might not become too insolent, and that none might factiously aspire to public employments; which ought neither to be sold, nor made burdensome by a great expense; since otherwise those that serve in them would be tempted to reimburse themselves by cheats and violence, and it would become necessary to find out rich men for undergoing those employments which ought rather to be trusted to the wise—these laws, I say, might have such effects, as good diet and care might have on a sick man, whose recovery is desperate: they might allay and mitigate the disease, but it could never be quite healed, nor the body politic be brought again to a good habit, as long as property remains; and it will fall out as in a complication of diseases, that by applying a remedy to one sore, you will provoke another; and that which removes the one ill symptom produces others, while the strengthening one part of the body weakens the rest."

"On the contrary," answered I, "it seems to me that men cannot live conveniently where all things are common: how can there be any plenty, where every man will excuse himself from labor? For as the hope of gain doth not excite him, so the confidence that he has in other men's industry may make him slothful: if people come to be pinched with want, and yet cannot dispose of anything as their own; what can follow upon this but perpetual sedition and bloodshed, especially when the reverence and authority due to magistrates fall to the ground? For I cannot imagine how that can be kept up among those that are in all things equal to one another."

"I do not wonder," said he, "that it appears so to you, since you have no notion, or at least no right one, of such a constitution: but if you had been in Utopia with me, and had seen their laws and rules, as I did, for the space of five years, in which I lived among them; and during which time I was so delighted with them, that indeed I should never have left them, if it had not been to make the discovery of that new world to the Europeans; you would then confess that you had never seen a people so well constituted as they." . . .

BOOK II

[***]

Of Their Trades, and Manner of Life

Agriculture is that which is so universally understood among them that no person, either man or woman, is ignorant of it; they are instructed in it from their childhood, partly by what they learn at school and partly by practice; they being led out often into the fields, about the town, where they not only see others at work, but are likewise exercised in it themselves. Besides agriculture, which is so common to them all, every man has some peculiar trade to which he applies himself, such as the manufacture of wool, or flax, masonry, smith's work, or carpenter's work; for there is no sort of trade that is not in great esteem among them. Throughout the island they wear the same sort of clothes without any other distinction, except what is necessary to distinguish the two sexes, and the married and unmarried. The fashion never alters; and as it is neither disagreeable nor uneasy, so it is suited to the climate, and calculated both for their summers and winters. Every family makes their own clothes; but all among them, women as well as men, learn one or other of the trades formerly mentioned. Women, for the most part, deal in wool and flax, which suit best with their weakness, leaving the ruder trades to the men. The same trade generally passes down from father to son, inclinations often following descent; but if any man's genius lies another way, he is by adoption translated into a family that deals in the trade to which he is inclined: and when that is to be done, care is taken not only by his father, but by the magistrate, that he may be put to a discreet and good man. And if after a person has learned one trade, he desires to acquire another, that is also allowed, and is managed in the same manner as the former. When he has learned both, he follows that which he likes best, unless the public has more occasion for the other.

The chief, and almost the only business of the syphogrants, is to take care that no man may live idle, but that every one may follow his trade diligently: yet they do not wear themselves out with perpetual toil, from morning to night, as if they were beasts of burden, which, as it is indeed a heavy slavery, so it is everywhere the common course of life among all mechanics except the Utopians; but they dividing the day and night into twenty-four hours, appoint six of these for work; three of which are before dinner, and three after. They then sup, and at eight o'clock, counting from noon, go to bed and sleep eight hours. The rest of their time besides that taken up in work, eating and sleeping, is left to every man's discretion; yet they are not to abuse that interval to luxury and idleness, but must employ it in some proper exercise according to their various inclinations, which is for the most part reading. It is ordinary to have public lectures every morning before daybreak; at which none are obliged to appear but those who are marked out for literature; yet a great many, both men and women of all ranks, go to hear lectures of one sort of other, according to their inclinations. But if others, that are not made for contemplation, choose rather to employ themselves at that time in their trades, as many of them do, they are not hindered, but are rather commended, as men that take care to serve their country. After supper, they spend an hour in some diversion, in summer in their gardens, and in winter in the halls where they eat; where they entertain each other, either with music or discourse. They do not so much as know dice, or any such foolish and mischievous games: they have, however, two sorts of games not unlike our chess; the one is between several numbers, in which one number, as it were, consumes another: the other resembles a battle between the virtues and the vices, in which the enmity in the vices among themselves, and their agreement against virtue, is not unpleasantly represented; together with the special oppositions between the particular virtues and vices; as also the methods by which vice either openly assaults or secretly undermines virtue, and virtue on the other hand resists it. But the time appointed for labor is to be narrowly examined, otherwise you may imagine, that since there are only six hours appointed for work, they may fall under a scarcity of necessary provisions. But it is so far from being true, that this time is not sufficient for supplying them with plenty of all things, either necessary or convenient, that it is rather too much; and this you will easily apprehend, if you consider how great a part of all other nations is quite idle.

First, women generally do little, who are the half of mankind; and if some few women are diligent, their husbands are idle: then consider the great company of idle priests, and of those that are called religious men; add to these all rich men, chiefly those that have estates in land, who are called noblemen and gentlemen, together with their families, made up of idle persons, that are kept more for show than use; add to these, all those strong and lusty beggars, that go about pretending some disease, in excuse for their begging; and upon the whole account you will find that the number of those by whose labors mankind is supplied, is much less than you perhaps imagined. Then consider how few of those that work are employed in labors that are of real service; for we who measure all things by money, give rise to many trades that are both vain and superfluous, and serve only to support riot and luxury. For if those who work were employed only in such things as the conveniences of life require, there would be such an abundance of them that the prices of them would so sink that tradesmen could not be maintained by their gains; if all those who labor about useless things were set to more profitable employments, and if all they that languish out their lives in sloth and idleness, every one of whom consumes as much as any two of the men that are at work, were forced to labor, you may easily imagine that a small proportion of time would serve for doing all that is either necessary, profitable, or pleasant to mankind, especially while pleasure is kept within its due bounds.

This appears very plainly in Utopia, for there, in a great city, and in all the territory that lies round it, you can scarce find 500, either men or women, by their age and strength, are capable of labor, that are not engaged in it; even the syphogrants, though excused by the law, yet do not excuse themselves, but work, that by their examples they may excite the industry of the rest of the people. The like exemption is allowed to those who, being recommended to the people by the priests, are by the secret suffrages of the syphogrants privileged from labor, that they may apply themselves wholly to study; and if any of these fall short of those hopes that they seemed at first to give, they are obliged to return to work. And sometimes a mechanic, that so employs his leisure hours, as to make a considerable advancement in learning, is eased from being a tradesman, and ranked among their learned men. Out of these they choose their ambassadors, their priests, their tranibors, and the prince himself, anciently called their Barzenes, but is called of late their Ademus.

And thus from the great numbers among them that are neither suffered to be idle, nor to be employed in any fruitless labor, you may easily make the estimate how much may be done in those few hours in which they are obliged to labor. But besides all that has been already said, it is to be considered that the needful arts among them are managed with less labor than anywhere else. The building or the repairing of houses among us employ many hands, because often a thriftless heir suffers a house that his father built to fall into decay, so that his successor must, at a great cost, repair that which he might have kept up with a small charge: it frequently happens that the same house which one person built at a vast expense is neglected by another, who thinks he has a more delicate sense of the beauties of architecture; and he suffering it to fall to ruin, builds another at no less charge. But among the Utopians all things are so regulated that men very seldom build upon a new piece of ground; and are not only very quick in repairing their houses, but show their foresight in preventing their decay: so that their buildings are preserved very long, with but little labor, and thus the builders to whom that care belongs are often without employment, except the hewing of timber and the squaring of stones, that the materials may be in readiness for raising a building very suddenly when there is any occasion for it.

As to their clothes, observe how little work is spent in them: while they are at labor, they are clothed with leather and skins. cast carelessly about them, which will last seven years; and when they appear in public they put on an upper garment, which hides the other; and these are all of one color, and that is the natural color of the wool. As they need less woollen cloth than is used anywhere else, so that which they make use of is much less costly. They use linen cloth more; but that is prepared with less labor, and they value cloth only by the whiteness of the linen or the cleanness of the wool, without much regard to the fineness of the thread: while in other places, four or five upper garments of woollen cloth, of different colors, and as many vests of silk, will scarce serve one man; and while those that are nicer think ten are too few, every man there is content with one, which very often serves him two years. Nor is there anything that can tempt a man to desire more; for if he had them, he would neither be the warmer nor would he make one jot the better appearance for it. And thus, since they are all employed in some useful labor, and since they content themselves with fewer things, it falls out that there is a great abundance of all things among them: so that it frequently happens that, for want of other work, vast numbers are sent out to mend the highways. But when no public undertaking is to be performed, the hours of working are lessened. The magistrates never engage the people in unnecessary labor, since the chief end of the constitution is to regulate labor by the necessities of the public, and to allow all the people as much time as is necessary for the improvement of their minds, in which they think the happiness of life consists.

Of Their Traffic

But it is now time to explain to you the mutual intercourse of this people, their commerce, and the rules by which all things are distributed among them.

As their cities are composed of families, so their families are made up of those that are nearly related to one another. Their women, when they grow up, are married out; but all the males, both children and grandchildren, live still in the same house, in great obedience to their common parent, unless age has weakened his understanding: and in that case, he that is next to him in age comes in his room. But lest any city should become either too great, or by any accident be dispeopled, provision is made that none of their cities may contain above 6,000 families, besides those of the country round it. No family may have less than ten and more than sixteen persons in it; but there can be no determined number for the children under age. This rule is easily observed, by removing some of the children of a more fruitful couple to any other family that does not abound so much in them.

By the same rule, they supply cities that do not increase so fast, from others that breed faster; and if there is any increase over the whole island, then they draw out a number of their citizens out of the several towns, and send them over to the neighboring continent; where, if they find that the inhabitants have more soil than they can well cultivate, they fix a colony, taking the inhabitants into their society, if they are willing to live with them; and where they do that of their own accord, they quickly enter into their method of life, and conform to their rules, and this proves a happiness to both nations; for according to their constitution, such care is taken of the soil that it becomes fruitful enough for both, though it might be otherwise too narrow and barren for any one of them. But if the natives refuse to conform themselves to their laws, they drive them out of those bounds which they mark out for themselves, and use force if they resist. For they account it a very just cause of war, for a nation to hinder others from possessing a part of that soil of which they make no use, but which is suffered to lie idle and uncultivated; since every man has by the law of nature a right to such a waste portion of the earth as is necessary for his subsistence. If an accident has so lessened the number of the inhabitants of any of their towns that it cannot be made up from the other towns of the island, without diminishing them too much, which is said to have fallen out but twice since they were first a people, when great numbers were carried off by the plague, the loss is then supplied by recalling as many as are wanted from their colonies; for they will abandon these, rather than suffer the towns in the island to sink too low.

But to return to their manner of living in society, the oldest man of every family, as has been already said, is its governor. Wives serve their husbands, and children their parents, and always the younger serves the elder. Every city is divided into four equal parts, and in the middle of each there is a marketplace: what is brought thither, and manufactured by the several families, is carried from thence to houses appointed for that purpose, in which all things of a sort are laid by themselves; and thither every father goes and takes whatsoever he or his family stand in need of, without either paying for it or leaving anything in exchange. There is no reason for giving a denial to any person, since there is such plenty of everything among them; and there is no danger of a man's asking for more than he needs; they have no inducements to do this, since they are sure that they shall always be supplied. It is the fear of want that makes any of the whole race of animals either greedy or ravenous; but besides fear, there is in man a pride that makes him fancy it a particular glory to excel others in pomp and excess. But by the laws of the Utopians, there is no room for this. Near these markets there are others for all sorts of provisions, where there are not only herbs, fruits, and bread, but also fish, fowl, and cattle.

There are also, without their towns, places appointed near some running water, for killing their beasts, and for washing away their filth, which is done by their slaves: for they suffer none of their citizens to kill their cattle, because they think that pity and good-nature, which are among the best of those affections that are born with us, are much impaired by the butchering of animals: nor do they suffer anything that is foul or unclean to be brought within their towns, lest the air should be infected by ill-smells which might prejudice their health. In every street there are great halls that lie at an equal distance from each other, distinguished by particular names. The syphogrants dwell in those that are set over thirty families, fifteen lying on one side of it, and as many on the other. In these halls they all meet and have their repasts. The stewards of every one of them come to the market-place at an appointed hour; and according to the number of those that belong to the hall, they carry home provisions. But they take more care of their sick than of any others: these are lodged and provided for in public hospitals they have belonging to every town four hospitals, that are built without their walls, and are so large that they may pass for little towns: by this means, if they had ever such a number of sick persons, they could lodge them conveniently, and at such a distance, that such of them as are sick of infectious diseases may be kept so far from the rest that there can be no danger of contagion. The hospitals are furnished and stored with all things that are convenient for the ease and recovery of the sick; and those that are put in them are looked after with such tender and watchful care, and are so constantly attended by their skilful physicians, that as none is sent to them against their will, so there is scarce one in a whole town that, if he should fall ill, would not choose rather to go thither than lie sick at home.

After the steward of the hospitals has taken for the sick whatsoever the physician prescribes, then the best things that are left in the market are distributed equally among the halls, in proportion to their numbers, only, in the first place, they serve the Prince, the chief priest, the tranibors, the ambassadors, and strangers, if there are any, which indeed falls out but seldom, and for whom there are houses well furnished, particularly appointed for their reception when they come among them. At the hours of dinner and supper, the whole syphogranty being called together by sound of trumpet, they meet and eat together, except only such as are in the hospitals or lie sick at home. Yet after the halls are served, no man is hindered to carry provisions home from the market-place; for they know that none does that but for some good reason; for though any that will may eat at home, yet none does it willingly, since it is both ridiculous and foolish for any to give themselves the trouble to make ready an ill dinner at home, when there is a much more plentiful one made ready for him so near at hand. All the uneasy and sordid services about these halls are performed by their slaves; but the dressing and cooking their meat, and the ordering their tables, belong only to the women, all those of every family taking it by turns. They sit at three or more tables, according to their number; the men sit toward the wall, and the women sit on the other side, that if any of them should be taken suddenly ill, which is no uncommon case among women with child, she may, without disturbing the rest, rise and go to the nurses' room, who are there with the sucking children, where there is always clean water at hand, and cradles in which they may lay the young children, if there is occasion for it, and a fire that they may shift and dress them before it.

Every child is nursed by its own mother, if death or sickness does not intervene; and in that case the syphogrants' wives find out a nurse quickly, which is no hard matter; for anyone that can do it offers herself cheerfully; for as they are much inclined to that piece of mercy, so the child whom the nurse considers the nurse as its mother. All the children under five years old sit among the nurses, the rest of the younger sort of both sexes, till they are fit for marriage, either serve those that sit at table or, if they are not strong enough for that, stand by them in great silence, and eat what is given them; nor have they any other formality of dining. In the middle of the first table, which stands across the upper end of the hall, sit the syphogrant and his wife; for that is the chief and most conspicuous place: next to him sit two of the most ancient, for there go always four to a mess. If there is a temple within that syphogranty, the priest and his wife sit with the syphogrant above all the rest: next them there is a mixture of old and young, who are so placed, that as the young are set near others, so they are mixed with the more ancient; which they say was appointed on this account, that the gravity of the old people, and the reverence that is due to them, might restrain the younger from all indecent words and gestures. Dishes are not served up to the whole table at first, but the best are first set before the old, whose seats are distinguished from the young, and after them all the rest are served alike. The old men distribute to the younger any curious meats that happen to be set before them, if there is not such an abundance of them that the whole company may be served alike.

Thus old men are honored with a particular respect; yet all the rest fare as well as they. Both dinner and supper are begun with some lecture of morality that is read to them; but it is so short, that it is not tedious nor uneasy to them to hear it: from hence the old men take occasion to entertain those about them with some useful and pleasant enlargements; but they do not engross the whole discourse so to themselves, during their meals, that the younger may not put in for a share: on the contrary, they engage them to talk, that so they may in that free way of conversation find out the force of everyone's spirit and observe his temper. They despatch their dinners quickly, but sit long at supper; because they go to work after the one, and are to sleep after the other, during which they think the stomach carries on the concoction more vigorously. They never sup without music; and there is always fruit served up after meat; while they are at table, some burn perfumes and sprinkle about fragrant ointments and sweet waters: in short, they want nothing that may cheer up their spirits: they give themselves a large allowance that way, and indulge themselves in all such pleasures as are attended with no inconvenience. Thus do those that are in the towns live together; but in the country, where they live at great distance, everyone eats at home, and no family wants any necessary sort of provision, for it is from them that provisions are sent unto those that live in the towns.

Of the Travelling of the Utopians

If any man has a mind to visit his friends that live in some other town, or desires to travel and see the rest of the country, he obtains leave very easily from the syphogrant and tranibors when there is no particular occasion for him at home: such as travel, carry with them a passport from the Prince, which both certifies the license that is granted for travelling, and limits the time of their return. They are furnished with a wagon, and a slave who drives the oxen and looks after them; but unless there are women in the company, the wagon is sent back at the end of the journey as a needless encumbrance. While they are on the road, they carry no provisions with them; yet they want nothing, but are everywhere treated as if they were at home. If they stay in any place longer than a night, everyone follows his proper occupation, and is very well used by those of his own trade; but if any man goes out of the city to which he belongs, without leave, and is found rambling without a passport, he is severely treated, he is punished as a fugitive, and sent home disgracefully; and if he falls again into the like fault, is condemned to slavery. If any man has a mind to travel only over the precinct of his own city, he may freely do it, with his father's permission and his wife's consent; but when he comes into any of the country houses, if he expects to be entertained by them, he must labor with them and conform to their rules: and if he does this, he may freely go over the whole precinct; being thus as useful to the city to which he belongs, as if he were still within it. Thus you see that there are no idle persons among them, nor pretences of excusing any from labor. There are no taverns, no alehouses nor stews among them; nor any other occasions of corrupting each other, of getting into corners, or forming themselves into parties: all men live in full view, so that all are obliged, both to perform their ordinary tasks, and to employ themselves well in their spare hours. And it is certain that a people thus ordered must live in great abundance of all things; and these being equally distributed among them, no man can want, or be obliged to beg.

In their great Council at Amaurot, to which there are three sent from every town once a year, they examine what towns abound in provisions and what are under any scarcity, that so the one may be furnished from the other; and this is done freely, without any sort of exchange; for according to their plenty or scarcity they supply or are supplied from one another; so that indeed the whole island is, as it were, one family. When they have thus taken care of their whole country, and laid up stores for two years, which they do to prevent the ill-consequences of an unfavorable season, they order an exportation of the overplus, of corn, honey, wool, flax, wood, wax, tallow, leather, and cattle; which they send out commonly in great quantities to other nations. They order a seventh part of all these goods to be freely given to the poor of the countries to which they send them, and sell the rest at moderate rates. And by this exchange, they not only bring back those few things that they need at home (for indeed they scarce need anything but iron), but likewise a great deal of gold and silver; and by their driving this trade so long, it is not to be imagined how vast a treasure they have got among them: so that now they do not much care whether they sell off their merchandise for money in hand, or upon trust.

A great part of their treasure is now in bonds; but in all their contracts no private man stands bound, but the writing runs in the name of the town; and the towns that owe them money raise it from those private hands that owe it to them, lay it up in their public chamber, or enjoy the profit of it till the Utopians call for it; and they choose rather to let the greatest part of it lie in their hands who make advantage by it, than to call for it themselves: but if they see that any of their other neighbors stand more in need of it, then they call it in and lend it to them: whenever they are engaged in war, which is the only occasion in which their treasure can be usefully employed, they make use of it themselves. In great extremities or sudden accidents they employ it in hiring foreign troops, whom they more willingly expose to danger than their own people: they give them great pay, knowing well that this will work even on their enemies, that it will engage them either to betray their own side, or at least to desert it, and that it is the best means of raising mutual jealousies among them: for this end they have an incredible treasure; but they do not keep it as a treasure, but in such a manner as I am almost afraid to tell, lest you think it so extravagant, as to be hardly credible. This I have the more reason to apprehend, because if I had not seen it myself, I could not have been easily persuaded to have believed it upon any man's report.

It is certain that all things appear incredible to us, in proportion as they differ from our own customs. But one who can judge aright will not wonder to find that, since their constitution differs so much from ours, their value of gold and silver should be measured by a very different standard; for since they have no use for money among themselves, but keep it as a provision against events which seldom happen, and between which there are generally long intervening intervals, they value it no farther than it deserves, that is, in proportion to its use. So that it is plain they must prefer iron either to gold or silver; for men can no more live without iron than without fire or water, but nature has marked out no use for the other metals, so essential as not easily to be dispensed with. The folly of men has enhanced the value of gold and silver, because of their scarcity. Whereas, on the contrary, it is their opinion that nature, as an indulgent parent, has freely given us all the best things in great abundance, such as water and earth, but has laid up and hid from us the things that are vain and useless.

If these metals were laid up in any tower in the kingdom, it would raise a jealousy of the Prince and Senate, and give birth to that foolish mistrust into which the people are apt to fall, a jealousy of their intending to sacrifice the interest of the public to their own private advantage. If they should work it into vessels or any sort of plate, they fear that the people might grow too fond of it, and so be unwilling to let the plate be run down if a war made it necessary to employ it in paying their soldiers. To prevent all these inconveniences, they have fallen upon an expedient, which, as it agrees with their other policy, so is it very different from ours, and will scarce gain belief among us, who value gold so much and lay it up so carefully. They eat and drink out of vessels of earth, or glass, which make an agreeable appearance though formed of brittle materials: while they make their chamber-pots and close-stools of gold and silver; and that not only in their public halls, but in their private houses: of the same metals they likewise make chains and fetters for their slaves; to some of which, as a badge of infamy, they hang an earring of gold, and make others wear a chain or coronet of the same metal; and thus they take care, by all possible means, to render gold and silver of no esteem. And from hence it is that while other nations part with their gold and silver as unwillingly as if one tore out their bowels, those of Utopia would look on their giving in all they possess of those (metals, when there was any use for them) but as the parting with a trifle, or as we would esteem the loss of a penny. They find pearls on their coast, and diamonds and carbuncles on their rocks; they do not look after them, but, if they find them by chance, they polish them, and with them they adorn their children, who are delighted with them, and glory in them during their childhood; but when they grow to years, and see that none but children use such baubles, they of their own accord, without being bid by their parents, lay them aside; and would be as much ashamed to use them afterward as children among us, when they come to years, are of their puppets and other toys . . . .

[***]

. . . The Utopians wonder how any man should be so much taken with the glaring doubtful lustre of a jewel or a stone, that can look up to a star or to the sun himself; or how any should value himself because his cloth is made of a finer thread: for how fine soever that thread may be, it was once no better than the fleece of a sheep, and that sheep was a sheep still for all its wearing it. They wonder much to hear that gold which in itself is so useless a thing, should be everywhere so much esteemed, that even men for whom it was made, and by whom it has its value, should yet be thought of less value than this metal. That a man of lead, who has no more sense than a log of wood, and is as bad as he is foolish, should have many wise and good men to serve him, only because he has a great heap of that metal; and that if it should happen that by some accident or trick of law (which sometimes produces as great changes as chance itself) all this wealth should pass from the master to the meanest varlet of his whole family, he himself would very soon become one of his servants, as if he were a thing that belonged to his wealth, and so were bound to follow its fortune. But they much more admire and detest the folly of those who, when they see a rich man, though they neither owe him anything nor are in any sort dependent on his bounty, yet merely because he is rich give him little less than divine honors, even though they know him to be so covetous and base-minded that notwithstanding all his wealth he will not part with one farthing of it to them as long as he lives . . . .

. . . They seem, indeed, more inclinable to that opinion that places, if not the whole, yet the chief part of a man's happiness in pleasure; and, what may seem more strange, they make use of arguments even from religion, notwithstanding its severity and roughness, for the support of that opinion so indulgent to pleasure; for they never dispute concerning happiness without fetching some arguments from the principles of religion, as well as from natural reason, since without the former they reckon that all our inquiries after happiness must be but conjectural and defective.

These are their religious principles, that the soul of man is immortal, and that God of his goodness has designed that it should be happy; and that he has therefore appointed rewards for good and virtuous actions, and punishments for vice, to be distributed after this life. Though these principles of religion are conveyed down among them by tradition, they think that even reason itself determines a man to believe and acknowledge them, and freely confess that if these were taken away no man would be so insensible as not to seek after pleasure by all possible means, lawful or unlawful; using only this caution, that a lesser pleasure might not stand in the way of a greater, and that no pleasure ought to be pursued that should draw a great deal of pain after it; for they think it the maddest thing in the world to pursue virtue, that is a sour and difficult thing; and not only to renounce the pleasures of life, but willingly to undergo much pain and trouble, if a man has no prospect of a reward. And what reward can there be for one that has passed his whole life, not only without pleasure, but in pain, if there is nothing to be expected after death? Yet they do not place happiness in all sorts of pleasures, but only in those that in themselves are good and honest . . . .

A life of pleasure is either a real evil, and in that case we ought not to assist others in their pursuit of it, but on the contrary, to keep them from it all we can, as from that which is most hurtful and deadly; or if it is a good thing, so that we not only may, but ought to help others to it, why, then, ought not a man to begin with himself? Since no man can be more bound to look after the good of another than after his own; for nature cannot direct us to be good and kind to others, and yet at the same time to be unmerciful and cruel to ourselves. Thus, as they define virtue to be living according to nature, so they imagine that nature prompts all people on to seek after pleasure, as the end of all they do. They also observe that in order to our supporting the pleasures of life, nature inclines us to enter into society; for there is no man so much raised above the rest of mankind as to be the only favorite of nature who, on the contrary, seems to have placed on a level all those that belong to the same species. Upon this they infer that no man ought to seek his own conveniences so eagerly as to prejudice others; and therefore they think that not only all agreements between private persons ought to be observed, but likewise that all those laws ought to be kept, which either a good prince has published in due form, or to which a people that is neither oppressed with tyranny nor circumvented by fraud, has consented, for distributing those conveniences of life which afford us all our pleasures.

They think it is an evidence of true wisdom for a man to pursue his own advantages as far as the laws allow it. They account it piety to prefer the public good to one's private concerns; but they think it unjust for a man to seek for pleasure by snatching another man's pleasures from him. And on the contrary, they think it a sign of a gentle and good soul, for a man to dispense with his own advantage for the good of others; and that by this means a good man finds as much pleasure one way as he parts with another; for as he may expect the like from others when he may come to need it, so if that should fail him, yet the sense of a good action, and the reflections that he makes on the love and gratitude of those whom he has so obliged, gives the mind more pleasure than the body could have found in that from which it had restrained itself. They are also persuaded that God will make up the loss of those small pleasures, with a vast and endless joy, of which religion easily convinces a good soul.

Thus, upon an inquiry into the whole matter, they reckon that all our actions, and even all our virtues, terminate in pleasure, as in our chief end and greatest happiness; and they call every motion or state, either of body or mind, in which nature teaches us to delight, a pleasure. Thus they cautiously limit pleasure only to those appetites to which nature leads us; for they say that nature leads us only to those delights to which reason as well as sense carries us, and by which we neither injure any other person nor lose the possession of greater pleasures, and of such as draw no troubles after them; but they look upon those delights which men by a foolish though common mistake call pleasure, as if they could change as easily the nature of things as the use of words; as things that greatly obstruct their real happiness instead of advancing it, because they so entirely possess the minds of those that are once captivated by them with a false notion of pleasure, that there is no room left for pleasures of a truer or purer kind . . . .

The Utopians have no better opinion of those who are much taken with gems and precious stones, and who account it a degree of happiness, next to a divine one, if they can purchase one that is very extraordinary; especially if it be of that sort of stones that is then in greatest request; for the same sort is not at all times universally of the same value; nor will men buy it unless it be dismounted and taken out of the gold; the jeweller is then made to give good security, and required solemnly to swear that the stone is true, that by such an exact caution a false one might not be bought instead of a true: though if you were to examine it, your eye could find no difference between the counterfeit and that which is true; so that they are all one to you as much as if you were blind. Or can it be thought that they who heap up a useless mass of wealth, not for any use that it is to bring them, but merely to please themselves with the contemplation of it, enjoy any true pleasure in it? The delight they find is only a false shadow of joy. Those are no better whose error is somewhat different from the former, and who hide it, out of their fear of losing it; for what other name can fit the hiding it in the earth, or rather the restoring it to it again, it being thus cut off from being useful, either to its owner or to the rest of mankind? And yet the owner having hid it carefully, is glad, because he thinks he is now sure of it. If it should be stolen, the owner, though he might live perhaps ten years after the theft, of which he knew nothing, would find no difference between his having or losing it; for both ways it was equally useless to him . . . .

[***]

Of Their Slaves, and of Their Marriages

. . . For the most part, slavery is the punishment even of the greatest crimes; for as that is no less terrible to the criminals themselves than death, so they think the preserving them in a state of servitude is more for the interest of the commonwealth than killing them; since as their labor is a greater benefit to the public than their death could be, so the sight of their misery is a more lasting terror to other men than that which would be given by their death. If their slaves rebel, and will not bear their yoke and submit to the labor that is enjoined them, they are treated as wild beasts that cannot be kept in order, neither by a prison nor by their chains, and are at last put to death. But those who bear their punishment patiently, and are so much wrought on by that pressure that lies so hard on them that it appears they are really more troubled for the crimes they have committed than for the miseries they suffer, are not out of hope but that at last either the Prince will, by his prerogative, or the people by their intercession, restore them again to their liberty, or at least very much mitigate their slavery. He that tempts a married woman to adultery is no less severely punished than he that commits it; for they believe that a deliberate design to commit a crime is equal to the fact itself: since its not taking effect does not make the person that miscarried in his attempt at all the less guilty.

[***]

Of the Religions of the Utopians

[***]

Thus have I described to you, as particularly as I could, the constitution of that commonwealth, which I do not only think the best in the world, but indeed the only commonwealth that truly deserves that name. In all other places it is visible, that while people talk of a commonwealth, every man only seeks his own wealth; but there, where no man has any property, all men zealously pursue the good of the public: and, indeed, it is no wonder to see men act so differently; for in other commonwealths, every man knows that unless he provides for himself, how flourishing soever the commonwealth may be, he must die of hunger; so that he sees the necessity of preferring his own concerns to the public; but in Utopia, where every man has a right to everything, they all know that if care is taken to keep the public stores full, no private man can want anything; for among them there is no unequal distribution, so that no man is poor, none in necessity; and though no man has anything, yet they are all rich; for what can make a man so rich as to lead a serene and cheerful life, free from anxieties; neither apprehending want himself, nor vexed with the endless complaints of his wife? He is not afraid of the misery of his children, nor is he contriving how to raise a portion for his daughters, but is secure in this, that both he and his wife, his children and grandchildren, to as many generations as he can fancy, will all live both plentifully and happily; since among them there is no less care taken of those who were once engaged in labor, but grow afterward unable to follow it, than there is elsewhere of these that continue still employed.

I would gladly hear any man compare the justice that is among them with that of all other nations; among whom, may I perish, if I see anything that looks either like justice or equity: for what justice is there in this, that a nobleman, a goldsmith, a banker, or any other man, that either does nothing at all, or at best is employed in things that are of no use to the public, should live in great luxury and splendor, upon what is so ill acquired; and a mean man, a carter, a smith, or a ploughman, that works harder even than the beasts themselves, and is employed in labors so necessary, that no commonwealth could hold out a year without them, can only earn so poor a livelihood, and must lead so miserable a life, that the condition of the beasts is much better than theirs? For as the beasts do not work so constantly, so they feed almost as well, and with more pleasure; and have no anxiety about what is to come, whilst these men are depressed by a barren and fruitless employment, and tormented with the apprehensions of want in their old age; since that which they get by their daily labor does but maintain them at present, and is consumed as fast as it comes in, there is no overplus left to lay up for old age.

Is not that government both unjust and ungrateful, that is so prodigal of its favors to those that are called gentlemen, or goldsmiths, or such others who are idle, or live either by flattery, or by contriving the arts of vain pleasure; and on the other hand, takes no care of those of a meaner sort, such as ploughmen, colliers, and smiths, without whom it could not subsist? But after the public has reaped all the advantage of their service, and they come to be oppressed with age, sickness, and want, all their labors and the good they have done is forgotten; and all the recompense given them is that they are left to die in great misery. The richer sort are often endeavoring to bring the hire of laborers lower, not only by their fraudulent practices, but by the laws which they procure to be made to that effect; so that though it is a thing most unjust in itself, to give such small rewards to those who deserve so well of the public, yet they have given those hardships the name and color of justice, by procuring laws to be made for regulating them.

Therefore I must say that, as I hope for mercy, I can have no other notion of all the other governments that I see or know, than that they are a conspiracy of the rich, who on pretence of managing the public only pursue their private ends, and devise all the ways and arts they can find out; first, that they may, without danger, preserve all that they have so ill acquired, and then that they may engage the poor to toil and labor for them at as low rates as possible, and oppress them as much as they please. And if they can but prevail to get these contrivances established by the show of public authority, which is considered as the representative of the whole people, then they are accounted laws. Yet these wicked men after they have, by a most insatiable covetousness, divided that among themselves with which all the rest might have been well supplied, are far from that happiness that is enjoyed among the Utopians: for the use as well as the desire of money being extinguished, much anxiety and great occasions of mischief is cut off with it. And who does not see that the frauds, thefts, robberies, quarrels, tumults, contentions, seditions, murders, treacheries, and witchcrafts, which are indeed rather punished than restrained by the severities of law, would all fall off, if money were not any more valued by the world? Men's fears, solicitudes, cares, labors, and watchings, would all perish in the same moment with the value of money: even poverty itself, for the relief of which money seems most necessary, would fall. But, in order to the apprehending this aright, take one instance.

Consider any year that has been so unfruitful that many thousands have died of hunger; and yet if at the end of that year a survey was made of the granaries of all the rich men that have hoarded up the corn, it would be found that there was enough among them to have prevented all that consumption of men that perished in misery; and that if it had been distributed among them, none would have felt the terrible effects of that scarcity; so easy a thing would it be to supply all the necessities of life, if that blessed thing called money, which is pretended to be invented for procuring them, was not really the only thing that obstructed their being procured!

I do not doubt but rich men are sensible of this, and that they well know how much a greater happiness it is to want nothing necessary than to abound in many superfluities, and to be rescued out of so much misery than to abound with so much wealth; and I cannot think but the sense of every man's interest, added to the authority of Christ's commands, who as He was infinitely wise, knew what was best, and was not less good in discovering it to us, would have drawn all the world over to the laws of the Utopians, if pride, that plague of human nature, that source of so much misery, did not hinder it; for this vice does not measure happiness so much by its own conveniences as by the miseries of others; and would not be satisfied with being thought a goddess, if none were left that were miserable, over whom she might insult. Pride thinks its own happiness shines the brighter by comparing it with the misfortunes of other persons; that by displaying its own wealth, they may feel their poverty the more sensibly. This is that infernal serpent that creeps into the breasts of mortals, and possesses them too much to be easily drawn out; and therefore I am glad that the Utopians have fallen upon this form of government, in which I wish that all the world could be so wise as to imitate them; for they have indeed laid down such a scheme and foundation of policy, that as men live happily under it, so it is like to be of great continuance; for they having rooted out of the minds of their people all the seeds both of ambition and faction, there is no danger of any commotion at home; which alone has been the ruin of many States that seemed otherwise to be well secured; but as long as they live in peace at home, and are governed by such good laws, the envy of all their neighboring princes, who have often though in vain attempted their ruin, will never be able to put their State into any commotion or disorder.

When Raphael had thus made an end of speaking, though many things occurred to me, both concerning the manners and laws of that people, that seemed very absurd, as well in their way of making war, as in their notions of religion and divine matters; together with several other particulars, but chiefly what seemed the foundation of all the rest, their living in common, without the use of money, by which all nobility, magnificence, splendor, and majesty, which, according to the common opinion, are the true ornaments of a nation, would be quite taken away;—yet since I perceived that Raphael was weary, and was not sure whether he could easily bear contradiction, remembering that he had taken notice of some who seemed to think they were bound in honor to support the credit of their own wisdom, by finding out something to censure in all other men's inventions, besides their own; I only commended their constitution, and the account he had given of it in general; and so taking him by the hand, carried him to supper, and told him I would find out some other time for examining this subject more particularly, and for discoursing more copiously upon it; and indeed I shall be glad to embrace an opportunity of doing it. In the meanwhile, though it must be confessed that he is both a very learned man, and a person who has obtained a great knowledge of the world, I cannot perfectly agree to everything he has related; however, there are many things in the Commonwealth of Utopia that I rather wish, than hope, to see followed in our governments.

AYN RAND

1905-1982

ATLAS SHRUGGED
1957

Born Alissa Zinovyevna Rosenbaum in St. Petersburg, Russia, Ayn (rhymes with 'mine') Rand was a Hollywood screenwriter, a novelist, and the creator of the philosophy called Objectivism. An unabashed champion of capitalism and the rational pursuit of self-interest, she is best known for her philosophical novels *The Fountainhead* (1943) and *Atlas Shrugged* (1957), the latter of which was ranked the second most influential book read by respondents to a joint Library of Congress/Book-of-the-Month Club survey.

The eldest of three daughters born to middle-class Jewish parents, Zinovny Zacharovich and Anna Borisovna, Rand taught herself to read at age 6 and decided at age nine to become a writer. The family enjoyed a comfortable life, living in a large apartment, entertaining frequently, spending summers in the country and vacationing abroad. This lifestyle declined precipitously when, in the wake of the 1917 Russian Revolution, her father's pharmacy was confiscated "in the name of the people." As hunger and fear overcame the city, renamed Petrograd, the family struggled to survive on their accumulated savings. Twelve years old at the time, the brutality and injustice Rand witnessed at the hands of the Bolsheviks produced in her an antipathy for collectivism, a theme that reverberates throughout her writing.

Many years later, in her testimony before the House Un-American Activities Committee, she described her experience (Rand, 1947):

> In my time we were a bunch of ragged, starved, dirty, miserable people who had only two thoughts in our mind.

> That was our complete terror—afraid to look at one another, afraid to say anything for fear of who is listening and would report us—and where to get the next meal. You have no idea what it means to live in a country where nobody has any concern except food, where all the conversation is about food because everybody is so hungry that that is all they can think about . . . .

Rand shared a special bond with her father, a self-made man whose commercial success she deeply admired. Following the Revolution, the two spent long hours in political discussion and formed a strong intellectual friendship based in part on their mutual and profound belief in individualism. In 1926, at the age of 21, she traveled to the United States, ostensibly to visit relatives for a short time, but with the secret intention of never returning to Russia. "Call it fate or irony," Rand remarked, "but I was born of all countries on earth in the one least suitable for a fanatic of individualism." Her relief at escaping the oppressive rule of collectivism must have been palpable.

While many scholars have defended capitalism on the grounds of economic efficiency, only Rand has argued that capitalism—a system based on voluntary exchange for mutual advantage—is superior on moral grounds.

Atlas Shrugged, Rand's epic novel, is a cautionary tale of America in the not-so-distant future, an America suffocating from an overly intrusive government whose redistributive policies stifle creativity and penalize initiative. What would happen if the producers and creators, the people of ability whom Rand refers to as the "motors of the world," no longer allowed the fruits of their labor to be appropriated by government for the use of others? The title of the book derives from this question, which Rand (1961, pp. 96-7) expresses metaphorically as follows:

> "If you saw Atlas, the giant who holds the world on his shoulders, if you saw that he stood, blood running down his chest, his knees buckling, his arms trembling but still trying to hold the world aloft with the last of his strength, and the greater the effort the heavier the world bore down upon his shoulders—what would you tell him to do?"
>
>   "I . . . don't know. What . . . could he do? What would *you* tell him?"
>
>   "To shrug."

This selection describes a social experiment conducted by the owners of the Twentieth Century Motor Company. The Company motto, "From each according to his ability, to each according to his need," one of the key organizing principles of Communism, is borrowed from *The Critique of the Gotha Programme*, written by Karl Marx in 1875. This excerpt—and, in fact, the entire novel itself—paints a vivid picture of Rand's idea of life in a collectivist society and sounds a warning signal regarding the direction in which she perceived America to be moving.

As you read this selection, consider the role that incentives play in shaping behavior and the implications of Rand's views for the equity-efficiency tradeoff described by Okun. Consider the extent to which rational self-interest, the centerpiece of Objectivism, parallels Adam Smith's Theory of the Invisible Hand. Compare Rand's scathing indictment of collectivism with More's utopian vision, and most importantly, evaluate the ethical implications of the idea that some people can morally lay claim to that which is produced by, and belongs to, others.

SELECTION FROM:

Rand, Ayn. (1957). *Atlas Shrugged.* New York: Dutton (Penguin Group). 660-670.

CHAPTER X
THE SIGN OF THE DOLLAR

[***]

"Well, there was something that happened at that plant where I worked for twenty years. It was when the old man died and his heirs took over. There were three of them, two sons and a daughter, and they brought a new plan to run the factory. They let us vote on it, too, and everybody—almost everybody—voted for it. We didn't know. We thought it was good. No, that's not true, either. We thought that we were supposed to think it was good. The plan was that everybody in the factory would work according to his ability, but would be paid according to his need. We—what's the matter ma'am? Why do you look like that?"

"What was the name of the factory?" she asked, her voice barely audible.

"The Twentieth Century Motor Company, ma'am, of Starnesville, Wisconsin."

"Go on."

"We voted for that plan at a big meeting, with all of us present, six thousand of us, everybody that worked in the factory. The Starnes heirs made long speeches about it, and it wasn't too clear, but nobody asked any questions. None of us knew just how the plan would work, but every one of us thought that the next fellow knew it. And if anybody had doubts, he felt guilty and kept his mouth shut—because they made it sound like anyone who'd oppose the plan was a child-killer at heart and less than a human being. They told us that this plan would achieve a noble ideal. Well, how were we to know otherwise? Hadn't we heard it all our lives—from our parents and our schoolteachers and our ministers, and in every newspaper we ever read and every movie and every public speech? Hadn't we always been told that this was righteous and just? Well, maybe there's some excuse for what we did at that meeting. Still, we voted for the plan—and what we got, we had it coming to us. You know, ma'am, we are marked men, in a way, those of us who lived through the four years of that plan in the Twentieth Century factory. What is it that hell is supposed to be? Evil—plain, naked, smirking evil, isn't it? Well, that's what we saw and helped to make—and I think we're damned, every one of us, and maybe we'll never be forgiven . . . .

"Do you know how it worked, that plan, and what it did to people? Try pouring water into a tank where there's a pipe at the bottom draining it out faster than you pour it, and each bucket you bring breaks that pipe an inch wider, and the harder you work the more is demanded of you, and you stand slinging buckets forty hours a week, then forty-eight, then fifty-six—for your neighbor's supper—for his wife's operation—for his child's measles—for his mother's wheel chair—for his uncle's shirt—for his nephew's schooling—for the baby next door—for the baby to be born—for anyone anywhere around you—it's theirs to receive, from diapers to dentures—and yours to work, from sunup to sundown, month after month, year after year, with nothing to show for it but your sweat, with nothing in sight for you but their pleasure, for the whole of your life, without rest, without hope, without end . . . . From each according to his ability, to each according to his need . . . .

"We're all one big family, they told us, we're all in this together. But you don't all stand working an acetylene torch ten hours a day—together, and you don't all get a bellyache—together. What's whose ability and which of whose needs comes first? When it's all one pot, you can't let any man decide what his own needs are, can you? If you did, he might claim that he needs a yacht—and if his feelings is all you have to go by, he might prove it, too. Why not? If it's not right for me to own a car until I've worked myself into a hospital ward, earning a car for every loafer and every naked savage on earth—why can't he demand a yacht from me, too, if I still have the ability not to have collapsed? No? He can't? Then why can he demand that I go without cream for my coffee until he's replastered his living room? . . . Oh well . . . Well, anyway, it was decided that nobody had the right to judge his own need or ability. We *voted* on it. Yes, ma'am, we voted on it in a public meeting twice a year. How else could it be done? Do you care to think what would happen at such a meeting? It took us just one meeting to discover that we had become beggars—rotten, whining, sniveling beggars, all of us, because no man could claim his pay as his rightful earning, he had no rights and no earnings, his work didn't belong to him, it belonged to 'the family,' and they owed him nothing in return, and the only claim he had on them was his 'need'—so he had to beg in public for relief from his needs, like any lousy moocher, listing all his troubles and miseries, down to his patched drawers and his wife's head colds, hoping that 'the family' would throw him the alms. He had to claim miseries, because it's miseries, not work, that had become the coin of the realm—so it turned into a contest among six thousand panhandlers, each claiming that *his* need was worse than his brother's. How else could it be done? Do you care to guess what happened, what sort of men kept quiet, feeling shame, and what sort got away with the jackpot?

"But that wasn't all. There was something else that we discovered at the same meeting. The factory's production had fallen by forty per cent, in that first half-year, so it was decided that somebody hadn't delivered 'according to his ability.' Who? How would you tell it? 'The family' voted on that, too. They voted which men were the best, and these men were sentenced to work overtime each night for the next six months. Overtime without pay—because you weren't paid by time and you weren't paid by work, only by need.

"Do I have to tell you what happened after that—and into what sort of creatures we all started turning, we who had once been human? We began to hide whatever ability we had, to slow down and watch like hawks that we never worked any faster or better than the next fellow. What else could we do, when we knew that if we did our best for 'the family,' it's not thanks or rewards that we'd get, but punishment? We knew that for every stinker who'd ruin a batch of motors and cost the company money—either through his sloppiness, because he didn't have to care, or through plain incompetence—it's we who'd have to pay with our nights and our Sundays. So we did our best to be no good.

"There was one young boy who started out, full of fire for the noble ideal, a bright kid without any schooling, but with a wonderful head on his shoulders. The first year, he figured out a work process that saved us thousands of man-hours. He gave it to 'the family,' didn't ask anything for it, either, couldn't ask, but that was all right with him. It was for the ideal, he said. But when he found himself voted as one of our ablest and sentenced to night work, because we hadn't gotten enough from him, he shut his mouth and his brain. You can bet he didn't come up with any ideas, the second year.

"What was it they'd always told us about the vicious competition of the profit system, where men had to compete for who'd do a better job than his fellows? Vicious, wasn't it? Well, they should have seen what it was like when we all had to compete with one another for who'd do the worst job possible. There's no surer way to destroy a man than to force him into a spot where he has to aim at *not* doing his best, where he has to struggle to do a bad job, day after day. That will finish him quicker than drink or idleness or pulling stick-ups for a living. But there was nothing else for us to do except to fake unfitness. The one accusation we feared was to be suspected of ability. Ability was like a mortgage on you that you could never pay off. And what was there to work for? You knew that your basic pittance would be given to you anyway, whether you worked or not—your 'housing and feeding allowance,' it was called—and above that pittance, you had no chance to get anything, no matter how hard you tried. You couldn't count on buying a new suit of clothes next year—they might give you a 'clothing allowance' or they might not, according to whether nobody broke a leg, needed an operation or gave birth to more babies. And if there wasn't enough money for new suits for everybody, then you couldn't get yours, either.

"There was one man who'd worked hard all his life, because he'd always wanted to send his son through college. Well, the boy graduated from high school in the second year of the plan—but 'the family' wouldn't give the father any 'allowance' for the college. They said his son couldn't go to college, until we had enough to send everybody's sons to college—and that we first had to send everybody's children through high school, and we didn't even have enough for that. The father died the following year, in a knife fight with somebody in a saloon, a fight over nothing in particular—such fights were beginning to happen among us all the time.

"Then there was an old guy, a widower with no family, who had one hobby: phonograph records. I guess that was all he ever got out of life. In the old days, he used to skip meals just to buy himself some new recording of classical music. Well, they didn't give him any 'allowance' for records—'personal luxury,' they called it. But at that same meeting, Millie Bush, somebody's daughter, a mean, ugly little eight-year-old, was voted a pair of gold braces for her buck teeth—this was 'medical need,' because the staff psychologist had said that the poor girl would get an inferiority complex if her teeth weren't straightened out. The old guy who loved music, turned to drink, instead. He got so you never saw him fully conscious any more. But it seems like there was one thing he couldn't forget. One night, he came staggering down the street, saw Millie Bush, swung his fist and knocked all her teeth out. Every one of them.

"Drink, of course, was what we all turned to, some more, some less. Don't ask how we got the money for it. When all the decent pleasures are forbidden, there's always ways to get the rotten ones. You don't break into grocery stores after dark and you don't pick your fellow's pockets to buy classical symphonies or fishing tackle, but if it's to get stinking drunk and forget—you do. Fishing tackle? Hunting guns? Snapshot cameras? Hobbies? There wasn't any 'amusement allowance' for anybody. 'Amusement' was the first thing they dropped. Aren't you always supposed to be ashamed to object when anybody asks you to give up anything, if it's something that gave you pleasure? Even our 'tobacco allowance' was cut to where we got two packs of cigarettes a month—and this, they told us, was because the money had to go into the babies' milk fund. Babies was the only item of production that didn't fall, but rose and kept on rising—because people had nothing else to do, I guess, and because they didn't have to care, the baby wasn't their burden, it was 'the family's.' In fact, the best chance you had of getting a raise and breathing easier for a while was a 'baby allowance.' Either that, or a major disease.

"It didn't take us long to see how it all worked out. Any man who tried to play straight, had to refuse himself everything. He lost his taste for any pleasure, he hated to smoke a nickel's worth of tobacco or chew a stick of gum, worrying whether somebody had more need for that nickel. He felt ashamed of every mouthful of food he swallowed, wondering whose weary nights of overtime had paid for it, knowing that his food was not his by right, miserably wishing to be cheated rather than to cheat, to be a sucker, but not a blood-sucker. He wouldn't marry, he wouldn't help his folks back home, he wouldn't put an extra burden on 'the family.' Besides, if he still had some sort of sense of responsibility, he couldn't marry or bring children into the world, when he could plan nothing, promise nothing, count on nothing. But the shiftless and the irresponsible had a field day of it. They bred babies, they got girls into trouble, they dragged in every worthless relative they had from all over the country, every unmarried pregnant sister, for an extra 'disability allowance,' they got more sicknesses than any doctor could disprove, they ruined their clothing, their furniture, their homes—what the hell, 'the family' was paying for it! They found more ways of getting in 'need' than the rest of us could ever imagine—they developed a special skill for it, which was the only ability *they* showed.

"God help us, ma'am! Do you see what we saw? We saw that we'd been given a law to live by, a *moral* law, they called it, which punished those who observed it—for observing it. The more you tried to live up to it, the more you suffered; the more you cheated it, the bigger reward you got. Your honesty was like a tool left at the mercy of the next man's dishonesty. The honest ones paid, the dishonest collected. The honest lost, the dishonest won. How long could men stay good under this sort of a law of goodness? We were a pretty decent bunch of fellows when we started. There weren't many chiselers among us. We knew our jobs and we were proud of it and we worked for the best factory in the country, where old man Starnes hired nothing but the pick of the country's labor. Within one year under the new plan, there wasn't an honest man left among us. *That* was the evil, the sort of hell-horror evil that preachers used to scare you with, but you never thought to see alive. Not that the plan encouraged a few bastards, but that it turned decent people into bastards, and there was nothing else that it could do—and it was called a moral ideal!

"What was it we were supposed to want to work for? For the love of our brothers? What brothers? For the bums, the loafers, the moochers we saw all around us? And whether they were cheating or plain incompetent, whether they were unwilling or unable—what difference did that make to us? If we were tied for life to the level of their unfitness, faked or real, how long could we care to go on? We had no way of knowing their ability, we had no way of controlling their needs—all we knew was that we were beasts of burden struggling blindly in some sort of place that was half-hospital, half-stockyards—a place geared to nothing but disability, disaster, disease—beasts put there for the relief of whatever whoever chose to say was whichever's need.

"Love of our brothers? That's when we learned to hate our brothers for the first time in our lives. We began to hate them for every meal they swallowed, for every small pleasure they enjoyed, for one man's new shirt, for another's wife's hat, for an outing with their family, for a paint job on their house was taken from us, it was paid for by our privations, our denials, our hunger. We began to spy on one another, each hoping to catch the others lying about their needs, so as to cut their 'allowance' at the next meeting. We began to have stool pigeons who informed on people, who reported that some body had bootlegged a turkey to his family on some Sunday—which he'd paid for by gambling, most likely. We began to meddle into one another's lives. We provoked family quarrels, to get somebody's relatives thrown out. Any time we saw a man starting to go steady with a girl, we made life miserable for him. We broke up many engagements. We didn't want anyone to marry, we didn't want any more dependents to feed.

"In the old days, we used to celebrate if somebody had a baby, we used to chip in and help him out with the hospital bills, if he happened to be hard-pressed for the moment. Now, if a baby was born, we didn't speak to the parents for weeks. Babies, to us, had become what locusts were to farmers. In the old days, we used to help a man if he had a bad illness in the family. Now—well, I'll tell you about just one case. It was the mother of a man who had been with us for fifteen years. She was a kindly old lady, cheerful and wise, she knew us all by our first names and we all liked her—we used to like her. One day, she slipped on the cellar stairs and fell and broke her hip. We knew what that meant at her age. The staff doctor said that she'd have to be sent to a hospital in town, for expensive treatments that would take a long time. The old lady died the night before she was to leave for town. They never established the cause of death. No, I don't know whether she was murdered. Nobody said that. Nobody would talk about it at all. All I know is that I—and that's what I can't forget!—I, too, had caught myself wishing that she would die. This—may God forgive us!—was the brotherhood, the security, the abundance that the plan was supposed to achieve for us!

"Was there any reason why this sort of horror would ever be preached by anybody? Was there anybody who got any profit from it? There was. The Starnes heirs. I hope you're not going to remind me that they'd sacrificed a fortune and turned the factory over to us as a gift. We were fooled by that one, too. Yes, they gave up the factory. But profit, ma'am, depends on what it is you're after. And what the Starnes heirs were after, no money on earth could buy. Money is too clean and innocent for that.

"Eric Starnes, the youngest—he was a jellyfish that didn't have the guts to be after anything in particular. He got himself voted as Director of our Public Relations Department, which didn't do anything, except that he had a staff for the not doing of anything, so he didn't have to bother sticking around the office. The pay he got—well, I shouldn't call it 'pay,' none of us was 'paid'—the alms voted to him was fairly modest, about ten times what I got, but that wasn't riches. Eric didn't care for money—he wouldn't have known what to do with it. He spent his time hanging around among us, showing how chummy he was and democratic. He wanted to be loved, it seems. The way he went about it was to keep reminding us that he had given us the factory. We couldn't stand him.

"Gerald Starnes was our Director of Production. We never learned just what the size of his rake-off—his alms—had been. It would have taken a staff of accountants to figure that out, and a staff of engineers to trace the way it was piped, directly or indirectly, into his office. None of it was supposed to be for him—it was all for company expenses. Gerald had three cars, four secretaries, five telephones, and he used to throw champagne and caviar parties that no tax-paying tycoon in the country could have afforded. He spent more money in one year than his father had earned in profits in the last two years of his life. We saw a hundred-pound stack—a hundred pounds, we weighed them—of magazines in Gerald's office, full of stories about our factory and our noble plan, with big pictures of Gerald Starnes, calling him a great social crusader. Gerald liked to come into the shops at night, dressed in his formal clothes, flashing diamond cuff links the size of a nickel and shaking cigar ashes all over. Any cheap show-off who's got nothing to parade but his cash, is bad enough—except that he makes no bones about the cash being his, and you're free to gape at him or not, as you wish, and mostly you don't. But when a bastard like Gerald Starnes puts on an act and keeps spouting that he doesn't care for material wealth, that he's only serving 'the family,' that all the lushness is not for himself, but for our sake and for the common good, because it's necessary to keep up the prestige of the company and of the noble plan in the eyes of the public—then that's when you learn to hate the creature as you've never hated anything human.

"But his sister Ivy was worse. She really did not care for material wealth. The aims she got was no bigger than ours, and she went about in scuffed, flat-heeled shoes and shirtwaists—just to show how selfless she was. She was our Director of Distribution. She was the lady in charge of our needs. She was the one who held us by the throat. Of course, distribution was supposed to be decided by voting—by the voice of the people. But when the people are six thousand howling voices, trying to decide without yardstick, rhyme or reason, when there are no rules to the game and each can demand anything, but has a right to nothing, when everybody holds power over everybody's life except his own—then it turns out, as it did, that the voice of the people is Ivy Starnes. By the end of the second year, we dropped the pretense of the 'family meetings'—in the name of 'production efficiency and time economy,' one meeting used to take ten days—and all the petitions of need were simply sent to Miss Starnes' office. No, not sent. They had to be recited to her in person by every petitioner. Then she made up a distribution list, which she read to us for our vote of approval at a meeting that lasted three-quarters of an hour. We voted approval. There was a ten-minute period on the agenda for discussion and objections. We made no objections. We knew better by that time. Nobody can divide a factory's income among thousands of people, without some sort of a gauge to measure people's value. Her gauge was bootlicking. Selfless? In her father's time, all of his money wouldn't have given him a chance to speak to his lousiest wiper and get away with it, as she spoke to our best skilled workers and their wives. She had pale eyes that looked fishy, cold and dead. And if you ever want to see pure evil, you should have seen the way her eyes glinted when she watched some man who'd talked back to her once and who'd just heard his name on the list of those getting nothing above basic pittance. And when you saw it, you saw the real motive of any person who's ever preached the slogan: 'From each according to his ability, to each according to his need.'

"This was the whole secret of it. At first, I kept wondering how it could be possible that the educated, the cultured, the famous men of the world could make a mistake of this size and preach, as righteousness, this sort of abomination—when five minutes of thought should have told them what would happen if somebody tried to practice what they preached. Now I know that they didn't do it by any kind of mistake. Mistakes of this size are never made innocently. If men fall for some vicious piece of insanity, when they have no way to make it work and no possible reason to explain their choice—it's because they have a reason that they do not wish to tell. And we weren't so innocent either, when we voted for that plan at the first meeting. We didn't do it just because we believed that the drippy old guff they spewed was good. We had another reason, but the guff helped us to hide it from our neighbors and from ourselves. The guff gave us a chance to pass off as virtue something that we'd be ashamed to admit otherwise. There wasn't a man voting for it who didn't think that under a setup of this kind he'd muscle in on the profits of the men abler than himself. There wasn't a man rich and smart enough but that he didn't think that somebody was richer and smarter, and this plan would give him a share of his better's wealth and brain. But while he was thinking that he'd get unearned benefits from the men above, he forgot about the men below who'd get unearned benefits, too. He forgot about all his inferiors who'd rush to drain him just as he hoped to drain his superiors. The worker who liked the idea that his need entitled him to a limousine like his boss's, forgot that every bum and beggar on earth would come howling that *their* need entitled them to an icebox like his own. *That* was our real motive when we voted—that was the truth of it—but we didn't like to think it, so the less we liked it, the louder we yelled about our love for the common good.

"Well, we got what we asked for. By the time we saw what it was that we'd asked for, it was too late. We were trapped, with no place to go. The best men among us left the factory in the first week of the plan. We lost our best engineers, superintendents, foremen and highest-skilled workers. A man of self-respect doesn't turn into a milch cow for anybody. Some able fellows tried to stick it out, but they couldn't take it for long. We kept losing our men, they kept escaping from the factory like from a pesthole—till we had nothing left except the men of need, but none of the men of ability.

"And the few of us who were still any good, but stayed on, were only those who had been there too long. In the old days, nobody ever quit the Twentieth Century—and, somehow, we couldn't make ourselves believe that it was gone. After a while, we couldn't quit, because no other employer would have us—for which I can't blame him. Nobody would deal with us in any way, no respectable person or firm. All the small shops, where we traded, started moving out of Starnesville fast—till we had nothing left but saloons, gambling joints and crooks who sold us trash at gouging prices. The alms we got kept falling, but the cost of our living went up. The list of the factory's needy kept stretching, but the list of its customers shrank. There was less and less income to divide among more and more people. In the old days, it used to be said that the Twentieth Century Motor trademark was as good as the karat mark on gold. I don't know what it was that the Starnes heirs thought, if they thought at all, but I suppose that like all social planners and like savages, the thought that this trademark was a magic stamp which did the trick by some sort of voodoo power and that it would keep them rich, as it had kept their father. Well, when our customers began to see that we never delivered an order on time and never put out a motor that didn't have something wrong with it—the magic stamp began to work the other way around: people wouldn't take a motor as a gift, if it was marked Twentieth Century. And it came to where our only customers were men who never paid and never meant to pay their bills. But Gerald Starnes, doped by his own publicity, got huffy and went around, with an air of moral superiority, demanding that businessmen place orders with us, not because our motors were good, but because we *needed* the orders so badly.

"By that time, a village half-wit could see what generations of professors had pretended not to notice. What good would our need do to a power plant when its generators stopped because of our defective engines? What good would it do to a man caught on an operating table when the electric light went out? What good would it do to the passengers of a plane when its motor failed in mid-air? And if they bought our product, not because of its merit, but because of our need, would that be the good, the right, the moral thing to do for the owner of that power plant, the surgeon in that hospital, the maker of that plane?

"Yet this was the moral law that the professors and leaders and thinkers had wanted to establish all over the earth. If this is what it did in a single small town where we all knew one another, do you care to think what it would do on a world scale? Do you care to imagine what it would be like, if you had to live and to work, when you're tied to all the disasters and all the malingering of the globe? To work—and whenever any men failed anywhere, it's you who would have to make up for it. To work—with no chance to rise, with your meals and your clothes and your home and your pleasure depending on any swindle, any famine, any pestilence anywhere on earth. To work—with no chance for an extra ration, till the Cambodians have been fed and the Patagonians have been sent through college. To work—on a blank check held by every creature born, by men whom you'll never see, whose needs you'll never know, whose ability or laziness or sloppiness or fraud you have no way to learn and no right to question—just to work and work and work—and leave it up to the Ivys and the Geralds of the world to decide whose stomach will consume the effort, the dreams and the days of your life. And *this* is the moral law to accept? *This*—a moral ideal?

"Well, we tried it—and we learned. Our agony took four years, from our first meeting to our last, and it ended the only way it could end: in bankruptcy. At our last meeting, Ivy Starnes was the one who tried to brazen it out. She made a short, nasty, snippy little speech in which she said that the plan had failed because the rest of the country had not accepted it, that a single community could not succeed in the midst of a selfish, greedy world—and that the plan was a noble ideal, but human nature was not good enough for it. A young boy—the one who had been punished for giving us a useful idea in our first year—got up, as we all sat silent, and walked straight to Ivy Starnes on the platform. He said nothing. He spat in her face. That was the end of the noble plan and of the Twentieth Century."

Milton Friedman

1912-2006

The Social Responsibility of Business is to Increase its Profits
1970

Biographical information on Milton Friedman can be found in the introduction to his "The Role of Government" found in Section I of this volume.

Friedman's argument in this essay is based on the shareholder theory of the firm, which says that the firm's first and only obligation is to those individuals who have an ownership interest in the business, i.e., they hold shares of the company's stock. He was writing in opposition to the corporate social responsibility (CSR) movement that originated with Frank Abrams (1951, 29), Chairman of Standard Oil of New Jersey, who wrote:

> The job of professional management, as I see it, is to conduct the affairs of the enterprise in its charge in such a way as to maintain an equitable and workable balance among the claims of the various directly interested groups. Business firms are man-made instruments of society. They can be made to achieve their greatest social usefulness—and thus their future can be best assured—when management succeeds in finding a harmonious balance among the claims of the various interested groups: the stockholders, employees, customers, and the public at large.

Friedman's position contrasts with the stakeholder theory of the firm (Freeman, 1984), which assumes a much broader set of obligations. At minimum, the firm's stakeholders include its shareholders, employees, customers, and suppliers, as well as the communities within which it operates.[1] According to this view, which is an offshoot of corporate social responsibility, the firm's managers must balance the interests of competing stakeholders when making their decisions. It is worth noting that a firm's "obligations" under stakeholder theory are moral rather than legal, and would not stand up in a court of law. Only the firm's fiduciary responsibilities to its owners, i.e., its obligations under shareholder theory, are legally enforceable.

Stakeholder theory doesn't explain how the interests of competing groups should be balanced. It "leaves open the question of . . . whose need is greater or whose interest is stronger, and to which needs or interests managers should respond in specific situations where stakes conflict" (Weiss, 1995, 10). The answer to this question may depend, too, on the cultural context in which it is considered, e.g., it has been suggested that shareholders hold more sway in the United States than they do in Europe, where workers enjoy significant influence (*Economist*, 1992, 52).

The arguments in support of social responsibility are varied and complex. At one extreme, it is observed that the corporation is afforded special advantages under the law, e.g., it has many of the same rights as individuals, yet it lives forever and its stockholders enjoy limited liability. Since the corporation is a fictitious person, a legal entity created by society, it is argued that these advantages carry with them social responsibilities. At the opposite extreme, proponents of CSR challenge the assumption that the interests of corporations and society are in opposition to one another and argue that socially responsible behavior is good business (Porter and Kramer, 2006). The distinction between Friedman and CSR has become increasingly blurred of late. Reich (1996), for example, writes, "If we want companies to do things which do not necessarily improve the returns to shareholders but which are beneficial for the economy and society as a whole . . . we have to give business an economic reason to do so."

As you read this essay, speculate about the impact of "socially responsible behavior" on a firm's ability to raise money in financial markets or to compete in an increasingly globalized marketplace. Ask yourself how "socially responsible businesses" should weight the

---

[1]   At the opposite extreme, there is some concern that the tendency to define stakeholders as "'anything influencing or influenced by' the firm" results in a list that is too long to be operationally meaningful (Donaldson and Preston, 1995, 86).

competing interests of different groups when making decisions. Finally, consider the extent to which governmental regulations designed to promote workplace safety or control environmental pollution come at the expense of economic growth and jobs.

Selection From:

Friedman, Milton, (1970). *The Social Responsibility of Business is to Increase its Profits. The New York Times Magazine*, September 13, 1970.[2]

The Social Responsibility of Business is to Increase its Profits

When I hear businessmen speak eloquently about the "social responsibilities of business in a free-enterprise system," I am reminded of the wonderful line about the Frenchman who discovered at the age of 70 that he had been speaking prose all his life. The businessmen believe that they are defending free enterprise when they declaim that business is not concerned "merely" with profit but also with promoting desirable "social" ends; that business has a "social conscience" and takes seriously its responsibilities for providing employment, eliminating discrimination, avoiding pollution and whatever else may be the catchwords of the contemporary crop of reformers. In fact they are—or would be if they or anyone else took them seriously—preaching pure and unadulterated socialism. Businessmen who talk this way are unwitting puppets of the intellectual forces that have been undermining the basis of a free society these past decades.

The discussions of the "social responsibilities of business" are notable for their analytical looseness and lack of rigor. What does it mean to say that "business" has responsibilities? Only people can have responsibilities. A corporation is an artificial person and in this sense may have artificial responsibilities, but "business" as a whole cannot be said to have responsibilities, even in this vague sense. The first step toward clarity in examining the doctrine of the social responsibility of business is to ask precisely what it implies for whom.

Presumably, the individuals who are to be responsible are businessmen, which means individual proprietors or corporate executives. Most of the

---

discussion of social responsibility is directed at corporations, so in what follows I shall mostly neglect the individual proprietors and speak of corporate executives.

In a free-enterprise, private-property system, a corporate executive is an employee of the owners of the business. He has direct responsibility to his employers. That responsibility is to conduct the business in accordance with their desires, which generally will be to make as much money as possible while conforming to the basic rules of the society, both those embodied in law and those embodied in ethical custom. Of course, in some cases his employers may have a different objective. A group of persons might establish a corporation for an eleemosynary purpose—for example, a hospital or a school. The manager of such a corporation will not have money profit as his objective but the rendering of certain services.

In either case, the key point is that, in his capacity as a corporate executive, the manager is the agent of the individuals who own the corporation or establish the eleemosynary institution, and his primary responsibility is to them.

Needless to say, this does not mean that it is easy to judge how well he is performing his task. But at least the criterion of performance is straightforward, and the persons among whom a voluntary contractual arrangement exists are clearly defined.

Of course, the corporate executive is also a person in his own right. As a person, he may have many other responsibilities that he recognizes or assumes voluntarily—to his family, his conscience, his feelings of charity, his church, his clubs, his city, his country. He may feel impelled by these responsibilities to devote part of his income to causes he regards as worthy, to refuse to work for particular corporations, even to leave his job, for example, to join his country's armed forces. If we wish, we may refer to some of these responsibilities as "social responsibilities." But in these respects he is acting as a principal, not an agent; he is spending his own money or time or energy, not the money of his employers or the time or energy he has contracted to devote to their purposes. If these are "social responsibilities," they are the social responsibilities of individuals, not of business.

What does it mean to say that the corporate executive has a "social responsibility" in his capacity as businessman? If this statement is not pure rhetoric, it must mean that he is to act in some way that is not in the interest of his employers. For example, that he is to refrain from increasing the price of the product in order to contribute to the social objective of preventing inflation, even though a price increase would be in the best interests of the corporation. Or that he is to make expenditures on reducing pollution beyond the amount that is in the best interests of the corporation or that is required by law in order to contribute to the social objective of improving the environment. Or that, at the expense of corporate profits, he is to hire "hardcore" unemployed instead of better qualified available workmen to contribute to the social objective of reducing poverty.

In each of these cases, the corporate executive would be spending someone else's money for a general social interest. Insofar as his actions in accord with his "social responsibility" reduce returns to stockholders, he is spending their money. Insofar as his actions raise the price to customers, he is spending the customers' money. Insofar as his actions lower the wages of some employees, he is spending their money.

The stockholders or the customers or the employees could separately spend their own money on the particular action if they wished to do so. The executive is exercising a distinct "social responsibility," rather than serving as an agent of the stockholders or the customers or the employees, only if he spends the money in a different way than they would have spent it.

But if he does this, he is in effect imposing taxes, on the one hand, and deciding how the tax proceeds shall be spent, on the other.

This process raises political questions on two levels: principle and consequences. On the level of political principle, the imposition of taxes and the expenditure of tax proceeds are governmental functions. We have established elaborate constitutional, parliamentary and judicial provisions to control these functions, to assure that taxes are imposed so far as possible in accordance with the preferences and desires of the public—after all, "taxation without representation" was one of the battle cries of the American Revolution. We have a system of checks and balances to separate the legislative function of imposing taxes and enacting expenditures from the executive function of collecting taxes and administering expenditure programs and from the judicial function of mediating disputes and interpreting the law.

Here the businessman—self-selected or appointed directly or indirectly by stockholders—is to be simultaneously legislator, executive and, jurist. He is to decide whom to tax by how much and for what purpose, and he is to spend the proceeds—all this guided only by general exhortations from on high to restrain inflation, improve the environment, fight poverty and so on and on.

The whole justification for permitting the corporate executive to be selected by the stockholders is that the executive is an agent serving the interests of his principal. This justification disappears when the corporate executive imposes taxes and spends the proceeds for "social" purposes. He becomes in effect a public employee, a civil servant, even though he remains in name an employee of a private enterprise. On grounds of political principle, it is intolerable that such civil servants—insofar as their actions in the name of social responsibility are real and not just window-dressing—should be selected as they are now. If they are to be civil servants, then they must be elected through a political process. If they are to impose taxes and make expenditures to foster "social" objectives, then political machinery must be set up to make the assessment of taxes and to determine through a political process the objectives to be served.

This is the basic reason why the doctrine of "social responsibility" involves the acceptance of the socialist view that political mechanisms, not market mechanisms, are the appropriate way to determine the allocation of scarce resources to alternative uses.

On the grounds of consequences, can the corporate executive in fact discharge his alleged "social responsibilities?" On the other hand, suppose he could get away with spending the stockholders' or customers' or employees' money. How is he to know how to spend it? He is told that he must contribute to fighting inflation. How is he to know what action of his will contribute to that end? He is presumably an expert in running his company—in producing a product or selling it or financing it. But nothing about his selection makes him an expert on inflation. Will his holding down the price of his product reduce inflationary pressure? Or, by leaving more spending power in the hands of his customers, simply divert it elsewhere? Or, by forcing him to produce less because of the lower price, will it simply contribute to shortages? Even if he could answer these questions, how much cost is he justified in imposing on his stockholders, customers and employees for this social purpose? What is his appropriate share and what is the appropriate share of others?

And, whether he wants to or not, can he get away with spending his stockholders,' customers' or employees' money? Will not the stockholders fire him? (Either the present ones or those who take over when his actions in the name of social responsibility have reduced the corporation's profits and the price of its stock.) His customers and his employees can desert him for other producers and employers less scrupulous in exercising their social responsibilities.

This facet of "social responsibility" doctrine is brought into sharp relief when the doctrine is used to justify wage restraint by trade unions. The conflict of interest is naked and clear when union officials are asked to subordinate the interest of their members to some more general purpose. If the union officials try to enforce wage restraint, the consequence is likely to be wildcat strikes, rank-and-file revolts and the emergence of strong competitors for their jobs. We thus have the ironic phenomenon that union leaders—at least in the U.S.—have objected to Government interference with the market far more consistently and courageously than have business leaders.

The difficulty of exercising "social responsibility" illustrates, of course, the great virtue of private competitive enterprise—it forces people to be responsible for their own actions and makes it difficult for them to "exploit" other people for either selfish or unselfish purposes. They can do good—but only at their own expense.

Many a reader who has followed the argument this far may be tempted to remonstrate that it is all well and good to speak of Government's having the responsibility to impose taxes and determine expenditures for such "social" purposes as controlling pollution or training the hard-core unemployed, but that the problems are too urgent to wait on the slow course of political processes, that the exercise of social responsibility by businessmen is a quicker and surer way to solve pressing current problems.

Aside from the question of fact—I share Adam Smith's skepticism about the benefits that can be expected from "those who affected to trade for the public good"—this argument must be rejected on grounds of principle. What it amounts to is an assertion that those who favor the taxes and expenditures in question have failed to persuade a majority of their fellow citizens to be of like mind and that they are seeking to attain by undemocratic procedures what they cannot attain by democratic procedures. In a free society, it is hard for "evil" people to do "evil," especially since one man's good is another's evil.

I have, for simplicity, concentrated on the special case of the corporate executive, except only for the brief digression on trade unions. But precisely the same argument applies to the newer phenomenon of calling upon stockholders to require corporations to exercise social responsibility (the recent GM crusade for example). In most of these cases, what is in effect involved is some stockholders trying to get other stockholders (or customers or employees) to contribute against their will to "social" causes favored by the activists. Insofar as they succeed, they are again imposing taxes and spending the proceeds.

The situation of the individual proprietor is somewhat different. If he acts to reduce the returns of his enterprise in order to exercise his "social responsibility," he is spending his own money, not someone else's. If he wishes to spend his money on such purposes, that is his right, and I cannot see that there is any objection to his doing so. In the process, he, too, may impose costs on employees and customers. However, because he is far less likely than a large corporation or union to have monopolistic power, any such side effects will tend to be minor.

Of course, in practice the doctrine of social responsibility is frequently a cloak for actions that are justified on other grounds rather than a reason for those actions.

To illustrate, it may well be in the long run interest of a corporation that is a major employer in a small community to devote resources to providing amenities to that community or to improving its government. That may make it easier to attract desirable employees, it may reduce the wage bill or lessen losses from pilferage and sabotage or have other worthwhile effects. Or it may be that, given the laws about the deductibility of corporate charitable contributions, the stockholders can contribute more to charities they favor by having the corporation make the gift than by doing it themselves, since they can in that way contribute an amount that would otherwise have been paid as corporate taxes.

In each of these—and many similar—cases, there is a strong temptation to rationalize these actions as an exercise of "social responsibility." In the present climate of opinion, with its wide spread aversion to "capitalism," "profits," the "soulless corporation" and so on, this is one way for a corporation to generate goodwill as a by-product of expenditures that are entirely justified in its own self-interest.

It would be inconsistent of me to call on corporate executives to refrain from this hypocritical window-dressing because it harms the foundations of a free society. That would be to call on them to exercise a "social responsibility"! If our institutions, and the attitudes of the public make it in their self-interest to cloak their actions in this way, I cannot summon much indignation to denounce them. At the same time, I can express admiration for those individual proprietors or owners of closely held corporations or stockholders of more broadly held corporations who disdain such tactics as approaching fraud.

Whether blameworthy or not, the use of the cloak of social responsibility, and the nonsense spoken in its name by influential and prestigious businessmen, does clearly harm the foundations of a free society. I have been impressed time and again by the schizophrenic character of many businessmen. They are capable of being extremely farsighted and clearheaded in matters that are internal to their businesses. They are incredibly shortsighted and muddleheaded in matters that are outside their businesses but affect the possible survival of business in general. This shortsightedness is strikingly exemplified in the calls from many businessmen for wage and price guidelines or controls or income policies. There is nothing that could do more in a brief period to destroy a market system and replace it by a centrally controlled system than effective governmental control of prices and wages.

The shortsightedness is also exemplified in speeches by businessmen on social responsibility. This may gain them kudos in the short run. But it helps to strengthen the already too prevalent view that the pursuit of profits is wicked and immoral and must be curbed and controlled by external forces. Once this view is adopted, the external forces that curb the market will not be the social consciences, however highly developed, of the pontificating executives; it will be the iron fist of Government bureaucrats. Here, as with price and wage controls, businessmen seem to me to reveal a suicidal impulse.

The political principle that underlies the market mechanism is unanimity. In an ideal free market resting on private property, no individual can coerce any other, all cooperation is voluntary, all parties to such cooperation benefit or they need not participate. There are no values, no "social" responsibilities in any sense other than the shared values and responsibilities of individuals. Society is a collection of individuals and of the various groups they voluntarily form.

The political principle that underlies the political mechanism is conformity. The individual must serve a more general social interest—whether that be determined by a church or a dictator or a majority. The individual may have a vote and say in what is to be done, but if he is overruled, he must conform. It is appropriate for some to require others to contribute to a general social purpose whether they wish to or not.

Unfortunately, unanimity is not always feasible. There are some respects in which conformity appears unavoidable, so I do not see how one can avoid the use of the political mechanism altogether.

But the doctrine of "social responsibility" taken seriously would extend the scope of the political mechanism to every human activity. It does not differ in philosophy from the most explicitly collectivist doctrine. It differs only by professing to believe that collectivist ends can be attained without collectivist means. That is why, in my book

Capitalism and Freedom, I have called it a "fundamentally subversive doctrine" in a free society, and have said that in such a society, "there is one and only one social responsibility of business—to use it resources and engage in activities designed to increase its profits so long as it stays within the rules of the game, which is to say, engages in open and free competition without deception or fraud."

HENRY D. THOREAU

1817-1862

WALDEN
1854

Born just outside of Boston in Concord, Massachusetts, David Henry Thoreau[1] was an essayist, philosopher, and naturalist. A New England Transcendentalist and one of the first environmental scientists, he is best known for *Civil Disobedience* (1849) and *Walden* (1854). He is perhaps best remembered for these words, which will be familiar even to those who have never read his work: "If a man does not keep pace with his companions, perhaps it is because he hears a different drummer. Let him step to the music which he hears, however measured or far away"[2] (Thoreau, 1854, x).

Searching for business opportunities, Thoreau's shopkeeper father moved the family repeatedly. Ultimately, they returned to Concord, where they began the manufacture of pencils. His mother took in boarders to supplement the income from the family business. After graduating from the Concord Academy, a private school, at 16, it was

---

[1] Named "David Henry" after his paternal uncle, he was always called Henry as a child. He didn't change his name until after graduating college—and, even then, he didn't fill out the papers to change it legally. The name "Thoreau" is pronounced like the word "thorough," with the accent on the first syllable, and rhymes with "furrow"

[2] We may perhaps see here the influence of his friend and mentor, Ralph Waldo Emerson, who wrote in his 1841 essay *Self-Reliance*: "Trust thyself: every heart vibrates to that iron string."

decided that he would attend Harvard University. The cost of his college education was partly paid by the earnings of his two older siblings, Helen and John, both of whom were teachers. After graduation, he taught at the Concord Center School but quickly ran afoul of the superintendent when he refused to flog his students. After only two weeks, he was again looking for a job. Thoreau worked for a year in the pencil factory, then opened his own school. He met with considerable success, took over Concord Academy, and was soon joined by his brother. Unfortunately, John's health began to fail and they were forced to close their doors in April, 1841.

While at Harvard, Thoreau had read "Nature," Ralph Waldo Emerson's essay on the philosophical foundations of Transcendentalism. "The stars awaken a certain reverence," wrote Emerson, "but all natural objects make a kindred impression, when the mind is open to their influence" (Emerson, 1965, 188). We can almost imagine young Thoreau—the future author of *Walden*—reading these words and yearning to make such a connection with nature. "I wanted to live deep and suck out all the marrow of life," he later wrote (Thoreau, 91).

When Emerson moved to Concord in 1837, he and Thoreau spent considerable time together, each learning from the other. Despite this early closeness, Thoreau eventually began to distance himself from Emerson. Fiercely independent, "He could not endure following any master lest he should lose himself" (Moore, 1932).

From 1841 to 1843, Thoreau worked as a gardener and handyman for his neighbor and mentor, Ralph Waldo Emerson. He then moved to Staten Island where he tutored Emerson's nephew, hoping meanwhile to establish contacts in New York that would launch his literary career. He returned to Concord and resumed work in the pencil factory—modifying the production process so as to increase the quality of the final product—making valuable modifications to the production process and taught himself to be a land surveyor.

It took Thoreau four months to build the cabin in which he would live from July 4, 1845, to September 6, 1847. His intention was to use this time to write a book (eventually published as *A Week on the Concord and Merrimack Rivers*) memorializing John, whose death in 1842 had left him traumatized, and to simplify his life. Some readers are disappointed to learn that his life "in the woods" was anything but reclusive. Situated on the north shore of Walden Pond only 1.5 miles from Concord, he had frequent visitors and he often walked into town to dine with friends, obtain needed supplies, or visit his family.

In fact, during one foray into town to have his shoes repaired, Thoreau was arrested and spent a night in jail for failing to pay the poll tax. He had purposely withheld the tax as a form of protest against the Mexican-American War, which was sparked by the U.S. annexation of Texas. An vocal abolitionist, Thoreau (and others) feared that the newly acquired territory would fuel the expansion of slavery. Legend has it that his maiden aunt Maria paid his delinquent taxes "under cover of darkness," resulting in his release the next morning (Harding, 1959, 9). His anger at being denied the opportunity for effective protest dissipated, but the incident itself led him to write *Civil Disobedience*, the classic essay on passive resistance which later inspired the protest movements led by such great leaders as Mahatma Gandhi and Martin Luther King, Jr.

Both Thoreau's cabin on Walden Pond and his family home in Concord were part of the Underground Railroad, helping fugitive slaves escape to Canada. An outspoken opponent of slavery like his mother, Thoreau railed against the Fugitive Slave Act of 1850 and publicly defended John Brown's raid at Harpers Ferry.

Thoreau, unable to find a publisher for *A Week on the Concord and Merrimack Rivers*, took Emerson's advice and had the book published at his own expense. Only 200 copies sold, putting Thoreau into debt and creating ill-will between the two friends. When the publisher returned the remaining copies to Thoreau, he recorded in his Journal that "I have now a library of nearly 900 volumes over 700 of which I wrote myself."

As a philosopher, Thoreau made original contributions to ontology and the philosophy of science; as an environmental scientist, he applied scientific methods to the systematic study of woodland ecology, analyzing the process by which forests regenerate (in "Succession of Forest Trees"), and advanced the proposition that forest management systems follow existing ecological patters (in "Excursions"). He regarded government with distrust, championed freedom, and supported individuality in opposition to social conformity. As a transcendentalist, Thoreau believed that it is possible to experience the divine personally and intuitively. *Walden*, the record of his spiritual odyssey, took him nine years to write.

A self-taught naturalist, over a 24 year period, he had recorded two million words in his journal, producing an extensively detailed natural history of his observations and travels. While Thoreau produced only two published books in his lifetime, his posthumously published works fill more than 20 volumes.

As you read this selection, consider whether Thoreau's beliefs constitute a repudiation of Bentham's principle of utility. Ask yourself what he might have to say about the plight of the Lithuanian family described in *The Jungle* and try to determine the extent to which he and Veblen would agree. To what degree is the significance of Thoreau's message diminished by the fact that he regularly visited town to socialize with friends and purchase necessary items?

SELECTION FROM:

Thoreau, H. D. (1929). *A Week on the Concord and Merrimack Rivers and Walden.* 3, 4-6, 6-10, 12-16, 17-18, 20-21, 23-25, 29, 37-40, 50-51, 58-59, 77-78.

ECONOMY

WHEN I wrote the following pages, or rather the bulk of them, I lived alone, in the woods, a mile from any neighbor, in a house which I had built myself, on the shore of Walden Pond, in Concord, Massachusetts, and earned my living by the labor of my hands only. I lived there two years and two months. At present I am a sojourner in civilized life again . . . .

. . . I have travelled a good deal in Concord; and everywhere, in shops, and offices, and fields, the inhabitants have appeared to me to be doing penance in a thousand remarkable ways. What I have heard of Bramins sitting exposed to four fires and looking in the face of the sun; or hanging suspended, with their heads downward, over flames; or looking at the heavens over their shoulders "until it becomes impossible for them to resume their natural position, while from the twist of the neck nothing but liquids can pass into the stomach;" or dwelling, chained for life, at the foot of a tree; or measuring with their bodies, like caterpillars, the breadth of vast empires; or standing on one leg on the tops of pillars,—even these forms of conscious penance are hardly more incredible and astonishing than the scenes which I daily witness. The twelve labors of Hercules were trifling in comparison with those which my neighbors have undertaken; for they were only twelve, and had an end; but I could never see that these men slew or captured any monster or finished any labor. They have no friend Iolaus to burn with a hot iron the root of the hydras head, but as soon as one head is crushed, two spring up.

I see young men, my townsmen, whose misfortune it is to have inherited farms, houses, barns, cattle, and farming tools; for these are more easily acquired than got rid of. Better if they had been born in the open pasture and suckled by a wolf, that they might have seen with clearer eyes what field they were called to labor in. Who made them serfs of the soil? Why should they eat their sixty acres, when man is condemned to eat only his peck of dirt? Why should they begin digging their graves as soon as they are born? They have got to live a man's life, pushing all these things before them, and get on as well as they can. How many a poor immortal soul have I met well-nigh crushed and smothered under its load, creeping down the road of life, pushing before it a barn seventy-five feet by forty, its Augean stables never cleansed, and one hundred acres of land, tillage, mowing, pasture, and wood-lot! The portionless, who struggle with no such unnecessary inherited encumbrances, find it labor enough to subdue and cultivate a few cubic feet of flesh.

But men labor under a mistake. The better part of the man is soon plowed into the soil for compost. By a seeming fate, commonly called necessity, they are employed, as it says in an old book, laying up treasures which moth and rust will corrupt and thieves break through and steal. It is a fool's life, as they will find when they get to the end of it, if not before . . . .

Most men, even in this comparatively free country, through mere ignorance and mistake, are so occupied with the factitious cares and superfluously coarse labors of life that its finer fruits cannot be plucked by them. Their fingers, from excessive toil, are too clumsy and tremble too much for that. Actually, the laboring man has not leisure for a true integrity day by day; he cannot afford to sustain the manliest relations to men; his labor would be depreciated in the market. He has no time to be anything but a machine. How can he remember well his ignorance—which his growth requires—who has so often to use his knowledge? We should feed and clothe him gratuitously sometimes, and recruit him with our cordials, before we judge of him. The finest qualities of our nature, like the bloom on fruits, can be preserved only by the most delicate handling. Yet we do not treat ourselves nor one another thus tenderly.

Some of you, we all know, are poor, find it hard to live, are sometimes, as it were, gasping for breath. I have no doubt that some of you who read this book are unable to pay for all the dinners which you have actually eaten, or for the coats and shoes which are fast wearing or are already worn out, and have come to this page to spend borrowed or stolen time, robbing your creditors of an hour. It is very evident what mean and sneaking lives many of you live, for my sight has been whetted by experience; always on the limits, trying to get into business and trying to get out of debt, a very ancient slough, called by the Latins *aes alienum*, another's brass, for some of their coins were made of brass; still living, and dying, and buried by this other's brass; always promising to pay, promising to pay, to-morrow, and dying to-day, insolvent; seeking to curry favor, to get custom, by how many modes, only not state-prison offences; lying, flattering, voting, contracting yourselves into a nutshell of civility or dilating into an atmosphere of thin and vaporous generosity, that you may persuade your neighbor to let you make his shoes, or his hat, or his coat, or his carriage, or import his groceries for him; making yourselves sick, that you may lay up something against a sick day, something to be tucked away in an old chest, or in a stocking behind the plastering, or, more safely, in the brick bank; no matter where, no matter how much or how little.

I sometimes wonder that we can be so frivolous, I may almost say, as to attend to the gross but somewhat foreign form of servitude called Negro Slavery, there are so many keen and subtle masters that enslave both North and South. It is hard to have a Southern overseer; it is worse to have a Northern one; but worst of all when you are the slave-driver of yourself. Talk of a divinity in man! Look at the teamster on the highway, wending to market by day or night; does any divinity stir within him? His highest duty to fodder and water his horses! What is his destiny to him compared with the shipping interests? Does not he drive for Squire Make-a-stir? How godlike, how immortal, is he? See how he cowers and sneaks, how vaguely all the day he fears, not being immortal nor divine, but the slave and prisoner of his own opinion of himself, a fame won by his own deeds. Public opinion is a weak tyrant compared with our own private opinion. What a man thinks of himself, that it is which determines, or rather indicates, his fate . . . .

The mass of men lead lives of quiet desperation. What is called resignation is confirmed desperation. From the desperate city you go into the desperate country, and have to console yourself with the bravery of minks and muskrats. A stereotyped but unconscious despair is concealed even under what are called the games and amusements of mankind. There is no play in them, for this comes after work. But it is a characteristic of wisdom not to do desperate things.

When we consider what, to use the words of the catechism, is the chief end of man, and what are the true necessaries and means of life, it appears as if men had deliberately chosen the common mode of living because they preferred it to any other. Yet they honestly think there is no choice left. But alert and healthy natures remember that the sun rose clear. It is never too late to give up our prejudices. No way of thinking or doing, however ancient, can be trusted without proof. What everybody echoes or in silence passes by as true to-day may turn out to be falsehood to-morrow, mere smoke of opinion, which some had trusted for a cloud that would sprinkle fertilizing rain on their fields. What old people say you cannot do, you try and find that you can. Old deeds for old people, and new deeds for new. Old people did not know enough once, perchance, to fetch fresh fuel to keep the fire a-going; new people put a little dry wood under a pot, and are whirled round the globe with the speed of birds, in a way to kill old people, as the phrase is. Age is no better, hardly so well, qualified for an instructor as youth, for it has not profited so much as it has lost. One may almost doubt if the wisest man has learned anything of absolute value by living. Practically, the old have no very important advice to give the young, their own experience has been so partial, and their lives have been such miserable failures, for private reasons, as they must believe; and it may be that they have some faith left which belies that experience, and they are only less young than they were. I have lived some thirty years on this planet, and I have yet to hear the first syllable of valuable or even earnest advice from my seniors. They have told me nothing, and probably cannot tell me anything to the purpose. Here is life, an experiment to a great extent untried by me; but it does not avail me that they have tried it. If I have any experience which I think valuable, I am sure to reflect that this my Mentors said nothing about.

One farmer says to me, "You cannot live on vegetable food solely, for it furnishes nothing to make bones with"; and so he religiously devotes a part of his day to supplying his system with the raw material of bones; walking all the while he talks behind his oxen, which, with vegetable-made bones, jerk him and his lumbering plow along in spite of every obstacle. Some things are really necessaries of life in some circles, the most helpless and diseased, which in others are luxuries merely, and in others still are entirely unknown.

[***]

Let us consider for a moment what most of the trouble and anxiety which I have referred to is about, and how much it is necessary that we be troubled, or at least careful. It would be some advantage to live a primitive and frontier life, though in the midst of an outward civilization, if only to learn what are the gross necessaries of life and what methods have been taken to obtain them; or even to look over the old day-books of the merchants, to see what it was that men most commonly bought at the stores, what they stored, that is, what are the grossest groceries. For the improvements of ages have had but little influence on the essential laws of man's existence" as our skeletons, probably, are not to be distinguished from those of our ancestors.

By the words, *necessary of life*, I mean whatever, of all that man obtains by his own exertions, has been from the first, or from long use has become, so important to human life that few, if any, whether from savageness, or poverty, or philosophy, ever attempt to do without it. To many creatures there is in this sense but one necessary of life, Food. To the bison of the prairie it is a few inches of palatable grass, with water to drink; unless he seeks the Shelter of the forest or the mountain's shadow. None of the brute creation requires more than Food and Shelter. The necessaries of life for man in this climate may, accurately enough, be distributed under the several heads of Food, Shelter, Clothing, and Fuel; for not till we have secured these are we prepared to entertain the true problems of life with freedom and a prospect of success. Man has invented, not only houses, but clothes and cooked food; and possibly from the accidental discovery of the warmth of fire, and the consequent use of it, at first a luxury, arose the present necessity to sit by it. We observe cats and dogs acquiring the same second nature. By proper Shelter and Clothing we legitimately retain our own internal heat; but with an excess of these, or of Fuel, that is, with an external heat greater than our own internal, may not cookery properly be said to begin? Darwin, the naturalist, says of the inhabitants of Tierra del Fuego, that while his own party, who were well clothed and sitting close to a fire, were far from too warm, these naked savages, who were farther off, were observed, to his great surprise, "to be streaming with perspiration at undergoing such a roasting." So, we are told, the New Hollander goes naked with impunity, while the European shivers in his clothes. Is it impossible to combine the hardiness of these savages with the intellectualness of the civilized man? According to Liebig, man's body is a stove, and food the fuel which keeps up the internal combustion in the lungs. In cold weather we eat more, in warm less. The animal heat is the result of a slow combustion, and disease and death take place when this is too rapid; or for want of fuel, or from some defect in the draught, the fire goes out. Of course the vital heat is not to be confounded with fire; but so much for analogy. It appears, therefore, from the above list, that the expression, *animal life*, is nearly synonymous with the expression, *animal heat*; for while Food may be regarded as the Fuel which keeps up the fire within us,—and Fuel serves only to prepare that Food or to increase the warmth of our bodies by addition from without,—Shelter and Clothing also serve only to retain the *heat* thus generated and absorbed.

The grand necessity, then, for our bodies, is to keep warm, to keep the vital heat in us. What pains we accordingly take, not only with our Food, and Clothing, and Shelter, but with our beds, which are our night-clothes, robbing the nests and breasts of birds to prepare this shelter within a shelter, as the mole has its bed of grass and leaves at the end of its burrow! The poor man is wont to complain that this is a cold world; and to cold, no less physical than social, we refer directly a great part of our ails. The summer, in some climates, makes possible to man a sort of Elysian life. Fuel, except to cook his Food, is then unnecessary; the sun is his fire, and many of the fruits are sufficiently cooked by its rays; while Food generally is more various, and more easily obtained, and Clothing and Shelter are wholly or half unnecessary. At the present day, and in this country, as I find by my own experience, a few implements, a knife, an axe, a spade, a wheelbarrow, etc., and for the studious, lamplight, stationery, and access to a few books, rank next to necessaries, and can all be obtained at a trifling cost. Yet some, not wise, go to the other side of the globe, to barbarous and unhealthy regions, and devote themselves to trade for ten or twenty years, in order that they may live,—that is, keep comfortably warm,—and die in New England at last. The luxuriously rich are not simply kept comfortably warm, but unnaturally hot; as I implied before, they are cooked, of course *à la mode*.

Most of the luxuries, and many of the so-called comforts of life, are not only not indispensable, but positive hindrances to the elevation of mankind. With respect to luxuries and comforts, the wisest have ever lived a more simple and meagre life than the poor. The ancient philosophers, Chinese, Hindoo, Persian, and Greek, were a class than which none has been poorer in outward riches, none so rich in inward. We know not much about them. It is remarkable that *we* know so much of them as we do. The same is true of the more modern reformers and benefactors of their race. None can be an impartial or wise observer of human life but from the vantage ground of what *we* should call voluntary poverty. Of a life of luxury the fruit is luxury, whether in agriculture, or commerce, or literature, or art. There are nowadays professors of philosophy, but not philosophers. Yet it is admirable to profess because it was once admirable to live. To be a philosopher is not merely to have subtle thoughts, nor even to found a school, but so to love wisdom as to live according to its dictates, a life of simplicity, independence, magnanimity, and trust.

It is to solve some of the problems of life, not only theoretically, but practically. The success of great scholars and thinkers is commonly a courtier-like success, not kingly, not manly. They make shift to live merely by conformity, practically as their fathers did, and are in no sense the progenitors of a noble race of men. But why do men degenerate ever? What makes families run out? What is the nature of the luxury which enervates and destroys nations? Are we sure that there is none of it in our own lives? The philosopher is in advance of his age even in the outward form of his life. He is not fed, sheltered, clothed, warmed, like his contemporaries. How can a man be a philosopher and not maintain his vital heat by better methods than other men? . . .

I do not mean to prescribe rules to strong and valiant natures, who will mind their own affairs whether in heaven or hell, and perchance build more magnificently and spend more lavishly than the richest, without ever impoverishing themselves, not knowing how they live,—if, indeed, there are any such, as has been dreamed; nor to those who find their encouragement and inspiration in precisely the present condition of things, and cherish it with the fondness and enthusiasm of lovers,—and, to some extent, I reckon myself in this number; I do not speak to those who are well employed, in whatever circumstances, and they know whether they are well employed or not;—but mainly to the mass of men who are discontented, and idly complaining of the hardness of their lot or of the times, when they might improve them. There are some who complain most energetically and inconsolably of any, because they are, as they say, doing their duty. I also have in my mind that seemingly wealthy, but most terribly impoverished class of all, who have accumulated dross, but know not how to use it, or get rid of it, and thus have forged their own golden or silver fetters.

[***]

Not long since, a strolling Indian went to sell baskets at the house of a well-known lawyer in my neighborhood. "Do you wish to buy any baskets?" he asked. "No, we do not want any," was the reply. "What!" exclaimed the Indian as he went out the gate, "do you mean to starve us?" Having seen his industrious white neighbors so well off,—that the lawyer had only to weave arguments, and, by some magic, wealth and standing followed,—he had said to himself: I will go into business; I will weave baskets; it is a thing which I can do. Thinking that when he had made the baskets he would have done his part, and then it would be the white man's to buy them. He had not discovered that it was necessary for him to make it worth the other's while to buy them, or at least make him think that it was so, or to make something else which it would be worth his while to buy. I too had woven a kind of basket of a delicate texture, but I had not made it worth any one's while to buy them. Yet not the less, in my case, did I think it worth my while to weave them, and instead of studying how to make it worth men's while to buy my baskets, I studied rather how to avoid the necessity of selling them. The life which men praise and regard as successful is but one kind. Why should we exaggerate any one kind at the expense of the others.

[***]

As this business was to be entered into without the usual capital, it may not be easy to conjecture where those means, that will still be indispensable to every such undertaking, were to be obtained. As for Clothing, to come at once to the practical part of the question, perhaps we are led oftener by the love of novelty and a regard for the opinions of men, in procuring it, than by a true utility. Let him who has work to do recollect that the object of clothing is, first, to retain the vital heat, and secondly, in this state of society, to cover nakedness, and he may judge how much of any necessary or important work may be accomplished without adding to his wardrobe. Kings and queens who wear a suit but once, though made by some tailor or dressmaker to their majesties, cannot know the comfort of wearing a suit that fits. They are no better than wooden horses to hang the clean clothes on. Every day our garments become more assimilated to ourselves, receiving the impress of the wearer's character, until we hesitate to lay them aside without such delay and medical appliances and some such solemnity even as our bodies. No man ever stood the lower in my estimation for having a patch in his clothes; yet I am sure that there is greater anxiety, commonly, to have fashionable, or at least clean and unpatched clothes, than to have a sound conscience. But even if the rent is not mended, perhaps the worst vice betrayed is improvidence. I sometimes try my acquaintances by such tests as this,—Who could wear a patch, or two extra seams only, over the knee? Most behave as if they believed that their prospects for life would be ruined if they should do it. It would be easier for them to hobble to town with a broken leg than with a broken pantaloon. Often if an accident happens to a gentleman's legs, they can be mended; but if a similar accident happens to the legs of his pantaloons, there is no help for it; for he considers, not what is truly respectable, but what is respected. We know but few men, a great many coats and breeches. Dress a scarecrow in your last shift, you standing shiftless by, who would not soonest salute the scarecrow? Passing a cornfield the other day, close by a hat and coat on a stake, I recognized the owner of the farm. He was only a little more weather-beaten than when I saw him last. I have heard of a dog that barked at every stranger who approached his master's premises with clothes on, but was easily quieted by a naked thief. It is an interesting question how far men would retain their relative rank if they were divested of their clothes. Could you, in such a case, tell surely of any company of civilized men which belonged to the most respected class? When Madam Pfeiffer, in her adventurous travels round the world, from east to west, had got so near home as Asiatic Russia, she says that she felt the necessity of wearing other than a travelling dress, when she went to meet the authorities, for she "was now in a civilized country, where . . . people are judged of by their clothes." Even in our democratic New England towns the accidental possession of wealth, and its manifestation in dress and equipage alone, obtain for the possessor almost universal respect. But they yield such respect, numerous as they are, are so far heathen, and need to have a missionary sent to them. Beside, clothes introduced sewing, a kind of work which you may call endless; a woman's dress, at least, is never done.

[***]

I cannot believe that our factory system is the best mode by which men may get clothing. The condition of the operatives is becoming every day more like that of the English; and it cannot be wondered at, since, as far as I have heard or observed, the principal object is, not that mankind may be well and honestly clad, but, unquestionably, that corporations may be enriched. In the long run men hit only what they aim at. Therefore, though they should fail immediately, they had better aim at something high.

[***]

But how do the poor *minority* fare? Perhaps it will be found that just in proportion as some have been placed in outward circumstances above the savage, others have been degraded below him. The luxury of one class is counterbalanced by the indigence of another. On the one side is the palace, on the other are the almshouse and "silent poor." The myriads who built the pyramids to be the tombs of the Pharaohs were fed on garlic, and it may be were not decently buried themselves. The mason who finishes the cornice of the palace returns at night perchance to a hut not so good as a wigwam. It is a mistake to suppose that, in a country where the usual evidences of civilization exist, the condition of a very large body of the inhabitants may not be as degraded as that of savages. I refer to the degraded poor, not now to the degraded rich. To know this I should not need to look farther than to the shanties which everywhere border our railroads, that last improvement in civilization; where I see in my daily walks human beings living in sties, and all winter with an open door, for the sake of light, without any visible, often imaginable, wood-pile, and the forms of both old and young are permanently contracted by the long habit of shrinking from cold and misery, and the development of all their limbs and faculties is checked. It certainly is fair to look at that class by whose labor the works which distinguish this generation are accomplished. Such too, to a greater or less extent, is the condition of the operatives of every denomination in England, which is the great workhouse of the world. Or I could refer you to Ireland, which is marked as one of the white or enlightened spots on the map. Contrast the physical condition of the Irish with that of the North American Indian, or the South Sea Islander, or any other savage race before it was degraded by contact with the civilized man. Yet I have no doubt that that people's rulers are as wise as the average of civilized rulers. Their condition only proves what squalidness may consist with civilization. I hardly need refer now to the laborers in our Southern States who produce the staple exports of this country, and are themselves a staple production of the South. But to confine myself to those who are said to be in *moderate* circumstances.

Most men appear never to have considered what a house is, and are actually though needlessly poor all their lives because they think that they must have such a one as their neighbors have. As if one were to wear any sort of coat which the tailor might cut out for him, or, gradually leaving off palm-leaf hat or cap of woodchuck skin, complain of hard times because he could not afford to buy him a crown! It is possible to invent a house still more convenient and luxurious than we have, which yet all would admit that man could not afford to pay for. Shall we always study to obtain more of these things, and not sometimes to be content with less? Shall the respectable citizen thus gravely teach, by precept and example, the necessity of the young man's providing a certain number of superfluous glow-shoes, and umbrellas, and empty guest chambers for empty guests, before he dies? Why should not our furniture be as simple as the Arab's or the Indian's? When I think of the benefactors of the race, whom we have apotheosized as messengers from heaven, bearers of divine gifts to man, I do not see in my mind any retinue at their heels, any carload of fashionable furniture. Or what if I were to allow—would it not be a singular allowance?—that our furniture should be more complex than the Arab's, in proportion as we are morally and intellectually his superiors! At present our houses are cluttered and defiled with it, and a good housewife would sweep out the greater part into the dust hole, and not leave her morning's work undone. Morning work! By the blushes of Aurora and the music of Memnon, what should be man's *morning work* in this world? I had three pieces of limestone on my desk, but I was terrified to find that they required to be dusted daily, when the furniture of my mind was all undusted still, and threw them out the window in disgust. How, then, could I have a furnished house? I would rather sit in the open air, for no dust gathers on the grass, unless where man has broken ground.

[***]

It would be worth the while to build still more deliberately than I did, considering, for instance, what foundation a door, a window, a cellar, a garret, have in the nature of man, and perchance never raising any superstructure until we found a better reason for it than our temporal necessities even. There is some of the same fitness in a man's building his own house that there is in a bird's building its own nest. Who knows but if men constructed their dwellings with their own hands, and provided food for themselves and families simply and honestly enough, the poetic faculty would be universally developed, as birds universally sing when they are so engaged? But alas! we do like cowbirds and cuckoos, which lay their eggs in nests which other birds have built, and cheer no traveller with their chattering and unmusical notes. Shall we forever resign the pleasure of construction to the carpenter? What does architecture amount to in the experience of the mass of men? I never in all my walks came across a man engaged in so simple and natural an occupation as building his house. We belong to the community. It is not the tailor alone who is the ninth part of a man; it is as much the preacher, and the merchant, and the farmer. Where is this division of labor to end? and what object does it finally serve? No doubt another *may* also think for me; but it is not therefore desirable that he should do so to the exclusion of my thinking for myself.

[***]

One says to me, "I wonder that you do not lay up money; you love to travel; you might take the cars and go to Fitchburg today and see the country." But I am wiser than that. I have learned that the swiftest traveller is he that goes afoot. I say to my friend, Suppose we try who will get there first. The distance is thirty miles; the fare ninety cents. That is almost a day's wages. I remember when wages were sixty cents a day for laborers on this very road. Well, I start now on foot, and get there before night; I have travelled at that rate by the week together. You will in the meanwhile have earned your fare, and arrive there some time tomorrow, or possibly this evening, if you are lucky enough to get a job in season. Instead of going to Fitchburg, you will be working here the greater part of the day. And so, if the railroad reached round the world, I think that I should keep ahead of you; and as for seeing the country and getting experience of that kind, I should have to cut your acquaintance altogether.

[***]

As I preferred some things to others, and especially valued my freedom, as I could fare hard and yet succeed well, I did not wish to spend my time in earning rich carpets or other fine furniture, or delicate cookery, or a house in the Grecian or the Gothic style just yet. If there are any to whom it is no interruption to acquire these things, and who know how to use them when acquired, I relinquish to them the pursuit. Some are "industrious," and appear to love labor for its own sake, or perhaps because it keeps them out of worse mischief; to such I have at present nothing to say. Those who would not know what to do with more leisure than they now enjoy, I might advise to work twice as hard as they do,—work till they pay for themselves, and get their free papers. For myself I found that the occupation of a day-laborer was the most independent of any, especially as it required only thirty or forty days in a year to support one. The laborer's day ends with the going down of the sun, and he is then free to devote himself to his chosen pursuit, independent of his labor; but his employer, who speculates from month to month, has no respite from one end of the year to the other.

In short, I am convinced, both by faith and experience, that to maintain one's self on this earth is not a hardship but a pastime, if we will live simply and wisely; as the pursuits of the simpler nations are still the sports of the more artificial. It is not necessary that a man should earn his living by the sweat of his brow, unless he sweats easier than I do . . . .

SECTION III

CONFRONTING THE CAUSES OF INEQUALITY

Thorstein Veblen
   The Theory of the Leisure Class (1899)
J. J. Rousseau
   On the Origin and Foundation of the Inequality of Mankind (1754)
Kingsley Davis & Wilbert E. Moore
   "Some Principles of Stratification" (1944)
Upton Sinclair
   The Jungle (1946)
W.E.B. Du Bois
   The Souls of Black Folks (1903)

The causes of inequality are numerous and defy simple classification. It is easy to see that innate differences in ability are partly responsible for observed differences in wealth and status. Relative advantages and disadvantages, however, change over time and with economic conditions. The competitive edge provided by physical strength and speed, for example, diminished as the economy evolved from the early hunter-gatherer stage to today's Information Age, where brains dominate brawn in the battle for survival. Yet as important as are our differing gifts, we must still recognize the critical role played by both luck and personal connections. Success often depends on "being in the right place at the right time," and young people are still told that "it's not what you know, but who you know" that matters. But even superior natural gifts and good fortune may be insufficient to overcome historical, institutional, or attitudinal obstacles to success. This last point is guaranteed to spark controversy for it forces us to ask whether responsibility for success (or failure) belongs to the individual or to the society as a whole.

Veblen starts off this section with a probing inquiry into the motives that drive people to acquire and accumulate wealth. His exploration of the intimate connection between the property ownership, popular esteem, and self respect meshes well with many of the observations made by Thoreau in the last section. Searching for the roots of inequality in the historical evolution of civil society, Rousseau points an accusing finger at the political institutions men created to preserve and protect their common interests. The third reading in this section adopts a somewhat unconventional stance: not only is inequality a necessary feature of any social system, it exists because it serves an important function in society. Sinclair's harrowing narrative vividly illustrates the difficulty of rising above one's circumstances when confronted by overwhelming odds. Du Bois closes this section with a description of the plight of the Negro during the period following the abolition of slavery and the Reconstruction. Like Sinclair, Du Bois helps us feel the desperation and frustration that people experience when fighting to overcome powerful social forces that would diminish their lives.

THORSTEIN VEBLEN

1957-1929

THE THEORY OF THE LEISURE CLASS
1899

Economist, sociologist and social critic, Thorstein Bunde Veblen was born in Cato, Wisconsin, to poor Norwegian immigrants at a time when "money was the stepping-stone to social recognition in the United States" and fortunes were being made by unscrupulous means (Heilbroner, 1992, 214). In 1865, his parents packed up their belongings and their 12 children, and moved to another farm in the Norwegian township of Wheeling in Rice County, Minnesota. Since Norwegian was the only language spoken in both of these tight-knit communities, Veblen was forced to learn English as a second language, a feat he didn't perfect until he went off to college.

At age 17, Veblen was sent to Carleton College Academy, a small Congregational school in nearby Northfield, to prepare himself for entry into the ministry. A brilliant student, he was an irreverent and insufferable prankster (he is said to have advocated cannibalism and drunkenness during public declamations) and did not fit in well with the pious atmosphere at Carleton. He did, however, manage to romance the niece of the president of the college, Ellen Rolfe, who many years later would become his wife. After completing his degree, he matriculated at Johns Hopkins University to study philosophy and political economy. He was unable to remain there without a scholarship, and transferred to Yale where he got his PhD in philosophy in 1884. Degree in hand, he went looking for a teaching position but was unable to find one. Having contracted malaria while in Baltimore, he returned home to recuperate.

He spent the next seven years loafing around the family farm, reading voraciously. In 1888, he married Ellen despite being unemployed. Finally, in 1891, at the age of 34, he was sent back to graduate school by a decision of the family council.

Veblen took up graduate studies in economics at Cornell University, where he met J. Laurence Laughlin, the man who was to become his mentor. The following year, the newly established University of Chicago hired Laughlin to head its economics department, and Veblen was offered an assistant professorship as part of the deal. He taught political economy at Chicago from 1892 to 1906, editing the *Journal of Political Economy* for nine of these years. During this time, Ellen repeatedly left him for his frequent marital indiscretions. It was this scandalous behavior that eventually led University of Chicago President Harper to dismiss Veblen. He managed to get a job at Stanford University, but was forced to leave after three years as a result of his continued philandering. His marriage was dissolved in 1911 and he moved on to the University of Missouri, where he stayed for the next seven years, until making his final move to the New School for Social Research in New York City. In 1925, he turned down an opportunity to be president of the American Economic Association, the most highly respected professional organization for economists.

By all accounts, Veblen was a very strange man. "The first time I saw him," remembers one of his students, "ambling along the Quad, with a slouch hat pulled down over his brow, with coat and trousers hanging with untrimmed hair and moustache creating a general unkempt appearance, I thought he was a tramp" (Breit and Ransom, 1971, 35). "He allowed the dishes to accumulate until the cupboard was bare and then washed the whole messy heap by turning the hose on them" (Heilbroner, 1992, 219). He has been described as neurotic, taciturn, and cruelly sadistic. "His students thought him dull, and he did not pretend to be fond of them" (Mills, 1953, viii). He was a terrible teacher, mumbling, rambling and digressing, and he derived tremendous pleasure from driving students away. He gave the same grade to everyone, regardless of the quality of the work turned in.

Veblen's ability to see below the surface, to challenge conventional interpretations and to comfortably move back-and-forth between economics and sociology may be attributable to the unique perspective he "enjoyed" as an outsider, a stranger in a strange land. "He walked through life as if he had descended from another world," observes Heilbroner (1992, 219), "and the going on that appeared so natural to the eyes of his contemporaries appeared to him as piquant, exotic, and curious as the rituals of a savage community to the eye of an anthropologist."

While best known for *The Theory of the Leisure Class* (1899), in which he coined the terms "conspicuous consumption" and "captains of industry," Veblen's *The Theory of Business Enterprise* (1904), *The Higher Learning In America* (1918), and *The Engineers and the Price System* (1921) are also well regarded. In addition to his six other books, he wrote more than 50 academic papers for such publications as *The Journal of Speculative Philosophy*, *Quarterly Journal of Economics*, *Journal of Political Economy*, *American Journal of Sociology*, *Political Science Quarterly*, and *The International Journal of Ethics*.

As you read this selection, try to identify the similarities between Veblen's theories and those advanced by Marx and Engels in *The Communist Manifesto*. To what extent would Veblen and Thoreau find themselves in agreement, and on what points? Consider the possibility that the phenomenon of pecuniary emulation may have contributed to the race riots discussed in the Kerner Report and ask yourself how the insights you gain from reading Veblen impact your assessment of the amount of inequality that exists in our society. Finally, compare and contrast the role of private property in Rand's, Rousseau's and Veblen's writings.

SELECTION FROM:

Veblen, Thorstein. (1912). *The Theory of the Leisure Class*. New York: The Macmillan Company. Reprinted by the New York: New American Library, 1953. 33-40.

2
PECUNIARY EMULATION

IN THE sequence of cultural evolution the emergence of a leisure class coincides with the beginning of ownership. This is necessarily the case, for these two institutions result from the same set of economic forces. In the inchoate phase of their development they are but different aspects of the same general facts of social structure.

It is as elements of social structure—conventional facts—that leisure and ownership are matters of interest for the purpose in hand. An habitual neglect of work does not constitute a leisure class; neither does the mechanical fact of use and consumption constitute ownership. The present inquiry, therefore, is not concerned with the beginning of indolence, nor with the beginning of the appropriation of useful articles to individual consumption. The point in question is the origin and nature of a conventional leisure class on the one hand and the beginnings of individual ownership as a conventional right or equitable claim on the other hand.

The early differentiation out of which the distinction between a leisure and a working class arises is a division maintained between men's and women's work in the lower stages of barbarism. Likewise the earliest form of ownership is an ownership of the women by the able bodied men of the community. The facts may be expressed in more general terms. and truer to the import of the barbarian theory of life, by saying that it is an ownership of the woman by the man.

There was undoubtedly some appropriation of useful articles before the custom of appropriating women arose. The usages of existing archaic communities in which there is no ownership of women is warrant for such a view. In all communities the members, both male and female, habitually appropriate to their individual use a variety of useful things; but these useful things are not thought of as owned by the person who appropriates and consumes them. The habitual appropriation and consumption of certain slight personal effects goes on without raising the question of ownership; that is to say, the question of a conventional, equitable claim to extraneous things.

The ownership of women begins in the lower barbarian stages of culture, apparently with the seizure of female captives. The original reason for the seizure and appropriation of women seems to have been their usefulness as trophies. The practice of seizing women from the enemy as trophies, gave rise to a form of ownership-marriage, resulting in a household with a male head. This was followed by an extension of slavery to other captives and inferiors, besides women, and by an extension of ownership-marriage to other women than those seized from the enemy. The outcome of emulation under the circumstances of a predatory life, therefore, has been on the one hand a form of marriage resting on coercion, and on the other hand the custom of ownership. The two institutions are not distinguishable in the initial phase of their development; both arise from the desire of the successful men to put their prowess in evidence by exhibiting some durable result of their exploits. Both also minister to that propensity for mastery which pervades all predatory communities. From the ownership of women the concept of ownership extends itself to include the products of their industry, and so there arises the ownership of things as well as of persons.

In this way a consistent system of property in goods is gradually installed. And although in the latest stages of the development, the serviceability of goods for consumption has come to be the most obtrusive element of their value, still, wealth has by no means yet lost its utility as a honorific evidence of the owner's prepotence.

Wherever the institution of private property is found, even in a slightly developed form, the economic process bears the character of a struggle between men for the possession of goods. It has been customary in economic theory, and especially among those economists who adhere with least faltering to the body of modernized classical doctrines, to construe this struggle for wealth as being substantially a struggle for subsistence. Such is, no doubt, its character in large part during the earlier and less efficient phases of industry. Such is also its character in all cases where the "niggardliness of nature" is so strict as to afford but a scanty livelihood to the community in return for strenuous and unremitting application to the business of getting the means of subsistence. But in all progressing communities an advance is presently made beyond this early stage of technological development. Industrial efficiency is presently carried to such a pitch as to afford something appreciably more than a bare livelihood to those engaged in the industrial process. It has not been unusual for economic theory to speak of the further struggle for wealth on this new industrial basis as a competition for an increase of the comforts of life—primarily for an increase of the physical comforts which the consumption of goods affords.

The end of acquisition and accumulation is conventionally held to be the consumption of the goods accumulated—whether it is consumption directly by the owner of the goods or by the household attached to him and for this purpose identified with him in theory. This is at least felt to be the economically legitimate end of acquisition, which alone it is incumbent on the theory to take account of. Such consumption may of course be conceived to serve the consumer's physical wants—his physical comfort—or his so-called higher wants—spiritual, aesthetic, intellectual, or what not; the latter class of wants being served indirectly by an expenditure of goods, after the fashion familiar to all economic readers.

But it is only when taken in a sense far removed from its naive meaning that consumption of goods can be said to afford the incentive from which accumulation invariably proceeds. The motive that lies at the root of ownership is emulation; and the same motive of emulation continues active in the further development of the institution to which it has given rise and in the development of all those features of the social structure which this institution of ownership touches. The possession of wealth confers honor; it is an invidious distinction. Nothing equally cogent can be said for the consumption of goods, nor for any other conceivable incentive to acquisition, and especially not for any incentive to accumulation of wealth.

It is of course not to be overlooked that in a community where nearly all goods are private property the necessity of earning a livelihood is a powerful and ever present incentive for the poorer members of the community. The need of subsistence and of an increase of physical comfort may for a time be the dominant motive of acquisition for those classes who are habitually employed at manual labor, whose subsistence is on a precarious footing, who possess little and ordinarily accumulate little; but it will appear in the course of the discussion that even in the case of these impecunious classes the predominance of the motive of physical want is not so decided as has sometimes been assumed. On the other hand, so far as regards those members and classes of the community who are chiefly concerned in the accumulation of wealth, the incentive of subsistence or of physical comfort never plays a considerable part. Ownership began and grew into a human institution on grounds unrelated to the subsistence minimum. The dominant incentive was from the outset the invidious distinction attaching to wealth, and, save temporarily and by exception, no other motive has usurped the primacy at any later stage of the development.

Property set out with being booty held as trophies of the successful raid. So long as the group had departed and so long as it still stood in close contact with other hostile groups, the utility of things or persons owned lay chiefly in an invidious comparison between their possessor and the enemy from whom they were taken. The habit of distinguishing between the interests of the individual and those of the group to which he belongs is apparently a later growth. Invidious comparison between the possessor of the honorific booty and his less successful neighbors within the group was no doubt present early as an element of the utility of the things possessed, though this was not at the outset the chief element of their value. The man's prowess was still primarily the group's prowess, and the possessor of the booty felt himself to be primarily the keeper of the honor of his group. This appreciation of exploit from the communal point of view is met with also at later stages of social growth, especially as regards the laurels of war.

But as soon as the custom of individual ownership begins to gain consistency, the point of view taken in making the invidious comparison on which private property rests will begin to change. Indeed, the one change is but the reflex of the other. The initial phase of ownership, the phase of acquisition by naive seizure and conversion, begins to pass into the subsequent stage of an incipient organization of industry on the basis of private property (in slaves); the horde develops into a more or less self-sufficing industrial community; possessions then come to be valued not so much as evidence of successful foray, but rather as evidence of the prepotence of the possessor of these goods over other individuals within the community. The invidious comparison now becomes primarily a comparison of the owner with the other members of the group. Property is still of the nature of trophy, but, with the cultural advance, it becomes more and more a trophy of successes scored in the game of ownership carried on between the members of the group under the quasi-peaceable methods of nomadic life.

Gradually, as industrial activity further displaced predatory activity in the community's everyday life and in men's habits of thought, accumulated property more and more replaces trophies of predatory exploit as the conventional exponent of prepotence and success. With the growth of settled industry, therefore, the possession of wealth gains in relative importance and effectiveness as a customary basis of repute and esteem. Not that esteem ceases to be awarded on the basis of other, more direct evidence of prowess; not that successful predatory aggression or warlike exploit ceases to call out the approval and admiration of the crowd, or to stir the envy of the less successful competitors; but the opportunities for gaining distinction by means of this direct manifestation of superior force grow less available both in scope and frequency. At the same time opportunities for industrial aggression, and for the accumulation of property, increase in scope and availability. And it is even more to the point that property now becomes the most easily recognized evidence of a reputable degree of success as distinguished from heroic or signal achievement. It therefore becomes the conventional basis of esteem. Its possession in some amount becomes necessary in order to any reputable standing in the community. It becomes indispensable to accumulate, to acquire property, in order to retain one's good name. When accumulated goods have in this way once become the accepted badge of efficiency, the possession of wealth presently assumes the character of an independent and definitive basis of esteem. The possession of goods, whether acquired aggressively by one's own exertion or passively by transmission through inheritance from others, becomes a conventional basis of reputability. The possession of wealth, which was at the outset valued simply as an evidence of efficiency, becomes, in popular apprehension, itself a meritorious act. Wealth is now itself intrinsically honorable and confers honor on its possessor. By a further refinement, wealth acquired passively by transmission from ancestors or other antecedents presently becomes even more honorific than wealth acquired by the possessor's own effort; but this distinction belongs at a later stage in the evolution of the pecuniary culture and will be spoken of in its place.

Prowess and exploit may still remain the basis of award of the highest popular esteem, although the possession of wealth has become the basis of common place reputability and of a blameless social standing. The predatory instinct and the consequent approbation of predatory efficiency are deeply ingrained in the habits of thought of those peoples who have passed under the discipline of a protracted predatory culture. According to popular award, the highest honors within human reach may, even yet, be those gained by an unfolding of extraordinary predatory efficiency in war, or by a quasi-predatory efficiency in statecraft; but for the purposes of a commonplace decent standing in the community these means of repute have been replaced by the acquisition and accumulation of goods. In order to stand well in the eyes of the community, it is necessary to come up to a certain, somewhat indefinite, conventional standard of wealth; just as in the earlier predatory stage it is necessary for the barbarian man to come up to the tribe's standard of physical endurance, cunning, and skill at arms. A certain standard of wealth in the one case, and of prowess in the other, is a necessary condition of reputability, and anything in excess of this normal amount is meritorious.

Those members of the community who fall short of this, somewhat indefinite, normal degree of prowess or of property suffer in the esteem of their fellowmen; and consequently they suffer also in their own esteem, since the usual basis of self-respect is the respect accorded by one's neighbors. Only individuals with an aberrant temperament can in the long run retain their self-esteem in the face of the disesteem of their fellows. Apparent exceptions to the rule are met with, especially among people with strong religious convictions. But these apparent exceptions are scarcely real exceptions, since such persons commonly fall back on the putative approbation of some supernatural witness of their deeds.

So soon as the possession of property becomes the basis of popular esteem, therefore, it becomes also a requisite to the complacency which we call self-respect. In any community where goods are held in severalty it is necessary, in order to his own peace of mind, that an individual should possess as large a portion of goods as others with whom he is accustomed to class himself; and it is extremely gratifying to possess something more than others. But as fast as a person makes new acquisitions, and becomes accustomed to the resulting new standard of wealth, the new standard forthwith ceases to afford appreciably greater satisfaction than the earlier standard did. The tendency in any case is constantly to make the present pecuniary standard the point of departure for a fresh increase of wealth; and this in turn gives rise to a new standard of sufficiency and a new pecuniary classification of one's self as compared with one's neighbors. So far as concerns the present question, the end sought by accumulation is to rank high in comparison with the rest of the community in point of pecuniary strength. So long as the comparison is distinctly unfavorable to himself, the normal, average individual will live in chronic dissatisfaction with his present lot; and when he has reached what may be called the normal pecuniary standard of the community, or of his class in the community, this chronic dissatisfaction will give place to a restless straining to place a wider and ever-widening pecuniary interval between himself and this average standard. The invidious comparison can never become so favorable to the individual making it that he would not gladly rate himself still higher relatively to his competitors in the struggle for pecuniary reputability.

In the nature of the case, the desire for wealth can scarcely be satiated in any individual instance, and evidently a satiation of the average or general desire for wealth is out of the question. However widely, or equally, or "fairly," it may be distributed, no general increase of the community's wealth can make any approach to satiating this need, the ground of which approach to satiating this need, the ground of which is the desire of every one to excel every one else in the accumulation of goods. If, as is sometimes assumed, the incentive to accumulation were the want of subsistence or of physical comfort, then the aggregate economic wants of a community might conceivably be satisfied at some point in the advance of industrial efficiency; but since the struggle is substantially a race for reputability on the basis of an invidious comparison, no approach to a definitive attainment is possible.

What has just been said must not be taken to mean that there are no other incentives to acquisition and accumulation than this desire to excel in pecuniary standing and so gain the esteem and envy of one's fellowmen. The desire for added comfort and security from want is present as a motive at every stage of the process of accumulation in a modern industrial community; although the standard of sufficiency in these respects is in turn greatly affected by the habit of pecuniary emulation. To a great extent this emulation shapes the methods and selects the objects of expenditure for personal comfort and decent livelihood.

Besides this, the power conferred by wealth also affords a motive to accumulation. That propensity for purposeful activity and that repugnance to all futility of effort which belong to man by virtue of his character as an agent do not desert him when he emerges from the naïve communal culture where the dominant note of life is the unanalyzed and undifferentiated solidarity of the individual with the group with which his life is bound up. When he enters upon the predatory stage, where self-seeking in the narrower sense becomes the dominant note, this propensity goes with him still, as the pervasive trait that shapes his scheme of life. The propensity for achievement and the repugnance to futility remain the underlying economic motive. The propensity changes only in the form of its expression and in the proximate objects to which it directs the man's activity. Under the regime of individual ownership the most available means of visibly achieving a purpose is that afforded by the acquisition and accumulation of goods; and as the self-regarding antithesis between man and man reaches fuller consciousness, the propensity for achievement—the instinct of workmanship—tends more and more to shape itself into a straining to excel others in pecuniary achievement. Relative success, tested by an invidious pecuniary comparison with other men, becomes the conventional end of action. The currently accepted legitimate end of effort becomes the achievement of a favorable comparison with other men; and therefore the repugnance to futility to a good extent coalesces with the incentive of emulation. It acts to accentuate the struggle for pecuniary reputability by visiting with a sharper disapproval all shortcoming and all evidence of shortcoming in point of pecuniary success. Purposeful effort comes to mean, primarily, effort directed to or resulting in a more creditable showing of accumulated wealth. Among the motives which lead men to accumulate wealth, the primacy, both in scope and intensity, therefore, continues to belong to this motive of pecuniary emulation.

In making use of the term "invidious," it may perhaps be unnecessary to remark, there is no intention to extol or depreciate, or to commend or deplore any of the phenomena which the word is used to characterize. The term is used in a technical sense as describing a comparison of persons with a view to rating and grading them in respect of relative worth or value—in an æsthetic or moral sense—and so awarding and defining the relative degrees of complacency with which they may legitimately be contemplated by themselves and by others. An invidious comparison is a process of valuation of persons in respect of worth.

JEAN-JACQUES ROUSSEAU

1712-1778

THE SOCIAL CONTRACT AND DISCOURSES
1817-1862

ON THE ORIGIN AND FOUNDATION OF THE INEQUALITY OF MANKIND
1754

Political philosopher and novelist, Jean-Jacques Rousseau was an important Enlightenment thinker whose ideas helped lay the foundation for ninth-century Romanticism. Born in Geneva, Switzerland, his passionate rhetoric is said to have inspired the leaders of the French Revolution. While best known for his classic *On Social Contract* (1762)—with its famous opening line "Man is born free, but everywhere is in chains"—and his *Confessions* (1782), Rousseau considered *Émile, or On Education* (1762) to be his most important work.

Rousseau's mother died shortly after he was born, leaving him to be raised by his father, an irresponsible and "pleasure-loving" watchmaker with a penchant for dueling.[1] Their house originally belonged to his mother's uncle, a prominent scholar and a member of the Genevan upper class. Taking full advantage of its extensive library, his father instilled in him a love of reading and exposed him to the classics, of which Plutarch's *Lives* was a favorite. When Rousseau was

---

[1] Rousseau himself describes his father as a pleasure-lover (Cohen, 1953, 34).

quite young, his father, falsely accused by a French captain of having drawn his weapon during a quarrel, was forced to flee the city to avoid imprisonment.[2] Left in the care of his uncle, he and his cousin were sent to Bossey, where they were to live with, and be educated by, the pastor Lambercier and his sister.

Rousseau's recollection of being punished unjustly by Lambercier left an impression that may have influenced his later thinking on the problem of governmental abuses of power. This incident, he wrote, "ended the serenity of my childish life."

> I feel my pulse beat faster once more as I write. I shall always remember that time if I live to be a thousand. That first meeting with violence and injustice has remained so deeply engraved on my heart that any thought which recalls it summons back the first emotion. The feeling was only a personal one in its origins, but it has since assumed such a consistency and has become so divorced from personal interests that my blood boils at the sight or the tale of any injustice, whoever may be the sufferer and wherever it may have taken place, in just the same way as if I were myself its victim. (Rousseau, 1953, 30)

Apprenticed by his uncle to an engraver, Rousseau ran away from this violent and abusive man when an opportunity unexpectedly presented itself. Wandering Europe, he found himself in Annecy, where he met Louise Éléonore de Warens, who arranged for him to travel to Turin to be baptized. Being all alone and in need of support from "some charitable Christians," he overcame his aversion to Catholicism and made the conversion, renouncing Calvinism and forfeiting his Genevan citizenship in the process. He later returned to Annecy and, in 1729, moved into the house of Madame de Warens (almost twice his age, she referred to him as

---

2   While most sources indicate that Rousseau's father fled Geneva in 1922, making Rousseau ten years old at the time, *The Confessions* suggest otherwise. The following passage describes his experience of being spanked by Mlle Lambercier: "Who could have supposed that this childish punishment, *received at the age of eight* at the hands of a woman of thirty, would determine my tastes and desires, my passions, my very self for the rest of my life . . . ." (Cohen, 1953, 26), [emphasis added]. Since Rousseau and his cousin were sent to Bossey soon after he arrived at this uncle's home, he couldn't possibly have been ten years old when he was first placed in his uncle's care.

"Child" and to herself as "Mamma"), who cultivated his love of music, provided him with an education and, later, became his lover.

Moving to Paris in 1742, he held a variety of odd jobs, including copying music and tutoring, and became friendly with Denis Diderot, François-Marie Arouet de Voltaire, Étienne Bonnot de Condillac and other French Enlightenment philosophers. In 1745, he met Thérèse Levasseur, a hotel maid whom he eventually married in 1768 and who bore him five children, all of whom were placed in a foundling home.

In 1750, Rousseau achieved fame with the publication of *Discourse on the Arts and Sciences* (also called the "First Discourse"), his winning submission to an essay contest sponsored by the Academy of Dijon, which posed the question "Has the restoration of the sciences and the arts had a purifying effect upon morals?" He answered in the negative, arguing that the refinement of tastes had corrupted humanity, leading people to speak an affected language, encouraging pretentiousness and pomposity, producing false respectability, and undercutting trust. In his own words,

> a vile and misleading uniformity governs our customs, and all minds seem to have been cast in the same mould: . . . incessantly people follow customary usage, never their own inclinations. One does not dare to appear as what one is. And in this perpetual constraint, men who make up this herd we call society, placed in the same circumstances, will all do the same things, unless more powerful motives prevent them. Thus, one will never know well the person one is dealing with. (Rousseau, 1953, 30)

The Academy of Dijon sponsored another essay contest in 1753, and Rousseau again entered. Having already achieved fame and respectability on the basis of his First Discourse, he was able to arrange for the independent publication of his essay before submitting it to the Academy. This decision proved prescient. The judges thought that his response to the question "What is the origin of inequality among men, and is it authorized by the natural law?" was too long and excessively bold, and didn't even finish reading it. His submission, *On the Origin and Foundation of the Inequality of Mankind* (also called the "Second Discourse"), challenged conventional beliefs and was widely read by the public.

The Second Discourse, the Third Discourse (*A Discourse on Political Economy*, 1755), and *On Social Contract* present and develop Rousseau's political philosophy. In contrast to Hobbes (1651), he believed that human beings in the "state of nature" are essentially good, peaceful, content and amoral (the idea of the "noble savage"), but were corrupted by society. Nonetheless, he strongly believed that a proper education could free people from the oppressive influence of civilization. He observed that people were willing to sacrifice some of their freedom to rulers in exchange for protection of their lives and property. This "exchange" constituted a "social contract" that obligated government to work to promote the general well-being of society as a whole. If the state fails to fulfill its side of the bargain, said Rousseau, it loses its moral authority to rule, leaving the people free to dissolve the government and select new rulers.

Rousseau's two masterpieces, *On Social Contract* and *Émile*, were highly controversial. Both were banned by French authorities, in part for their attacks on traditional religious and political beliefs. His books were burned and he was ordered arrested. Forced into exile, he fled first to Switzerland and then, at the invitation of David Hume, to England. Suffering from both a persecution complex and paranoia, his psychological state become increasingly unstable. He accused Hume of plotting against him and fled once again, this time back to Paris, where he wandered in poverty until he died.

Ask yourself, after reading the following excerpt from his *Second Discourse*, how Rousseau's explanation for the existence of inequality compares with those advanced by Eitzen and by Marx and Engels. Consider the extent to which Rousseau and Friedman would agree about the proper role of government in a civil society and try to determine whether Rousseau would agree or disagree with Davis and Moore about the consequence of inequality.

SELECTION FROM:

Rousseau, Jean Jacques. (1754). *The Social Contract and Discourses.* New York: E. P. Dutton and Company, Inc. 1950. 234-272.

THE SECOND PART

THE first man who, having enclosed a piece of ground, bethought himself of saying "This is mine," and found people simple enough to believe him, was the real founder of civil society. From how many crimes, wars, and murders, from how many horrors and misfortunes might not any one have saved mankind, by pulling up the stakes, or filling up the ditch, and crying to his fellows: "Beware of listening to this impostor;

you are undone if you once forget that the fruits of the earth belong to us all, and the earth itself to nobody." But there is great probability that things had then already come to such a pitch, that they could no longer continue as they were; for the idea of property depends on many prior ideas, which could only be acquired successively, and cannot have been formed all at once in the human mind. Mankind must have made very considerable progress, and acquired considerable knowledge and industry which they must also have transmitted and increased from age to age, before they arrived at this last point of the state of nature. Let us then go farther back, and endeavour to unify under a single point of view that slow succession of events and discoveries in the most natural order.

Man's first feeling was that of his own existence, and his first care that of self-preservation. The produce of the earth furnished him with all he needed, and instinct told him how to use it. Hunger and other appetites made him at various times experience various modes of existence; and among these was one which urged him to propagate his species—a blind propensity that, having nothing to do with the heart, produced a merely animal act. The want once gratified, the two sexes knew each other no more; and even the offspring was nothing to its mother, as soon as it could do without her.

Such was the condition of infant man; the life of an animal limited at first to mere sensations, and hardly profiting by the gifts nature bestowed on him, much less capable of entertaining a thought of forcing anything from her. But difficulties soon presented themselves, and it became necessary to learn how to surmount them: the height of the trees, which prevented him from gathering their fruits, the competition of other animals desirous of the same fruits, and the ferocity of those who needed them for their own preservation, all obliged him to apply himself to bodily exercises. He had to be active, swift of foot, and vigorous in fight. Natural weapons, stones, and sticks, were easily found: he learnt to surmount the obstacles of nature, to contend in case of necessity with other animals, and to dispute for the means of subsistence even with other men, or to indemnify himself for what he was forced to give up to a stronger.

In proportion as the human race grew more numerous, men's cares increased. The difference of soils, climates, and seasons, must have introduced some differences into their manner of living. Barren years, long and sharp winters, scorching summers which parched the fruits of the earth, must have demanded a new industry. On the seashore and the banks of rivers, they invented the hook and line, and became fishermen and eaters of fish. In the forests they made bows and arrows, and became huntsmen and warriors. In cold countries they clothed themselves with the skins of the beasts they had slain. The lightning, a volcano, or some lucky chance acquainted them with fire, a new resource against the rigours of winter: they next learned how to preserve this element, then how to reproduce it, and finally how to prepare with it the flesh of animals which before they had eaten raw.

[***]

Taught by experience that the love of well-being is the sole motive of human actions, he found himself in a position to distinguish the few cases, in which mutual interest might justify him in relying upon the assistance of his fellows; and also the still fewer cases in which a conflict of interests might give cause to suspect them. In the former case, he joined in the same herd with them, or at most in some kind of loose association, that laid no restraint on its members, and lasted no longer than the transitory occasion that formed it. In the latter case, every one sought his own private advantage, either by open force, if he thought himself strong enough, or by address and cunning, if he felt himself the weaker.

In this manner, men may have insensibly acquired some gross ideas of mutual undertakings, and of the advantages of fulfilling them: that is, just so far as their present and apparent interest was concerned: for they were perfect strangers to foresight, and were so far from troubling themselves about the distant future, that they hardly thought of the morrow. If a deer was to be taken, every one saw that, in order to succeed, he must abide faithfully by his post: but if a hare happened to come within the reach of any one of them, it is not to be doubted that he pursued it without scruple, and, having seized his prey, cared very little, if by so doing he caused his companions to miss theirs.

[***]

The first expansions of the human heart were the effects of a novel situation, which united husbands and wives, fathers and children, under one roof. The habit of living together soon gave rise to the finest feelings known to humanity, conjugal love and paternal affection. Every family became a little society, the more united because liberty and reciprocal attachment were the only bonds of its union. The sexes, whose manner of life had been hitherto the same, began now to adopt different ways of living. The women became more sedentary, and accustomed themselves to mind the hut and their children, while the men went abroad in search of their common subsistence. From living a softer life, both sexes also began to lose something of their strength and ferocity: but, if individuals became to some extent less able to encounter wild beasts separately, they found it, on the other hand, easier to assemble and resist in common.

The simplicity and solitude of man's life in this new condition, the paucity of his wants, and the implements he had invented to satisfy them, left him a great deal of leisure, which he employed to furnish himself with many conveniences unknown to his fathers: and this was the first yoke he inadvertently imposed on himself, and the first source of the evils he prepared for his descendants. For, besides continuing thus to enervate both body and mind, these conveniences lost with use almost all their power to please, and even degenerated into real needs, till the want of them became far more disagreeable than the possession of them had been pleasant. Men would have been unhappy at the loss of them, though the possession did not make them happy.

[***]

Everything now begins to change its aspect. Men, who have up to now been roving in the woods, by taking to a more settled manner of life, come gradually together, form separate bodies, and at length in every country arises a distinct nation, united in character and manners, not by regulations or laws, but by uniformity of life and food, and the common influence of climate. Permanent neighbourhood could not fail to produce, in time, some connection between different families. Among young people of opposite sexes, living in neighbouring huts, the transient commerce required by nature soon led, through mutual intercourse, to another kind not less agreeable, and more permanent. Men began now to take the difference between objects into account, and to make comparisons; they acquired imperceptibly the ideas of beauty and merit, which soon gave rise to feelings of preference. In consequence of seeing each other often, they could not do without seeing each other constantly. A tender and pleasant feeling insinuated itself into their souls, and the least opposition turned it into an impetuous fury: with love arose jealousy; discord triumphed, and human blood was sacrificed to the gentlest of all passions.

As ideas and feelings succeeded one another, and heart and head were brought into play, men continued to lay aside their original wildness; their private connections became every day more intimate as their limits extended. They accustomed themselves to assemble before their huts round a large tree; singing and dancing, the true offspring of love and leisure, became the amusement, or rather the occupation, of men and women thus assembled together with nothing else to do. Each one began to consider the rest, and to wish to be considered in turn; and thus a value came to be attached to public esteem. Whoever sang or danced best, whoever was the handsomest, the strongest, the most dexterous, or the most eloquent, came to be of most consideration; and this was the first step towards inequality, and at the same time towards vice. From these first distinctions arose on the one side vanity and contempt and on the other shame and envy: and the fermentation caused by these new leavens ended by producing combinations fatal to innocence and happiness.

As soon as men began to value one another, and the idea of consideration had got a footing in the mind, every one put in his claim to it, and it became impossible to refuse it to any with impunity. Hence arose the first obligations of civility even among savages; and every intended injury became an affront; because, besides the hurt which might result from it, the party injured was certain to find in it a contempt for his person, which was often more insupportable than the hurt itself.

Thus, as every man punished the contempt shown him by others, in proportion to his opinion of himself, revenge became terrible, and men bloody and cruel. This is precisely the state reached by most of the savage nations known to us: and it is for want of having made a proper distinction in our ideas, and seen how very far they already are from the state of nature, that so many writers have hastily concluded that man is naturally cruel, and requires civil institutions to make him more mild; whereas nothing is more gentle than man in his primitive state, as he is placed by nature at an equal distance from the stupidity of brutes, and the fatal ingenuity of civilized man. Equally confined by instinct and reason to the sole care of guarding himself against the mischiefs which threaten him, he is restrained by natural compassion from doing any injury to others, and is not led to do such a thing even in return for injuries received. For, according to the axiom of the wise Locke, "There can be no injury, where there is no property."

But it must be remarked that the society thus formed, and the relations thus established among men, required of them qualities different from those which they possessed from their primitive constitution. Morality began to appear in human actions, and every one, before the institution of law, was the only judge and avenger of the injuries done him, so that the goodness which was suitable in the pure state of nature was no longer proper in the new-born state of society. Punishments had to be made more severe, as opportunities of offending became more frequent, and the dread of vengeance had to take the place of the rigour of the law. Thus, though men had become less patient, and their "natural compassion had already suffered some diminution, this period of expansion of the human faculties, keeping a just mean between the indolence of the primitive state and the petulant activity of our egoism, must, have been the happiest and most stable of epochs. The more we reflect on it, the more we shall find that this state was the least subject to revolutions, and altogether the very best man could experience; so that he can have departed from it only through some fatal accident, which, for the public good, should never have happened. The example of savages, most of whom have been found in this state, seems to prove that men were meant to remain in it, that it is the real youth of the world, and that all subsequent advances have been apparently so many steps towards the perfection of the individual, but in reality towards the decrepitude of the species.

So long as men remained content with their rustic huts, so long as they were satisfied with clothes made of the skins of animals and sewn together with thorns and fishbones, adorned themselves only with feathers and shells, and continued to paint their bodies different colours, to improve and beautify their bows and arrows, and to make with sharp-edged stones fishing boats or clumsy musical instruments; in a word, so long as they undertook only what a single person could accomplish, and confined themselves to such arts as did not require the joint labour of several hands, they lived free, healthy, honest, and happy lives, so long as their nature allowed, and as they continued to enjoy the pleasures of mutual and independent intercourse. But from the moment one man began to stand in need of the help of another; from the moment it appeared advantageous to any one man to have enough provisions for two, equality disappeared, property was introduced, work became indispensable, and vast forests became smiling fields, which man had to water with the sweat of his brow, and where slavery and misery were soon seen to germinate and grow up with the crops.

Metallurgy and agriculture were the two arts which produced this great revolution. The poets tell us it was gold and silver, but, for the philosophers, it was iron and corn, which first civilized men, and ruined humanity . . . .

[***]

When they grew more industrious, it is natural to believe that they began with the help of sharp stones and pointed sticks, to cultivate a few vegetables or roots around their huts; though it was long before they knew how to prepare corn, or were provided with the implement necessary for raising it in any large quantity; not to mention how essential it is, for husbandry, to consent to immediate loss, in order to reap a future gain—a precaution very foreign to the turn of a savage's mind; for, as I have said, he hardly foresees in the morning what he will need at night.

The invention of the other arts must therefore have been necessary to compel mankind to apply themselves to agriculture. No sooner were artificers wanted to smelt and forge iron, than others were required to maintain them; the more hands that were employed in manufactures, the fewer were left to provide for the common subsistence, though the number of mouths to be furnished with food remained the same: and as some require commodities in exchange for their iron, the rest at length discovered the method of making iron serve for the multiplication of commodities. By this means the arts of husbandry and agriculture were established on the one hand, and the art of working metals and multiplying their uses on the other.

The cultivation of the earth necessarily brought about its distribution; and property, once recognized, gave rise to the first rules of justice; for, to secure each man his own, it had to be possible for each to have something. Besides, as men began to look forward to the future, and all had something to lose, every one had reason to apprehend that reprisals would follow any injury he might do to another. This origin is so much the more natural, as it is impossible to conceive how property can come from anything but manual labour: for what else can a man add to things which he does not originally create, so as to make them his own property? It is the husbandman's labour alone that, giving him a title to the produce of the ground he has tilled, gives him a claim also to the land itself, at least till harvest; and so, from year to year, a constant possession which is easily transformed into property. When the ancients, says Grotius, gave to Ceres the title of Legislatrix, and to a festival celebrated in her honour the name of Thesmophoria, they meant by that that the distribution of lands had produced a new kind of right: that is to say, the right of property, which is different from the right deducible from the law of nature.

In this state of affairs, equality might have been sustained, had the talents of individuals been equal, and had, for example, the use of iron and the consumption of commodities always exactly balanced each other; but, as there was nothing to preserve this balance, it was soon disturbed; the strongest did most work; the most skilful turned his labour to best account; the most ingenious devised methods of diminishing his labour:

the husbandman wanted more iron, or the smith more corn, and, while both laboured equally, the one gained a great deal by his work, while the other could hardly support himself. Thus natural inequality unfolds itself insensibly with that of combination, and the difference between men, developed by their different circumstances, becomes more sensible and permanent in its effects, and begins to have an influence, in the same proportion, over the lot of individuals.

Matters once at this pitch, it is easy to imagine the rest. I shall not detain the reader with a description of the successive invention of other arts, the development of language, the trial and utilization of talents, the inequality of fortunes, the use and abuse of riches, and all the details connected with them which the reader can easily supply for himself. I shall confine myself to a glance at mankind in this new situation.

Behold then all human faculties developed, memory and imagination in full play, egoism interested, reason active, and the mind almost at the highest point of its perfection. Behold all the natural qualities in action, the rank and condition of every man assigned him; not merely his share of property and his power to serve or injure others, but also his wit, beauty, strength or skill, merit or talents: and these being the only qualities capable of commanding respect, it soon became necessary to possess or to affect them.

It now became the interest of men to appear what they really were not. To be and to seem became two totally different things; and from this distinction sprang insolent pomp and cheating trickery, with all the numerous vices that go in their train. On the other hand, free and independent as men were before, they were now, in consequence of a multiplicity of new wants, brought into subjection, as it were, to all nature, and particularly to one another; and each became in some degree a slave even in becoming the master of other men: if rich, they stood in need of the services of others; if poor, of their assistance; and even a middle condition did not enable them to do without one another. Man must now, therefore, have been perpetually employed in getting others to interest themselves in his lot, and in making them, apparently at least, if not really, find their advantage in promoting his own. Thus he must have been sly and artful in his behaviour to some, and imperious and cruel to others; being under a kind of necessity to ill-use all the persons of whom he stood in need, when he could not frighten them into compliance, and did not judge it his interest to be useful to them. Insatiable ambition, the thirst of raising their respective fortunes, not so much from real want as from the desire to surpass others, inspired all men with a vile propensity to injure one another, and with a secret jealousy, which is the more dangerous, as it puts on the mask of benevolence, to carry its point with greater security. In a word, there arose rivalry and competition on the one hand, and conflicting interests on the other, together with a secret desire on both of profiting at the expense of others. All these evils were the first effects of property, and the inseparable attendants of growing inequality.

Before the invention of signs to represent riches, wealth could hardly consist in anything but lands and cattle, the only real possessions men can have. But, when inheritances so increased in number and extent as to occupy the whole of the land, and to border on one another, one man could aggrandize himself only at the expense of another; at the same time the supernumeraries, who had been too weak or too indolent to make such acquisitions, and had grown poor without sustaining any loss, because, while they saw everything change around them, they remained still the same, were obliged to receive their subsistence, or steal it, from the rich; and this soon bred, according to their different characters, dominion and slavery, or violence and rapine. The wealthy, on their part, had no sooner begun to taste the pleasure of command than they disdained all others, and, using their old slaves to acquire new, thought of nothing but subduing and enslaving their neighbours; like ravenous wolves, which, having once tasted human flesh, despise every other food and thenceforth seek only men to devour.

Thus, as the most powerful or the most miserable considered their might or misery as a kind of right to the possessions of others, equivalent, in their opinion, to that of property, the destruction of equality was attended by the most terrible disorders. Usurpations by the rich, robbery by the poor, and unbridled passions of both, suppressed the cries of natural compassion and the still feeble voice of justice, and filled men with avarice, ambition, and vice. Between the title of the strongest and that of the first occupier, there arose perpetual conflicts, which never ended but in battles and bloodshed. The new-born state of society thus gave rise to a horrible state of war; men thus harassed and depraved were no longer capable of retracing their steps or renouncing the fatal acquisitions they had made, but, labouring by the abuse of the faculties which do them honour, merely to their own confusion, brought themselves to the brink of ruin.

> *Attonitus novitate mali, divesque miserque,*
> *Effugere optat opes; et quae modo voverat odit.*[3]

---

[3]   [Ovid, *Metamorposes*, xi. 127. Both rich and poor, shocked at their new-found ill, Would fly from wealth, and lose what they had sought.]

It is impossible that men should not at length have reflected on so wretched a situation, and on the calamities that overwhelmed them. The rich, in particular, must have felt how much they suffered by a constant state of war, of which they bore all the expense; and in which, though all risked their lives, they alone risked their property. Besides, however speciously they might disguise their usurpations, they knew that they were founded on precarious and false titles; so that, if others took from them by force what they themselves had gained by force, they would have no reason to complain. Even those who had been enriched by their own industry, could hardly base their proprietorship on better claims. It was in vain to repeat: "I built this well; I gained this spot by my industry." Who gave you your standing, it might be answered, and what right have you to demand payment of us for doing what we never asked you to do? Do you not know that numbers of your fellow-creatures are starving, for want of what you have too much of? You ought to have had the express and universal consent of mankind, before appropriating more of the common subsistence than you needed for your own maintenance. Destitute of valid reasons to justify and sufficient strength to defend himself, able to crush individuals with ease, but easily crushed himself by a troop of bandits, one against all, and incapable, on account of mutual jealousy, of joining with his equals against numerous enemies united by the common hope of plunder, the rich man, thus urged by necessity, conceived at length the profoundest plan that ever entered the mind of man: this was to employ in his favour the forces of those who attacked him, to make allies of his adversaries, to inspire them with different maxims, and to give them other institutions as favourable to himself as the law of nature was unfavourable.

With this view, after having represented to his neighbours the horror of a situation which armed every man against the rest, and made their possessions as burdensome to them as their wants, and in which no safety could be expected either in riches or in poverty, he readily devised plausible arguments to make them close with his design. "Let us join," said he, "to guard the weak from oppression, to restrain the ambitious, and secure to every man the possession of what belongs to him: let us institute rules of justice and peace, to which all without exception may be obliged to conform; rules that may in some measure make amends for the caprices of fortune, by subjecting equally the powerful and the weak to the observance of reciprocal obligations. Let us, in a word, instead of turning our forces against ourselves, collect them in a supreme power which may govern us by wise laws, protect and defend all the members of the association, repulse their common enemies, and maintain eternal harmony among us."

Far fewer words to this purpose would have been enough to impose on men so barbarous and easily seduced; especially as they had too many disputes among themselves to do without arbitrators, and too much ambition and avarice to go long without masters. All ran headlong to their chains, in hopes of securing their liberty; for they had just wit enough to perceive the advantages of political institutions, without experience enough to enable them to foresee the dangers. The most capable of foreseeing the dangers were the very persons who expected to benefit by them; and even the most prudent judged it not inexpedient to sacrifice one part of their freedom to ensure the rest; as a wounded man has his arm cut off to save the rest of his body.

Such was, or may well have been, the origin of society and law, which bound new fetters on the poor, and gave new powers to the rich; which irretrievably destroyed natural liberty, eternally fixed the law of property and inequality, converted clever usurpation into unalterable right, and, for the advantage of a few ambitious individuals, subjected all mankind to perpetual labour, slavery, and wretchedness. It is easy to see how the establishment of one community made that of all the rest necessary, and how, in order to make head against united forces, the rest of mankind had to unite in turn. Societies soon multiplied and spread over the face of the earth, till hardly a corner of the world was left in which a man could escape the yoke, and withdraw his head from beneath the sword which he saw perpetually hanging over him by a thread. Civil right having thus become the common rule among the members of each community, the law of nature maintained its place only between different communities, where, under the name of the right of nations, it was qualified by certain tacit conventions, in order to make commerce practicable, and serve as a substitute for natural compassion, which lost, when applied to societies, almost all the influence it had over individuals, and survived no longer except in some great cosmopolitan spirits, who, breaking down the imaginary barriers that separate different peoples, follow the example of our Sovereign Creator, and include the whole human race in their benevolence.

But bodies politic, remaining thus in a state of nature among themselves, presently experienced the inconveniences which had obliged individuals to forsake it; for this state became still more fatal to these great bodies than it had been to the individuals of whom they were composed. Hence arose national wars, battles, murders, and reprisals, which shock nature and outrage reason; together with all those horrible prejudices which class among the virtues the honour of shedding human blood. The most distinguished men hence learned to consider cutting each other's throats a duty; at length men massacred their fellow-creatures by thousands without so much as knowing why, and committed more murders in a single day's fighting, and more violent outrages in the sack of a single town, than were committed in the state of nature during whole ages over the whole earth. Such were the first effects which we can see to have followed the division of mankind into different communities. But let us return to their institutions.

I know that some writers have given other explanations of the origin of political societies, such as the conquest of the powerful, or the association of the weak. It is, indeed, indifferent to my argument which of these causes we choose. That which I have just laid down, however, appears to me the most natural for the following reasons. First: because, in the first case, the right of conquest, being no right in itself, could not serve as a foundation on which to build any other; the victor and the vanquished people still remained with respect to each other in the state of war, unless the vanquished, restored to the full possession of their liberty, voluntarily made choice of the victor for their chief. For till then, whatever capitulation may have been made being founded on violence, and therefore ipso facto void, there could not have been on this hypothesis either a real society or body politic, or any law other than that of the strongest. Secondly: because the words "strong" and "weak" are, in the second case, ambiguous; for during the interval between the establishment of a right of property, or prior occupancy, and that of political government, the meaning of these words is better expressed by the terms "rich" and "poor"; because, in fact, before the institution of laws, men had no other way of reducing their equals to submission, than by attaching their goods, or making some of their own over to them. Thirdly: because, as the poor had nothing but their freedom to lose, it would have been in the highest degree absurd for them to resign voluntarily the only good they still enjoyed, without getting anything in exchange: whereas the rich having feelings, if I may so express myself, in every part of their possessions, it was much easier to harm them, and therefore more necessary for them to take precautions against it; and, in short, because it is more reasonable to suppose a thing to have been invented by those to whom it would be of service, than by those whom it must have harmed.

. . . Society consisted at first merely of a few general conventions, which every member bound himself to observe; and for the performance of covenants the whole body went security to each individual. Experience only could show the weakness of such a constitution, and how easily it might be infringed with impunity, from the difficulty of convicting men of faults, where the public alone was to be witness and judge: the laws could not but be eluded in many ways; disorders and inconveniences could not but multiply continually, till it became necessary to commit the dangerous trust of public authority to private persons, and the care of enforcing obedience to the deliberations of the people to the magistrate. For to say that chiefs were chosen before the confederacy was formed, and that the administrators of the laws were there before the laws themselves, is too absurd a supposition to consider seriously.

It would be as unreasonable to suppose that men at first threw themselves irretrievably and unconditionally into the arms of an absolute master, and that the first expedient which proud and unsubdued men hit upon for their common security was to run headlong into slavery. For what reason, in fact, did they take to themselves superiors, if it was not in order that they might be defended from oppression, and have protection for their lives, liberties, and properties, which are, so to speak, the constituent elements of their being? Now, in the relations between man and man, the worst that can happen is for one to find himself at the mercy of another, and it would have been inconsistent with common sense to begin by bestowing on a chief the only things they wanted his help to preserve. What equivalent could he offer them for so great a right? And if he had presumed to exact it under pretext of defending them, would he not have received the answer recorded in the fable: "What more can the enemy do to us?" It is therefore beyond dispute, and indeed the fundamental maxim of all political right, that people have set up chiefs to protect their liberty, and not to enslave them. "If we have a prince," said Pliny to Trajan "it is to save ourselves from having a master."

[***]

The different forms of government owe their origin to the differing degrees of inequality which existed between individuals at the time of their institution. If there happened to be any one man among them pre-eminent in power, virtue, riches, or personal influence, he became sole magistrate, and the State assumed the form of monarchy. If several, nearly equal in point of eminence, stood above the rest, they were elected jointly, and formed an aristocracy. Again, among a people who had deviated less from a state of nature, and between whose fortune or talents there was less disproportion, the supreme administration was retained in common, and a democracy was formed. It was discovered in process of time which of these forms suited men the best. Some peoples remained altogether subject to the laws; others soon came to obey their magistrates. The citizens laboured to preserve their liberty; the subjects, irritated at seeing others enjoying a blessing they had lost, thought only of making slaves of their neighbours. In a word, on the one side arose riches and conquests, and on the other happiness and virtue.

In these different governments, all the offices were at first elective; and when the influence of wealth was out of the question, the preference was given to merit, which gives a natural ascendancy, and to age, which is experienced in business and deliberate in council. The Elders of the Hebrews, the Gerontes at Sparta, the Senate at Rome, and the very etymology of our word Seigneur, show how old age was once held in veneration. But the more often the choice fell upon old men, the more often elections had to be repeated, and the more they became a nuisance; intrigues set in, factions were formed, party feeling grew bitter, civil war broke out; the lives of individuals were sacrificed to the pretended happiness of the State; and at length men were on the point of relapsing into their primitive anarchy. Ambitious chiefs profited by these circumstances to perpetuate their offices in their own families: at the same time the people already used to dependence, ease and the conveniences of life, and already incapable of breaking its fetters, agreed to an increase of its slavery, in order to secure its tranquillity. Thus magistrates, having become hereditary, contracted the habit of considering their offices as a family estate, and themselves as proprietors of the communities of which they were at first only the officers, of regarding their fellow-citizens as their slaves, and numbering them, like cattle, among their belongings, and of calling themselves the equals of the gods and kings of kings.

If we follow the progress of inequality in these various revolutions, we shall find that the establishment of laws and of the right of property was its first term, the institution of magistracy the second, and the conversion of legitimate into arbitrary power the third and last; so that the condition of rich and poor was authorized by the first period; that of powerful and weak by the second; and only by the third that of master and slave, which is the last degree of inequality, and the term at which all the rest remain, when they have got so far, till the government is either entirely dissolved by new revolutions or brought back again to legitimacy.

To understand this progress as necessary we must consider not so much the motives of the establishment of the body politic, as the forms it assumes in actuality, and the faults that necessarily attend it: for the flaws which make social institutions necessary are the same as make the abuse of them unavoidable. If we except Sparta, where the laws were mainly concerned with the education of children, and where Lycurgus established such morality as practically made laws needless—for laws as a rule, being weaker than the passions, restrain men without altering them—it would not be difficult to prove that every government, which scrupulously complied with the ends for which it was instituted, and guarded carefully against change and corruption, was set up unnecessarily. For a country, in which no one either evaded the laws or made a bad use of magisterial power, could require neither laws nor magistrates.

Political distinctions necessarily produce civil distinctions. The growing equality between the chiefs and the people is soon felt by individuals, and modified in a thousand ways according to passions talents, and circumstances. The magistrate could not usurp any illegitimate power, without giving distinction to the creatures with whom he must share it. Besides, individuals only allow themselves to be oppressed so far as they are hurried on by blind ambition, and, looking rather below than above them, come to love authority more than independence, and submit to slavery, that they may in turn enslave others. It is no easy matter to reduce to obedience a man who has no ambition to command; nor could the most adroit politician find it possible to enslave a people whose only desire was to be independent. But inequality easily makes its way among cowardly and ambitious minds, which are ever ready to run the risks of fortune, and almost indifferent whether they command or obey, as it is favourable or adverse. Thus, there must have been a time, when the eyes of the people were so fascinated, that their rulers had only to say to the least of men, "Be great, you and all your posterity," to make him immediately appear great in the eyes of every one as well as in his own. His descendants took still more upon them, in proportion to their distance from him; the more obscure and uncertain the cause, the greater the effect: the greater the number of idlers one could count in a family, the more illustrious it was held to be.

If this were the place to go into details, I could readily explain how, even without the intervention of government, inequality of credit and authority became unavoidable among private persons, as soon as their union in a single society made them compare themselves one with another, and take into account the differences which they found out from the continual intercourse every man had to have with his neighbours.[4] These differences

---

4   Distributive justice would oppose this rigorous equality of the state of nature, even were it practicable in civil society; as all the members of the state owe it their services in proportion to their talents and abilities, they ought, on their side, to be distinguished and favoured in proportion to the services they have actually rendered. It is in this sense we must understand that passage of Isocrates, in which he extols the primitive Athenians, for having determined which of the two kinds of equality was the most useful, viz. that which consists in dividing the same advantages indiscriminately among all the citizens, or that which consists in distributing them to each according to his deserts. These able politicians, adds the orator, banishing that unjust inequality which makes no distinction between good and bad men, adhered inviolably to that which rewards and punishes every man according to his deserts.

are of several kinds; but riches, nobility or rank, power and personal merit being the principal distinctions by which men form an estimate of each other in society, I could prove that the harmony or conflict of these different forces is the surest indication of the good or bad constitution of a State. I could show that among these four kinds of inequality, personal qualities being the origin of all the others, wealth is the one most immediately to the prosperity of individuals, and are easiest to communicate, they are used to purchase every other distinction. By this observation we are enabled to judge pretty exactly how far a people has departed from its primitive constitution, and of its progress towards the extreme term of corruption. I could explain how much this universal desire for reputation, honours, and advancement, which inflames us all, exercises and holds up to comparison our faculties and powers; how it excites and multiplies our passions, and, by creating universal competition and rivalry, or rather enmity, among men, occasions numberless failures, successes, and disturbances of all kinds by making so many aspirants run the same course. I could show that it is to this desire of being talked about, and this unremitting rage of distinguishing ourselves, that we owe the best and the worst things we possess, both our virtues and our vices, our science and our errors, our conquerors and our philosophers; that is to say, a great many bad things, and a very few good ones. In a word, I could prove that, if we have a few rich and powerful men on the pinnacle of fortune and grandeur, while the crowd grovels in want and obscurity, it is because the former prize what they enjoy only in so far as others are destitute of it; and because, without changing their condition, they would cease to be happy the moment the people ceased to be wretched.

But in the first place, there never existed a society, however corrupt some may have become, where no difference was made between the good and the bad; and with regard to morality, where no measures can be prescribed by law exact enough to serve as a practical rule for a magistrate, it is with great prudence that, in order not to leave the fortune or quality of the citizens to his discretion, it prohibits him from passing judgment on persons and confines his judgment to actions. Only morals such as those of the ancient Romans can bear censors, and such a tribunal among us would throw everything into confusion. The difference between good and bad men is determined by public esteem; the magistrate being strictly a judge of right alone; whereas the public is the truest head, that although it may be sometimes deceived, it can never be corrupted. The rank of citizens ought, therefore, to be regulated, not according to the actual services done to the State, which are capable of being more exactly estimated.

These details alone, however, would furnish matter for a considerable work, in which the advantages and disadvantages of every kind of government might be weighed, as they are related to man in the state of nature, and at the same time all the different aspects, under which inequality has up to the present appeared, or may appear in ages yet to come, according to the nature of the several governments, and the alterations which time must unavoidably occasion in them, might be demonstrated. We should then see the multitude oppressed from within, in consequence of the very precaution it had taken to guard against foreign tyranny. We should see oppression continually gain ground without it being possible for the oppressed to know where it would stop, or what legitimate means was left them of checking its progress. We should see the rights of citizens, and the freedom of nations slowly extinguished, and the complaints, protests, and appeals of the weak treated as seditions murmurings. We should see the honour of defending the common cause confined by statecraft to a mercenary part of the people. We should see taxes made necessary by such means, and the disheartened husbandman deserting his fields even in the midst of peace, and leaving the plough to gird on the sword. We should see fatal and capricious codes of honour established; and the champions of their country sooner or later becoming its enemies, and for ever holding their daggers to the breasts of their fellow-citizens. The time would come when they would be heard saying to the oppressor of their country:

Pectore si fratris gladium juguloque parentis
Condere me jubeas, gravidæque in viscera partu
Conjugis, invitâ peragam tamen omnia dextra.
Lucan. i. 376

From great inequality of fortunes and conditions, from the vast variety of passions and of talents, of useless and pernicious arts, of vain sciences, would arise a multitude of prejudices equally contrary to reason, happiness, and virtue. We should see the magistrates fomenting every thing that might weaken men united in society, by promoting dissension among them; everything that might sow in it the seeds of actual division, while it gave society the air of harmony; everything that might inspire the different ranks of people with mutual hatred and distrust, by setting the rights and interests of one against those of another, and so strengthen the power which comprehended them all.

It is from the midst of this disorder and these revolutions, that despotism, gradually raising up its hideous head and devouring everything that remained sound and untainted in any part of the State, would at length trample on both the laws and the people, and establish itself on the ruins of the republic. The times which immediately preceded this last change would be times of trouble and calamity; but at length the monster would swallow up everything, and the people would no longer have either chiefs or laws, but only tyrants. From this moment there would be no question of virtue or morality; for despotism *(cui ex honesto nulla est spes),* wherever it prevails, admits no other master; it no sooner speaks than probity and duty lose their weight and blind obedience is the only virtue which slaves can still practise.

[***]

If the reader thus discovers and retraces the lost and forgotten road, by which man must have passed from the state of nature to the state of society; if he carefully restores, along with the intermediate situations which I have just described, those which want of time has compelled me to suppress, or my imagination has failed to suggest, he cannot fail to be struck by the vast distance which separates the two states . . . .

The savage and the civilized man differ so much in the bottom of their hearts and in their inclinations, that what constitutes the supreme happiness of one would reduce the other to despair. The former breathes only peace and liberty; he desires only to live and be free from labour; even the *ataraxia* of the Stoic falls far short of his profound indifference to every other object. Civilized man, on the other hand, is always moving, sweating, toiling, and racking his brains to find still more laborious occupations: he goes on in drudgery to his last moment, and even seeks death to put himself in a position to live, or renounces life to acquire immortality. He pays his court to men in power, whom he hates, and to the wealthy, whom he despises; he stops at nothing to have the honour of serving them; he is not ashamed to value himself on his own meanness and their protection; and, proud of his slavery, he speaks with disdain of those, who have not the honour of sharing it. What a sight would the perplexing and envied labours of a European minister of State present to the eyes of a Caribbean! How many cruel deaths would not this indolent savage prefer to the horrors of such a life, which is seldom even sweetened by the pleasure of doing good! But, for him to see into the motives of all this solicitude the words "power" and "reputation" would have to bear some meaning in his mind; he would have to know that there are men who set a value on the opinion of the rest of the world; who can be made happy and satisfied with themselves rather on the testimony of other people than on their own. In reality, the source of all these differences is, that the savage lives within himself, while social man lives constantly outside himself, and only knows how to live in the opinion of others so that he seems to receive the consciousness of his on existence merely from the judgment of others concerning him. It is not to my present purpose to insist on the indifference to good and evil which arises from this disposition, in spite of our many fine works on morality, or to show how, everything being reduced to appearances, there is but art and mummery in even honour, friendship, virtue, and often vice itself, of which we at length learn the secret of boasting; to show, in short, how, always asking others what we are, and never daring to ask ourselves, in the midst of so much philosophy humanity, and civilization, and of such sublime codes of morality, we have nothing to show for ourselves but a frivolous and deceitful appearance, honour without virtue, reason without wisdom, and pleasure without happiness. It is sufficient that I have proved that this is not by any means the original state of man, but that it is merely the spirit of society, and the inequality which society produces, that thus transform and alter all our natural inclinations.

I have endeavoured to trace the origin and progress of inequality, and the institution and abuse of political societies, as far as these are capable of being deduced from the nature of man merely by the light of reason, and independently of those sacred dogmas which give the sanction of divine right to sovereign authority. It follows from this survey that, as there is hardly any inequality in the state of nature, all the inequality which now prevails owes its strength and growth to the development of our faculties and the advance of the human mind, and becomes at last permanent and legitimate by the establishment of property and laws. Secondly, it follows that moral inequality, authorized by positive right alone, clashes with natural right, whenever it is not proportionate to physical inequality—a distinction which sufficiently determines what we ought to think of that species of inequality which prevails in all civilized countries; since it is plainly contrary to the law of nature, however defined, that children should command old men, fools wise men, and that the privileged few should gorge themselves with superfluities, while the starving multitude are in want of the bare necessities of life.

KINGSLEY DAVIS

1908-1997
and

WILBERT E. MOORE

1914-1987

"SOME PRINCIPLES OF STRATIFICATION"
1944

An American sociologist and demographer, Kingsley Davis specialized in the study of international population dynamics, urbanization, family structure, and population policy. He is credited with coining the term "population explosion" and is "especially remembered for his arresting and forceful critique of family-planning programs intended to achieve zero population growth" (Heer, 2005). A consultant to India, Nepal, Bahrain, and parts of Latin American, he advocated the use of incentives as a means of curtailing fertility.

Davis attended Harvard, where he studied under Talcott Parsons, receiving both his masters and doctorate in sociology. During his career, he taught at Pennsylvania State University, Princeton (where he was a visiting research associate in the Office of Population Research), Columbia (where he was director of the Bureau of Applied Social Research), the University of California at Berkeley, and the University of Southern California, having over the years held appointments in sociology, public affairs, anthropology, and political science. The Ford Professor Emeritus of Sociology and Comparative Studies at Berkeley, he helped to establish their programs in international population research and demography.

His books include *Human Society* (1949), *The Population of India and Pakistan* (1951), *World Urbanization 1950-1970* (1972), and *Cities: Their Origin, Growth and Human Impact* (1973). In addition to the numerous scholarly journals in which he published, his writing also appeared in *Scientific American, Science,* the *New York Times Magazine, Commentary,* and *Foreign Affairs.*

Davis served as president of both the Population Association of America and the American Sociological Association, as U.S. representative to the United Nations Population Commission, and as a member of the Census Bureau's Advisory Committee on Population.

Wilbert Ellis Moore was an American sociologist who specialized in the study of industrialization and social change. He received his PhD from Harvard University in 1940, also studying under Parsons, and then went on to teach at Pennsylvania State University. Shortly thereafter, he moved to Princeton University, where he worked in the Office of Population Research and taught in the Department of Sociology. He did a six-year stint at the Russell Sage Foundation as a staff researcher, after which time he moved on to the University of Denver to begin working on the sociology of law.

Moore served as director of the Social Science Research Council and as president of both the American Sociological Association and the Eastern Sociological Association. He wrote almost a dozen major books, including *Industrial Relations and the Social Order* (1946), *Industrialization and Labor* (1951), *Economy and Society* (1955), *The Conduct of the Corporation* (1962), and *Social Change* (1963). *Indicators of Social Change: Concepts and Measurements,* which he co-edited with Eleanor Sheldon in 1968, is considered a landmark in the field.

The essay that follows is "perhaps the single most widely cited paper in American introductory sociology and stratification textbooks and constitutes 'required reading' in hundreds, if not thousands, of undergraduate and graduate courses throughout the United States" (Hauhart, 2003, 5). In it, Davis and Moore use the theoretical perspective known as functionalism to explore the meaning and purpose of stratification in society. Significantly, this essay, and the functionalist perspective generally, has been widely criticized. Some detractors argue that it is incapable of explaining social change, while others decry what they perceive as its inherent conservative bias.

Social systems, according to the functionalist perspective, are similar to living organisms whose continued survival is dependent upon the ability of their constituent parts to work together to maintain the whole successfully. In this view, the existence of any given structure (e.g., behavior, institution, or social phenomenon) is understood in terms of its contribution to societal stability. The tendency to explain structures in terms of the status quo accounts for the allegations of bias mentioned above.

Merton (1957) expanded on earlier work by distinguishing between manifest functions (explicit or intended consequences) and latent functions (implicit or unintended consequences). The manifest function of education, for example, is to provide young people with the intellectual tools needed to become effective citizens and productive workers. The latent function of education supports societal stability through the transmission of core cultural values. Children in American classrooms, for example, are taught to value competition (and winning), revere individualism, respond to extrinsic motivators, and respect authority and follow directions.

As you read the following selection, consider the political implications of the functionalist perspective on stratification. Ask yourself how Hacker or Eitzen might respond to Davis and Moore, and whether Bentham's "greatest happiness principle" would support the views advanced in the authors.

SELECTION FROM:

Davis, K. and Moore, W. (1944). Some Principles of Stratification. *American Sociological Review*, Vol. 10, No. 2 Annual Meeting Papers (Apr., 1945). 242-249. Retrieved June 13, 2005, from http://links. jstor.org/sici.

SOME PRINCIPLES OF STRATIFICATION

KINGSLEY DAVIS AND WILBERT E. MOORE
Princeton University

IN A PREVIOUS PAPER some concepts for handling the phenomena of social inequality were presented.[1] In the present paper a further step in stratification theory is undertaken—an attempt to show the relationship between stratification and the rest of the social order.[2] Starting from the proposition that no society is "classless," or unstratified,

---

[1]   Kingsley Davis, "A Conceptual Analysis of Stratification," *American Sociological Review.* 7: 309-321, June, 1942.

[2]   The writers regret (and beg indulgence) that the present essay, a condensation of a longer study, covers so much in such short space that adequate evidence and qualification cannot be given and that as a result what is actually very tentative is presented in an unfortunately dogmatic manner.

an effort is made to explain, in functional terms, the universal necessity which calls forth stratification in any social system. Next, an attempt is made to explain the roughly uniform distribution of prestige as between the major types of positions in every society. Since, however, there occur between one society and another great differences in the degree and kind of stratification, some attention is also given to the varieties of social inequality and the variable factors that give rise to them.

Clearly, the present task requires two different lines of analysis—one to understand the universal, the other to understand the variable features of stratification. Naturally each line of inquiry aids the other and is indispensable, and in the treatment that follows the two will be interwoven, although, because of space limitations, the emphasis will be on the universals.

Throughout, it will be necessary to keep in mind one thing—namely, that the discussion relates to the system of positions, not to the individuals occupying those positions. It is one thing to ask why different positions carry different degrees of prestige, and quite another to ask how certain individuals get into those positions. Although, as the argument will try to show, both questions are related, it is essential to keep them separate in our thinking. Most of the literature on stratification has tried to answer the second question (particularly with regard to the ease or difficulty of mobility between strata) without tackling the first. The first question, however, is logically prior and, in the case of any particular individual or group, factually prior.

THE FUNCTIONAL NECESSITY
OF STRATIFICATION

Curiously, however, the main functional necessity explaining the universal presence of stratification is precisely the requirement faced by any society of placing and motivating individuals in the social structure. As a functioning mechanism a society must somehow distribute its members in social positions and induce them to perform the duties of these positions. It must thus concern itself with motivation at two different levels: to instill in the proper individuals the desire to fill certain positions, and, once in these positions, the desire to perform the duties attached to them. Even though the social order may be relatively static in form, there is a continuous process of metabolism as new individuals are born into it, shift with age, and die off. Their absorption into the positional system must somehow be arranged and motivated. This is true whether the system is competitive or non-competitive. A competitive system gives greater importance to the motivation to achieve positions, whereas a non-competitive system gives perhaps greater importance to the motivation to perform the duties of the positions; but in any system both types of motivation are required.

If the duties associated with the various positions were all equally pleasant to the human organism, all equally important to societal survival, and all equally in need of the same ability or talent, it would make no difference who got into which positions, and the problem of social placement would be greatly reduced. But actually it does make a great deal of difference who gets into which positions, not only because some positions are inherently more agreeable than others, but also because some require special talents or training and some are functionally more important than others. Also, it is essential that the duties of the positions be performed with the diligence that their importance requires. Inevitably, then, a society must have, first, some kind of rewards that it can use as inducements, and, second, some way of distributing these rewards differentially according to positions. The rewards and their distribution become a part of the social order, and thus give rise to stratification.

One may ask what kind of rewards a society has at its disposal in distributing its personnel and securing essential services. It has, first of all, the things that contribute to sustenance and comfort. It has, second, the things that contribute to humor and diversion. And it has, finally, the things that contribute to self respect and ego expansion. The last, because of the peculiarly social character of the self, is largely a function of the opinion of others, but it nonetheless ranks in importance with the first two. In any social system all three kinds of rewards must be dispensed differentially according to positions.

In a sense the rewards are "built into" the position. They consist in the "rights" associated with the position, plus what may be called its accompaniments or perquisites. Often the rights, and sometimes the accompaniments, are functionally related to the duties of the position. (Rights as viewed by the incumbent are usually duties as viewed by other members of the community.) However, there may be a host of subsidiary rights and perquisites that are not essential to the function of the position and have only an indirect and symbolic connection with its duties, but which still may be of considerable importance in inducing people to seek the positions and fulfil the essential duties.

If the rights and perquisites of different positions in a society must be unequal, then the society must be stratified, because that is precisely what stratification means. Social inequality is thus an unconsciously evolved

device by which societies insure that the most important positions are
conscientiously filled by the most qualified persons. Hence every society,
no matter how simple or complex, must differentiate persons in terms of
both prestige and esteem, and must therefore possess a certain amount
of institutionalized inequality.

It does not follow that the amount or type of inequality need be
the same in all societies. This is largely a function of factors that will be
discussed presently.

THE TWO DETERMINANTS OF
POSITIONAL RANK

Granting the general function that inequality subserves, one can
specify the two factors that determine the relative rank of different
positions. In general those positions convey the best reward, and hence
have the highest rank, which (a) have the greatest importance for the
society and (b) require the greatest training or talent. The first factor
concerns function and is a matter of relative significance; the second
concerns means and is a matter of scarcity.

Differential Functional Importance. Actually a society does not need to
reward positions in proportion to their functional importance. It merely
needs to give sufficient reward to them to insure that they will be filled
competently. In other words, it must see that less essential positions do not
compete successfully with more essential ones. If a position is easily filled,
it need not be heavily rewarded, even though important. On the other
hand, if it is important but hard to fill, the reward must be high enough
to get it filled anyway. Functional importance is therefore a necessary but
not a sufficient cause of high rank being assigned to a position.[3]

Differential Scarcity of Personnel. Practically all positions, no matter
how acquired, require some form of skill or capacity for performance. This

---

[3]   Unfortunately, functional importance is difficult to establish. To use
the position's prestige to establish it, as is often unconsciously done,
constitutes circular reasoning from our point of view. There are, however,
two independent clues: (a) the degree to which a position is functionally
unique, there being no other positions that can perform the same function
satisfactorily; (b) the degree to which other positions are dependent on
the one in question. Both clues are best exemplified in organized systems
of positions built around one major function. Thus, in most complex
societies the religious, political, economic, and educational functions are

is implicit in the very notion of position, which implies that the incumbent must, by virtue of his incumbency, accomplish certain things.

There are, ultimately, only two ways in which a person's qualifications come about: through inherent capacity or through training. Obviously, in concrete activities both are always necessary, but from a practical standpoint the scarcity may lie primarily in one or the other, as well as in both. Some positions require innate talents of such high degree that the persons who fill them are bound to be rare. In many cases, however, talent is fairly abundant in the population but the training process is so long, costly, and elaborate that relatively few can qualify. Modern medicine, for example, is within the mental capacity of most individuals, but a medical education is so burdensome and expensive that virtually none would undertake it if the position of the M.D. did not carry a reward commensurate with the sacrifice.

If the talents required for a position are abundant and the training easy, the method of acquiring the position may have little to do with its duties. There may be, in fact, a virtually accidental relationship. But if the skills required are scarce by reason of the rarity of talent or the costliness of training, the position, if functionally important, must have an attractive power that will draw the necessary skills in competition with other positions. This means, in effect, that the position must be high in the social scale—must command great prestige, high salary, ample leisure, and the like.

How Variations Are to Be Understood. In so far as there is a difference between one system of stratification and another, it is attributable to whatever factors affect the two determinants of differential reward—namely, functional importance and scarcity of personnel. Positions important in one society may not be important in another, because the conditions faced by the societies, or their degree of internal development, may be different. The same conditions, in turn, may affect the question of scarcity;

handled by distinct structures not easily interchangeable. In addition, each structure possesses many different positions, some clearly dependent on, if not subordinate to, others. In sum, when an institutional nucleus becomes differentiated around one main function, and at the same time organizes a large portion of the population into its relationships, the key positions in it are of the highest functional importance. The absence of such specialization does not prove functional unimportance, for the whole society may be relatively unspecialized; but it is safe to assume that the more important functions receive the first and clearest structural differentiation.

for in some societies the stage of development, or the external situation, may wholly obviate the necessity of certain kinds of skill or talent. Any particular system of stratification, then, can be understood as a product of the special conditions affecting the two aforementioned grounds of differential reward.

MAJOR SOCIETAL FUNCTIONS AND STRATIFICATION

Religion. The reason why religion is necessary is apparently to be found in the fact that human society achieves its unity primarily through the possession by its members of certain ultimate values and ends in common. Although these values and ends are subjective, they influence behavior, and their integration enables the society to operate as a system. Derived neither from inherited nor from external nature, they have evolved as a part of culture by communication and moral pressure. They must, however, appear to the members of the society to have some reality, and it is the role of religious belief and ritual to supply and reinforce this appearance of reality. Through belief and ritual the common ends and values are connected with an imaginary world symbolized by concrete sacred objects, which world in turn is related in a meaningful way to the facts and trials of the individual's life. Through the worship of the sacred objects and the beings they symbolize, and the acceptance of supernatural prescriptions that are at the same time codes of behavior, a powerful control over human conduct is exercised, guiding it along lines sustaining the institutional structure and conforming to the ultimate ends and values.

If this conception of the role of religion is true, one can understand why in every known society the religious activities tend to be under the charge of particular persons, who tend thereby to enjoy greater rewards than the ordinary societal member. Certain of the rewards and special privileges may attach to only the highest religious functionaries, but others usually apply, if such exists, to the entire sacerdotal class.

Moreover, there is a peculiar relation between the duties of the religious official and the special privileges he enjoys. If the supernatural world governs the destinies of men more ultimately than does the real world, its earthly representative, the person through whom one may communicate with the supernatural, must be a powerful individual. He is a keeper of sacred tradition, a skilled performer of the ritual, and an interpreter of lore and myth. He is in such close contact with the gods that he is viewed as possessing some of their characteristics. He is, in short, a bit sacred, and hence free from some of the more vulgar necessities and controls.

It is no accident, therefore, that religious functionaries have been associated with the very highest positions of power, as in theocratic regimes. Indeed, looking at it from this point of view, one may wonder why it is that they do not get *entire* control over their societies. The factors that prevent this are worthy of note.

In the first place, the amount of technical competence necessary for the performance of religious duties is small. Scientific or artistic capacity is not required. Anyone can set himself up as enjoying an intimate relation with deities, and nobody can successfully dispute him. Therefore, the factor of scarcity of personnel does not operate in the technical sense.

One may assert, on the other hand, that religious ritual is often elaborate and religious lore abstruse, and that priestly ministrations require tact, if not intelligence. This is true, but the technical requirements of the profession are for the most part adventitious, not related to the end in the same way that science is related to air travel. The priest can never be free from competition, since the criteria of whether or not one has genuine contact with the supernatural are never strictly clear. It is this competition that debases the priestly position below what might be expected at first glance. That is why priestly prestige is highest in those societies where membership in the profession is rigidly controlled by the priestly guild itself. That is why, in part at least, elaborate devices are utilized to stress the identification of the person with his office—spectacular costume, abnormal conduct, special diet, segregated residence, celibacy, conspicuous leisure, and the like. In fact, the priest is always in danger of becoming somewhat discredited—as happens in a secularized society—because in a world of stubborn fact, ritual and sacred knowledge alone will not grow crops or build houses. Furthermore, unless he is protected by a professional guild, the priest's identification with the supernatural tends to preclude his acquisition of abundant wordly [*sic*] goods.

As between one society and another it seems that the highest general position awarded the priest occurs in the medieval type of social order. Here there is enough economic production to afford a surplus, which can be used to support a numerous and highly organized priesthood; and yet the populace is unlettered and therefore credulous to a high degree. Perhaps the most extreme example is to be found in the Buddhism of Tibet, but others are encountered in the Catholicism of feudal Europe, the Inca regime of Peru, the Brahminism of India, and the Mayan priesthood of Yucatan. On the other hand, if the society is so crude as to have no surplus and little differentiation, so that every priest must be also a cultivator or hunter, the separation of the priestly status from the others has hardly gone far enough for priestly prestige to mean much. When the priest actually has high prestige under these circumstances, it is because he also performs other important functions (usually political and medical).

In an extremely advanced society built on scientific technology, the priesthood tends to lose status, because sacred tradition and supernaturalism drop into the background. The ultimate values and common ends of the society tend to be expressed in less anthropomorphic ways, by officials who occupy fundamentally political, economic, or educational rather than religious positions. Nevertheless, it is easily possible for intellectuals to exaggerate the degree to which the priesthood in a presumably secular milieu has lost prestige. When the matter is closely examined the urban proletariat, as well as the rural citizenry, proves to be suprisingly [sic] god-fearing and priest-ridden. No society has become so completely secularized as to liquidate entirely the belief in transcendental ends and supernatural entities. Even in a secularized society some system must exist for the integration of ultimate values, for their ritualistic expression, and for the emotional adjustments required by disappointment, death, and disaster.

Government. Like religion, government plays a unique and indispensable part in society. But in contrast to religion, which provides integration in terms of sentiments, beliefs, and rituals, it organizes the society in terms of law and authority. Furthermore, it orients the society to the actual rather than the unseen world.

The main functions of government are, internally, the ultimate enforcement of norms, the final arbitration of conflicting interests, and the overall planning and direction of society; and externally, the handling of war and diplomacy. To carry out these functions it acts as the agent of the entire people, enjoys a monopoly of force, and controls all individuals within its territory.

Political action, by definition, implies authority. An official can command because he has authority, and the citizen must obey because he is subject to that authority. For this reason stratification is inherent in the nature of political relationships.

So clear is the power embodied in political position that political inequality is sometimes thought to comprise all inequality. But it can be shown that there are other bases of stratification, that the following controls operate in practice to keep political power from becoming complete: (a) The fact that the actual holders of political office, and especially those determining top policy must necessarily be few in number compared to the total population. (b) The fact that the rulers represent the interest of the group rather than of themselves, and are therefore restricted in their behavior by rules and mores designed to enforce this limitation of interest. (c) The fact that the holder of political office has his authority by virtue of his office and nothing else, and therefore any special knowledge, talent, or capacity he may claim is purely incidental, so that he often has to depend upon others for technical assistance.

In view of these limiting factors, it is not strange that the rulers often have less power and prestige than a literal enumeration of their formal rights would lead one to expect.

Wealth, Property, and Labor. Every position that secures for its incumbent a livelihood is, by definition, economically rewarded. For this reason there is an economic aspect to those positions (e.g. political and religious) the main function of which is not economic. It therefore becomes convenient for the society to use unequal economic returns as a principal means of controlling the entrance of persons into positions and stimulating the performance of their duties. The amount of the economic return therefore becomes one of the main indices of social status.

It should be stressed, however, that a position does not bring power and prestige *because* it draws a high income. Rather, it draws a high income because it is functionally important and the available personnel is for one reason or another scarce. It is therefore superficial and erroneous to regard high income as the cause of a man's power and prestige, just as it is erroneous to think that a man's fever is the cause of his disease.[4]

The economic source of power and prestige is not income primarily, but the ownership of capital goods (including patents, good will, and professional reputation). Such ownership should be distinguished from the possession of consumers' goods, which is an index rather than a cause of social standing. In other words, the ownership of producers' goods is properly speaking, a source of income like other positions, the income itself remaining an index. Even in situations where social values are

---

[4]   The symbolic rather than intrinsic role of income in social stratification has been succinctly summarized by Talcott Parsons, "An Analytical Approach to the Theory of Social Stratification," *American Journal of Sociology.* 45:842-862, May, 1940.

widely commercialized and earnings are the readiest method of judging social position, income does not confer prestige on a position so much as it induces people to compete for the position. It is true that a man who has a high income as a result of one position may find this money helpful in climbing into another position as well, but this again reflects the effect of his initial, economically advantageous status, which exercises its influence through the medium of money.

In a system of private property in productive enterprise, an income above what an individual spends can give rise to possession of capital wealth. Presumably such possession is a reward for the proper management of one's finances originally and of the productive enterprise later. But as social differentiation becomes highly advanced and yet the institution of inheritance persists, the phenomenon of pure ownership, and reward for pure ownership, emerges. In such a case it is difficult to prove that the position is functionally important or that the scarcity involved is anything other than extrinsic and accidental. It is for this reason, doubtless, that the institution of private property in productive goods becomes more subject to criticism as social development proceeds toward industrialization. It is only this pure, that is, strictly legal and functionless ownership, however, that is open to attack; for some form of active ownership, whether private or public, is indispensable.

One kind of ownership of production goods consists in rights over the labor of others. The most extremely concentrated and exclusive of such rights are found in slavery, but the essential principle remains in serfdom, peonage, encomienda, and indenture. Naturally this kind of ownership has the greatest significance for stratification, because it necessarily entails an unequal relationship.

But property in capital goods inevitably introduces a compulsive element even into the nominally free contractual relationship. Indeed, in some respects the authority of the contractual employer is greater than that of the feudal landlord, inasmuch as the latter is more limited by traditional reciprocities. Even the classical economics recognized that competitors would fare unequally, but it did not pursue this fact to its necessary conclusion that, however it might be acquired, unequal control of goods and services must give unequal advantage to the parties to a contract.

Technical Knowledge. The function of finding means to single goals, without any concern with the choice between goals, is the exclusively technical sphere. The explanation of why positions requiring great technical skill receive fairly high rewards is easy to see, for it is the simplest case of the rewards being so distributed as to draw talent and motivate training. Why they seldom if ever receive the highest rewards is also clear: the importance of technical knowledge from a societal point of view is never so great as the integration of goals, which takes place on the religious, political, and economic levels. Since the technological level is concerned solely with means, a purely technical position must ultimately be subordinate to other positions that are religious, political, or economic in character.

Nevertheless, the distinction between expert and layman in any social order is fundamental, and cannot be entirely reduced to other terms. Methods of recruitment, as well as of reward, sometimes lead to the erroneous interpretation that technical positions are economically determined. Actually, however, the acquisition of knowledge and skill cannot be accomplished by purchase, although the opportunity to learn may be. The control of the avenues of training may inhere as a sort of property right in certain families or classes, giving them power and prestige in consequence. Such a situation adds an artificial scarcity to the natural scarcity of skills and talents. On the other hand, it is possible for an opposite situation to arise. The rewards of technical position may be so great that a condition of excess supply is created, leading to at least temporary devaluation of the rewards. Thus "unemployment in the learned professions" may result in a debasement of the prestige of those positions. Such adjustments and readjustments are constantly occurring in changing societies; and it is always well to bear in mind that the efficiency of a stratified structure may be affected by the modes of recruitment for positions. The social order itself, however, sets limits to the inflation or deflation of the prestige of experts: an over-supply tends to debase the rewards and discourage recruitment or produce revolution, whereas an under-supply tends to increase the rewards or weaken the society in competition with other societies.

Particular systems of stratification show a wide range with respect to the exact position of technically competent persons. This range is perhaps most evident in the degree of specialization. Extreme division of labor tends to create many specialists without high prestige since the training is short and the required native capacity relatively small. On the other hand it also tends to accentuate the high position of the true experts—scientists, engineers, and administrators—by increasing their authority relative to other functionally important positions. But the idea of a technocratic social order or a government or priesthood of engineers or social scientists neglects the limitations of knowledge and skills as a basic for performing social functions. To the extent that the social structure is truly specialized the prestige of the technical person must also be circumscribed.

VARIATION IN STRATIFIED SYSTEMS

The generalized principles of stratification here suggested form a necessary preliminary to a consideration of types of stratified systems, because it is in terms of these principles that the types must be described. This can be seen by trying to delineate types according to certain modes of variation. For instance, some of the most important modes (together with the polar types in terms of them) seem to be as follows:

(a) *The Degree of Specialization.* The degree of specialization affects the fineness and multiplicity of the gradations in power and prestige. It also influences the extent to which particular functions may be emphasized in the invidious system, since a given function cannot receive much emphasis in the hierarchy until it has achieved structural separation from the other functions. Finally, the amount of specialization influences the bases of selection. Polar types: *Specialized, Unspecialized.*

(b) *The Nature of the Functional Emphasis.* In general when emphasis is put on sacred matters, a rigidity is introduced that tends to limit specialization and hence the development of technology. In addition, a brake is placed on social mobility, and on the development of bureaucracy. When the preoccupation with the sacred is withdrawn, leaving greater scope for purely secular preoccupations, a great development, and rise in status, of economic and technological positions seemingly takes place. Curiously, a concomitant rise in political position is not likely, because it has usually been allied with the religious and stands to gain little by the decline of the latter. It is also possible for a society to emphasize family functions—as in relatively undifferentiated societies where high mortality requires high fertility and kinship forms the main basis of social organization. Main types: *Familistic, Authoritarian* (*Theocratic* or sacred, and *Totalitarian* or secular), *Capitalistic.*

(c) *The Magnitude of Invidious Differences.* What may be called the amount of social distance between positions, taking into account the entire scale, is something that should lend itself to quantitative measurement. Considerable differences apparently exist between different societies in this regard, and also between parts of the same society. Polar types: *Equalitarian, Inequalitarian.*

(d) *The Degree of Opportunity.* The familiar question of the amount of mobility is different from the question of the comparative equality or inequality of rewards posed above, because the two criteria may vary independently up to a point. For instance, the tremendous divergences in monetary income in the United States are far greater than those found in primitive societies, yet the equality of opportunity to move from one rung to the other in the social scale may also be greater in the United States than in a hereditary tribal kingdom. Polar types: *Mobile* (open), *Immobile* (closed).

(e) *The Degree of Stratum Solidarity.* Again, the degree of "class solidarity" (or the presence of specific organizations to promote class interests) may vary to some extent independently of the other criteria, and hence is an important principle in classifying systems of stratification. Polar types: *Class organized, Class unorganized.*

EXTERNAL CONDITIONS

What state any particular system of stratification is in with reference to each of these modes of variation depends on two things: (1) its state with reference to the other ranges of variation, and (2) the conditions outside the system of stratification which nevertheless influence that system. Among the latter are the following:

(a) *The Stage of Cultural Development.* As the cultural heritage grows, increased specialization becomes necessary, which in turn contributes to the enhancement of mobility, a decline of stratum solidarity, and a change of functional emphasis.

(b) *Situation with Respect to Other Societies.* The presence or absence of open conflict with other societies, of free trade relations or cultural diffusion, all influence the class structure to some extent. A chronic state of warfare tends to place emphasis upon the military functions, especially when the opponents are more or less equal. Free trade, on the other hand, strengthens the hand of the trader at the expense of the warrior and priest. Free movement of ideas generally has an equalitarian effect. Migration and conquest create special circumstances.

(c) *Size of the Society.* A small society limits the degree to which functional specialization can go, the degree of segregation of different strata, and the magnitude of inequality.

COMPOSITE TYPES

Much of the literature on stratification has attempted to classify concrete systems into a certain number of types. This task is deceptively simple, however, and should come at the end of an analysis of elements and principles, rather than at the beginning. If the preceding discussion has any validity, it indicates that there are a number of modes of variation between different systems, and that any one system is a composite of the society's status with reference to all these modes of variation. The danger of trying to classify whole societies under such rubrics as caste, feudal, or open class is that one or two criteria are selected and others ignored, the result being an unsatisfactory solution to the problem posed. The present discussion has been offered as a possible approach to the more systematic classification of composite types.

Upton Sinclair

1878-1968

The Jungle
1946

A novelist, social reformer, and political activist, Upton Beall Sinclair, Jr., was born into a poor Baltimore family whose financial situation was made even more precarious by his father's alcoholism. Best known for his "muckraking" novel *The Jungle*, which describes the oppressive and unsanitary working conditions in Chicago's meat packing industry, he also received the Pulitzer Prize in Fiction for his novel about the rise of Nazism, *Dragon's Teeth* (1942).

The Jungle, originally published in serial form by the Socialist journal *Appeal to Reason*, was intended as a critique of capitalism. It tells the story of Lithuanian immigrants who come to America in search of a better life and find themselves forced to fight tooth-and-nail for their survival. If Sinclair's portrayal of society's underbelly seems particularly evocative, it is because he drew upon personal experience when constructing these passages. In his own words,

> I wrote with tears and anguish, pouring into the pages all that pain which life had meant to me. Externally the story had to do with a family of stockyard workers, but internally it was the story of my own family. Did I wish to know how the poor suffered in winter time in Chicago? I only had to recall the previous winter in the cabin, when we had only cotton blankets, and had rags on top of us. It was the same with hunger, with illness, with fear. Our little boy was down

with pneumonia that winter, and nearly died, and the grief
of that went into the book.[1]

The book, published one year later, sold over 150,000 copies and
was translated into seventeen languages. An investigation of the meat
packing industry, ordered by President Theodore Roosevelt after reading
the book, supported all of Sinclair's accusations *except* the claim that
workers who fell into the processing tanks were left there and made into
lard. The results of the investigation and the public outcry prompted by
the book's more horrific details, coupled with a precipitous decline in
foreign sales of American beef, contributed to the passage of the Pure Food
and Drug Act, which established the Food and Drug Administration,
and the Federal Meat Inspection Act of 1906.

A member of the Socialist Party since 1902, Sinclair wanted to draw
attention to the inhumane treatment of the workers, but people focused
instead on the disgusting conditions under which their food was being
produced. He was disappointed that the ensuing legislation addressed
the problem of unsanitary conditions in the packing plants, but not the
scandalous way in which workers were treated by ruthless and corrupt
employers. "I aimed at the public's heart," he commented wistfully, "and
by accident I hit it in the stomach."

In 1906, the five largest producers controlled 55 percent of the beef
market. Today, with the four largest producers controlling more than 80
percent of beef processing, the American beef industry is less competitive
than it was when *The Jungle* was written. Workers in meatpacking plants
now earn less than workers in other factories, while sustaining injury rates
that are among the highest in the nation. The movement of plants to
small towns in nonunion states has further reduced the bargaining power
of labor, which is already weakened by the fact that approximately 80
percent of the nation's meatpacking workers are illegal immigrants who
can't speak English and are reluctant to report injuries and hazardous
work conditions for fear of deportation.

As you read this selection, consider the extent to which our lives
are determined by forces beyond our direct control, such as market
realities, social institutions and government policies. Compare Sinclair's

---

[1]   From Upton Sinclair's *American Outpost: A Book of Reminiscences*. Quotation
obtained from http://chicagolaborarts.org/jungle.html.

perspective on the dehumanizing effects of capitalism with Marx's description of the plight of the proletariat, and ask yourself whether Sinclair and Smith would disagree about the social and economic effects of specialization and division of labor in the workplace. Finally, consider whether Sinclair's indictment of capitalism is sufficiently compelling to warrant more aggressive government intervention in the marketplace.

In the selection that follows, you will meet Jurgis and his wife Ona, their son Antanas, Jurgis's father Dede Antanas, Ona's cousin Marija Berczynskas, Uncle Jonas, and stepmother Teta Elzbieta, whose six children (Stanislovas, Kotrina, Kristoforas, Vilimas, Nikalojus, and Juozapas) round out the family.

SELECTION FROM:

Sinclair, U. (1946). *The Jungle*. New York: Viking Press. 119-140

CHAPTER
12

FOR three weeks after his injury Jurgis never got up from bed. It was a very obstinate sprain; the swelling would not go down, and the pain still continued. At the end of that time, however, he could contain himself no longer, and began trying to walk a little every day, laboring to persuade himself that he was better. No arguments could stop him, and three or four days later he declared that he was going back to work. He limped to the cars and got to Brown's, where he found that the boss had kept his place—that is, was, willing to turn out into the snow the poor devil he had hired in the meantime. Every now and then the pain would force Jurgis to stop work, but he stuck it out till nearly an hour before closing. Then he was forced to acknowledge that he could not go on without fainting; it almost broke his heart to do it, and he stood leaning against a pillar and weeping like a child. Two of the men had to help him to the car, and when he got out he had to sit down and wait in the snow till some one came along.

So they put him to bed again, and sent for the doctor, as they ought to have done in the beginning. It transpired that he had twisted a tendon out of place, and could never have gotten well without attention. Then he gripped the sides of the bed, and shut his teeth together, and turned white with agony, while the doctor pulled and wrenched away at his swollen ankle. When finally the doctor left, he told him that he would have to lie quiet for two months, and that if he went to work before that time he might lame himself for life.

Three days later there came another heavy snowstorm, and Jonas and Marija and Ona and little Stanislovas all set out together, an hour before daybreak, to try to get to the yards. About noon the last two came back, the boy screaming with pain. His fingers were all frosted, it seemed. They had had to give up trying to get to the yards, and had nearly perished in a drift. All that they knew how to do was to hold the frozen fingers near the fire, and so little Stanislovas spent most of the day dancing about in horrible agony, till Jurgis flew a passion of nervous rage and swore like a madman, declaring that he would kill him if he did not stop. All that day and night the family was half-crazed with fear that Ona and the boy had lost their places; and in the morning they set out earlier than ever, after the little fellow had been beaten with a stick by Jurgis. There could be no trifling in a case like this, it was a matter of life and death; little Stanislovas could not be expected to realize that he might a great deal better freeze in the snowdrift than lose his job at the lard machine. Ona was quite certain that she would find her place gone, and was all unnerved when she finally got to Brown's, and found that the forelady herself had failed to come, and was therefore compelled to be lenient.

One of the consequences of this episode was that the first joints of three of the little boy's fingers were permanently disabled, and another that thereafter he always had to be beaten before he set out to work, whenever there was fresh snow on the ground. Jurgis was called upon to do the beating, and as it hurt his foot he did it with a vengeance; but it did not tend to add to the sweetness of his temper. They say that the best dog will turn cross if he be kept chained all the time, and it was the same with the man; he had not a thing to do all day but lie and curse his fate, and the time came when he wanted to curse everything.

This was never for very long, however, for when Ona began to cry, Jurgis could not stay angry. The poor fellow looked like a homeless ghost, with his cheeks sunken in and his long black hair straggling into his eyes; he was too discouraged to cut it, or to think about his appearance. His muscles were wasting away, and what were left were soft and flabby. He had no appetite, and they could not afford to tempt him with delicacies. It was better, he said, that he should not eat, it was a saving. About the end of March he had got hold of Ona's bankbook, and learned that there was only three dollars left to them in the world.

But perhaps the worst of the consequences of this long siege was that they lost another member of their family; Brother Jonas disappeared. One Saturday night he did not come home, and thereafter all their efforts to get trace of him were futile. It was said by the boss at Durham's that he had gotten his week's money and left there. That might not be true, of course, for sometimes they would say that when a man had been killed; it was the easiest way out of it for all concerned. When, for instance, a man had fallen into one of the rendering tanks and had been made into pure leaf lard and peerless fertilizer, there was no use letting the fact out and making his family unhappy. More probable, however, was the theory that Jonas had deserted them, and gone on the road, seeking happiness. He had been discontented for a long time, and not without some cause. He paid good board, and was yet obliged to live in a family where nobody had enough to eat. And Marija would keep giving them all her money, and of course he could not but feel that he was called upon to do the same. Then there were crying brats, and all sorts of misery; a man would have had to be a good deal of a hero to stand it all without grumbling, and Jonas was not in the least a hero—he was simply a weatherbeaten old fellow who liked to have a good supper and sit in the corner by the fire and smoke his pipe in peace before he went to bed. Here there was not room by the fire, and through the winter the kitchen had seldom been warm enough for comfort. So, with the springtime, what was more likely than that the wild idea of escaping had come to him? Two years he had been yoked like a horse to a half-ton truck in Durham's dark cellars, with never a rest, save on Sundays and four holidays in the year, and with never a word of thanks—only kicks and blows and curses, such as no decent dog would have stood. And now the winter was over, and the spring winds were blowing—and with a day's walk a man might put the smoke of Packingtown behind him forever, and be where the grass was green and the flowers all the colors of the rainbow!

But now the income of the family was cut down more than one-third, and the food demand was cut only one-eleventh, so that they were worse off than ever. Also they were borrowing money from Marija, and eating up her bank account, and spoiling once again her hopes of marriage and happiness. And they were even going into debt to Tamoszius Kuszleika and letting him impoverish himself. Poor Tamoszius was a man without any relatives, and with a wonderful talent besides, and he ought to have made money and prospered; but he had fallen in love, and so given hostages to fortune, and was doomed to be dragged down too.

So it was finally decided that two more of the children would have to leave school. Next to Stanislovas, who was now fifteen, there was a girl, little Kotrina, who was two years younger, and then, two boys, Vilimas, who was eleven, and Nikalojus, who was ten. Both of these last were bright boys, and there was no reason why their family should starve when tens of thousands of children no older were earning their own livings. So one morning they were given a quarter apiece and a roll with a sausage in it, and, with their minds top-heavy with good advice, were sent out to make their way to the city and learn to sell newspapers. They came back late at night in tears, having walked the five or six miles to report that a man had offered to take them to a place where they sold newspapers, and had taken their money and gone into a store to get them, and nevermore been seen. So they both received a whipping, and the next morning set out again. This time they found the newspaper place, and procured their stock; and after wandering about till nearly noontime, saying "Paper?" to every one they saw, they had all their stock taken away and received a thrashing besides from a big newsman upon whose territory they had trespassed. Fortunately, however, they had already sold some papers, and came back with nearly as much as they started with.

After a week of mishaps such as these, the two little fellows began to learn the ways of the trade—the names of the different papers, and how many of each to get, and what sort of people to offer them to, and where to go and where to stay away from. After this, leaving home at four o'clock in the morning, and running about the streets, first with morning papers and then with evening, they might come home late at night with twenty or thirty cents apiece—possibly as much as forty cents. From this they had to deduct their carfare, since the distance was so great; but after a while they made friends, and learned still more, and then they would save their carfare. They would get on a car when the conductor was not looking, and hide in the crowd; and three times out of four he would not ask for their fares, either not seeing them, or thinking they had already paid; or if he did ask, they would hunt through their pockets, and then begin to cry, and either have their fares paid by some kind old lady, or else try the trick again on a new car. All this was fair play, they felt. Whose fault was it that at the hours when workingmen were going to their work and back, the cars were so crowded that the conductors could not collect all the fares? And besides, the companies were thieves, people said—had stolen all their franchises with the help of scoundrelly politicians!

Now that the winter was by, and there was no more danger of snow, and no more coal to buy, and another room warm enough to put the children into when they cried, and enough money to get along from week to week with, Jurgis was less terrible than he had been. A man can get used to anything in the course of time, and Jurgis had gotten used to lying about the house. Ona saw this, and was very careful not to destroy his peace of mind, by letting him know how very much pain she was suffering. It was now the time of the spring rains, and Ona had often to ride to her work, in spite of the expense; she was getting paler every day, and sometimes, in spite of her good resolutions, it pained her that Jurgis did not notice it. She wondered if he cared for her as much as ever, if all this misery was not wearing out his love. She had to be away from him all the time, and bear her own troubles while he was bearing his; and then, when she came home, she was so worn out; and whenever they talked they had only their worries to talk of—truly it was hard, in such a life, to keep any sentiment alive. The woe of this would flame up in Ona sometimes—at night she would suddenly clasp her big husband in her arms and break into passionate weeping, demanding to know if he really loved her. Poor Jurgis, who had in truth grown more matter-of-fact, under the endless pressure of penury, would not know what to make of these things, and could only try to recollect when he had last been cross; and so Ona would have to forgive him and sob herself to sleep.

The latter part of April Jurgis went to see the doctor, and was given a bandage to lace about his ankle, and told that he might go back to work. It needed more than the permission of the doctor, however, for when he showed up on the killing floor of Brown's, he was told by the foreman that it had not been possible to keep his job for him. Jurgis knew that this meant simply that the foreman had found some one else to do the work as well and did not want to bother to make a change. He stood in the doorway, looking mournfully on, seeing his friends and companions at work, and feeling like an outcast. Then he went out and took his place with the mob of the unemployed.

This time, however, Jurgis did not have the same fine confidence, nor the same reason for it. He was no longer the finest-looking man in the throng, and the bosses no longer made for him; he was thin and haggard, and his clothes were seedy, and he looked miserable. And there were hundreds who looked and felt just like him, and who had been wandering about Packingtown for months begging for work. This was a critical time in Jurgis' life, and if he had been a weaker man he would have gone the way the rest did. Those out-of-work wretches would stand about the packing houses every morning till the police drove them away, and then they would scatter among the saloons. Very few of them had the nerve to face the rebuffs that they would encounter by trying to get into the buildings to interview the bosses; if they did not get a chance in the morning, there would be nothing to do but hang about the saloons the rest of the day and night. Jurgis was saved from all this—partly, to be sure, because it was pleasant weather, and there was no need to be indoors; but mainly because he carried with him always the pitiful little face of his wife. He must get work, he told himself, fighting the battle with despair every hour of the day. He must get work! He must have a place again and some money saved up, before the next winter came.

But there was no work for him. He sought out all the members of his union—Jurgis had stuck to the union through all this—and begged them to speak a word for him. He went to every one he knew, asking for a chance, there or anywhere. He wandered all day through the buildings; and in a week or two, when he had been all over the yards, and into every room to which he had access, and learned that there was not a job anywhere, he persuaded himself that there might have been a change in the places he had first visited, and began the round all over; till finally the watchmen and the "spotters" of the companies came to know him by sight and to order him out with threats. Then there was nothing more for him to do but go with the crowd in the morning, and keep in the front row and look eager, and when he failed, go back home, and play with little Kotrina and the baby.

The peculiar bitterness of all this was that Jurgis saw so plainly the meaning of it. In the beginning he had been fresh and strong, and he had gotten a job the first day; but now he was secondhand, a damaged article, so to speak, and they did not want him. They had got the best out of him—they had worn him out, with their speeding-up and their carelessness, and now they had thrown him away! And Jurgis would make the acquaintance of others of these unemployed men and find that they had all had the same experience. There were some, of course, who had wandered in from other places, who had been ground up in other mills; there were others who were out from their own fault—some, for instance, who had not been able to stand the awful grind without drink. The vast majority, however, were simply the worn-out parts of the great merciless packing machine; they had toiled there, and kept up with the pace, some of them for ten or twenty years, until finally the time had come when they could not keep up with it any more. Some had been frankly told that they were too old, that a sprier man was needed; others had given occasion, by some act of carelessness or incompetence; with most, however, the occasion had been the same as with Jurgis. They had been overworked and underfed so long, and finally some disease had laid them on their backs; or they had cut themselves, and had blood poisoning, or met with some other accident. When a man came back after that, he would get his place back only by the courtesy of the boss. To this there was no exception, save when the accident was one for which the firm was liable; in that case they would send a slippery lawyer to see him, first to try to get him to sign away his claims, but if he was too smart for that, to promise him that he and his should always be provided with work. This promise they would keep, strictly and to the letter—for two years. Two years was the "statute of limitations," and after that the victim could not sue.

What happened to a man after any of these things, all depended upon the circumstances. If he were of the highly skilled workers, he would probably have enough saved up to tide him over. The best-paid men, the "splitters," made fifty cents an hour, which would be five or six dollars a day in the rush seasons, and one or two in the dullest. A man could live and save on that; but then there were only half a dozen splitters in each place, and one of them that Jurgis knew had a family of twenty-two children, all hoping to grow up to be splitters like their father. For an unskilled man, who made ten dollars a week in the rush seasons and five in the dull, it all depended upon his age and the number he had dependent upon him. (An unmarried man could save, if he did not drink, and if he was absolutely selfish—that is, if he paid no heed to the demands of his old parents, or of his little brothers and sisters, or of any other relatives he might have, as well as of the members of his union, and his chums, and the people who might be starving to death next door.

CHAPTER
13

DURING this time that Jurgis was looking for work occurred the death of little Kristoforas, one of the children of Teta Elzbieta. Both Kristoforas and his brother, Juozapas, were cripples, the latter having lost one leg by having it run over, and Kristoforas having congenital dislocation of the hip, which made it impossible for him ever to walk. He was the last of Teta Elzbieta's children, and perhaps he had been intended by nature to let her know that she had had enough. At any rate he was wretchedly sick and undersized; he had the rickets, and though he was over three years old, he was no bigger than an ordinary child of one. All day long he would crawl around the floor in a filthy little dress, whining and fretting; because the floor was full of drafts he was always catching cold, and snuffling because his nose ran. This made him a nuisance, and a source of endless trouble in the family. For his mother, with unnatural perversity, loved him best of all her children, and made a perpetual fuss over him—would let him do anything undisturbed, and would burst into tears when his fretting drove Jurgis wild.

And now he died. Perhaps it was the smoked sausage he had eaten that morning—which may have been made out of some of the tubercular pork that was condemned as unfit for export. At any rate, an hour after eating it, the child had begun to cry with pain, and in another hour he was rolling about on the floor in convulsions. Little Kotrina, who was all alone with him, ran out screaming for help, and after a while a doctor came, but not until Kristoforas had howled his last howl. No one was really sorry about this except poor Elzbieta, who was inconsolable. Jurgis announced that so far as he was concerned the child would have to be buried by the city, since they had no money for a funeral; and at this the poor woman almost went out of her senses, wringing her hands and screaming with grief and despair. Her child to be buried in a pauper's grave! And her stepdaughter to stand by and hear it said without protesting! It was enough to make Ona's father rise up out of his grave to rebuke her! If it had come to this, they might as well give up at once, and be buried all of them together! . . . In the end Marija said that she would help with ten dollars; and Jurgis being still obdurate, Elzbieta went in tears and begged the money from the neighbors, and so little Kristoforas had a mass and a hearse with white plumes on it, and a tiny plot in a graveyard with a wooden cross to mark the place. The poor mother was not the same for months after that; the mere sight of the floor where little Kristoforas had crawled about would make her weep. He had never had a fair chance, poor little fellow, she would say. He had been handicapped from his birth. If only she had heard about it in time, so that she might have had that great doctor to cure him of his lameness! . . . Some time ago, Elzbieta was told, a Chicago billionaire had paid a fortune to bring a great European surgeon over to cure his little daughter of the same disease from which Kristoforas had suffered. And because this surgeon had to have bodies to demonstrate upon, he announced that he would treat the children of the poor, a piece of magnanimity over which the papers became quite eloquent. Elzbieta, alas, did not read the papers, and no one had told her; but perhaps it was as well, for just then they would not have had the carfare to spare to go every day to wait upon the surgeon, nor for that matter anybody with the time to take the child.

All this while that he was seeking for work, there was a dark shadow hanging over Jurgis; as if a savage beast were lurking somewhere in the pathway of his life, and he knew it, and yet could not help approaching the place. There are all stages of being out of work in Packingtown, and he faced in dread the prospect of reaching the lowest. There is a place that waits for the lowest man—the fertilizer plant!

The men would talk about it in awe-stricken whispers. Not more than one in ten had ever really tried it; the other nine had contented themselves with hearsay evidence and a peep through the door. There were some things worse than even starving to death. They would ask Jurgis if he had worked there yet, and if he meant to; and Jurgis would debate the matter with himself. As poor as they were, and making all the sacrifices that they were, would he dare to refuse any sort of work that was offered to him, be it as horrible as ever it could? Would he dare to go home and eat bread that had been earned by Ona, weak and complaining as she was, knowing that he had been given a chance, and had not had the nerve to take it?—And yet he might argue that way with himself all day, and one glimpse into the fertilizer works would send him away again shuddering. He was a man, and he would do his duty; he went and made application—but surely he was not also required to hope for success!

The fertilizer works of Durham's lay away from the rest of the plant. Few visitors ever saw them, and the few who did would come out looking like Dante, of whom the peasants declared that he had been into hell. To this part of the yards came all the "tankage" and the waste products of all sorts; here they dried out the bones,—and in suffocating cellars where the daylight never came you might see men and women and children bending over whirling machines and sawing bits of bone into all sorts of shapes, breathing their lungs full of the fine dust, and doomed to die, every one of them, within a certain definite time. Here they made the blood into albumen, and made other foul-smelling things into things still more foul-smelling. In the corridors and caverns where it was done you might lose yourself as in the great caves of Kentucky. In the dust and the steam the electric lights would shine like far-off twinkling stars—red and blue-green and purple stars, according to the color of the mist and the brew from which it came. For the odors in these ghastly charnel houses there may be words in Lithuanian, but there are none in English. The person entering would have to summon his courage as for a cold-water plunge. He would go on like a man swimming under water; he would put his handkerchief over his face, and begin to cough and choke; and then, if he were still obstinate, he would find his head beginning to ring, and the veins in his forehead to throb, until finally he would be assailed by an overpowering blast of ammonia fumes, and would turn and run for his life, and come out half-dazed.

On top of this were the rooms where they dried the "tankage," the mass of brown stringy stuff that was left after the waste portions of the carcasses had had the lard and tallow tried out of them. This dried material they would then grind to a fine powder, and after they had mixed it up well with a mysterious but inoffensive brown rock which they brought in and ground up by the hundreds of carloads for that purpose, the substance was ready to be put into bags and sent out to the world as any one of a hundred different brands of standard bone phosphate. And then the farmer in Maine or California or Texas would buy this, at say twenty-five dollars a ton, and plant it with his corn; and for several days after the operation the fields would have a strong odor, and the farmer and his wagon and the very horses that had hauled it would all have it too. In Packingtown the fertilizer is pure, instead of being a flavoring, and instead of a ton or so spread out on several acres under the open sky, there are hundreds and thousands of tons of it in one building, heaped here and there in haystack piles, covering the floor several inches deep, and filling the air with a choking dust that becomes a blinding sandstorm when the wind stirs.

It was to this building that Jurgis came daily, as if dragged by an unseen hand. The month of May was an exceptionally cool one, and his secret prayers were granted; but early in June there came a record-breaking hot spell, and after that there were men wanted in the fertilizer mill.

The boss of the grinding room had come to know Jurgis by this time, and had marked him for a likely man; and so when he came to the door about two o'clock this breathless hot day, he felt a sudden spasm of pain shoot through him—the boss beckoned to him! In ten minutes more Jurgis had pulled off his coat and overshirt, and set his teeth together and gone to work. Here was one more difficulty for him to meet and conquer!

His labor took him about one minute to learn. Before him was one of the vents of the mill in which the fertilizer was being ground—rushing forth in a great brown river, with a spray of the finest dust flung forth in clouds. Jurgis was given a shovel, and along with half a dozen others it was his task to shovel this fertilizer into carts. That others were at work he knew by the sound, and by the fact that he sometimes collided with them; otherwise they might as well not have been there, for in the blinding dust storm a man could not see six feet in front of his face.

When he had filled one cart he had to grope around him until another came, and if there was none on hand he continued to grope till one arrived. In five minutes he was, of course, a mass of fertilizer from head to feet; they gave him a sponge to tie over his mouth, so that he could breathe, but the sponge did not prevent his lips and eyelids from caking up with it and his ears from filling solid. He looked like a brown ghost at twilight—from hair to shoes he became the color of the building and of everything in it, and for that matter a hundred yards outside it. The building had to be left open, and when the wind blew Durham and Company lost a great deal of fertilizer.

Working in his shirt sleeves, and with the thermometer at over a hundred, the phosphates soaked in through every pore of Jurgis' skin, and in five minutes he had a headache, and in fifteen was almost dazed. The blood was pounding in his brain like an engine's throbbing; there was a frightful pain in the top of his skull, and he could hardly control his hands. Still, with the memory of his four months' siege behind him, he fought on, in a frenzy of determination; and half an hour later he began to vomit—he vomited until it seemed as if his inwards must be torn into shreds. A man could get used to the fertilizer mill, the boss had said, if he would only make up his mind to it; but Jurgis now began to see that it was a question of making up his stomach.

At the end of that day of horror, he could scarcely stand. He had to catch himself now and then, and lean against a building and get his bearings. Most of the men, when they came out, made straight for a saloon—they seemed to place fertilizer and rattlesnake poison in one class. But Jurgis was too ill to think of drinking—he could only make his way to the street and stagger on to a car. He had a sense of humor, and later on, when he became an old hand, he used to think it fun to board a streetcar and see what happened. Now, however, he was too ill to notice it—how the people in the car began to gasp and sputter, to put their handkerchiefs to their noses, and transfix him with furious glances. Jurgis only knew that a man in front of him immediately got up and gave him a seat; and that half a minute later the two people on each side of him got up; and that in a full minute the crowded car was nearly empty—those passengers who could not get room on the platform having gotten out to walk.

Of course Jurgis had made his home a miniature fertilizer mill a minute after entering. The stuff was half an inch deep in his skin—his whole system was full of it, and it would have taken a week not merely of scrubbing, but of vigorous exercise, to get it out of him. As it was, he could be compared with nothing known to men, save that newest discovery of the savants, a substance which emits energy for an unlimited time, without being itself in the least diminished in power. He smelled so that he made all the food at the table taste, and set the whole family to vomiting; for himself it was three days before he could keep anything upon his stomach—he might wash his hands, and use a knife and fork, but were not his mouth and throat filled with the poison?

And still Jurgis stuck it out! In spite of splitting headaches he would stagger down to the plant and take up his stand once more, and begin to shovel in the blinding clouds of dust. And so at the end of the week he was a fertilizer man for life—he was able to eat again, and though his head never stopped aching, it ceased to be so bad that he could not work.

So there passed another summer. It was a summer of prosperity, all over the country, and the country ate generously of packing house products, and there was plenty of work for all the family, in spite of the packers' efforts to keep a superfluity of labor. They were again able to pay their debts and to begin to save a little sum; but there were one or two sacrifices they considered too heavy to be made for long—it was too bad that the boys should have to sell papers at their age. It was utterly useless to caution them and plead with them; quite without knowing it, they were taking on the tone of their new environment. They were learning to swear in voluble English; they were learning to pick up cigar stumps and smoke them, to pass hours of their time gambling with pennies and dice and cigarette cards; they were learning the location of all the houses of prostitution on the "Levee," and the names of the "madames" who kept them, and the days when they gave their state banquets, which the police captains and the big politicians all attended. If a visiting "country customer" were to ask them, they could show him which was "Hinkydink's" famous saloon, and could even point out to him by name the different gamblers and thugs and "hold-up men" who made the place their headquarters. And worse yet, the boys were getting out of the habit of coming home at night. What was the use, they would ask, of wasting time and energy and a possible carfare riding out to the stockyards every night when the weather was pleasant and they could crawl under a truck or into an empty doorway and sleep exactly as well? So long as they brought home a half dollar for each day, what mattered it when they brought it? But Jurgis declared that from this to ceasing to come at all would not be a very long step, and so it was decided that Vilimas and Nikalojus should return to school in the fall, and that instead Elzbieta should go out and get some work, her place at home being taken by her younger daughter.

Little Kotrina was like most children of the poor, prematurely made old; she had to take care of her little brother, who was a cripple, and also of the baby; she had to cook the meals and wash the dishes and clean house, and have supper ready when the workers came home in the evening. She was only thirteen, and small for her age, but she did all this without a murmur; and her mother went out, and after trudging a couple of days about the yards, settled down as a servant of a "sausage machine."

Elzbieta was used to working, but she found this change a hard one, for the reason that she had to stand motionless upon her feet from seven o'clock in the morning till half-past twelve, and again from one till half-past five. For the first few days it seemed to her that she could not stand it—she suffered almost as much as Jurgis had from the fertilizer, and would come out at sundown with her head fairly reeling. Besides this, she was working in one of the dark holes, by electric light, and the dampness, too, was deadly—there were always puddles of water on the floor, and a sickening odor of moist flesh in the room. The people who worked here followed the ancient custom of nature, whereby the ptarmigan is the color of dead leaves in the fall and of snow in the winter, and the chameleon, who is black when he lies upon a stump and turns green when he moves to a leaf. The men and women who worked in this department were precisely the color of the "fresh country sausage" they made.

The sausage room was an interesting place to visit, for two or three minutes, and provided that you did not look at the people; the machines were perhaps the most wonderful things in the entire plant. Presumably sausages were once chopped and stuffed by hand, and if so it would be interesting to know how many workers had been displaced by these inventions. On one side of the room were the hoppers, into which men shoveled loads of meat and wheelbarrows full of spices; in these great bowls were whirling knives that made two thousand revolutions a minute, and when the meat was ground fine and adulterated with potato flour, and well mixed with water, it was forced to the stuffing machines on the other side of the room. The latter were tended by women; there was a sort of spout, like the nozzle of a hose, and one of the women would take a long string of" "casing" and put the end over the nozzle and then work the whole thing on, as one works on the finger of a tight glove. This string would be twenty or thirty feet long, but the woman would have it all on in a jiffy; and when she had several on, she would press a lever, and a stream of sausage meat would be shot out, taking the casing with it as it came. Thus one might stand and see appear, miraculously born from the machine, a wriggling snake of sausage of incredible length. In front was a big pan which caught these creatures, and two more women who seized them as fast as they appeared and twisted them into links. This was for the uninitiated the most perplexing work of all; for all that the woman had to give was a single turn of the wrist; and in some way she contrived to give it so that instead of an endless chain of sausages, one after another, there grew under her hands a bunch of strings, all dangling from a single center. It was quite like the feat of a prestidigitator—for the woman worked so fast that the eye could literally not follow her, and there was only a mist of motion, and tangle after tangle of sausages appearing. In the midst of the mist, however, the visitor would suddenly notice the tense set face, with the two wrinkles graven in the forehead, and the ghastly pallor of the cheeks; and then he would suddenly recollect that it was time he was going on. The woman did not go on; she stayed right there—hour after hour, day after day, year after year, twisting sausage links and racing with death. It was piecework, and she was apt to have a family to keep alive; and stern and ruthless economic laws had arranged it that she could only do this by working just as she did, with all her soul upon her work, and with never an instant for a glance at the well-dressed ladies and gentlemen who came to stare at her, as at some wild beast in a menagerie.

CHAPTER
14

WITH one member trimming beef in a cannery, and another working in a sausage factory, the family had a first-hand knowledge of the great majority of Packingtown swindles. For it was the custom, as they found, whenever meat was so spoiled that it could not be used for anything else, either to can it or else to chop it up into sausage. With what had been told them by Jonas, who had worked in the pickle rooms, they could now study the whole of the spoiled-meat industry on the inside, and read a new and grim meaning into that old Packingtown jest—that they use everything of the pig except the squeal.

Jonas had told them how the meat that was taken out of pickle would often be found sour, and how they would rub it up with soda to take away the smell, and sell it to be eaten on free-lunch counters; also of all the miracles of chemistry which they performed, giving to any sort of meat, fresh or salted, whole or chopped, any color and any flavor and any odor they chose. In the pickling of hams they had an ingenious apparatus, by which they saved time and increased the capacity of the plant—a machine consisting of a hollow needle attached to a pump; by plunging this needle into the meat and working with his foot, a man could fill a ham with pickle in a few seconds. And yet, in spite of this, there would be hams found spoiled, some of them with an odor so bad that a man could hardly bear to be in the room with them. To pump into these the packers had a second and much stronger pickle which destroyed the odor—a process known to the workers as "giving them thirty per cent." Also, after the hams had been smoked, there would be found some that had gone to the bad. Formerly these had been sold as "Number Three Grade," but later on some ingenious person had hit upon a new device, and now they would extract the bone, about which the bad part generally lay, and insert in the hole a white-hot iron. After this invention there was no longer Number One, Two, and Three Grade—there was only Number One Grade. The packers were always originating such schemes—they had what they called "boneless hams," which were all the odds and ends of pork stuffed into casings; and "California hams," which were the shoulders, with big knuckle joints, and nearly all the meat cut out; and fancy "skinned hams," which were made of the oldest hogs, whose skins were so heavy and coarse that no one would buy them—that is, until they had been cooked and chopped fine and labeled "head cheese!"

It was only when the whole ham was spoiled that it came into the department of Elzbieta. Cut up by the two-thousand-revolutions-a-minute flyers, and mixed with half a ton of other meat, no odor that ever was in a ham could make any difference. There was never the least attention paid to what was cut up for sausage; there would come all the way back from Europe old sausage that had been rejected, and that was moldy and white—it would be dosed with borax and glycerine, and dumped into the hoppers, and made over again for home consumption. There would be meat that had tumbled out on the floor, in the dirt and sawdust, where the workers had tramped and spit uncounted billions of consumption germs. There would be meat stored in great piles in rooms; and the water from leaky roofs would drip over it, and thousands of rats would race about on it. It was too dark in these storage places to see well, but a man could run his hand over these piles of meat and sweep off handfuls of the dried dung of rats. These rats were nuisances, and the packers would put poisoned bread out for them; they would die, and then rats, bread, and meat would go into the hoppers together. This is no fairy story and no joke; the meat would be shoveled into carts, and the man who did the shoveling would not trouble to lift out a rat even when he saw one—there were things that went into the sausage in comparison with which a poisoned rat was a tidbit. There was no place for the men to wash their hands before they ate their dinner, and so they made a practice of washing them in the water that was to be ladled into the sausage. There were the butt-ends of smoked meat, and the scraps of corned beef, and all the odds and ends of the waste of the plants, that would be dumped into old barrels in the cellar and left there. Under the system of rigid economy which the packers enforced, there were some jobs that it only paid to do once in a long time, and among these was the cleaning out of the waste barrels. Every spring they did it; and in the barrels would be dirt and rust and old nails and stale water—and cartload after cartload of it would be taken up and dumped into the hoppers with fresh meat, and sent out to the public's breakfast. Some of it they would make into "smoked" sausage—but as the smoking took time, and was therefore expensive, they would call upon their chemistry department, and preserve it with borax and color it with gelatine to make it brown. All of their sausage came out of the same bowl, but when they came to wrap it they would stamp some of it "special," and for this they would charge two cents more a pound.

Such were the new surroundings in which Elzbieta was placed, and such was the work she was compelled to do. It was stupefying, brutalizing work; it left her no time to think, no strength for anything. She was part of the machine she tended, and every faculty that was not needed for the machine was doomed to be crushed out of existence. There was only one mercy about the cruel grind—that it gave her the gift of insensibility. Little by little she sank into a torpor—she fell silent. She would meet Jurgis and Ona in the evening, and the three would walk home together, often without saying a word. Ona, too, was falling into a habit of silence—Ona, who had once gone about singing like a bird. She was sick and miserable, and often she would barely have strength enough to drag herself home. And there they would eat what they had to eat, and afterward, because there was only their misery to talk of, they would crawl into bed and fall into a stupor and never stir until it was time to get up again, and dress by candlelight, and go back to the machines. They were so numbed that they did not even suffer much from hunger, now; only the children continued to fret when the food ran short.

Yet the soul of Ona was not dead—the souls of none of them were dead, but only sleeping; and now and then they would waken, and these were cruel times. The gates of memory would roll open—old joys would stretch out their arms to them, old hopes and dreams would call to them,

They wanted to be nums [handwritten annotation]

and they would stir beneath the burden that lay upon them, and feel its forever immeasurable weight. They could not even cry out beneath it; but anguish would seize them, more dreadful than the agony of death. It was a thing scarcely to be spoken—a thing never spoken by all the world, that will not know its own defeat.

They were beaten; they had lost the game, they were swept aside. It was not less tragic because it was so sordid, because it had to do with wages and grocery bills and rents. They had dreamed of freedom; of a chance to look about them and learn something; to be decent and clean, to see their child grow up to be strong. And now it was all gone—it would never be! They had played the game and they had lost. Six years more of toil they had to face before they could expect the least respite, the cessation of the payments upon the house; and how cruelly certain it was that they could never stand six years of such a life as they were living! They were lost, they were going down—and there was no deliverance for them, no hope; for all the help it gave them the vast city in which they lived might have been an ocean waste, a wilderness, a desert, a tomb. So often this mood would come to Ona, in the nighttime, when something wakened her; she would lie, afraid of the beating of her own heart, fronting the blood-red eyes of the old primeval terror of life. Once she cried aloud, and woke Jurgis, who was tired and cross. After that she learned to weep silently—their moods so seldom came together now! It was as if their hopes were buried in separate graves. *drinking* [handwritten annotation]

Jurgis, being a man, had troubles of his own. There was another specter following him. He had never spoken of it, nor would he allow any one else to speak of it—he had never acknowledged its existence to himself. Yet the battle with it took all the manhood that he had—and once or twice, alas, a little more. Jurgis had discovered drink.

He was working in the steaming pit of hell; day after day, week after week—until now there was not an organ of his body that did its work without pain, until the sound of ocean breakers echoed in his head day and night, and the buildings swayed and danced before him as he went down the street. And from all the unending horror of this there was a respite, a deliverance—he could drink! He could forget the pain, he could slip off the burden; he would see clearly again, he would be master of his brain, of his thoughts, of his will. His dead self would stir in him, and he would find himself laughing and cracking jokes with his companions—he would be a man again, and master of his life.

It was not an easy thing for Jurgis to take more than two or three drinks. With the first drink he could eat a meal, and he could persuade himself that that was economy; with the second he could eat another meal—but there would come a time when he could eat no more, and then to pay for a drink was an unthinkable extravagance, a defiance of the agelong instincts of his hunger-haunted class. One day, however, he took the plunge, and drank up all that he had in his pockets, and went home half "piped," as the men phrase it. He was happier than he had been in a year; and yet, because he knew that the happiness would not last, he was savage, too—with those who would wreck it, and with the world, and with his life; and then again, beneath this, he was sick with the shame of himself. Afterward, when he saw the despair of his family, and reckoned up the money he had spent, the tears came into his eyes, and he began the long battle with the specter.

It was a battle that had no end, that never could have one. But Jurgis did not realize that very clearly; he was not given much time for reflection. He simply knew that he was always fighting. Steeped in misery and despair as he was, merely to walk down the street was to be put upon the rack. There was surely a saloon on the corner—perhaps on all four corners, and some in the middle of the block as well; and each one stretched out a hand to him—each one had a personality of its own, allurements unlike any other. Going and coming—before sunrise and after dark—there was warmth and a glow of light, and the steam of hot food, and perhaps music, or a friendly face, and a word of good cheer. Jurgis developed a fondness for having Ona on his arm whenever he went out on the street, and he would hold her tightly, and walk fast. It was pitiful to have Ona know of this—it drove him wild to think of it; the thing was not fair, for Ona had never tasted drink, and so could not understand. Sometimes, in desperate hours, he would find himself wishing that she might learn what it was, so that he need not be ashamed in her presence. They might drink together, and escape from the horror—escape for a while, come what would.

So there came a time when nearly all the conscious life of Jurgis consisted of a struggle with the craving for liquor. He would have ugly moods, when he hated Ona and the whole family, because they stood in his way. He was a fool to have married; he had tied himself down, had made himself a slave. It was all because he was a married man that he was compelled to stay in the yards; if it had not been for that he might have gone off like Jonas, and to hell with the packers. There were few single men in the fertilizer mill—and those few were working only for a chance to escape. Meantime, too, they had something to think about while they worked,—they had the memory of the last time they had been drunk, and the hope of the time when they would be drunk again. As for Jurgis, he was expected to bring home every penny; he could not even go with the men at noontime—he was supposed to sit down and eat his dinner on a pile of fertilizer dust.

This was not always his mood, of course; he still loved his family. But just now was a time of trial. Poor little Antanas, for instance—who had never failed to win him with a smile—little Antanas was not smiling just now, being a mass of fiery red pimples. He had had all the diseases that babies are heir to, in quick succession, scarlet fever, mumps, and whooping cough in the first year, and now he was down with the measles. There was no one to attend him but Kotrina; there was no doctor to help him, because they were too poor, and children did not die of the measles—at least not often. Now and then Kotrina would find time to sob over his woes, but for the greater part of the time he had to be left alone, barricaded upon the bed. The floor was full of drafts, and if he caught cold he would die. At night he was tied down, lest he should kick the covers off him, while the family lay in their stupor of exhaustion. He would lie and scream for hours, almost in convulsions; and then, when he was worn out, he would lie whimpering and wailing in his torment. He was burning up with fever, and his eyes were running sores; in the daytime he was a thing uncanny and impish to behold, a plaster of pimples and sweat, a great purple lump of misery.

Yet all this was not really as cruel as it sounds, for, sick as he was, little Antanas was the least unfortunate member of that family. He was quite able to bear his sufferings—it was as if he had all these complaints to show what a prodigy of health he was. He was the child of his parents' youth and joy; he grew up like the conjurer's rosebush, and all the world was his oyster. In general, he toddled around the kitchen all day with a lean and hungry look—the portion of the family's allowance that fell to him was not enough, and he was unrestrainable in his demand for more. Antanas was but little over a year old, and already no one but his father could manage him.

It seemed as if he had taken all of his mother's strength—had left nothing for those that might come after him. Ona was with child again now, and it was a dreadful thing to contemplate; even Jurgis, dumb and despairing as he was, could not but understand that yet other agonies were on the way, and shudder at the thought of them.

For Ona was visibly going to pieces. In the first place she was developing a cough, like the one that had killed old Dede Antanas. She had had a trace of it ever since that fatal morning when the greedy streetcar corporation had turned her out into the rain; but now it was beginning to grow serious, and to wake her up at night. Even worse than that was the fearful nervousness from which she suffered; she would have frightful headaches and fits of aimless weeping; and sometimes she would come home at night shuddering and moaning, and would fling herself down upon the bed and burst into tears. Several times she was quite beside herself and hysterical; and then Jurgis would go half-mad with fright. Elzbieta would explain to him that it could not be helped, that a woman was subject to such things when she was pregnant; but he was hardly to be persuaded, and would beg and plead to know what had happened. She had never been like this before, he would argue—it was monstrous and unthinkable. It was the life she had to live, the accursed work she had to do, that was killing her by inches. She was not fitted for it—no woman was fitted for it, no woman ought to be allowed to do such work; if the world could not keep them alive any other way it ought to kill them at once and be done with it. They ought not to marry, to have children; no workingman ought to marry—if he, Jurgis, had known what a woman was like, he would have had his eyes torn out first. So he would carry on, becoming half hysterical himself, which was an unbearable thing to see in a big man; Ona would pull herself together and fling herself into his arms, begging him to stop, to be still, that she would be better, it would be all right. So she would lie and sob out her grief upon his shoulder, while he gazed at her, as helpless as a wounded animal, the target of unseen enemies.

W. E. Burghardt Du Bois

1868-1963

The Souls of Black Folk
1903

A sociologist, historian, civil rights activist and author, William Edward Burghardt Du Bois[1] was born in Great Barrington, Massachusetts, the intellectually gifted son of a Haitian father and an African-American mother. Raised in a primarily white community by his mother, whose circumstances bordered on destitution, he encountered little racism and enjoyed a happy childhood. It was only when he attended historically black Fisk College in Nashville, Tennessee, that he first came face-to-face with racial segregation and prejudice.

After receiving his bachelor's degree from Fisk, Du Bois went on to Harvard to earn a second undergraduate degree (graduating cum laude in philosophy) and an M.A. in history. For the next two years, as a Fellow in the graduate school, he studied history and political science.[2] With the support of the Slater Fund for the Education of Negroes, he was able to travel to Europe for additional graduate study. After only three semesters at the University of Berlin, studying under radical economist Gustave Schmoller, he wrote his doctoral dissertation (in German). Unfortunately for Du Bois, the Slater Fund's refusal to extend his grant for one more

---

[1] His father Alfred rejected the French pronunciation and chose "due boyss" instead (Pampel 2007, 214).

[2] Or, in his words, "what would have been sociology if Harvard had recognized such a field." (www2.pfeiffer.edu/~Iridener/DSS/DuBois/DUBOISP2.HTML).

semester made it impossible for him to satisfy the school's residency requirement and he was never awarded a PhD in economics. He returned to the United States, wrote a second doctoral dissertation, this one entitled "The Suppression of the African Slave Trade to the United States of America, 1638-1870," and became the first black to receive a PhD from Harvard. Over his academic career, he taught at Wilberforce University, the University of Pennsylvania, and (Clark) Atlanta University.

Best known for *The Souls of Black Folk* (1903), Du Bois also wrote *The Philadelphia Negro* (1899), the case study of a black community that helped define the field of urban sociology, and *Black Reconstruction* (1935), which he considered his greatest work. Overall, he wrote 19 books, edited 18 others, placed articles and essays in such publications as *The Nation*, *Atlantic Monthly*, *The American Historical Review*, and *The American Sociological Review*, and wrote weekly newspaper columns.

The father of empirical sociology, Du Bois pioneered the scientific approach to the study of racism. According to Poussaint (1969, xxxi),

> Du Bois genuinely believed that if he could utilize his training in gathering and presenting the facts concerning the misery of the black man in America, those facts, indisputable in their logic and clarity, would move the white man to right the wrongs now made visible to him. This belief was based on an assumption which presupposed the existence of willingness, a reservoir of goodwill and simple goodness, within the white man which would move him inevitably to correct the injustice of the black man's plight.

He presents these facts In *The Souls of Black Folk*, expecting his audience to rise to the challenge. While he initially believed that education and awareness could bring about racial justice, he eventually came to believe that social change would only occur through agitation and political protest. This view put him in conflict with Booker T. Washington, perhaps the most influential black leader of the time, who believed that blacks could win the respect of whites through hard work and acquiescence.

Co-founder of the National Association for the Advancement of Colored People (NAACP) in 1909, Du Bois edited its magazine, *Crisis: A Record of the Darker Races*, for almost 25 years. Ultimately, he decided that "to finally solve the problem of racism, . . . mankind must, sooner than later, come to the conclusion that this old structure is beyond effective reform . . . ."

In 1961, Du Bois joined the Communist Party, saying, "Today I have reached a firm conclusion: Capitalism cannot reform itself; it is doomed to self-destruction. No universal selfishness can bring social good to all." He and his wife moved to Ghana, where he died two years later.

The selection you're about to read originally appeared as Chapter 8 of *The Souls of Black Folk*, which, you will recall was written specifically for white readers. The forward invites the white reader into his world: "Herein lie buried many things which if read with patience may show the strange meaning of being black here at the dawning of the Twentieth Century. The meaning is not without interest to you, Gentle Reader, for the problem of the Twentieth Century is the problem of the color line." He then opens the book, saying,

> Between me and the other world there is ever an unasked question: unasked by some through feelings of delicacy; by others through the difficulty of rightly framing it. All, nevertheless, flutter round it. They approach me in a half-hesitant sort of way, eye me curiously or compassionately, and then, instead of saying directly, How does it feel to be a problem? they say, I know an excellent colored man in my town; or, I fought at Mechanicsville; or, Do not these Southern outrages make your blood boil? At these I smile, or am interested, or reduce the boiling to a simmer, as the occasion may require. To the real question, How does it feel to be a problem? I answer seldom a word. (1)

As you read this selection, try to imagine what life was like for a black person living during and after the period of Reconstruction. Compare the existence Du Bois is describing with that described by Hacker, and ask yourself whether the problem of the twenty-first century might also be the problem of the color line. Think about the extent to which racial prejudice and discrimination are consequences of our political, economic, or social institutions, and consider the kinds of changes that might be needed in order to ameliorate the problem.

SELECTION FROM:

Du Bois, W.E.B. (1903). *The Souls of Black Folk, Essays and Sketches.* Chicago: A. C. McClurg & Co. 135-162.

VIII
Of the Quest of the Golden Fleece

But the Brute said in his breast, "Till the mills I grind have ceased,
The riches shall be dust of dust, dry ashes be the feast!

"On the strong and cunning few
Cynic favors I will strew;
I will stuff their maw with overplus until their spirit dies;
From the patient and the low
I will take the joys they know;
They shall hunger after vanities and still an-hungered go.
Madness shall be on the people, ghastly jealousies arise;
Brother's blood shall cry on brother up the dead and empty skies.
WILLIAM VAUGHN MOODY.

HAVE you ever seen a cotton-field white with harvest,—its golden fleece hovering above the black earth like a silvery cloud edged with dark green, its bold white signals waving like the foam of billows from Carolina to Texas across that Black and human Sea? I have sometimes half suspected that here the winged ram Chrysomallus left that Fleece after which Jason and his Argonauts went vaguely wandering into the shadowy East three thousand years ago; and certainly one might frame a pretty and not far-fetched analogy of witchery and dragons' teeth, and blood and armed men, between the ancient and the modern quest of the Golden Fleece in the Black Sea.

And now the golden fleece is found; not only found, but, in its birthplace, woven. For the hum of the cotton-mills is the newest and most significant thing in the New South to-day. All through the Carolinas and Georgia, away down to Mexico, rise these gaunt red buildings, bare and homely, and yet so busy and noisy withal that they scarce seem to belong to the slow and sleepy land. Perhaps they sprang from dragons' teeth. So the Cotton Kingdom still lives; the world still bows beneath her sceptre. Even the markets that once defied the *parvenu* have crept one by one across the seas, and then slowly and reluctantly, but surely, have started toward the Black Belt.

To be sure, there are those who wag their heads knowingly and tell us that the capital of the Cotton Kingdom has moved from the Black to the White Belt,—that the Negro of to-day raises not more than half of the cotton crop. Such men forget that the cotton crop has doubled, and more than doubled, since the era of slavery, and that, even granting their contention, the Negro is still supreme in a Cotton Kingdom larger than that on which the Confederacy builded its hopes. So the Negro forms to-day one of the chief figures in a great world-industry; and this, for its own sake, and in the light of historic interest, makes the field-hands of the cotton country worth studying.

We seldom study the condition of the Negro to-day honestly and carefully. It is so much easier to assume that we know it all. Or perhaps, having already reached conclusions in our own minds, we are loth to have them disturbed by facts. And yet how little we really know of these millions,—of their daily lives and longings, of their homely joys and sorrows, of their real shortcomings and the meaning of their crimes! All this we can only learn by intimate contact with the masses, and not by wholesale arguments covering millions separate in time and space, and differing widely in training and culture. To-day, then, my reader, let us turn our faces to the Black Belt of Georgia and seek simply to know the condition of the black farm-laborers of one county there.

Here in 1890 lived ten thousand Negroes and two thousand whites. The country is rich, yet the people are poor. The keynote of the Black Belt is debt; not commercial credit, but debt in the sense of continued inability on the part of the mass of the population to make income cover expense. This is the direct heritage of the South from the wasteful economies of the slave *régime*; but it was emphasized and brought to a crisis by the Emancipation of the slaves. In 1860, Dougherty County had six thousand slaves, worth at least two and a half millions of dollars; its farms were estimated at three millions,—making five and a half millions of property, the value of which depended largely on the slave system, and on the speculative demand for land once marvellously rich but already partially devitalized by careless and exhaustive culture. The war then meant a financial crash; in place of the five and a half millions of 1860, there remained in 1870 only farms valued at less than two millions.

With this came increased competition in cotton culture from the rich lands of Texas; a steady fall in the normal price of cotton followed, from about fourteen cents a pound in 1860 until it reached four cents in 1898. Such a financial revolution was it that involved the owners of the cotton-belt in debt. And if things went ill with the master, how fared it with the man?

The plantations of Dougherty County in slavery days were not as imposing and aristocratic as those of Virginia. The Big House was smaller and usually one-storied, and sat very near the slave cabins. Sometimes these cabins stretched off on either side like wings; sometimes only on one side, forming a double row, or edging the road that turned into the plantation from the main thoroughfare. The form and disposition of the laborers' cabins throughout the Black Belt is to-day the same as in slavery days. Some live in the self-same cabins, others in cabins rebuilt on the sites of the old. All are sprinkled in little groups over the face of the land, centering about some dilapidated Big House where the head-tenant or agent lives. The general character and arrangement of these dwellings remains on the whole unaltered. There were in the county, outside the corporate town of Albany, about fifteen hundred Negro families in 1898. Out of all these, only a single family occupied a house with seven rooms; only fourteen have five rooms or more. The mass live in one—and two-room homes.

The size and arrangements of a people's homes are no unfair index of their condition. If, then, we inquire more carefully into these Negro homes, we find much that is unsatisfactory. All over the face of the land is the one-room cabin,—now standing in the shadow of the Big House, now staring at the dusty road, now rising dark and sombre amid the green of the cotton-fields. It is nearly always old and bare, built of rough boards, and neither plastered nor ceiled. Light and ventilation are supplied by the single door and by the square hole in the wall with its wooden shutter. There is no glass, porch, or ornamentation without. Within is a fireplace, black and smoky, and usually unsteady with age. A bed or two, a table, a wooden chest, and a few chairs compose the furniture; while a stray show-bill or a newspaper makes up the decorations for the walls. Now and then one may find such a cabin kept scrupulously neat, with merry steaming fireplaces and hospitable door; but the majority are dirty and dilapidated, smelling of eating and sleeping, poorly ventilated, and anything but homes.

Above all, the cabins are crowded. We have come to associate crowding with homes in cities almost exclusively. This is primarily because we have so little accurate knowledge of country life. Here in Dougherty County one may find families of eight and ten occupying one or two rooms, and for every ten rooms of house accommodation for the Negroes there are twenty-five persons. The worst tenement abominations of New York do not have above twenty-two persons for every ten rooms. Of course, one small, close room in a city, without a yard, is in many respects worse than the larger single country room. In other respects it is better; it has glass windows, a decent chimney, and a trustworthy floor. The single great advantage of the Negro peasant is that he may spend most of his life outside his hovel, in the open fields.

There are four chief causes of these wretched homes: First, long custom born of slavery has assigned such homes to Negroes; white laborers would be offered better accommodations, and might, for that and similar reasons, give better work. Secondly, the Negroes, used to such accommodations, do not as a rule demand better; they do not know what better houses mean. Thirdly, the landlords as a class have not yet come to realize that it is a good business investment to raise the standard of living among labor by slow and judicious methods; that a Negro laborer who demands three rooms and fifty cents a day would give more efficient work and leave a larger profit than a discouraged toiler herding his family in one room and working for thirty cents. Lastly, among such conditions of life there are few incentives to make the laborer become a better farmer. If he is ambitious, he moves to town or tries other labor; as a tenant-farmer his outlook is almost hopeless, and following it as a makeshift, he takes the house that is given him without protest.

In such homes, then, these Negro peasants live. The families are both small and large; there are many single tenants,—widows and bachelors, and remnants of broken groups. The system of labor and the size of the houses both tend to the breaking up of family groups: the grown children go away as contract hands or migrate to town, the sister goes into service; and so one finds many families with hosts of babies, and many newly married couples, but comparatively few families with half-grown and grown sons and daughters. The average size of Negro families has undoubtedly decreased since the war, primarily from economic stress. In Russia over a third of the bridegrooms and over half the brides are under twenty; the same was true of the ante-bellum Negroes. To-day, however, very few of the boys and less than a fifth of the Negro girls under twenty are married. The young men marry between the ages of twenty-five and thirty-five; the young women between twenty and thirty. Such postponement is due to the difficulty of earning sufficient to rear and support a family; and it undoubtedly leads, in the country districts, to sexual immorality. The form of this immorality, however, is very seldom that of prostitution, and less frequently that of illegitimacy than one would imagine. Rather, it takes the form of separation and desertion after a family group has been formed. The number of separated persons is thirty-five to the thousand,—a very large number. It would of course be unfair to compare this number with divorce statistics, for many of these separated women are in reality widowed, were the truth known, and in other cases the separation is not permanent. Nevertheless, here lies the seat of greatest moral danger. There is little or no prostitution among these Negroes, and over three-fourths of the families, as found by house-to-house investigation, deserve to be classed as decent people with considerable regard for female chastity. To be sure, the ideas of the mass would not suit New England, and there are many loose habits and notions. Yet the rate of illegitimacy is undoubtedly lower than in Austria or Italy, and the women as a class are modest. The plague-spot in sexual relations is easy marriage and easy separation. This is no sudden development, nor the fruit of Emancipation. It is the plain heritage from slavery. In those days Sam, with his master's consent, "took up" with Mary. No ceremony was necessary, and in the busy life of the great plantations of the Black Belt it was usually dispensed with. If now the master needed Sam's work in another plantation or in another part of the same plantation, or if he took a notion to sell the slave, Sam's married life with Mary was usually unceremoniously broken, and then it was clearly to the master's interest to have both of them take new mates. This widespread custom of two centuries has not been eradicated in thirty years. To-day Sam's grandson "takes up" with a woman without license or ceremony; they live together decently and honestly, and are, to all intents and purposes, man and wife. Sometimes these unions are never broken until death; but in too many cases family quarrels, a roving spirit, a rival suitor, or perhaps more frequently the hopeless battle to support a family, lead to separation, and a broken house-hold is the result. The Negro church has done much to stop this practice, and now most marriage ceremonies are performed by the pastors. Nevertheless, the evil is still deep seated, and only a general raising of the standard of living will finally cure it.

Looking now at the county black population as a whole, it is fair to characterize it as poor and ignorant. Perhaps ten per cent compose the well-to-do and the best of the laborers, while at least nine per cent are thoroughly lewd and vicious. The rest, over eighty per cent, are poor and ignorant, fairly honest and well meaning, plodding, and to a degree shiftless, with some but not great sexual looseness. Such class lines are by no means fixed; they vary, one might almost say, with the price of cotton. The degree of ignorance cannot easily be expressed. We may say, for instance, that nearly two-thirds of them cannot read or write. This but partially expresses the fact. They are ignorant of the world about them, of modern economic organization, of the function of government, of individual worth and possibilities,—of nearly all those things which slavery in self-defence had to keep them from learning. Much that the white boy imbibes from his earliest social atmosphere forms the puzzling problems of the black boy's mature years. America is not another word for Opportunity to *all* her sons.

It is easy for us to lose ourselves in details in endeavoring to grasp and comprehend the real condition of a mass of human beings. We often forget that each unit in the mass is a throbbing human soul. Ignorant it may be, and poverty stricken, black and curious in limb and ways and thought; and yet it loves and hates, it toils and tires, it laughs and weeps its bitter tears, and looks in vague and awful longing at the grim horizon of its life,—all this, even as you and I. These black thousands are not in reality lazy; they are improvident and careless; they insist on breaking the monotony of toil with a glimpse at the great town-world on Saturday; they have their loafers and their rascals; but the great mass of them work continuously and faithfully for a return, and under circumstances that would call forth equal voluntary effort from few if any other modern laboring class. Over eighty-eight per cent of them—men, women, and children—are farmers. Indeed, this is almost the only industry. Most of the children get their schooling after the "crops are laid by," and very few there are that stay in school after the spring work has begun. Child-labor is to be found here in some of its worst phases, as fostering ignorance and stunting physical development. With the grown men of the county there is little variety in work: thirteen hundred are farmers, and two hundred are laborers, teamsters, etc., including twenty-four artisans, ten merchants, twenty-one preachers, and four teachers. This narrowness of life reaches its maximum among the women: thirteen hundred and fifty of these are farm laborers, one hundred are servants and washerwomen, leaving sixty-five housewives, eight teachers, and six seamstresses.

Among this people there is no leisure class. We often forget that in the United States over half the youth and adults are not in the world earning incomes, but are making homes, learning of the world, or resting after the heat of the strife. But here ninety-six per cent are toiling; no one with leisure to turn the bare and cheerless cabin into a home, no old folks to sit beside the fire and hand down traditions of the past; little of careless happy childhood and dreaming youth. The dull monotony of daily toil is broken only by the gayety of the thoughtless and the Saturday trip to town. The toil, like all farm toil, is monotonous, and here there are little machinery and few tools to relieve its burdensome drudgery. But with all this, it is work in the pure open air, and this is something in a day when fresh air is scarce.

The land on the whole is still fertile, despite long abuse. For nine or ten months in succession the crops will come if asked: garden vegetables in April, grain in May, melons in June and July, hay in August, sweet potatoes in September, and cotton from then to Christmas. And yet on two-thirds of the land there is but one crop, and that leaves the toilers in debt. Why is this?

Away down the Baysan road, where the broad flat fields are flanked by great oak forests, is a plantation; many thousands of acres it used to run, here and there, and beyond the great wood. Thirteen hundred human beings here obeyed the call of one,—were his in body, and largely in soul. One of them lives there yet,—a short, stocky man, his dull-brown face seamed and drawn, and his tightly curled hair gray-white. The crops? Just tolerable, he said; just tolerable. Getting on? No—he wasn't getting on at all. Smith of Albany "furnishes" him, and his rent is eight hundred pounds of cotton. Can't make anything at that. Why didn't he buy land! *Humph!* Takes money to buy land. And he turns away. Free! The most piteous thing amid all the black ruin of war-time, amid the broken fortunes of the masters, the blighted hopes of mothers and maidens, and the fall of an empire,—the most piteous thing amid all this was the black freedman who threw down his hoe because the world called him free. What did such a mockery of freedom mean? Not a cent of money, not an inch of land, not a mouthful of victuals,—not even ownership of the rags on his back. Free! On Saturday, once or twice a month, the old master, before the war, used to dole out bacon and meal to his Negroes. And after the first flush of freedom wore off, and his true helplessness dawned on the freedman, he came back and picked up his hoe, and old master still doled out his bacon and meal. The legal form of service was theoretically far different; in practice, task-work or "cropping" was substituted for daily toil in gangs; and the slave gradually became a metayer, or tenant on shares, in name, but a laborer with indeterminate wages in fact.

Still the price of cotton fell, and gradually the landlords deserted their plantations, and the reign of the merchant began. The merchant of the Black Belt is a curious institution,—part banker, part landlord, part banker, and part despot. His store, which used most frequently to stand at the cross-roads and become the centre of a weekly village, has now moved to town; and thither the Negro tenant follows him. The merchant keeps everything,—clothes and shoes, coffee and sugar, pork and meal, canned and dried goods, wagons and ploughs, seed and fertilizer,—and what he has not in stock he can give you an order for at the store across the way. Here, then, comes the tenant, Sam Scott, after he has contracted with some absent landlord's agent for hiring forty acres of land; he fingers his hat nervously until the merchant finishes his morning chat with Colonel Saunders, and calls out, "Well, Sam, what do you want?" Sam wants him to "furnish" him,—i.e., to advance him food and clothing for the year, and perhaps seed and tools, until his crop is raised and sold. If Sam seems a favorable subject, he and the merchant go to a lawyer, and Sam executes a chattel mortgage on his mule and wagon in return for seed and a week's rations. As soon as the green cotton-leaves appear above the ground, another mortgage is given on the "crop." Every Saturday, or at longer intervals, Sam calls upon the merchant for his "rations"; a family of five usually gets about thirty pounds of fat side-pork and a couple of bushels of cornmeal a month. Besides this, clothing and shoes must be furnished; if Sam or his family is sick, there are orders on the druggist and doctor; if the mule wants shoeing, an order on the blacksmith, etc. If Sam is a hard worker and crops promise well, he is often encouraged to buy more,—sugar, extra clothes, perhaps a buggy. But he is seldom encouraged to save. When cotton rose to ten cents last fall, the shrewd merchants of Dougherty County sold a thousand buggies in one season, mostly to black men.

The security offered for such transactions—a crop and chattel mortgage—may at first seem slight. And, indeed, the merchants tell many a true tale of shiftlessness and cheating; of cotton picked at night, mules disappearing, and tenants absconding. But on the whole the merchant of the Black Belt is the most prosperous man in the section. So skilfully and so closely has he drawn the bonds of the law about the tenant, that the black man has often simply to choose between pauperism and crime; he "waives" all homestead exemptions in his contract; he cannot touch his own mortgaged crop, which the laws put almost in the full control of the land-owner and of the merchant. When the crop is growing the merchant watches it like a hawk; as soon as it is ready for market he takes possession of it, sells it, pays the landowner his rent, subtracts his bill for supplies, and if, as sometimes happens, there is anything left, he hands it over to the black serf for his Christmas celebration.

The direct result of this system is an all-cotton scheme of agriculture and the continued bankruptcy of the tenant. The currency of the Black Belt is cotton. It is a crop always salable for ready money, not usually subject to great yearly fluctuations in price, and one which the Negroes know how to raise. The landlord therefore demands his rent in cotton, and the merchant will accept mortgages on no other crop. There is no use asking the black tenant, then, to diversify his crops,—he cannot under this system. Moreover, the system is bound to bankrupt the tenant. I remember once meeting a little one-mule wagon on the River road. A young black fellow sat in it driving listlessly, his elbows on his knees. His dark-faced wife sat beside him, stolid, silent.

"Hello!" cried my driver,—he has a most imprudent way of addressing these people, though they seem used to it,—"what have you got there?"

"Meat and meal," answered the man, stopping. The meat lay uncovered in the bottom of the wagon,—a great thin side of fat pork covered with salt; the meal was in a white bushel bag.

"What did you pay for that meat?"

"Ten cents a pound." It could have been bought for six or seven cents cash.

"And the meal?"

"Two dollars." One dollar and ten cents is the cash price in town. Here was a man paying five dollars for goods which he could have bought for three dollars cash, and raised for one dollar or one dollar and a half.

Yet it is not wholly his fault. The Negro farmer started behind,—started in debt. This was not his choosing, but the crime of this happy-go-lucky nation which goes blundering along with its Reconstruction tragedies, its Spanish war interludes and Philippine matinees, just as though God really were dead. Once in debt, it is no easy matter for a whole race to emerge.

In the year of low-priced cotton, 1898, out of three hundred tenant families one hundred and seventy-five ended their year's work in debt to the extent of fourteen thousand dollars; fifty cleared nothing, and the remaining seventy-five made a total profit of sixteen hundred dollars. The net indebtedness of the black tenant families of the whole county must have been at least sixty thousand dollars. In a more prosperous year the situation is far better; but on the average the majority of tenants end the year even, or in debt, which means that they work for board and clothes. Such an economic organization is radically wrong. Whose is the blame?

The underlying causes of this situation are complicated but discernible. And one of the chief, outside the carelessness of the nation in letting the slave start with nothing, is the widespread opinion among the merchants and employers of the Black Belt that only by the slavery of debt can the Negro be kept at work. Without doubt, some pressure was necessary at the beginning of the free-labor system to keep the listless and lazy at work; and even to-day the mass of the Negro laborers need stricter guardianship than most Northern laborers. Behind this honest and widespread opinion dishonesty and cheating of the ignorant laborers have a good chance to take refuge. And to all this must be added the obvious fact that a slave ancestry and a system of unrequited toil has not improved the efficiency or temper of the mass of black laborers. Nor is this peculiar to Sambo; it has in history been just as true of John and Hans, of Jacques and Pat, of all ground-down peasantries. Such is the situation of the mass of the Negroes in the Black Belt to-day; and they are thinking about it. Crime, and a cheap and dangerous socialism, are the inevitable results of this pondering. I see now that ragged black man sitting on a log, aimlessly whittling a stick. He muttered to me with the murmur of many ages, when he said: "White man sit down whole year; Nigger work day and night and make crop; Nigger hardly gits bread and meat; white man sittin' down gits all. *It's wrong.*" And what do the better classes of Negroes do to improve their situation? One of two things: if any way possible, they buy land; if not, they migrate to town. Just as centuries ago it was no easy thing for the serf to escape into the freedom of town-life, even so to-day there are hindrances laid in the way of county laborers. In considerable parts of all the Gulf States, and especially in Mississippi, Louisiana, and Arkansas, the Negroes on the plantations in the back-country districts are still held at forced labor practically without wages. Especially is this true in districts where the farmers are composed of the more ignorant class of poor whites, and the Negroes are beyond the reach of schools and intercourse with their advancing fellows. If such a peon should run away, the sheriff, elected by white suffrage, can usually be depended on to catch the fugitive, return him, and ask no questions. If he escape to another county, a charge of petty thieving, easily true, can be depended upon to secure his return. Even if some unduly officious person insist upon a trial, neighborly comity will probably make his conviction sure, and then the labor due the county can easily be bought by the master. Such a system is impossible in the more civilized parts of the South, or near the large towns and cities; but in those vast stretches of land beyond the telegraph and the newspaper the spirit of the Thirteenth Amendment is sadly broken. This represents the lowest economic depths of the black American peasant; and in a study of the rise and condition of the Negro freeholder we must trace his economic progress from the modern serfdom.

Even in the better-ordered country districts of the South the free movement of agricultural laborers is hindered by the migration-agent laws. The "Associated Press" recently informed the world of the arrest of a young white man in Southern Georgia who represented the "Atlantic Naval Supplies Company," and who "was caught in the act of enticing hands from the turpentine farm of Mr. John Greer." The crime for which this young man was arrested is taxed five hundred dollars for each county in which the employment agent proposes to gather laborers for work outside the State. Thus the Negroes' ignorance of the labor-market outside his own vicinity is increased rather than diminished by the laws of nearly every Southern State.

Similar to such measures is the unwritten law of the back districts and small towns of the South, that the character of all Negroes unknown to the mass of the community must be vouched for by some white man. This is really a revival of the old Roman idea of the patron under whose protection the new-made freedman was put. In many instances this system has been of great good to the Negro, and very often under the protection and guidance of the former master's family, or other white friends, the freedman progressed in wealth and morality. But the same system has in other cases resulted in the refusal of whole communities to recognize the right of a Negro to change his habitation and to be master of his own fortunes. A black stranger in Baker County, Georgia, for instance, is liable to be stopped anywhere on the public highway and made to state his business to the satisfaction of any white interrogator. If he fails to give a suitable answer, or seems too independent or "sassy," he may be arrested or summarily driven away.

Thus it is that in the country districts of the South, by written or unwritten law, peonage, hindrances to the migration of labor, and a system of white patronage exists over large areas. Besides this, the chance for lawless oppression and illegal exactions is vastly greater in the country than in the city, and nearly all the more serious race disturbances of the last decade have arisen from disputes in the count between master and man,—as, for instance, the Sam Hose affair. As a result of such a situation, there arose, first, the Black Belt; and, second, the Migration to Town. The Black Belt was not, as many assumed, a movement toward fields of labor under more genial climatic conditions; it was primarily a huddling for self-protection,—a massing of the black population for mutual defence in order to secure the peace and tranquillity necessary to economic advance. This movement took place between Emancipation and 1880, and only partially accomplished the desired results. The rush to town since 1880 is the counter-movement of men disappointed in the economic opportunities of the Black Belt.

In Dougherty County, Georgia, one can see easily the results of this experiment in huddling for protection. Only ten per cent of the adult population was born in the county, and yet the blacks outnumber the whites four or five to one. There is undoubtedly a security to the blacks in their very numbers,—a personal freedom from arbitrary treatment, which makes hundreds of laborers cling to Dougherty in spite of low wages and economic distress. But a change is coming, and slowly but surely even here the agricultural laborers are drifting to town and leaving the broad acres behind. Why is this? Why do not the Negroes become land-owners, and build up the black landed peasantry, which has for a generation and more been the dream of philanthropist and statesman?

To the car-window sociologist, to the man who seeks to understand and know the South by devoting the few leisure hours of a holiday trip to unravelling the snarl of centuries,—to such men very often the whole trouble with the black field-hand may be summed up by Aunt Ophelia's word, "Shiftless!" They have noted repeatedly scenes like one I saw last summer. We were riding along the highroad to town at the close of a long hot day. A couple of young black fellows passed us in a mule-team, with several bushels of loose corn in the ear. One was driving, listlessly bent forward, his elbows on his knees,—a happy-go-lucky, careless picture of irresponsibility. The other was fast asleep in the bottom of the wagon. As we passed we noticed an ear of corn fall from the wagon. They never saw it,—not they. A rod farther on we noted another ear on the ground; and between that creeping mule and town we counted twenty-six ears of corn. Shiftless? Yes, the personification of shiftlessness. And yet follow those boys: they are not lazy; to-morrow morning they'll be up with the sun; they work hard when they do work, and they work willingly. They have no sordid, selfish, money-getting ways, but rather a fine disdain for mere cash. They'll loaf before your face and work behind your back with good-natured honesty. They'll steal a watermelon, and hand you back your lost purse intact. Their great defect as laborers lies in their lack of incentive beyond the mere pleasure of physical exertion. They are careless because they have not found that it pays to be careful; they are improvident because the improvident ones of their acquaintance get on about as well as the provident. Above all, they cannot see why they should take unusual pains to make the white man's land better, or to fatten his mule, or save his corn. On the other hand, the white land-owner argues that any attempt to improve these laborers by increased responsibility, or higher wages, or better homes, or land of their own, would be sure to result in failure. He shows his Northern visitor the scarred and wretched land; the ruined mansions, the worn-out soil and mortgaged acres, and says, This is Negro freedom!

Now it happens that both master and man have just enough argument on their respective sides to make it difficult for them to understand each other. The Negro dimly personifies in the white man all his ills and misfortunes; if he is poor, it is because the white man seizes the fruit of his toil; if he is ignorant, it is because the white man gives him neither time nor facilities to learn; and, indeed, if any misfortune happens to him, it is because of some hidden machinations of "white folks." On the other hand, the masters and the masters' sons have never been able to see why the Negro, instead of settling down to be day-laborers for bread and clothes, are infected with a silly desire to rise in the world, and why they are sulky, dissatisfied, and careless, where their fathers were happy and dumb and faithful. "Why, you niggers have an easier time than I do," said a puzzled Albany merchant to his black customer. "Yes," he replied, "and so does yo' hogs."

Taking, then, the dissatisfied and shiftless field-hand as a starting-point, let us inquire how the black thousands of Dougherty have struggled from him up toward their ideal, and what that ideal is. All social struggle is evidenced by the rise, first of economic, then of social classes, among a homogeneous population. To-day the following economic classes are plainly differentiated among these Negroes.

A "submerged tenth" of croppers, with a few paupers; forty per cent who are metayers and thirty-nine per cent of semi-metayers and wage-laborers. There are left five per cent of money-renters and six per cent of freeholders,—the "Upper Ten" of the land. The croppers are entirely without capital, even in the limited sense of food or money to keep them from seed-time to harvest. All they furnish is their labor; the land-owner furnishes land, stock, tools, seed, and house; and at the end of the year the laborer gets from a third to a half of the crop. Out of his share, however, comes pay and interest for food and clothing advanced him during the year. Thus we have a laborer without capital and without wages, and an employer whose capital is largely his employees' wages. It is an unsatisfactory arrangement, both for hirer and hired, and is usually in vogue on poor land with hard-pressed owners.

Above the croppers come the great mass of the black population who work the land on their own responsibility, paying rent in cotton and supported by the crop-mortgage system. After the war this system was attractive to the freedmen on account of its larger freedom and its possibility for making a surplus. But with the carrying out of the crop-lien system, the deterioration of the land, and the slavery of debt, the position of the metayers has sunk to a dead level of practically unrewarded toil. Formerly all tenants had some capital, and often considerable; but absentee landlordism, rising rack-rent, and failing cotton have stripped them well-nigh of all, and probably not over half of them to-day own their mules. The change from cropper to tenant was accomplished by fixing the rent. If, now, the rent fixed was reasonable, this was an incentive to the tenant to strive. On the other hand, if the rent was too high, or if the land deteriorated, the result was to discourage and check the efforts of the black peasantry. There is no doubt that the latter case is true; that in Dougherty County every economic advantage of the price of cotton in market and of the strivings of the tenant has been taken advantage of by the landlords and merchants, and swallowed up in rent and interest. If cotton rose in price, the rent rose even higher; if cotton fell, the rent remained or followed reluctantly. If the tenant worked hard and raised a large crop, his rent was raised the next year; if that year the crop failed, his corn was confiscated and his mule sold for debt. There were, of course, exceptions to this,—cases of personal kindness and forbearance; but in the vast majority of cases the rule was to extract the uttermost farthing from the mass of the black farm laborers.

The average metayer pays from twenty to thirty per cent of his crop in rent. The result of such rack-rent can only be evil,—abuse and neglect of the soil, deterioration in the character of the laborers, and a widespread sense of injustice. "Wherever the country is poor," cried Arthur Young, "it is in the hands of metayers," and "their condition is more wretched than that of day-laborers." He was talking of Italy a century ago; but he might have been talking of Dougherty County to-day. And especially is that true to-day which he declares was true in France before the Revolution: "The metayers are considered as little better than menial servants, removable at pleasure, and obliged to conform in all things to the will of the landlords." On this low plane half the black population of Dougherty County—perhaps more than half the black millions of this land—are to-day struggling.

A degree above these we may place those laborers who receive money wages for their work. Some receive a house with perhaps a garden-spot;

then supplies of food and clothing are advanced, and certain fixed wages are given at the end of the year, varying from thirty to sixty dollars, out of which the supplies must be paid for, with interest. About eighteen per cent of the population belong to this class of semi-metayers, while twenty-two per cent are laborers paid by the month or year, and are either "furnished" by their own savings or perhaps more usually by some merchant who takes his chances of payment. Such laborers receive from thirty-five to fifty cents a day during the working season. They are usually young unmarried persons, some being women; and when they marry they sink to the class of metayers, or, more seldom, become renters.

The renters for fixed money rentals are the first of the emerging classes, and form five per cent of the families. The sole advantage of this small class is their freedom to choose their crops, and the increased responsibility which comes through having money transactions. While some of the renters differ little in condition from the metayers, yet on the whole they are more intelligent and responsible persons, and are the ones who eventually become land-owners. Their better character and greater shrewdness enable them to gain, perhaps to demand, better terms in rents; rented farms, varying from forty to a hundred acres, bear an average rental of about fifty-four dollars a year. The men who conduct such farms do not long remain renters; either they sink to metayers, or with a successful series of harvests rise to be land-owners.

In 1870 the tax-books of Dougherty report no Negroes as landholders. If there were any such at that time,—and there may have been a few,—their land was probably held in the name of some white patron,—a method not uncommon during slavery. In 1875 ownership of land had begun with seven hundred and fifty acres; ten years later this had increased to over sixty-five hundred acres, to nine thousand acres in 1890 and ten thousand in 1900. The total assessed property has in this same period risen from eighty thousand dollars in 1875 to two hundred and forty thousand dollars in 1900.

Two circumstances complicate this development and make it in some respects difficult to be sure of the real tendencies; they are the panic of 1893, and the low price of cotton in 1898. Besides this, the system of assessing property in the country districts of Georgia is somewhat antiquated and of uncertain statistical value; there are no assessors, and each man makes a sworn return to a tax-receiver. Thus public opinion plays a large part, and the returns vary strangely from year to year. Certainly these figures show the small amount of accumulated capital among the Negroes, and the consequent large dependence of their property on temporary prosperity. They have little to tide over a few years of economic depression, and are at the mercy of the cotton-market far more than the whites. And thus the land-owners, despite their marvellous efforts, are really a transient class, continually being depleted by those who fall back into the class of renters or metayers, and augmented by newcomers from the masses. Of one hundred land-owners in 1898, half had bought their land since 1893, a fourth between 1890 and 1893, a fifth between 1884 and 1890, and the rest between 1870 and 1884. In all, one hundred and eighty-five Negroes have owned land in this county since 1875.

If all the black land-owners who had ever held land here had kept it or left it in the hands of black men, the Negroes would have owned nearer thirty thousand acres than the fifteen thousand they now hold. And yet these fifteen thousand acres are a creditable showing,—a proof of no little weight of the worth and ability of the Negro people. If they had been given an economic start at Emancipation, if they had been in an enlightened and rich community which really desired their best good, then we might perhaps call such a result small or even insignificant. But for a few thousand poor ignorant field-hands, in the face of poverty, a falling market, and social stress, to save and capitalize two hundred thousand dollars in a generation has meant a tremendous effort. The rise of a nation, the pressing forward of a social class, means a bitter struggle, a hard and soul-sickening battle with the world such as few of the more favored classes know or appreciate.

Out of the hard economic conditions of this portion of the Black Belt, only six per cent of the population have succeeded in emerging into peasant proprietorship; and these are not all firmly fixed, but grow and shrink in number with the wavering of the cotton-market. Fully ninety-four per cent have struggled for land and failed, and half of them sit in hopeless serfdom. For these there is one other avenue of escape toward which they have turned in increasing numbers, namely, migration to town. A glance at the distribution of land among the black owners curiously reveals this fact. In 1898 the holdings were as follows: Under forty acres, forty-nine families; forty to two hundred and fifty acres, seventeen families; two hundred and fifty to one thousand acres, thirteen families; one thousand or more acres, two families. Now in 1890 there were forty-four holdings, but only nine of these were under forty acres. The great increase of holdings, then, has come in the buying of small homesteads near town, where their owners really share in the town life; this is a part of the rush to town. And for every land-owner who has thus hurried away from the narrow and hard conditions of country life, how many field-hands, how many tenants, how many ruined renters, have joined that long procession? Is it not strange compensation? The sin of the country districts is visited on the town, and the social sores of city life to-day may, here in Dougherty County, and perhaps in many places near and far, look for their final healing without the city walls.

SECTION IV

EXPLORING THE CONSEQUENCES OF INEQUALITY

Andrew Hacker
  Two Nations, "Being Black in America" (1992)
The Kerner Commission
  "Report of the National Advisory Commission on Civil
  Disorders" (1968)
Karl Marx & Friedrich Engels
  The Communist Manifesto (1848)
D. Stanley Eitzen
  "The Fragmentation of Social Life" (2000)

There is a large—albeit controversial—literature tying poverty to a wide range of social ills, from criminal behavior and teen pregnancy to shortened lifespan and reduced educational attainment. Ideological differences aside, most people would agree that poverty is an undesirable state of affairs and one to be assiduously avoided. The same cannot be said of inequality, the consequences of which are at least as difficult to identify as the causes. The harmful effects of inequality are not obvious to most people, and too much talk of equality makes many in our fiercely individualistic society a bit uncomfortable. It is hardly surprising that there is so little national interest in reducing inequality.

In some cases, the causes and consequences of inequality appear to be inextricably linked. For example, to the extent that social stratification serves an important function in societies, the article by Davis and Moore (see Section III) could just as easily have been located in this section. If racial discrimination contributes to the disadvantaged position of blacks in our society, it is probably also true that the disproportionate representation of blacks among the lower strata of our society reinforces the prejudice and bigotry that fuels discrimination. Hacker's essay, which follows nicely on the heels of Du Bois's, provides a compelling perspective for white readers and will almost surely produce some level of discomfort among all readers. The Kerner Commission Report, which describes the urban violence that gripped the nation during the height of the Civil Rights Movement, provides a riveting analysis of the causes of this unrest. Considerable attention is devoted to disparities in wealth and power between white and blacks. The suggestion that political violence might flow from class conflict has important roots in the work of Marx and Engels, whose ideas influenced global politics for much of the twentieth century. The final selection by Eitzen addresses the consequences of reduced societal cohesion, one component of which is increasing inequality. His conclusion that we need to become more accepting of our differences or face continued fragmentation ends the book on an ominous, though perhaps hopeful, note.

Andrew Hacker

1929-

Two Nations: Black and White, Separate, Hostile, Unequal
1992

Andrew Hacker, an American social scientist with a background in political science, psychology, and sociology, specializes in the study of race, class, and gender relations. Born in New York City, he taught at Cornell University from 1955 to 1971, after which time he joined the faculty of Queens College, City University of New York (CUNY), where he currently holds the position of professor emeritus of political science.

Hacker did his undergraduate work at Amherst College, where he received the Robert Frost Fork Award, presented to the student "who had done the most to promote academics" on the campus. He received his Master's degree from Oxford University and his doctorate from Princeton University.

The author of ten books, Hacker has published articles in such peer-reviewed journals as *The American Political Science Review*, *Yale Law Journal*, *Contemporary Sociology*, and *The International Journal of Social Psychiatry*. His writing has also appeared broadly in the popular press, from *The New York Review of Books*, the *Wall Street Journal*, and the *Chronicle of Higher Education* to *Atlantic Monthly*, *Commentary*, and *New York Times Magazine*.

In 1968, the members of the National Advisory Commission on Civil Disorders, also known as the Kerner Commission, famously concluded that "Our nation is moving toward two societies, one black, one white—separate and unequal." Writing 24 years later, Hacker's assessment of race relations in *Two Nations: Black and White, Separate, Hostile, Unequal* argued that blacks and whites remained "dangerously far apart in their ability to participate fully in the American Dream."

In *Two Nations,* Hacker (1992, 19) attributes the persistence of racial attitudes to that fact that they arise from "outlooks and assumptions of which we are largely unaware" and suggests that blacks and whites experience our society in very different ways. Hacker, himself white, points out that:

> Most whites will protest that they bear neither responsibility nor blame for the conditions blacks face. Neither they nor their forebears ever owned slaves, nor can they see themselves as having held anyone back or down. Most white Americans believe that for at least the last generation blacks have been given more than a fair chance and at least equal opportunity, if not outright advantage. (4)

If Hacker is right, this may explain why some whites believe that blacks who are unemployed, impoverished, or homeless are themselves responsible for their own circumstances, victims of choices that they themselves have made.

Do blacks, in fact, perceive the world differently than whites, seeing obstacles where whites see opportunities? Do black children—many of whom grow up in single-parent households with fewer economic resources than their white counterparts—have difficulty reconciling their own personal experiences with the notion that America is the land of opportunity? Do white children, taught from an early age that "hard work results in success" and that "in this country, anyone can grow up to be president," understand that the environment in which you're raised can hold you back as well as propel you forward? Is Barry Switzer's quip that "Some people are born on third base and go through life thinking they hit a triple" closer to the truth than some of us are comfortable admitting?

Hacker (1992, 60) writes:

> It will be proposed here that all white Americans, regardless of their political persuasions, are well aware of how black people have suffered due to inequities imposed upon them by white America . . . . Yet white people who disavow responsibility deny an everyday reality: that to be black is to be consigned to

the margins of American life. It is because of this that no white American, including those who insist that opportunities exist for persons of every race, would change places with even the most successful black American. All white Americans realize that their skin comprises an inestimable asset. It opens doors and facilitates freedom of movement.

In a just society, Rawls (1971) expects rights to be more evenly distributed. His argument, in a nutshell, proceeds as follows: if your place in society—for example, whether you are black or white, old or young, male or female—is going to be determined by a throw of the dice and you had to agree to the "rules of the game" before throwing those dice, most people would choose rules that are fair and do not disadvantage particular individuals or groups within society. Hacker's observation that no white American would willingly trade places with even the most successful black American would, in Rawls' view, suggest that our society is lacking in social justice.

In the reading that follows, Hacker asks you to imagine what it would be like to be a member of a racial minority in a society characterized by significant economic and social inequality. Consider whether, and to what extent, Friedman might be willing to support a public policy solution to the problems of inequality and discrimination. What about you? Would you support such a remedy?

Selection From:

Hacker, A. (1992). *Two Nations: black and white, separate, hostile, unequal.* New York: Charles Scribner's Sons. 39-49.

Two Nations

[***]

Except when you are in your own neighborhood, you feel always on display. On many occasions, you find you are the only person of your race present. You may be the only black student in a college classroom, the only black on a jury, the sole black at a corporate meeting, the only one at a social gathering. With luck, there may be one or two others. You feel every eye is on you, and you are not clear what posture to present. You realize that your presence makes whites uncomfortable; most of them

probably wish you were not there at all. But since you are, they want to
see you smile, so they can believe that you are being treated well. Not
only is an upbeat air expected, but you must never show exasperation or
anger, let alone anything that could look like a chip on your shoulder. Not
everyone can keep such tight control. You don't find it surprising that so
many black athletes and entertainers seek relief from those tensions.

Even when not in white company, you know that you are forever in
their conversations. Ralph Ellison once said that to whites, you are an
"invisible man." You know what he meant. Yet for all that, you and your
people have been studied and scrutinized and dissected, caricatured, and
pitied or deplored, as no other group ever has. You see yourself reduced to
data in research, statistics in reports. Each year, the nation asks how many
of your teenagers have become pregnant, how many of your young men are
in prison. Not only are you continually on view; you are always on trial.

What we have come to call the media looms large in the lives of
almost all Americans. Television and films, newspapers and magazines,
books and advertising, all serve as windows on a wider world, providing
real and fantasized images of the human experience. The media also help
us to fill out our own identities, telling us about ourselves, or the selves
we might like to be.

If you are black, most of what is available for you to read and
watch and hear depicts the activities of white people, with only rare and
incidental allusions to persons like yourself. Black topics and authors and
performers appear even less than your share of the population, not least
because the rest of America doesn't care to know about you. Whites will
be quick to point out that there have been successful "black" programs on
radio and television, as well as popular black entertainers and best-selling
authors. Yet in these and other instances, it is whites who decide which
people and productions will be underwritten, which almost always usually
means that "black" projects will have to appeal to whites as well. You
sometimes sense that much that is "black" is missing in artists like Jessye
Norman and Toni Morrison, Paul Robeson, and Bill Cosby, who you
sense must tailor their talents to white audiences. You often find yourself
wishing they could just be themselves, among their own people.

At the same time, you feel frustration and disgust when white America
appropriates your music, your styles, indeed your speech and sexuality.
At times, white audiences will laud the originality of black artists and
performers and athletes. But in the end, they feel more comfortable when
white musicians and designers and writers—and athletic coaches—adapt
black talents to white sensibilities.

Add to this your bemusement when movies and television series cast more blacks as physicians and attorneys and executives than one will ever find in actual hospitals or law firms or corporations. True, these depictions can serve as role models for your children, encouraging their aspirations. At the same time, you do not want white audiences to conclude that since so many of your people seem to be doing well, little more needs to be done.

Then there are those advertisements showing groups of people. Yes, one of them may be black, although not too black, and always looking happy to be in white company. Still, these blacks are seldom in the front row, or close to the center. Even worse, you think you have detected a recent trend: in advertisements that include a person of color, you see Asians being used instead of blacks.

To be sure, textbooks and lesson plans now include allusions to "contributions" made by Americans of many ancestries. Children are taught how the Chinese built the railroads, and that Hispanics have a vibrant and varied culture. Even acknowledging these nods, the curriculums of the nation's schools and colleges focus mainly on the achievements of white people . . . .

[***]

Whether you would like to know more white people is not an easy question to answer. So many of the contacts you have with them are stiff and uneasy, hardly worth the effort. If you are a woman, you may have developed some cordial acquaintances among white women at your place of work, since women tend to be more relaxed when among themselves. Still, very few black men and women can say that they have white "friends," if by that is meant people they confide in or entertain in their homes.

Of course, friendships often grow out of shared experiences. People with similar backgrounds can take certain things for granted when with one another. In this respect, you and white people may not have very much in common. At the same time, by no means all your outlooks and interests relate to your race. There probably are at least a few white people you would like to know better. It just might be that some of them would like to know you. But as matters now stand, the chances that these barriers will be broken do not appear to be very great.

Societies create vocabularies, devising new terms when they are needed, and retaining old ones when they serve a purpose. Dictionaries list words as obsolete or archaic, denoting that they are no longer used or heard. But one epithet survives, because people want it to. Your vulnerability to humiliation can be summed up in a single word. That word, of course, is "nigger."

When a white person voices it, it becomes a knife with a whetted edge. No black person can hear it with equanimity or ignore it as "simply a word." This word has the force to pierce, to wound, to penetrate, as no other has. There have, of course, been terms like "kike" and "spic" and "chink." But these are less frequently heard today, and they lack the same emotional impact. Some nonethnic terms come closer, such as "slut" and "fag" and "cripple." Yet, "nigger" stands alone with its power to tear at one's insides. It is revealing that whites have never created so wrenching an epithet for even the most benighted members of their own race.

Black people may use "nigger" among themselves, but with a tone and intention that is known and understood. Even so, if you are black, you know white society devised this word and keeps it available for use. (Not officially, of course, or even in print; but you know it continues to be uttered behind closed doors.) Its persistence reminds you that you are still perceived as a degraded species of humanity, a level to which whites can never descend.

You and your people have problems, far more than your share. And it is not as if you are ignorant of them, or wish to sweep them under a rug. But how to frame your opinions is not an easy matter. For example, what should you say about black crime or addiction or out-of-wedlock pregnancies? Of course, you have much to say on these and other topics, and you certainly express your ideas when you are among your own people. And you can be critical—very critical—of a lot of behavior you agree has become common among blacks.

However, the white world also asks that black people conduct these discussions in public. In particular, they want to hear you condemn black figures they regard as outrageous or irresponsible. This cannot help but annoy you. For one thing, you have never asked for white advice. Yet whites seem to feel that you stand in need of their tutelage, as if you lack the insight to understand your own interests. Moreover, it makes sense for members of a minority to stand together, especially since so many whites delight in magnifying differences among blacks. Your people have had a long history of being divided and conquered. At the same time, you have no desire to be held responsible for what every person of your color thinks or does. You cannot count how many times you have been asked to atone for some utterances of Louis Farrakhan, or simply to assert that he does not speak for you. You want to retort that you will choose your own causes and laments. Like other Americans, you have no obligation to follow agendas set by others.

As it happens, black Americans can and do disagree on racial matters, not to mention a host of other issues. Thus a survey conducted in 1990 found that 78 percent of those polled said they preferred to think of themselves as "black," and another 20 percent chose "African-American," while the remaining 2 percent stayed with "Negro." Another study by a team of black social scientists found that less than a quarter of the blacks they polled felt that black parents should give their children African names. Indeed, on a wide range of matters, there is no fixed, let alone official, black position. Yet it is amazing how often white people ask you to tell them how "black people" think about some individual or issue.

Then there are the accusations of inconsistency. As when you seem to favor taking race into consideration in some areas, but not in others. Or that you support a double standard, which allows separate criteria to be used for blacks in employment or education. Well, as it happens, you do believe:

- That discrimination against blacks remains real and calls for radical remedies; yet you cannot take seriously the argument that these compensatory actions will cause whites to suffer from "reverse" discrimination.
- That blacks have every right to attend dominantly white schools; yet once they are there, they should not be taken to task for spending much of their time with classmates of their own race.
- That it is important to preserve historically black colleges; yet you would feel entitled to object if some other schools were to designate themselves as "historically white."
- That racism is often the key reason why white voters rally behind white candidates; yet when blacks support a candidate of their own race, you do not see this as expressing racism.
- That while you reject censorship, you would prefer that a book like *Huckleberry Finn* not be assigned in high school classes, since its ubiquitous use of "nigger" sustains a view of blacks that can only hurt your people. Nor are you persuaded that the typical teacher can make clear Mark Twain's intentions, or put them in perspective, for white teenagers.

It will often seem to you as if black people's opinions are constantly under scrutiny by the white world. Every time you express an opinion, whites seem to slap it on their dissecting table, showing that blacks want the best of both ways. In fact, you have answers on these issues, but whites take so much delight in citing alleged "inconsistencies" that they hardly hear what you have to say.

You may, by a combination of brains and luck and perseverance, make it into the middle class. And like all middle-class Americans, you will want to enjoy the comforts and pleasures that come with that status. One downside is that you will find many white people asking why you aren't doing more to help members of your race whom you have supposedly left behind. There is even the suggestion that, by moving to a safer or more spacious area, you have callously deserted your own people.

Yet hardly ever do middle-class whites reflect on the fact that they, too, have moved to better neighborhoods, usually far from poorer and less equable persons of their own race or ethnic origins. There is little evidence that middle-class whites are prepared to give much of themselves in aid of fellow whites who have fallen on misfortune. Indeed, the majority of white Americans have chosen to live in sequestered suburbs, where they are insulated from the nation's losers and failures.

Compounding these expectations, you find yourself continually subjected to comparisons with other minorities or even members of your own race. For example, you are informed that blacks who have emigrated from the Caribbean earn higher incomes than those born in the United States. Here the message seems to be that color by itself is not an insurmountable barrier. Most stinging of all are contrasts with recent immigrants. You hear people just off the boat (or, nowadays, a plane) extolled for building businesses and becoming productive citizens. Which is another way of asking why you haven't matched their achievements, considering how long your people have been here.

Moreover, immigrants are praised for being willing to start at the bottom. The fact that so many of them manage to find jobs is taken as evidence that the economy still has ample opportunities for employment. You want to reply that you are not an immigrant, but as much a citizen as any white person born here. Perhaps you can't match the mathematical skills of a teenager from Korea, but then neither can most white kids at suburban high schools. You feel much like a child being chided because she has not done as well as a precocious sister. However, you are an adult, and do not find such scolding helpful or welcome.

No law of humanity or nature posits a precise format for the family. Throughout history and even in our day, households have had many shapes and structures. The same strictures apply to marriage and parental relationships. All this requires some emphasis, given concerns expressed about "the black family" and its presumed disintegration. In fact, the last several decades have seen a weakening of domestic ties in all classes and races.

Black Americans are fully aware of what is happening in this sphere. They know that most black children are being born out of wedlock and that these youngsters will spend most of their growing years with a single parent. They understand that a majority of their marriages will dissolve in separation or divorce, and that many black men and women will never marry at all. Black Americans also realize that tensions between men and women sometimes bear a violence and bitterness that can take an awful toll.

If you are black, you soon learn it is safest to make peace with reality: to acknowledge that the conditions of your time can undercut dreams of enduring romance and "happily ever after." This is especially true if you are a black woman, since you may find yourself spending many of your years without a man in your life. Of course, you will survive and adapt, as your people always have. Central in this effort will be joining and sustaining a community of women—another form of a family—on whom you can rely for love and strength and support.

If you are a black woman, you can expect to live five fewer years than your white counterpart. Among men, the gap is seven years. Indeed, a man living in New York's Harlem is less likely to reach sixty-five than is a resident of Bangladesh. Black men have a three times greater chance of dying of AIDS, and outnumber whites as murder victims by a factor of seven. According to studies, you get less sleep, are more likely to be overweight, and to develop hypertension. This is not simply due to poverty. Your shorter and more painful life results, in considerable measure, from the anxieties that come with being black in America.

If you are a black young man, life can be an interlude with an early demise. Black youths do what they must to survive in a hostile world, with the prospect of violence and death on its battlefields. Attitudes can turn fatalistic, even suicidal: gladiators without even the cheers of an audience.

When white people hear the cry, "the police are coming!" for them it almost always means, "help is on the way." Black citizens cannot make the same assumption. If you have been the victim of a crime, you cannot presume that the police will actually show up; or, if they do, that they will take much note of your losses or suffering. You sense police officials feel that blacks should accept being robbed or raped as one of life's everyday risks. It seems to you obvious that more detectives are assigned to a case when a white person is murdered.

If you are black and young and a man, the arrival of the police does not usually signify help, but something very different. If you are a teenager simply socializing with some friends, the police may order you to disperse and get off the streets. They may turn on a searchlight, order you against a wall. Then comes the command to spread your legs and empty out your pockets, and stand splayed there while they call in your identity over their radio. You may be a college student and sing in a church choir, but that will not overcome the police presumption that you have probably done something they can arrest you for.

If you find yourself caught up in the system, it will seem like alien terrain. Usually your judge and prosecutor will be white, as will most members of the jury, as well as your attorney. In short, your fate will be decided by a white world.

This may help to explain why you have so many harsh words for the police, even though you want and need their protection more than white people do. After all, there tends to be more crime in areas where you live, not to mention drug dealing and all that comes in its wake. Black citizens are at least twice as likely as whites to become victims of violent crimes. Moreover, in almost all of these cases, the person who attacks you will be black. Since this is so, whites want to know, why don't black people speak out against the members of their race who are causing so much grief? The reason is partly that you do not want to attack other blacks while whites are listening. At least equally important is that while you obviously have no taste for violence, you are also wary of measures that might come with a campaign to stamp out "black crime." These reasons will receive fuller consideration in a later chapter. At this point you might simply say that you are not sure you want a more vigorous police presence, if those enforcers are unable to distinguish between law-abiding citizens and local predators. Of course, you want to be protected. But not if it means that you and your friends and relatives end up included among those the police harass or arrest.

[***]

We know from surveys that during the Cold War era, black Americans felt less antipathy toward nations then designated as our enemies, since they saw themselves less threatened by the Soviet Union or Cuba or China than did most white Americans. Nor were they so sure why they or their children were asked to risk their lives fighting people of color in places like Vietnam and Panama and the Middle East. And if the United States finds itself increasingly at odds with Islamic countries or other movements in the Third World, even more black Americans may find themselves wondering where their own allegiances lie.

As you look back on the way this nation has treated your people, you wonder how so many have managed to persevere amid so much adversity. About slavery, of course, too much cannot be said. Yet even within living memory, there were beaches and parks—in the North as well as in the South—where black Americans simply could not set foot. Segregation meant separation without even a pretense of equal facilities. In Southern communities that had only a single public library or swimming pool, black residents and taxpayers could never borrow a book or go for a swim. Indeed, black youths were even forbidden to stroll past the pool, lest they catch a glimpse of white girls in their bathing costumes.

How did they endure the endless insults and humiliations? Grown people being called by their first names, having to avert their eyes when addressed by white people, even being expected to step off a sidewalk when whites walked by. Overarching it all was the terror, with white police and prosecutors and judges possessing all but total power over black lives. Not to mention the lynchings by white mobs, with victims even chosen at random, to remind all blacks of what could happen to them if they did not remain compliant and submissive.

You wonder how much that has changed. Suppose, for example, you find yourself having to drive across the country, stopping at gasoline stations and restaurants and motels. As you travel across the heart of white America, you can never be sure of how you will be received. While the odds are that you will reach your destination alive, you cannot be so sure that you will not be stopped by the police or spend a night in a cell. So you would be well advised to keep to the speed limit, and not exceed it by a single mile. Of course, white people are pulled over by state troopers; but how often are their cars searched? Or if a motel clerk cannot "find" your reservation, is it because she has now seen you in person? And are all the toilet facilities at this service station really out of order?

The day-to-day aggravations and humiliations add up bit by bitter bit. To take a depressingly familiar example, you stroll into a shop to look at the merchandise, and it soon becomes clear that the clerks are keeping a watchful eye on you. Too quickly, one of them comes over to inquire what it is you might want, and then remains conspicuously close as you continue your search. It also seems that they take an unusually long time verifying your credit card. And then you and a black friend enter a restaurant, and find yourselves greeted warily, with what is obviously a more anxious reception than that given to white guests. Yes, you will be served, and your table will not necessarily be next to the kitchen. Still, you sense that they would rather you had chosen some other eating place. Or has this sort of thing happened so often that you are growing paranoid?

So there is the sheer strain of living in a white world, the rage that you must suppress almost every day. No wonder black Americans, especially black men, suffer so much from hypertension. (If ever an illness had social causes, this is certainly one.) To be black in America means reining in your opinions and emotions as no whites ever have to do. Not to mention the forced and false smiles you are expected to contrive, to assure white Americans that you harbor no grievances against them.

Along with the tension and the strain and the rage, there come those moments of despair. At times, the conclusion seems all but self-evident that white America has no desire for your presence or any need for your people. Can this nation have an unstated strategy for annihilating your people? How else, you ask yourself, can one explain the incidence of death and debilitation from drugs and disease; the incarceration of a whole generation of your men; the consignment of millions of women and children to half-lives of poverty and dependency?* Each of these debilities has its causes; indeed, analyzing them has become a minor industry. Yet with so much about these conditions that is so closely related to race, they say something about the larger society that has allowed them to happen . . . .

---

*   In 1990, when a sample of black Americans were asked if they thought that the government was deliberately encouraging drug use among black people, 64 percent felt that this might be true. When asked if they suspected that AIDS had been purposely created by scientists to infect black people, 32 percent believed there might be some truth in this view.

KERNER COMMISSION

Chairman: Otto Kerner, Governor of Illinois
Vice Chairman: John Lindsay, Mayor of New York City

REPORT OF THE NATIONAL ADVISORY
COMMISSION ON CIVIL DISORDERS
1968

When he wrote those famous words, "It was the best of times, it was the worst of times," Charles Dickens could have been talking about the sixties, one of the most tumultuous periods in the history of the United States. It was during this time that students, overcome by idealistic fervor, took to the streets in massive numbers, demonstrating against U.S. involvement in Vietnam, racism, and social injustice. Meanwhile, tensions escalated as the Civil Rights Movement drew attention to the second-class status of the black population and the Supreme Court mandated school desegregation, while the emergence of the hippie counterculture challenged dominant cultural values and the authority of the political establishment. The assassinations of President John F. Kennedy in 1963 and of the Reverend Martin Luther King, Jr. in 1968 added to the general sense of anxiety and confusion.

The cauldron came to a boil in July of 1967 when violence erupted in many of the nation's inner cities. But this was not the first incident of racial violence, nor would it be the last. Almost two years earlier, on August 11, 1965, violence exploded in the Watts section of Los Angeles, when an estimated 35,000 blacks took to the streets, looting and burning stores. The incident, sparked by an act of police brutality, lasted five days, took 34 lives, injured as many as 1,000 people, and destroyed approximately $200 million in property. Between 1965 and 1968, "329 'important' racial disturbances took place in 257 cities, resulting in nearly 300 deaths, 8,000 injuries, 60,000 arrests, and property losses in the hundreds of millions of dollars" (Thernstrom et al., 1998). The assassination of Martin Luther King prompted rioting in more than 120 cities.

Shortly after the 1967 riots, President Lyndon Baines Johnson established the National Advisory Commission on Civil Disorders—also known as the Kerner Commission—to investigate the cause of the riots and to suggest a strategy for ensuring that they did not happen again. After eight months of study, the Commission famously concluded that "Our nation is moving toward two societies, one black, one white—separate and unequal" (*Report*, 1968, 1). The trend could be reversed, the report suggested, but it would require a massive and sustained national commitment and an unprecedented investment of national resources.

It attributed the riots to the pent-up rage and frustration of inner city blacks who had endured the indignities of prejudice and discrimination and been denied access to basic social and economic opportunities. According to the Commission,

> Segregation and poverty have created in the racial ghetto a destructive environment totally unknown to most white Americans. What white Americans have never fully understood but what the Negro can never forget is that white society is deeply implicated in the ghetto. White institutions created it, white institutions maintain it, and white society condones it. (*Report*, 1968, 2)

At first glance, it might seem odd that most of these riots occurred *after* passage of the Civil Rights Act of 1964 and the Voting Rights Act of 1965, which, together, ended legal discrimination. In fact, the Johnson Administration had already launched its Great Society initiative, which put into place a vast array of government programs to combat poverty, improve education, eliminate hunger, provide medical care for the indigent, foster urban economic development, subsidize job training, and make available pre-school education for the poor.

The Kerner Commission itself addressed this question, noting that "frustrated hopes are the residue of the unfulfilled expectations aroused by the judicial and legislative victories of the Civil Rights Movement" (*Report*, 1968, 10). History reveals that many Great Society reforms, including the War on Poverty, had only limited impact because they were not fully funded. This problem was further compounded by the

decision to divert resources away from social programs in order to finance
the country's escalating involvement in Vietnam. Finally, it is likely that
frustration levels remained high because of the glacial pace at which racial
attitudes and social structures change.

The findings of the Kerner Commission remain controversial to this
day. Thernstrom, for example, contends that the commission was "wildly
mistaken in its claims . . . that the country was splitting into 'two societies'"
and takes issue with others who argue that conditions in the inner cities are,
once again, deteriorating (Thernstrom et al., 1998). The accompanying
public policy debate, which is as much ideological as it is historical, turns
on the question of whether and to what degree government should be
actively involved in promoting economic and social equality.

The Kerner Commission recommended that the government
improve inner city schools, expand opportunities for higher education for
disadvantaged students, create incentives for people to seek employment,
expand public housing outside of the ghetto, expand opportunities for
interaction between the races, increase communication across racial
lines to destroy stereotypes, create jobs for the hard-core unemployed,
subsidize job training, set welfare standards at or above the poverty level,
eliminate illiteracy, and eliminate racial discrimination in employment
and housing (this is only a partial listing).

The delicate and incendiary nature of the questions asked by
the Kerner Commission demanded a high degree of objectivity
and detachment. Any sense that the Commission's findings and
recommendations reflected a political or racial bias would have doomed
the enterprise from the start. As a result, the Kerner Report rests heavily
on mountains of statistical evidence, some of which is included in the
following reading. These data paint a stark picture of the disparity
between blacks and whites. Consider, for example, that, in 1966, 23.7
percent of nonwhite families were headed by females, while the same was
true of only 8.9 percent of white families. It is a sobering fact that, by
1999, the percentage of black households and white households headed
by women had risen, respectively, to 45.1 and 14.2.[1]

As you read this selection, consider the extent to which Eitzen's
concerns parallel those raised by the members of the Kerner Commission.
Compare and contrast the description of the immigrant experience in this
reading with that provided by Sinclair in The Jungle. Try to determine

[1]   Census Data (2001) Accessed May 23, 2008 at http://www.census.
gov/prod/2001pubs/statab/sec02.pdf

how many of the Commission's recommendations Friedman would support.

SELECTIONS FROM:

Kerner, O., Chairman. (1968). *Report of the National Advisory Commission on Civil Disorders*. Washington, D.C.: U.S. Government Printing Office. 91-93, 123-145.

PART II: WHY DID IT HAPPEN?

CHAPTER 4
THE BASIC CAUSES

We have seen what happened. Why did it happen?

In addressing this question we shift our focus from the local to the national scene, from the particular events of the summer of 1967 to the factors within the society at large that created a mood for violence among so many urban Negroes.

The record before this Commission reveals that the causes of recent racial disorders are imbedded in a massive tangle of issues and circumstances—social, economic, political, and psychological—which arise out of the historical pattern of Negro-white relations in America.

These factors are both complex and interacting; they vary significantly in their effect from city to city and from year to year; and the consequences of one disorder, generating new grievances and new demands, become the causes of the next. It is this which creates the "thicket of tension, conflicting evidence, and extreme opinions" cited by the President.

Despite these complexities, certain fundamental matters are clear. Of these, the most fundamental is the racial attitude and behavior of white Americans toward black Americans. Race prejudice has shaped our history decisively in the past; it now threatens to do so again. White racism is essentially responsible for the explosive mixture which has been accumulating in our cities since the end of World War II. At the base of this mixture are three of the most bitter fruits of white racial attitudes:

Pervasive discrimination and segregation. The first is surely the continuing exclusion of great numbers of Negroes from the benefits of economic progress through discrimination in employment and education and their enforced confinement in segregated housing and schools. The corrosive and degrading effects of this condition and the attitudes that underlie it are the source of the deepest bitterness and at the center of the problem of racial disorder.

Black migration and white exodus. The second is the massive and growing concentration of impoverished Negroes in our major cities resulting from Negro migration from the rural South, rapid population growth, and the continuing movement of the white middle class to the suburbs. The consequence is a greatly increased burden on the already depleted resources of cities, creating a growing crisis of deteriorating facilities and services and unmet human needs.

Black ghettos. Third, in the teeming racial ghettos, segregation and poverty have intersected to destroy opportunity and hope and to enforce failure. The ghettos too often mean men and women without jobs, families without men, and schools where children are processed instead of educated, until they return to the street—to crime, to narcotics, to dependency on welfare, and to bitterness and resentment against society in general and white society in particular.

These three forces have converged on the inner city in recent years and on the people who inhabit it. At the same time, most whites and many Negroes outside the ghetto have prospered to a degree unparalleled in the history of civilization. Through television—the universal appliance in the ghetto—and the other media of mass communications, this affluence has been endlessly flaunted before the eyes of the Negro poor and the jobless ghetto youth.

As Americans, most Negro citizens carry within themselves two basic aspirations of our society. They seek to share in both the material resources of our system and its intangible benefits—dignity, respect, and acceptance. Outside the ghetto, many have succeeded in achieving a decent standard of life and in developing the inner resources which give life meaning and direction. Within the ghetto, however, it is rare that either aspiration is achieved.

Yet these facts alone—fundamental as they are—cannot be said to have caused the disorders. Other and more immediate factors help explain why these events happened now.

Recently, three powerful ingredients have begun to catalyze the mixture.

Frustrated hopes. The expectations aroused by the great judicial and legislative victories of the civil rights movement have led to frustration, hostility, and cynicism in the face of the persistent gap between promise and fulfillment. The dramatic struggle for equal rights in the South has sensitized northern Negroes to the economic inequalities reflected in the deprivations of ghetto life.

Legitimation of violence. A climate that tends toward the approval and encouragement of violence as a form of protest has been created by white terrorism directed against nonviolent protest, including instances of abuse and even murder of some civil rights workers in the South, by the open defiance of law and Federal authority by state and local officials resisting desegregation, and by some protest groups engaging in civil disobedience who turn their backs on nonviolence, go beyond the constitutionally protected rights of petition and free assembly and resort to violence to attempt to compel alteration of laws and policies with which they disagree. This condition has been reinforced by a general erosion of respect for authority in American society and reduced effectiveness of social standards and community restraints on violence and crime. This in turn has largely resulted from rapid urbanization and the dramatic reduction in the average age of the total population.

Powerlessness. Finally, many Negroes have come to believe that they are being exploited politically and economically by the white "power structure." Negroes, like people in poverty everywhere, in fact lack the channels of communication, influence and appeal that traditionally have been available to ethnic minorities within the city and which enabled them—unburdened by color—to scale the walls of the white ghettos in an earlier era. The frustrations of powerlessness have led some to the conviction that there is no effective alternative to violence as a means of expression and redress, as a way of "moving the system." More generally, the result is alienation and hostility toward the institutions of law and government and the white society which controls them. This is reflected in the reach toward racial consciousness and solidarity reflected in the slogan "Black Power."

These facts have combined to inspire a new mood among Negroes, particularly among the young. Self-esteem and enhanced racial pride are replacing apathy and submission to "the system." Moreover, Negro youth, who make up over half of the ghetto population, share the growing sense of alienation felt by many white youth in our country. Thus, their role in recent civil disorders reflects not only a shared sense of deprivation and victimization by white society but also the rising incidence of disruptive conduct by a segment of American youth throughout the society.

Incitement and encouragement of violence. These conditions have created a volatile mixture of attitudes and beliefs which needs only a spark to ignite mass violence. Strident appeals to violence, first heard from white racists, were echoed and reinforced last summer in the inflammatory rhetoric of black racists and militants. Throughout the year, extremists crisscrossed the country preaching a doctrine of black power and violence. Their rhetoric was widely reported in the mass media; it was echoed by local "militants" and organizations; it became the ugly background noise of the violent summer.

We cannot measure with any precision the influence of these organizations and individuals in the ghetto, but we think it clear that the intolerable and unconscionable encouragement of violence heightened tensions, created a mood of acceptance and an expectation of violence and thus contributed to the eruption of the disorders last summer.

The Police. It is the convergence of all these factors that makes the role of the police so difficult and so significant. Almost invariably the incident that ignites disorder arises from police action. Harlem, Watts, Newark and Detroit—all the major outbursts of recent years—were precipitated by routine arrests of Negroes for minor offenses by white police.

But the police are not merely the spark. In discharge of their obligation to maintain order and insure public safety in the disruptive conditions of ghetto life, they are inevitably involved in sharper and more frequent conflicts with ghetto residents than with the residents of other areas. Thus, to many Negroes, police have come to symbolize white power, white racism, and white repression. And the fact is that many police do reflect and express these white attitudes. The atmosphere of hostility and cynicism is reinforced by a widespread perception among Negroes of the existence of police brutality and corruption and of a "double standard" of justice and protection—one for Negroes and one for whites.

*   *   *

To this point, we have attempted only to identify the prime components of the "explosive mixture." In the chapter that follows we seek to analyze them in the perspective of history. Their meaning, however, is already clear:

In the summer of 1967, we have seen in our cities a chain reaction of racial violence. If we are heedless, none of us shall escape the consequences.

CHAPTER 7
UNEMPLOYMENT, FAMILY STRUCTURE AND SOCIAL DISORGANIZATION

RECENT ECONOMIC TRENDS

The Negro population in our country is as diverse in income, occupation, family composition, and other variables as the white community. Nevertheless, for purposes of analysis, three major Negro economic groups can be identified.

The first and smallest group consists of middle and upper income individuals and households whose educational, occupational, and cultural characteristics are similar to those of middle and upper income white groups.

The second and largest group contains Negroes whose incomes are above the "poverty level" but who have not attained the educational, occupational, or income status typical of middle-class Americans.

The third group has very low educational, occupational, and income attainments and lives below the "poverty level."

A recent compilation of data on American Negroes by the Departments of Labor and Commerce shows that although incomes of both Negroes and whites have been rising rapidly,

- Negro incomes still remain far below those of whites. Negro median family income was only 58 percent of the white median 1966.
- Negro family income is not keeping pace with white family income growth. In constant 1965 dollars, median nonwhite income in 1947 was $2,174 lower than median white income. By 1966, the gap had grown to $3,036.
- The Negro upper income group is expanding rapidly and achieving sizeable income gains. In 1966, 28 percent of all Negro families received incomes of $7,000 or more, compared with 55 percent of white families. This was 1.6 times the proportion of Negroes receiving comparable incomes in 1960, and four times greater than the proportion receiving such incomes in 1947. Moreover, the proportion of Negroes employed in high-skill, high-status, and well-paying jobs rose faster than comparable proportions among whites from 1960 to 1966.
- As Negro incomes have risen, the size of the lowest-income group has grown smaller, and the middle and upper groups have grown larger—both relatively and absolutely.

Group	Percentage of Negro families			Percentage of white families
	1947	1960	1966	1966
$7,000 and over	7	17	28	55
$3,000 to $6,999	29	40	41	33
Under $3,000	65	44	32	13

- About two-thirds of the lowest income group—or 20 percent of all Negro families—are making no significant economic gains despite continued general prosperity. Half of these "hard-core disadvantage"—more than 2 million persons—live in central-city neighborhoods. Recent special censuses in Los Angeles and Cleveland indicate that the incomes of persons living in the worst slum areas have not risen at all during this period, unemployment rates have declined only slightly, the proportion of families with female heads has increased, and housing conditions have worsened even though rents have risen.

Thus, between 2.0 and 2.5 million poor Negroes are living in disadvantaged neighborhoods of central cities in the United States. These persons comprise only slightly more than 1 percent of the nation's total population, but they make up about 16 to 20 percent of the total Negro population of all central cities, and a much higher proportion in certain cities.

UNEMPLOYMENT AND UNDEREMPLOYMENT

THE CRITICAL SIGNIFICANCE OF EMPLOYMENT

The capacity to obtain and hold a "good job" is the traditional test of participation in American society. Steady employment with adequate compensation provides both purchasing power and social status. It develops the capabilities, confidence, and self-esteem an individual needs to be a responsible citizen, and provides a basis for a stable family life. As Daniel P. Moynihan has written:

> The principal measure of progress toward equality will be that of employment. It is the primary source of individual or group identity. In America what you do is what you are: to do nothing is to be nothing; to do little is to be little. The equations are implacable and blunt, and ruthlessly public.
>
> For the Negro American it is already, and will continue to be, the master problem. It is the measure of white bona fides. It is the measure of Negro competence, and also of the competence of American society. Most importantly, the linkage between problems of employment and the range

of social pathology that afflicts the Negro community is unmistakable. Employment not only controls the present for the Negro American but, in a most profound way, it is creating the future as well.

For residents of disadvantaged Negro neighborhoods, obtaining good jobs is vastly more difficult than for most workers in society. For decades, social, economic, and psychological disadvantages surrounding the urban Negro poor have impaired their work capacities and opportunities. The result is a cycle of failure—the employment disabilities of one generation breed those of the next.

NEGRO UNEMPLOYMENT

Unemployment rates among Negroes have declined from a post-Korean War high of 12.6 percent in 1958 to 8.2 percent in 1967. Among married Negro men, the unemployment rate for 1967 was down to 3.2 percent.[2]

Notwithstanding this decline, unemployment rates for Negroes are still double those for whites in every category, including married men, as they have been throughout the postwar period. Moreover, since 1954, even during the current unprecedented period of sustained economic growth, unemployment among Negroes has been continuously above the 6 percent "recession" level widely regarded as a sign of serious economic weakness when prevalent for the entire work force.

While the Negro unemployment rate remains high in relation to the white rate, the number of additional jobs needed to lower this to the level of white unemployment is surprisingly small. In 1967, approximately 3 million persons were unemployed during an average week, of whom about 638,000, or 21 percent, were nonwhites. When corrected for undercounting, total nonwhite unemployment was approximately 712,000 or 8 percent of the nonwhite labor force. To reduce the unemployment rate to 3.4 percent, the rate prevalent among whites, jobs must be found for 57.5 percent of these unemployed persons. This amounts to nearly 409,000 jobs, or about 27 percent of the net number of new jobs added to the economy in the year 1967 alone and only slightly more than one-half of 1 percent of all jobs in the United States in 1967.

---

[2]   Adjusted for Census Bureau undercounting.

THE LOW-STATUS AND LOW-PAYING
NATURE OF MANY NEGRO JOBS

Even more important perhaps than unemployment is the related problem of the undesirable nature of many jobs open to Negroes. Negro workers are concentrated in the lowest skilled and lowest paying occupations. These jobs often involve substandard wages, great instability and uncertainty of tenure, extremely low status in the eyes of both employer and employee, little or no chance for meaningful advancement, and unpleasant or exhausting duties. Negro men in particular are more than twice as likely as whites to be in unskilled or service jobs which pay far less than most:

Type of Occupation	Percentage of Male Workers in Each Type of Occupation —1966		Median Earnings of All Male Civilians in Each Occupation —1965
	White	Nonwhite	
Professional, Technical, Managerial	27%	9%	$7,603[1]
Clerical and sales	14	9	$5,532[1]
Craftsmen and foremen	20	12	$6,270
Operatives	20	27	$5,046
Service Workers	6	16	$3,436
Non-farm laborers	6	20	$2,410
Farmers and farm workers	7	8	$1,699[1]

[1]   Average of two categories from normal Census Bureau categories as combined in data presented in *The Social and Economic Conditions of Negroes in the United States* (BLS #332).

This concentration in the least desirable jobs can be viewed another way by calculating the changes which would occur if Negro men were employed in various occupations in the same proportions as the male labor force as a whole (not solely the white labor force).

Type of Occupation	Number of Male Nonwhite Workers—1966			
	As Actually Distributed[2]	If Distributed the Same as All Male Workers	Difference No.	Percent
Professional, technical, managerial	415,000	1,173,000	+758,000	+183%
Clerical and sales	415,000	628,000	+213,000	+51%
Craftsmen and foremen	553,000	894,000	+341,000	+62%
Operatives	1,244,000	964,000	−280,000	−23%
Service workers	737,000	326,000	−411,000	−56%
Non-farm laborers	922,000	340,000	−582,000	−63%
Farmers and farm workers	369,000	330,000	−39,000	−11%

[2]   Estimates based upon percentages set forth in BLS #332, page 41.

Thus, upgrading the employment of Negro men to make their occupational distribution identical with that of the labor force as a whole would have an immense impact upon the nature of their occupations. About 1.3 million nonwhite men—or 28 percent of those employed in 1966—would move up the employment ladder into one of the higher status and higher paying categories. The effect of such a shift upon the incomes of Negro men would be very great. Using the 1966 job distribution, the shift indicated above would produce about $4.8 billion more earned income for nonwhite men alone if they received the 1965 median income in each occupation. This would be a rise of approximately 30 percent in the earnings actually received by all nonwhite men in 1965 (not counting any sources of income other than wages and salaries).

Of course, the kind of "instant upgrading" visualized in these calculations does not represent a practical alternative for national policy. The economy cannot drastically reduce the total number of low-status jobs it now contains, or shift large numbers of people upward in occupation in any short period. Therefore, major upgrading in the employment status of Negro men must come through a faster relative expansion of higher level jobs than lower level jobs (which has been occurring for several decades), an improvement in the skills of nonwhite workers so they can obtain a higher proportion of those added better jobs, and a drastic reduction of discriminatory hiring and promotion practices in all enterprises, both private and public.

Nevertheless, this hypothetical example clearly shows that the concentration of male Negro employment at the lowest end of the occupational scale is greatly depressing the incomes of U.S. Negroes in general. In fact, this is the single most important source of poverty among Negroes. It is even more important than unemployment, as can be shown by a second hypothetical calculation. In 1966, there were about 724,000 unemployed nonwhites in the United States on the average, including adults and teenagers, and allowing for the Census Bureau undercount of Negroes. If every one of these persons had been employed and had received the median amount earned by nonwhite males in 1966 ($3,864), this could have added a total of $2.8 billion to nonwhite income as a whole. If only enough of these persons had been employed at that wage to reduce nonwhite unemployment from 7.3 percent to 3.3 percent—the rate among whites in 1966—then the income gain for nonwhites would have totaled about $1.5 billion. But if nonwhite unemployment remained at 7.3 percent, and nonwhite men were upgraded so that they had the same occupational distribution and incomes as all men in the labor force considered together, this would have produced about $4.8 billion in additional income, as noted above (using 1965 earnings for calculation). Thus the potential income gains from upgrading the male nonwhite labor force are much larger than those from reducing nonwhite unemployment.

This conclusion underlines the difficulty of improving economic status of Negro men. It is far easier to create new jobs than either to create new jobs with relatively high status and earning power, or to upgrade existing employed or partly employed workers into such better-quality employment. Yet only such upgrading will eliminate the fundamental basis poverty and deprivation among Negro families.

Access to good-quality jobs clearly affects the willingness of Negro men actively to seek work. In riot cities surveyed by the Commission with the largest percentage of Negroes in skilled and semiskilled jobs, Negro men participated in the labor force to the same extent as, or greater than, white men. Conversely, where most Negro men were heavily concentrated in menial jobs, they participated less in the labor force than white men.

Even given similar employment, Negro workers with the same education as white workers are paid less. This disparity doubtless results to some extent from inferior training in segregated schools, and also from the fact that large numbers of Negroes are only now entering certain occupations for the first time. However, the differentials are so large and so universal at all educational levels that they clearly reflect the patterns of discrimination which characterize hiring and promotion practices in many segments of the economy. For example, in 1966 among persons who had completed high school, the median income of Negroes was only 73 percent that of whites. Even among persons with an eighth-grade education, Negro median income was only 80 percent of white median income.

At the same time, a higher proportion of Negro women than white women participates in the labor force at nearly all ages except 16 to 19. For instance, in 1966, 55 percent of nonwhite women from 25 to 34 years of age were employed, compared to only 38 percent of white women in the same age group. The fact that almost half of all adult Negro women work reflects the fact that so many Negro males have unsteady and low-paying jobs. Yet even though Negro women are often better able to find work than Negro men, the unemployment rate among adult nonwhite women

(20 years old and over) in 1967 was 7.1 percent, compared to the 4.3 percent rate among adult nonwhite men.

Unemployment rates are, of course, much higher among teenagers, both Negro and white, than among adults; in fact about one-third of all unemployed Negroes in 1967 were between 16 and 19 years old. During the first 9 months of 1967, the unemployment rate among nonwhite teenagers was 26.5 percent; for whites, it was 10.6 percent. About 219,300 nonwhite teenagers were unemployed.[3] About 58,300 were still in school but were actively looking for jobs.

SUBEMPLOYMENT IN DISADVANTAGED NEGRO NEIGHBORHOODS

In disadvantaged areas, employment conditions for Negroes are in a chronic state of crisis. Surveys in low-income neighborhoods of nine large cities made by the Department of Labor late in 1966 revealed that the rate of unemployment there was 9.3 percent, compared to 7.3 percent for Negroes generally and 3.3 percent for whites. Moreover, a high proportion of the persons living in these areas were "underemployed," that is they were either part-time workers looking for full-time employment, or full-time workers earning less than $3000 per year, or had dropped out of the labor force. The Department of Labor estimated that this underemployment is 2½ times greater than the number unemployed in these areas. Therefore, the "subemployment rate," including both the unemployed and the underemployed, was about 32.7 percent in the nine areas surveyed, or 8.8 times greater than the overall unemployment rate for all U.S. workers. Since underemployment also exists outside disadvantaged neighborhoods, comparing the full subemployment rate in these areas with the unemployment rate for the Nation as a whole is not entirely valid. However, it provides some measure of the enormous disparity between employment conditions in most of the nation those prevalent in disadvantaged Negro areas in our large cities.

The critical problem is to determine the actual number of those unemployed and underemployed in central city Negro ghettos. This involves a process of calculation which is detailed in the note at the end of this chapter. The outcome of this process is summarized in the following table:

---

3   After adjusting for Census Bureau undercounting.

Nonwhite Subemployment in Disadvantaged
Areas of All Central Cities—1967

Group	Unemployment	Underemployment	Total Subemployment
Adult men	102,000	230,000	332,000
Adult women	118,000	266,000	384,000
Teenagers	98,000	220,000	318,000
Total	318,000	716,000	1,034,000

Source: Social Security Administration

Therefore, in order to bring subemployment in these areas down to a level equal to unemployment alone among whites, enough steady, reasonably-paying jobs (and the training and motivation to perform them) must be provided to eliminate all underemployment and reduce unemployment by 65 percent. For all three age groups combined, this deficit amounted to 923,000 jobs in 1967.

THE MAGNITUDE OF POVERTY IN DISADVANTAGED NEIGHBORHOODS

The chronic unemployment problems in the central city, aggravated by the constant arrival of new unemployed migrants, is the fundamental cause of the persistent poverty in disadvantaged Negro areas.

"Poverty" in the affluent society is more than absolute deprivation. Many of the poor in the United States would be well off in other societies. Relative deprivation—inequality—is a more useful concept of poverty with respect to the Negro in America because it encompasses social and political exclusion as well as economic inequality. Because of the lack of data of this type, we have had to focus our analysis on a measure of poverty which is both economic and absolute—the Social Security Administration's "poverty level"[4] concept. It is clear, however, that broader measures of poverty would substantiate the conclusions that follow.

In 1966, there were 29.7 million persons in the United States—5.3 percent of the Nation's population—with incomes below the "poverty level," as defined by the Social Security Administration. Of these, 20.3 million were white (68.3 percent), and 9.3 million nonwhite (31.7 percent). Thus, about 11.9 percent of the Nation's whites and 40.6 percent of its nonwhites were poor under the Social Security definition.

The location of the nation's poor is best shown from 1964 data as indicated by the following table:

---

[4] $3335 per year for an urban family of four

	Percentage of Those in Poverty in Each Group Living in:			
	Metropolitan Areas			
Group	In Central Cities	Outside Central Cities	Other Areas	Total
Whites	23.8%	21.8%	54.4%	100%
Nonwhites	41.7	10.8	47.5	100
Total	29.4	18.4	52.2	100

Source: Social Security Administration

The following facts concerning poverty are relevant to an understanding of the problems faced by people living in disadvantaged neighborhoods.[5]

- In central cities 30.7 percent of nonwhite families of two or more persons lived in poverty compared to only 8.8 percent of whites.
- Of the 10.1 million poor persons in central cities in 1964, about 4.4 million of these (43.6 percent) were nonwhites, and 5.7 million (56.4 percent) were whites. The poor whites were much older on the average than the poor nonwhites. The proportion of poor persons 65 years old or older was 23.2 percent among whites, but only 6.8 percent among nonwhites.
- Poverty was more than twice as prevalent among nonwhite families with female heads than among those with male heads, 57 percent compared to 21 percent. In central cities, 26 percent of all nonwhite families of two or more persons had female heads, as compared to 12 percent of white families.
- Among nonwhite families headed by a female, and having children under 6, the incidence of poverty was 81 percent. Moreover, there were 243,000 such families living in poverty in central cities—or over 9 percent of all nonwhite families in those cities.
- Among all children living in poverty within central cities, nonwhites outnumbered whites by over 400,000. The number of poor nonwhite children equalled or surpassed the number of white poor children in every age group.

---

[5]   Source: Social Security Administration; based on 1964 data

Number of Children Living in Poverty (millions)

Age Group	White	Nonwhite	Percent of Total Nonwhite
Under 6	0.9	1.0	53%
6-15	1.0	1.3	57
16-21	0.4	0.4	50
Total	2.3	2.7	54%

Two stark facts emerge:

- 54 percent of all poor children in central cities in 1964 were nonwhites.
- Of the 4.4 million nonwhites living in poverty within central cities in 1964, 52 percent were children under 16, and 61 percent were under 21.

Since 1964, the number of nonwhite families living in poverty within central cities has remained about the same; hence, these poverty conditions are probably still prevalent in central cities in terms of absolute numbers of persons, although the proportion of persons in poverty may have dropped slightly.[6]

THE SOCIAL IMPACT OF EMPLOYMENT PROBLEMS IN DISADVANTAGED NEGRO AREAS

UNEMPLOYMENT AND THE FAMILY

The high rates of unemployment and underemployment in racial ghettos are evidence, in part, that many men living in these areas are

---

[6] For the Nation as a whole, the proportion of nonwhite families living in poverty dropped from 39 percent to 35 percent from 1964 to 1966 (defining "family" somewhat differently from the definition used in the data above). The number of such families declined from 1.9 million to 1.7 million. However, the number and proportion of all nonwhites living in central cities rose in the same period. As a result, the number of nonwhite families living in so-called "poverty areas" of large cities actually rose from 1,561,000 in 1960 to 1,588,000 in 1966.

seeking, but cannot obtain, jobs which will support a family. Perhaps equally important, most jobs they can get are at the low end of the occupational scale, and often lack the necessary status to sustain a worker's self-respect, or the respect of his family and friends. These same men are also constantly confronted with the message of discrimination: "You are inferior because of a trait you did not cause and cannot change." This message reinforces feelings of inadequacy arising from repeated failure to obtain and keep decent jobs.

Wives of these men are forced to work and usually produce more money. If men stay at home without working, their inadequacies constantly confront them and tensions arise between them and their wives and children. Under these pressures, it is not surprising that many of these men flee their responsibilities as husbands and fathers, leaving home, and drifting from city to city, or adopting the style of "street corner men."

Statistical evidence tends to document this. A close correlation exists between the number of nonwhite married women separated from their husbands each year and the unemployment rate among nonwhite males 20 years old and over. Similarly, from 1948 to 1962, the number of new Aid to Families with Dependent Children cases rose and fell with the nonwhite male unemployment rate. Since 1963, however, the number of new cases—most of them Negro children—has steadily increased even though the unemployment rate among nonwhite males has declined. The impact of marital status on employment among Negroes is shown by the fact that in 1967 the proportion of married men either divorced or separated from their wives was more than twice as high among unemployed nonwhite men as among employed nonwhite men. Moreover, among those participating in the labor force, there with a higher proportion of married men with wives present than with wives absent.

Unemployment Rate and Participation in Total Labor
Force, 25 to 54-Year-Old Nonwhite Men, by Marital
Status, March, 1967

	Unemployment Rate Nonwhite	Labor Force Participation (%) Nonwhite
Married, Wife Present	3.7	96.7
Other (Separated, Divorced, Widowed)	8.7	77.6

FATHERLESS FAMILIES

The abandonment of the home by many Negro males affects a great many children growing up in the racial ghetto. As previously indicated, most American Negro families are headed by men, just like most other American families. Yet the proportion of families with female heads is much greater among Negroes than among whites at all income levels, and has been rising in recent years.

Proportion of Families of Various Types

Date	Husband-Wife		Female Head	
	White	Nonwhite	White	Nonwhite
1950	88.0%	77.7%	8.5%	17.6%
1960	88.7	73.6	8.7	22.4
1966	88.8	72.7	8.9	23.7

during this time, howeve whites were forced to stay with their husbands....

This disparity between white and nonwhite families is far greater among the lowest income families—those most likely to reside in disadvantaged big-city neighborhoods—than among higher income families. Among families with incomes under $3,000 in 1966, the proportion with female heads was 42 percent for Negroes but only 23 percent for whites. In contrast, among families with incomes of $7,000 or more, 8 percent of Negro families had female heads compared to 4 percent of whites.

The problems of "fatherlessness" are aggravated by the tendency of the poor to have large families. The average poor, urban, nonwhite family contains 4.8 persons, as compared with 3.7 for the average poor, urban white family. This is one of the primary factors in the poverty status of nonwhite households in large cities.

The proportion of fatherless families appears to be increasing in the poorest Negro neighborhoods. In the Hough section of Cleveland, the proportion of families with female heads rose from 23 to 32 percent from 1960 to 1965. In the Watts section of Los Angeles it rose from 36 to 39 percent during the same period.

The handicap imposed on children growing up without fathers, in an atmosphere of poverty and deprivation, is increased because many mothers must work to provide support. The following table illustrates the disparity between the proportion of nonwhite women in the child-rearing ages who are in the labor force and the comparable proportion of white women:

Age Group	Percentage of Women in the Labor Force	
	Nonwhite	White
20-24	55%	51%
25-34	55	38
35-44	61	45

With the father absent and the mother working, many ghetto children spend the bulk of their time on the streets—the streets of a crime-ridden, violence-prone and poverty-stricken world. The image of success in this world is not that of the "solid citizen," the responsible husband and father, but rather that of the "hustler" who promotes his own interests by exploiting others. The dope sellers and the numbers runners are the "successful" men because their earnings far outstrip those men who try to climb the economic ladder in honest ways.

Young people in the ghetto are acutely conscious of a system which appears to offer rewards to those who illegally exploit others, and failure to those who struggle under traditional responsibilities. Under these circumstances, many adopt exploitation and the "hustle" as a way of life, disclaiming both work and marriage in favor of casual and temporary liaisons. This pattern reinforces itself from one generation to the next, creating a "culture of poverty" and an ingrained cynicism about society and its institutions.

THE "JUNGLE"

The culture of poverty that results from unemployment and family disorganization generates a system of ruthless, exploitative relationships within the ghetto. Prostitution, dope addiction, casual sexual affairs, and crime create an environmental jungle characterized by personal insecurity and tension. The effects of this development are stark:

- The rate of illegitimate births among nonwhite women has risen sharply in the past two decades. In 1940, 16.8 percent of all nonwhite births were illegitimate. By 1950 this proportion was 18 percent; by 1960, 21.6 percent; by 1966, 26.3 percent. In the ghettos of many large cities, illegitimacy rates exceed 50 percent.

- The rate of illegitimacy among nonwhite women is closely related to low income and high unemployment. In Washington, D. C., for example, an analysis of 1960 census tracts shows that in tracts with unemployment rates of 12 percent or more among nonwhite men, illegitimacy was over 40 percent. But in tracts with unemployment rates of 2.9 percent and below among nonwhite men, reported illegitimacy was under 20 percent. A similar contrast existed between tracts in which median nonwhite income was under $4,000 (where illegitimacy was 38 percent) and those in which it was $8,000 and over (where illegitimacy was 12 percent).

- Narcotics addiction is also heavily concentrated in low-income Negro neighborhoods, particularly in New York City. Of the 59,720 addicts known to the U. S. Bureau of Narcotics at the end of 1966, just over 50 percent were Negroes. Over 52 percent of all known addicts lived within New York State, mostly in Harlem and other Negro neighborhoods. These figures undoubtedly greatly understate the actual number of persons using narcotics regularly—especially those under 21.

- Not surprisingly, at every age from 6 through 19, the proportion of children from homes with both parents present who actually attend school is higher than the proportion of children from homes with only one parent or neither present.

- Rates of juvenile delinquency, venereal disease, dependency upon AFDC support, and use of public assistance in general are much higher in disadvantaged Negro areas than in other parts of large cities. Data taken from New York City contrasting predominantly Negro neighborhoods with the city as a whole clearly illustrate this fact.

Social Distress—Major Predominantly Negro
Neighborhoods in New York City and the City as a Whole

	Juvenile Delinquency[7]	Venereal Disease[8]	ADC[9]	Public Assistance[10]
Brownsville	125.3	609.9	459.0	265.8
East New York	98.6	207.5	148.6	71.8
Bedford Stuyvesant	115.2	771.3	337.1	197.2
Harlem	110.8	1,603.5	265.7	138.1
South Bronx	84.4	303.3	278.5	165.5
New York City	52.2	269.1	120.7	60.8

In conclusion: in 1965, 1.2 million nonwhite children under 16 lived in central city families headed by a woman under 65. The great majority of these children were growing up in poverty under conditions that make them better candidates for crime and civil disorder than for jobs providing an entry into American society. Because of the immense importance of this fact—the potential loss to the society of these young people—we describe these conditions in the next chapter.

NOTE: CALCULATIONS OF NONWHITE SUBEMPLOYMENT IN DISADVANTAGED AREAS OF ALL CENTRAL CITIES, 1967

In 1967, total unemployment in the United States was distributed as follows, by age and color:

Group	Nonwhite	White	Total
Adult men (20 and over)	193,000	866,000	1,059,000
Adult women (20 and over)	241,000	837,000	1,078,000
Teenagers (16-19)	204,000	635,000	839,000
Total	638,000	2,338,000	2,976,000

Adjustment for the Census Bureau undercount of nonwhite males in the labor force amounting to 7.5 percent for the teenage group, 18 percent for the adult male group and approximately 10 percent for adult females result in the following revised total employment:

Group	Nonwhite	White	Total
Adult men	228,000	866,000	1,094,000
Adult women	265,000	837,000	1,102,000
Teenagers	219,000	635,000	854,000
Total	712,000	2,338,000	3,050,000

These figures cover the entire United States. To provide an estimate of the number of unemployed in disadvantaged neighborhoods within central cities, it is necessary to discover what proportion of the nonwhite unemployed are in central cities and what proportion of those in central cities are within the most disadvantaged neighborhoods. The Department of Labor survey in nine large central cities covering the first 9 months of 1967 showed that these cities contained 27.3 percent of the total nonwhite labor force in the United States, and 26.4 percent of total nonwhite unemployment. Hence, it is reasonable to assume that nonwhite unemployment is concentrated in central cities to about the same degree as the nonwhite labor force. In turn, the nonwhite labor force is located in central cities in about the same proportion as the nonwhite population, or 57.1 percent in 1967. Thus central city unemployment among nonwhites was presumably about 57.1 percent of the national figures:

Nonwhite Unemployment in All Central Cities (Rounded)	
Adult men	130,000
Adult women	151,000
Teenagers	125,000
Total	406,000

Within large central cities, about 62 percent of all nonwhite families lived in certain Census Tracts which have been designated "poverty areas." These tracts ranked lowest in U. S. cities over 250,000 persons in size, according to an index of "deprivation" based upon family income, children in broken homes, persons with low educational attainment, males in unskilled jobs, and substandard housing. On the assumption that conditions in these poverty areas are comparable to those in the nine disadvantaged areas surveyed by the Department of Labor in 1966, the number of unemployed nonwhites in disadvantaged areas of central cities is as follows:[7]

Nonwhite Unemployment in Disadvantaged Areas of all Central Cities—1967

Adult men	102,000
Adult women	118,000
Teenagers	98,000
Total	318,000

The number of underemployed nonwhites in these areas was about 2.5 times larger than the number of unemployed. But we have already accounted for some underemployment in the adjustment for undercounting—so we will assume nonwhite underemployment was 2.25 times adjusted unemployment for all three age and sex groups. The resulting rough estimates are as follows:

Nonwhite Subemployment in Disadvantaged Areas of All Central Cities—1967

Group	Unemployment	Underemployment	Total Subemployment
Adult men	102,000	230,000	332,000
Adult women	118,000	266,000	384,000
Teenagers	98,000	220,000	318,000
Total	318,000	716,000	1,034,000

CHAPTER 8
CONDITIONS OF LIFE IN THE RACIAL GHETTO

The conditions of life in the racial ghetto are strikingly different from those to which most Americans are accustomed—especially white,

---

[7]   The number of nonwhite unemployed in the more disadvantaged areas was 26 percent higher than it would have been had it been proportional to the total population residing there. Therefore, the proportion of central city

middle-class Americans. We believe it important to describe these conditions and their effect on the lives of people who cannot escape from the ghetto.[8]

CRIME AND INSECURITY

Nothing is more fundamental to the quality of life in any area than the sense of personal security of its residents, and nothing affects this more than crime.

In general, crime rates in large cities are much higher than in other areas of our country. Within such cities, crime rates are higher in disadvantaged Negro areas than anywhere else.

The most widely used measure of crime is the number of "index crimes" (homicide, forcible rape, aggravated assault, robbery, burglary, grand larceny, and auto theft) in relation to population. In 1966, 1,754 such crimes were reported to police for every 100,000 Americans. In cities over 250,000, the rate was 3,153, and in cities over 1 million, it was 3,630—or more than double the national average. In suburban areas alone, including suburban cities, the rate was only 1,300, or just over one-third the rate in the largest cities.

Within larger cities, personal and property insecurity has consistently been highest in the older neighborhoods encircling the downtown business district. In most cities, crime rates for many decades have been higher in these inner areas than anywhere, except in downtown areas themselves, where they are inflated by the small number of residents.

High crime rates have persisted in these inner areas even though the ethnic character of their residents continually changed. Poor immigrants used these areas as "entry ports," then usually moved on to more desirable neighborhoods as soon as they acquired enough resources. Many "entry port" areas have now become racial ghettos.

The difference between crime rates in these disadvantaged neighborhoods and in other parts of the city is usually startling, as a comparison of crime rates in five police districts in Chicago for 1965

---

nonwhite unemployed in poverty areas is assumed to equal 78.1 percent (62 percent times 1.26).

[8]   We have not attempted here to describe conditions relating to the fundamental problems of housing, education, and welfare, which are treated in detail in later chapters.

illustrates. These five include one high-income, all-white district at the periphery of the city, two very low-income, virtually all-Negro districts near the city core with numerous public housing projects, and two predominantly white districts, one with mainly lower middle-income families, the other containing a mixture of very high-income and relatively low-income households. The table shows crime rates against persons and against property in these five districts, plus the number of patrolmen assigned to them per 100,000 residents, as follows:

Incidence of Index Crimes and Patrolmen Assignments per 100,000 Residents in 5 Chicago Police Districts, 1965

Number	High Income White District	Low-Middle-Income White District	Mixed High and Low-Income White District	Very Low Income Negro District No. 1	Very Low Income Negro District No. 2
Index crimes against persons	80	440	838	1,615	2,820
Index crimes against property	1,038	1,750	2,080	2,508	2,630
Patrolmen assigned	93	133	115	243	291

less likely to report (handwritten annotation)

These data indicate that:

- Variations in the crime rate against persons within the city are extremely large. One very low income Negro district had 35 times as many serious crimes against persons per 100,000 residents as did the high-income white district.
- Variations in the crime rate against property are much smaller. The highest rate was only 2.5 times larger than the lowest.
- The lower income in an area, the higher the crime rate there. Yet low-income Negro areas have significantly higher crime rates than low-income white areas. This reflects the high degree of social disorganization in Negro areas described in the previous chapter, as well as the fact that poor Negroes as a group have lower incomes than poor whites as a group.
- The presence of more police patrolmen per 100,000 residents does not necessarily offset high crime in certain parts of the city. Although the Chicago Police Department had assigned over three times as many patrolmen per 100,000 residents to the highest crime areas shown as to the lowest, crime rates in the

highest crime area for offenses against both persons and property combined were 4.9 times as high as in the lowest crime area.

Because most middle-class Americans live in neighborhoods similar to the more crime-free district described above, they have little comprehension of the sense of insecurity that characterizes the ghetto resident. Moreover, official statistics normally greatly understate actual crime rates because the vast majority of crimes are not reported to the police. For example, studies conducted for the President's Crime Commission in Washington, D. C., Boston, and Chicago, showed that three to six times as many crimes were actually committed against persons and homes as were reported to the police.

Two facts are crucial to understand the effects of high crime rates in racial ghettos; most of these crimes are committed by a small minority of the residents, and the principal victims are the residents themselves. Throughout the United States, the great majority of crimes committed by Negroes involve other Negroes as victims. A special tabulation made by the Chicago Police Department for the President's Crime Commission indicated that over 85 percent of the crimes committed against persons by Negroes between September, 1965, and March, 1966, involved Negro victims.

As a result, the majority of law-abiding citizens who live in disadvantaged Negro areas face much higher probabilities of being victimized than residents of most higher income areas, including almost all suburbs. For nonwhites, the probability of suffering from any index crime except larceny is 78 percent higher than for whites. The probability of being raped is 3.7 times higher among nonwhite women, and the probability of being robbed is 3.5 times higher for nonwhites in general.

The problems associated with high crime rates generate widespread hostility toward the police in these neighborhoods for reasons described elsewhere in this Report. Thus, crime not only creates an atmosphere of insecurity and fear throughout Negro neighborhoods but also causes continuing attrition of the relationship between Negro residents and police. This bears a direct relationship to civil disorder.

There are reasons to expect the crime situation in these areas to become worse in the future. First, crime rates throughout the United States have been rising rapidly in recent years. The rate of index crimes against persons rose 37 percent from 1960 to 1966, and the rate of index crimes against property rose 50 percent. In the first 9 months of 1967, the number of index crimes was up 16 percent over the same period in 1966, whereas the U.S. population rose about 1 percent. In cities of 250,000 to 1 million, index crime rose by over 20 percent, whereas it increased 4 percent in cities of over one million.[9]

Second, the number of police available to combat crime is rising much more slowly than the amount of crime. In 1966, there were about 20 percent more police employees in the United States than in 1960, and per capita expenditures for police rose from $15.29 in 1960 to $20.99 in 1966, a gain of 37 percent. But over the 6-year period, the number of reported index crimes had jumped 62 percent. In spite of significant improvements in police efficiency, it is clear that police will be unable to cope with their expanding workload unless there is a dramatic increase in the resources allocated by society to this task.

Third, in the next decade the number of young Negroes aged 14 to 24 will increase rapidly, particularly in central cities. This group is responsible for a disproportionately high share of crimes in all parts of the Nation. In 1966, persons under 25 years of age comprised the following proportions of those arrested for various major crimes: murder, 37 percent; forcible rape, 64 percent; robbery, 71 percent; burglary, 81 percent; larceny, about 77 percent; and auto theft, 89 percent. For all index crimes together, the arrest rate for Negroes is about four times higher than that for whites. Yet the number of young Negroes aged 14 to 24 in central cities will rise about 63 percent from 1966 to 1975, as compared to only 32 percent for the total Negro population of central cities.[10]

HEALTH AND SANITATION CONDITIONS

The residents of the racial ghetto are significantly less healthy than most other Americans. They suffer from higher mortality rates, higher incidence

[9]   The problem of interpreting and evaluating "rising" crime rates is complicated by the changing age distribution of the population, improvements in reporting methods, and the increasing willingness of victims to report crimes. Despite these complications, there is general agreement on the serious increase in the incidence of crime in the United States.

[10]   Assuming those cities will experience the same proportion of total United States Negro population growth that they did from 1960 to 1966. The calculations are derived from population projections in Bureau of the Census, *Population Estimates*, Current Population Reports, Series P-25, No. 381. Dec. 18, 1967, p.63.

of major diseases, and lower availability and utilization of medical services. They also experience higher admission rates to mental hospitals.

These conditions result from a number of factors.

POVERTY

From the standpoint of health, poverty means deficient diets, lack of medical care, inadequate shelter and clothing, and often lack of awareness of potential health needs. As a result, about 30 percent of all families with incomes less than $2,000 per year suffer from chronic health conditions that adversely affect their employment—as compared with less than 8 percent of the families with incomes of $7,000 or more.

Poor families have the greatest need for financial assistance in meeting medical expenses. Only about 34 percent of families with incomes of less than $2,000 per year use health insurance benefits, as compared to nearly 90 percent of those with incomes of $7,000 or more.[11]

These factors are aggravated for Negroes when compared to whites for the simple reason that the proportion of persons in the United States who are poor is 3.5 times as high among Negroes (41 percent in 1966) as among whites (12 percent in 1966).

MATERNAL MORTALITY

Maternal mortality rates for nonwhite mothers are four times as high as those for white mothers. There has been a sharp decline in such rates since 1940, when 774 nonwhite and 320 white mothers died per 100,000 live births—but the gap between nonwhites and whites actually increased.

INFANT MORTALITY

Mortality rates among nonwhite babies are 58 percent higher than among whites for those under 1 month old and almost three times as high among those from 1 month to 1 year old. This is true in spite of a large drop in infant mortality rates in both groups since 1940.

---

[11]   Public programs of various kinds have been providing significant financial assistance for medical care in recent years. In 1964, over $1.1 billion was paid out by various governments for such aid. About 52 percent of medical vendor payments came from Federal Government Agencies, 33 percent from states, and 12 percent from local governments. The biggest contributions

Number of Infants Who Died per 1,000 Live Births

Year	Less Than One Month Old White	Less Than One Month Old Nonwhite	One Month to One Year Old White	One Month to One Year Old Nonwhite
1940	27.2	39.7	16.0	84.1
1950	19.4	27.5	7.4	17.0
1960	17.2	26.9	5.7	16.4
1965	16.1	25.4	5.4	14.9

LIFE EXPECTANCY

To some extent because of infant mortality rates, life expectancy at birth was 6.9 years longer for whites (71.0 years) than for nonwhites (64.1 years) in 1965. Even in the prime working ages, life expectancy is significantly lower among nonwhites than among whites. In 1965, white persons 25 years old could expect to live an average of 48.6 more years; whereas nonwhites 25 years old could expect to live another 43.3 years, or 11 percent less. Similar but smaller discrepancies existed at all ages from 25 through 55; and were actually increased slightly between 1960 and 1965.

LOWER UTILIZATION OF HEALTH SERVICES

A fact that also contributes to poorer health conditions in the ghetto is that Negroes with incomes similar to those of whites spend less on medical services and visit medical specialists less often.

Income Group	Percent of Family Expenditures Spent for Medical Care 1960-61 White	Percent of Family Expenditures Spent for Medical Care 1960-61 Nonwhite	Ratio White: Nonwhite
Under $3,000	9	5	1.8:1
$3,000 to $7,499	7	5	1.4:1
$7,500 & over	6	4	1.5:1

Since the lowest income group contains a much larger proportion of nonwhite families than white families, the overall discrepancy in medical care spending between these two groups is very significant, as shown by the following table:

---

were made by the Old Age Assistance Program and the Medical Assistance for the Aged Program. The enactment of Medicare in 1965 has significantly added to this flow of public assistance for medical aid. However, it is too early to evaluate the results upon health conditions among the poor.

Health Expenses per Person per Year for the Period
From July to December 1962

Income Racial Group	Total Medical	Expenses Hospital	Doctor	Dental	Medicine
Under $2,000 per Family per Year:					
White	$130	$33	$41	$11	$32
Nonwhite	63	15	23	5	16
$10,000 and More per Family per Year:					
White	$179	$34	$61	$37	$31
Nonwhite	133	34	50	19	23

These data indicate that nonwhite families in the lower income group spent less than half as much per person on medical services as white families with similar incomes. This discrepancy sharply declines but is still significant in the higher income group, where total nonwhite medical expenditures per person equal, on the average, 74.3 percent of white expenditures.

Negroes spend less on medical care for several reasons. Negro households generally are larger, requiring greater nonmedical expenses for each household and leaving less money for meeting medical expenses. Thus, lower expenditures per person would result even if expenditures per household were the same. Negroes also often pay more for certain other basic necessities such as food and consumer durables, as is discussed in the next part of this chapter. In addition, fewer doctors, dentists, and medical facilities are conveniently available to Negroes than to most whites—a result of both geographic concentration of doctors in higher income areas in large cities and of discrimination against Negroes by doctors and hospitals. A survey in Cleveland indicated that there were 0.45 physicians per 1,000 people in poor neighborhoods, compared to 1.13 per 1,000 people in nonpoverty areas. The result nationally is fewer visits to physicians and dentists.

Percent of Population Making One or More
Visits to Indicated Type of Medical
Specialist from July 1963 to June 1964

Type of Medical Specialist	Family Incomes of $2,000 to $3,999 White	Nonwhite	Family Incomes of $7,000 to $9,999 White	Nonwhite
Physician	64	56	70	64
Dentist	31	20	52	33

Although widespread use of health insurance has led many hospitals to adopt nondiscriminatory policies, some private hospitals still refuse to admit Negro patients or to accept doctors with Negro patients. And many individual doctors still discriminate against Negro patients. As a result, Negroes are more likely to be treated in hospital clinics than whites and they are less likely to receive personalized service. This conclusion is confirmed by the following data:

Type of Visit to Physician	Percent of All Visits to Physicians from July 1963 to June 1964 Made in Indicated Ways			
	Family Incomes of $2,000 to $3,999		Family Incomes of $7,000 to $9,999	
	White	Nonwhite	White	Nonwhite
In Physician's Office	68	56	73	66
Hospital clinic	17	35	7	16
Other (mainly telephone)	15	9	20	18
Total	100	100	100	100

ENVIRONMENTAL FACTORS

Environmental conditions in disadvantaged Negro neighborhoods create further reasons for poor health conditions there. The level of sanitation is strikingly below that which is prevalent in most higher income areas. One simple reason is that residents lack proper storage facilities for food—adequate refrigerators, freezers, even garbage cans which are sometimes stolen as fast as landlords can replace them.

In areas where garbage collection and other sanitation services are grossly inadequate—commonly in the poorer parts of our large cities—rats proliferate. It is estimated that in 1965, there were over 14,000 cases of ratbite in the United States, mostly in such neighborhoods.

The importance of these conditions was outlined for the Commission as follows:[12]

Sanitation Commissioners of New York City and Chicago both feel this [sanitation] to be an important community problem and report themselves as being under substantial pressure to improve conditions. *It must be concluded that slum sanitation is a serious problem in the minds of the urban poor and well merits, at least on that ground, the attention of the Commission.* A related problem, according to one Sanitation Commissioner, is the fact that residents of areas bordering on slums feel that sanitation and neighborhood cleanliness is a crucial issue, relating to

---

[12]   Memorandum to the Commission dated Nov. 16, 1967, from Robert Patricelli, minority counsel, Subcommittee on Employment Manpower and Poverty, U.S. Senate.

the stability of their blocks and constituting an important psychological index of "how far gone" their area is.

[***]

There is no known study comparing sanitation services between slum and non-slum areas. The experts agree, however, that there are more services in the slums on a quantitative basis, although perhaps not on a per capita basis. In New York, for example, garbage pickups are supposedly scheduled for about six times a week in slums, compared to three times a week in other areas of the city; the comparable figures in Chicago are two to three times a week versus once a week.

The point, therefore, is not the relative quantitative level of services, but the peculiarly intense needs of ghetto areas for sanitation services. This high demand is the product of numerous factors including: (1) higher population density; (2) lack of well managed buildings and adequate garbage services provided by landlords, number of receptacles, carrying to curbside, number of electric garbage disposals; (3) high relocation rates of tenants and businesses, producing heavy volume of bulk refuse left on streets and in buildings; (4) different uses of the streets—as outdoor living rooms in summer, recreation areas—producing high visibility and sensitivity to garbage problems; (5) large numbers of abandoned cars; (6) severe rodent and pest problems; (7) traffic congestion blocking garbage collection; and (8) obstructed street cleaning and snow removal on crowded, car-choked streets. Each of these elements adds to the problem and suggests a different possible line of attack.

EXPLOITATION OF DISADVANTAGED CONSUMERS BY RETAIL MERCHANTS

Much of the violence in recent civil disorders has been directed at stores and other commercial establishments in disadvantaged Negro areas. In some cases, rioters focused on stores operated by white merchants who, they apparently believed, had been charging exorbitant prices or selling inferior goods. Not all the violence against these stores can be attributed to "revenge" for such practices. Yet it is clear that many residents of disadvantaged Negro neighborhoods believe they suffer constant abuses by local merchants.

Significant grievances concerning unfair commercial practices affecting Negro consumers were found in 11 of the 20 cities studied by the Commission. The fact that most of the merchants who operate stores in almost every Negro area are white undoubtedly contributes to the conclusion among Negroes that they are exploited by white society.

It is difficult to assess the precise degree and extent of exploitation. No systematic and reliable survey comparing consumer pricing and credit practices in all-Negro and other neighborhoods has ever been conducted on a nationwide basis. Differences in prices and credit practices between white middle-income areas and Negro low-income areas to some extent reflect differences in the real costs of serving these two markets (such as differential losses from pilferage in supermarkets), but the exact extent of these differential real costs has never been estimated accurately. Finally, an examination of exploitative consumer practices must consider the particular structure and functions of the low-income consumer durables market.

INSTALLMENT BUYING

This complex situation can best be understood by first considering certain basic facts:

- Various cultural factors generate constant pressure on low-income families to buy many relatively expensive durable goods and display them in their homes. This pressure comes in part from continuous exposure to commercial advertising, especially on television. In January, 1967, over 88 percent of all Negro households had TV sets. A 1961 study of 464 low-income families in New York City showed that 95 percent of these relatively poor families had TV sets.

- Many poor families have extremely low incomes, bad previous credit records, unstable sources of income, or other attributes which make it virtually impossible for them to buy merchandise from established large national or local retail firms. These families lack enough savings to pay cash, and they cannot meet the standard credit requirements of established general merchants because they are too likely to fall behind in their payments.

- Poor families in urban areas are far less mobile than others. A 1967 Chicago study of low-income Negro households indicated their low automobile ownership compelled them to patronize primarily local neighborhood merchants. These merchants typically provided smaller selection, poorer services and higher prices than big national outlets. The 1961 New York study also indicated that families who shopped outside their own neighborhoods were far less likely to pay exorbitant prices.

- Most low-income families are uneducated concerning the nature of credit purchase contracts, the legal rights and obligations of both buyers and sellers, sources of advice for consumers who are having difficulties with merchants and the operation of the courts concerned with these matters. In contrast, merchants engaged in selling goods to them are very well informed.
- In most states, the laws governing relations between consumers and merchants in effect offer protection only to informed, sophisticated parties with understanding of each other's rights and obligations. Consequently, these laws are little suited to protect the rights of most low-income consumers.

In this situation, exploitative practices flourish. Ghetto residents who want to buy relatively expensive goods cannot do so from standard retail outlets and are thus restricted to local stores. Forced to use credit, they have little understanding of the pitfalls of credit buying. But because they have unstable incomes and frequently fail to make payments, the cost to the merchants of serving them is significantly above that of serving middle-income consumers. Consequently, a special kind of merchant appears to sell them goods on terms designed to cover the high cost of doing business in ghetto neighborhoods.

Whether they actually gain higher profits, these merchants charge higher prices than those in other parts of the city to cover the greater credit risks and other higher operating costs inherent in neighborhood outlets. A recent study conducted by the Federal Trade Commission in Washington, D. C., illustrates this conclusion dramatically. The FTC identified a number of stores specializing in selling furniture and appliances to low-income households. About 92 percent of the sales of these stores were credit sales involving installment purchases, as compared to 27 percent of the sales in general retail outlets handling the same merchandise.

The median income annually of a sample of 486 customers of these stores was about $4,200, but one-third had annual incomes below $3,600, about 6 percent were receiving welfare payments, and another 76 percent were employed in the lowest paying occupations (service workers, operatives, laborers, and domestics), as compared to 36 percent of the total labor force in Washington in those occupations.

Definitely catering to a low-income group, these stores charged significantly higher prices than general merchandise outlets in the

Washington area. According to testimony by Paul Rand Dixon, Chairman of the FTC, an item selling wholesale at $100 would retail on the average for $165 in a general merchandise store, and for $250 in a low-income specialty store. Thus, the customers of these outlets were paying an average price premium of about 52 percent.

While higher prices are not necessarily exploitative in themselves, many merchants in ghetto neighborhoods take advantage of their superior knowledge of credit buying by engaging in various exploitative tactics—high-pressure salesmanship, "bait advertising," misrepresentation of prices, substitution of used goods for promised new ones, failure to notify consumers of legal actions against them, refusal to repair or replace substandard goods, exorbitant prices or credit charges, and use of shoddy merchandise. Such tactics affect a great many low-income consumers. In the New York study 60 percent of all households had suffered from consumer problems (some of which were purely their own fault). About 23 percent had experienced serious exploitation. Another 20 percent, many of whom were also exploited, had experienced repossession, garnishment, or threat of garnishment.

GARNISHMENT

Garnishment practices in many states allow creditors to deprive individuals of their wages through court action, without hearing or trial. In about 20 states, the wages of an employee can be diverted to a creditor merely upon the latter's deposition, with no advance hearing where the employee can defend himself. He often receives no prior notice of such action and is usually unaware of the law's operation and too poor to hire legal defense. Moreover, consumers may find themselves still owing money on a sales contract even after the creditor has repossessed the goods. The New York study cited earlier in this chapter indicated that 20 percent of a sample of low-income families had been subject to legal action regarding consumer purchases. And the Federal Trade Commission study in Washington, D.C., showed that, on average, retailers specializing in credit sales of furniture and appliances to low-income consumers resorted to court action once for every $2,200 of sales. Since their average sale was for $207, this amounted to using the courts to collect from one of every 11 customers. In contrast, department stores in the same area used court action against approximately one of every 14,500 customers.[13]

---

[13]   Assuming their sales also averaged $207 per customer.

VARIATIONS IN FOOD PRICES

Residents of low-income Negro neighborhoods frequently claim that they pay higher prices for food in local markets than wealthier white suburbanites and receive inferior quality meat and produce. Statistically reliable information comparing prices and quality in these two kinds of areas is generally unavailable. The U.S. Bureau of Labor Statistics, studying food prices in six cities in 1966, compared prices of a standard list of 18 items in low-income areas and higher-income areas in each city. In a total of 180 stores, including independent and chain stores, and for items of the same type sold in the same types of stores, there were no significant differences in prices between low-income and high-income areas. However, stores in low-income areas were more likely to be small independents (which had somewhat higher prices), to sell low-quality produce and meat at any given price, and to be patronized by people who typically bought smaller sized packages which are more expensive per unit of measure. In other words, many low-income consumers in fact pay higher prices, although the situation varies greatly from place to place.

Although these findings must be considered inconclusive, there are significant reasons to believe that poor households generally pay higher prices for the food they buy and receive per quality food. Low-income consumers buy more food at local groceries because they are less mobile. Prices in these small stores are significantly higher than in major supermarkets because they cannot achieve economies of scale and because real operating costs are higher in low-income Negro areas than in outlying suburbs. For instance, inventory "shrinkage" from pilfering and other causes is normally under 2 percent of sales but can run twice as much in high-crime areas. Managers seek to make up for these added costs by charging higher prices for food or by substituting lower grades.

These practices do not necessarily involve "exploitation," but they are often perceived as exploitative and unfair by those who are aware of the price and quality differences involved but unaware of operating costs. In addition, it is probable that genuinely exploitative pricing practices exist in some areas. In either case, differential food prices constitute another factor convincing urban Negroes in low-income neighborhoods that whites discriminate against them.

CHAPTER 9
COMPARING THE IMMIGRANT
AND NEGRO EXPERIENCE

In the preceding chapters we have surveyed the historical background of racial discrimination and traced its effects on Negro employment, on the social structure of the ghetto community and on the conditions of life that surround the urban Negro poor. Here we address a fundamental question that many white Americans are asking today: Why has the Negro been unable to escape from poverty and the ghetto like the European immigrants?

THE MATURING ECONOMY

The changing nature of the American economy is one major reason. When the European immigrants were arriving in large numbers, America was becoming an urban-industrial society. To build its major cities and industries, America needed great pools of unskilled labor. The immigrants provided the labor, gained an economic foothold and thereby enabled their children and grandchildren to move up to skilled, white collar, and professional employment.

Since World War II especially, America's urban-industrial society has matured; unskilled labor is far less essential than before, and blue-collar jobs of all kinds are decreasing in number and importance as a source of new employment. The Negroes who migrated to the great urban centers lacked the skills essential to the new economy, and the schools of the ghetto have been unable to provide the education that can qualify them for decent jobs. The Negro migrant, unlike the immigrant, found little opportunity in the city; he had arrived too late, and the unskilled labor he had to offer was no longer needed.

THE DISABILITY OF RACE

Racial discrimination is undoubtedly the second major reason why the Negro has been unable to escape from poverty. The structure of discrimination has persistently narrowed his opportunities and restricted his prospects. Well before the high tide of immigration from overseas, Negroes were already relegated to the poorly paid, low status occupations.

Had it not been for racial discrimination, the North might well have recruited Southern Negroes after the Civil War to provide the labor for building the burgeoning urban-industrial economy. Instead, Northern employers looked to Europe for their sources of unskilled labor. Upon the arrival of the immigrants, the Negroes were dislodged from the few urban occupations they had dominated. Not until World War II were Negroes generally hired for industrial jobs, and by that time the decline in the need for unskilled labor had already begun. European immigrants, too, suffered from discrimination, but never was it so pervasive. The prejudice against color in America, has formed a bar to advancement unlike any other

ENTRY INTO THE POLITICAL SYSTEM

Political opportunities also played an important role in enabling the European immigrants to escape from poverty. The immigrants settled for the most part in rapidly growing cities that had powerful and expanding political machines which gave them economic advantages in exchange for political support. The political machines were decentralized, and ward-level grievance machinery as well as personal representation enabled the immigrant to make his voice heard and his power felt. Since the local political organizations exercised considerable influence over public building in the cities, they provided employment in construction jobs for their immigrant voters. Ethnic groups often dominated one or more of the municipal services—police and fire protection, sanitation and even public education.

By the time the Negroes arrived, the situation had altered dramatically. The great wave of public building had virtually come to an end; reform groups were beginning to attack the political machines; the machines were no longer so powerful or so well equipped to provide jobs and other favors.

Although the political machines retained their hold over the areas settled by Negroes, the scarcity of patronage jobs made them unwilling to share with the Negroes the political positions they had created in these neighborhoods. For example, Harlem was dominated by white politicians for many years after it had become a Negro ghetto; even today, New York's Lower East Side, which is now predominantly Puerto Rican, is strongly influenced by politicians of the older immigrant groups.

This pattern exists in many other American cities. Negroes are still underrepresented in city councils and in most city agencies.

Segregation played a role here too. The immigrants and their descendants, who felt threatened by the arrival of the Negro, prevented a Negro-immigrant coalition that might have saved the old political machines. Reform groups, nominally more liberal on the race issue, were often dominated by businessmen and middle-class city residents who usually opposed coalition with any low-income group, white or black.

CULTURAL FACTORS

Cultural factors also made it easier for the immigrants to escape from poverty. They came to America from much poorer societies, with a low standard of living, and they came at a time when job aspirations were low. When most jobs in the American economy were unskilled, they sensed little deprivation in being forced to take the dirty and poorly paid jobs. Moreover, their families were large, and many breadwinners, some of whom never married, contributed to the total family income. As a result, family units managed to live even from the lowest paid jobs and still put some money aside for savings or investment, for example, to purchase a house or tenement or to open a store or factory. Since the immigrants spoke little English and had their own ethnic culture, they needed stores to supply them with ethnic foods and other services. Since their family structures were patriarchal, men found satisfactions in family life that helped compensate for the bad jobs they had to take and the hard work they had to endure.

Negroes came to the city under quite different circumstances. Generally relegated to jobs that others would not take, they were paid too little to be able to put money in savings for new enterprises. In addition, Negroes lacked the extended family characteristic of certain European groups; each household usually had only one or two breadwinners. Moreover, Negro men had fewer cultural incentive to work in a dirty job for the sake of the family. As a result of slavery and of long periods of male unemployment afterwards, the Negro family structure had become matriarchal; the man played a secondary and marginal role in his family. For many Negro men, then, there were few of the cultural and psychological rewards of family life; they abandoned their homes because they felt themselves useless to their families.

Although most Negro men worked as hard as the immigrants to support their families, their rewards were less. The jobs did not pay enough to enable them to support their families, for prices and living standards had risen since the immigrants had come, and the entrepreneurial opportunities that had allowed some immigrants to become independent, even rich, had vanished. Above all, Negroes suffered from segregation, which denied them access to the good jobs and the right unions and which deprived them of the opportunity to buy real estate or obtain business loans or move out of the ghetto and bring up their children in middle-class neighborhoods. Immigrants were able to leave their ghettos as soon as they had the money; segregation has denied Negroes the opportunity to live elsewhere.

THE VITAL ELEMENT OF TIME

Finally, nostalgia makes it easy to exaggerate the ease of escape of the white immigrants from the ghettos. When the immigrants were immersed in poverty, they, too, lived in slums, and these neighborhoods exhibited fearfully high rates of alcoholism, desertion, illegitimacy and the other pathologies associated with poverty. Just as some Negro men desert their families when they are unemployed and their wives can get jobs, so did the men of other ethnic groups, even though time and affluence has clouded white memories of the past.

Today, whites tend to contrast their experience with poverty-stricken Negroes. The fact is, among many of the Southern and Eastern Europeans who came to America in the last great wave of immigration, those who came already urbanized were the first to escape from poverty. The others who came to America from rural background, as Negroes did, are only now, after three generations, in the final stages of escaping from poverty. Until the last 10 years or so, most of these were employed in blue-collar jobs, and only a small proportion of their children were able or willing to attend college. In other words, only the third, and in many cases, only the fourth, generation has been able to achieve the kind of middle-class income and status that allows it to send its children to college. Because of favorable economic and political conditions, these ethnic groups were able to escape from lower-class status to working class and lower middle-class status, but it has taken them three generations.

Negroes have been concentrated in the city for only two generations, and they have been there under much less favorable conditions. Moreover, their escape from poverty has been blocked in part by the resistance of the European ethnic groups; they have been unable to enter some unions and to move into some neighborhoods outside the ghetto because descendants of the European immigrants who control these unions and neighborhoods have not yet abandoned them for middle-class occupations and areas.

Even so, some Negroes have escaped poverty, and they have done so in only two generations; their success is less visible than that of the immigrants in many cases, for residential segregation has forced them to remain in the ghetto. Still, the proportion of nonwhites employed in white-collar, technical and professional jobs has risen from 10.2 percent in 1950 to 20.8 percent in 1966 and the proportion attending college has risen an equal amount. Indeed, the development of a small but steadily increasing Negro middle class while the greater part of the Negro population is stagnating economically is creating a growing gap between Negro haves and have-nots.

The awareness of this gap by those left behind undoubtedly adds to the feelings of desperation and anger which breed civil disorders. Low-income Negroes realize that segregation and lack of job opportunities have made it possible for only a small proportion of all Negroes to escape poverty, and the summer disorders are at least in part a protest against being left behind and left out.

The immigrant who labored long hours at hard and often menial work had the hope of a better future, if not for himself then for his children. This was the promise of the "American dream"—the society offered to all a future that was open ended; with hard work and perseverance, a man and his family could in time achieve not only material well-being but "position" and status.

For the Negro family in the urban ghetto, there is a different vision—the future seems to lead only to a dead end.

What the American economy of the late 19th and early 20th century was able to do to help the European immigrants escape from poverty is now largely impossible. New methods of escape must be found for the majority of today's poor.

KARL MARX

1818-1883

FRIEDRICH ENGELS

1820-1895

THE COMMUNIST MANIFESTO
1848

Political economist, sociologist, historian, and philosopher, Karl Heinrich Marx changed the world with his revolutionary ideas.[1] Marx was born in Trier, Germany, to prosperous Jewish parents, though the family was forced by the Prussian government to convert to Christianity so that his father could continue practicing law. Marx himself began the study of law at the University of Bonn at age 17, but spent much of his time drinking and spending money. His father transferred him to the more academically oriented University of Berlin, where he came under the influence of Georg Hegel and joined the Young Hegelians. In 1841, he submitted his dissertation to the University of Jena, which granted him a doctorate in philosophy. Unable to get an academic job because of his radical leanings, he turned instead to journalism and began writing commentaries on social and political conditions. In

---

[1]   Until the fall of the Soviet Union, approximately half the world's population lived in countries with political regimes that considered themselves Marxist, e.g., China, Cuba, North Korea, Laos, Vietnam, and the now defunct Communist states, including the former Soviet Union, Poland, Yugoslavia, Czechoslovakia, and Hungary.

1843, he married his childhood sweetheart (after a seven-year engagement) and began reading Rousseau, Montesquieu, Machiavelli and numerous histories while living at his mother-in-law's house. Shortly thereafter, almost penniless, he moved the family to Paris. Mingling with other young radicals, he engaged in lively discussion and exposed himself to a wide range of ideas by reading Adam Smith, Ricardo, Proudhon, Saint-Simon, Bakunin, and Heinrich Heine. But, perhaps most important, he met Friedrich Engels.

Friedrich Engels, born in Barmen, Germany, was the son of a wealthy textile manufacturer with offices in Manchester, England. At the age of 18, he dropped out of high school and took a job as a clerk. In his spare time, he began studying philosophy, especially Hegel. Three years later, he moved to Berlin, where he attended lectures, joined the Young Hegelians, and started his own literary career, writing several articles for the newspaper being edited by Marx. His father, alarmed by his son's growing radicalism, sent him to England to work in the family's cotton factory. Shocked at the poverty he observed, he wrote a blistering expose on working conditions in England. Returning to Germany in 1844, he detoured to Paris to meet Marx, his soon-to-be lifelong friend and frequent co-author. His involvement in politics continued to create problems at home:

> The business of the meetings and the 'dissolute conduct' of several of our local communists, with whom I, of course, consort, have again aroused all my old man's religious fanaticism, which has been further exacerbated by my declared intention of giving up the huckstering business for good and all—while my public appearance as a communist has also fostered in him bourgeois fanaticism of truly splendid proportions. (Engels, 1845)

From that time on, the two friends worked together to advance their cause on behalf of the workers of the world. Marx and his family (only four of their seven children survived into adulthood) lived in constant poverty and might have starved were it not for the financial assistance provided by Engels and his meager earnings as a correspondent.

Marx and Engels are best known for their *Manifesto of the Communist Party* (1848). Individually, *Das Kapital* (1867) and *The Grundrisse* (1857) by Marx and *The Condition of the Working Class in England in 1844* (1844) and *The Origin of the Family, Private Property, and the State* (1884) by Engels stand out as especially significant.

It is not uncommon for readers to be put off when confronting Marxist (or radical), literature for the first time. The writing is replete with arcane terminology that appears to be "mere obfuscation and pointless complexity" (Heilbroner, 1980, 30). This is not the case. The special vocabulary has a very particular purpose—it is intended to disorient and to disarm. By depriving us of the opportunity to continue using familiar words, words with myriad meanings unconsciously attached to them, Marx forces us to see with a fresh set of eyes.

> His contribution . . . was the discovery of an unsuspected level of reality beneath the surface of history . . . What Marx invented . . . was a mode of inquiry to reach that buried reality, a mode we may call *socioanalysis*.

> *Capital* . . . begins with the misperceptions the system imposes on those who have not learned to penetrate its facade, and who therefore remain at the level of its surface manifestations. Marx's first purpose is to show how the everyday concepts by which we seek to elucidate society—concepts such as "labor" or "capital"—are, in fact, deceiving outward appearances that we must learn to pierce, if we are to understand the actual processes of social existence. (Heilbroner, 1980, 17)

As you read this selection, see if you can distinguish between the conventional meaning of the word "capitalist" and the meaning that Marx and Engels assign to the word. Try to determine the extent to which words traditionally associated with economics carry implicit meanings that say something about underlying social relationships. Consider whether Marx and Engels are more sociologists than economists, or vice versa.

SELECTION FROM:

Marx, Karl & Engels, Friedrich. (1848). *Manifesto of the Communist Party*. Retrieved August 9, 2007, from http://www.marxists. org/archive/marx/works/1848/communist-manifesto/.

MANIFESTO OF THE COMMUNIST PARTY

PREFACE BY FREDRICK ENGELS

The Manifesto was published as the platform of the Communist League, a working men's association, first exclusively German, later on international, and under the political conditions of the Continent before

1848, unavoidably a secret society. At a Congress of the League, held in November 1847, Marx and Engels were commissioned to prepare a complete theoretical and practical party programme . . . . [T}he history of the Manifesto reflects the history of the modern working-class movement; at present, it is doubtless the most wide spread, the most international production of all socialist literature, the common platform acknowledged by millions of working men from Siberia to California.

Yet, when it was written, we could not have called it a socialist manifesto. By Socialists, in 1847, were understood, on the one hand the adherents of the various Utopian systems: Owenites in England, Fourierists in France, both of them already reduced to the position of mere sects, and gradually dying out; on the other hand, the most multifarious social quacks who, by all manner of tinkering, professed to redress, without any danger to capital and profit, all sorts of social grievances, in both cases men outside the working-class movement, and looking rather to the "educated" classes for support. Whatever portion of the working class had become convinced of the insufficiency of mere political revolutions, and had proclaimed the necessity of total social change, called itself Communist. It was a crude, rough-hewn, purely instinctive sort of communism; still, it touched the cardinal point and was powerful enough amongst the working class to produce the Utopian communism of Cabet in France, and of Weitling in Germany. Thus, in 1847, socialism was a middle-class movement, communism a working-class movement. Socialism was, on the Continent at least, "respectable"; communism was the very opposite. And as our notion, from the very beginning, was that "the emancipation of the workers must be the act of the working class itself," there could be no doubt as to which of the two names we must take. Moreover, we have, ever since, been far from repudiating it.

The Manifesto being our joint production, I consider myself bound to state that the fundamental proposition which forms the nucleus belongs to Marx. That proposition is: That in every historical epoch, the prevailing mode of economic production and exchange, and the social organization necessarily following from it, form the basis upon which it is built up, and from that which alone can be explained the political and intellectual history of that epoch; that consequently the whole history of mankind (since the dissolution of primitive tribal society, holding land in common ownership) has been a history of class struggles, contests between exploiting and exploited, ruling and oppressed classes; That the history of these class struggles forms a series of evolutions in which, nowadays, a stage has been reached where the exploited and oppressed class—the proletariat—cannot attain its emancipation from the sway of the exploiting and ruling class—the bourgeoisie—without, at the same time, and once and for all, emancipating society at large from all exploitation, oppression, class distinction, and class struggles.

This proposition, which, in my opinion, is destined to do for history what Darwin's theory has done for biology, we both of us, had been gradually approaching for some years before 1845 . . . .

Friedrich Engels

JANUARY 30, 1888, LONDON

A spectre is haunting Europe—the spectre of communism. All the powers of old Europe have entered into a holy alliance to exorcise this spectre: Pope and Tsar, Metternich and Guizot, French Radicals and German police-spies.

Where is the party in opposition that has not been decried as communistic by its opponents in power? Where is the opposition that has not hurled back the branding reproach of communism, against the more advanced opposition parties, as well as against its reactionary adversaries?

Two things result from this fact:

I.   Communism is already acknowledged by all European powers to be itself a power.

II. It is high time that Communists should openly, in the face of the whole world, publish their views, their aims, their tendencies, and meet this nursery tale of the Spectre of Communism with a manifesto of the party itself.

To this end, Communists of various nationalities have assembled in London and sketched the following manifesto, to be published in the English, French, German, Italian, Flemish and Danish languages.

BOURGEOIS AND PROLETARIANS[2]

The history of all hitherto existing society[3] is the history of class struggles.

---

[2]   By bourgeoisie is meant the class of modern capitalists, owners of the means of social production and employers of wage labour. By proletariat, the class of modern wage labourers who, having no means of production of their own, are reduced to selling their labour power in order to live. [Engels, 1888 English edition]

[3]   That is, all written history. In 1847, the pre-history of society, the social organisation existing previous to recorded history, all but unknown. Since

Freeman and slave, patrician and plebeian, lord and serf, guild-master[4] and journeyman, in a word, oppressor and oppressed, stood in constant opposition to one another, carried on an uninterrupted, now hidden, now open fight, a fight that each time ended, either in a revolutionary reconstitution of society at large, or in the common ruin of the contending classes.

In the earlier epochs of history, we find almost everywhere a complicated arrangement of society into various orders, a manifold gradation of social rank. In ancient Rome we have patricians, knights, plebeians, slaves; in the Middle Ages, feudal lords, vassals, guild-masters, journeymen, apprentices, serfs; in almost all of these classes, again, subordinate gradations.

The modern bourgeois society that has sprouted from the ruins of feudal society has not done away with class antagonisms. It has but established new classes, new conditions of oppression, new forms of struggle in place of the old ones.

Our epoch, the epoch of the bourgeoisie, possesses, however, this distinct feature: it has simplified class antagonisms. Society as a whole is more and more splitting up into two great hostile camps, into two great classes directly facing each other—Bourgeoisie and Proletariat.

From the serfs of the Middle Ages sprang the chartered burghers of the earliest towns. From these burgesses the first elements of the bourgeoisie were developed.

The discovery of America, the rounding of the Cape, opened up fresh ground for the rising bourgeoisie. The East-Indian and Chinese markets, the

---

then, August von Haxthausen (1792-1866) discovered common ownership of land in Russia, Georg Ludwig von Maurer proved it to be the social foundation from which all Teutonic races started in history, and, by and by, village communities were found to be, or to have been, the primitive form of society everywhere from India to Ireland. The inner organisation of this primitive communistic society was laid bare, in its typical form, by Lewis Henry Morgan's (1818-1861) crowning discovery of the true nature of the gens and its relation to the tribe. With the dissolution of the primeval communities, society begins to be differentiated into separate and finally antagonistic classes. I have attempted to retrace this dissolution in The Origin of the Family, Private Property, and the State, second edition, Stuttgart, 1886. [Engels, 1888 English Edition and 1890 German Edition (with the last sentence omitted)]

4   Guild-master, that is, a full member of a guild, a master within, not a head of a guild. [Engels, 1888 English Edition]

colonisation of America, trade with the colonies, the increase in the means of exchange and in commodities generally, gave to commerce, to navigation, to industry, an impulse never before known, and thereby, to the revolutionary element in the tottering feudal society, a rapid development.

The feudal system of industry, in which industrial production was monopolised by closed guilds, now no longer sufficed for the growing wants of the new markets. The manufacturing system took its place. The guild-masters were pushed on one side by the manufacturing middle class; division of labour between the different corporate guilds vanished in the face of division of labour in each single workshop.

Meantime the markets kept ever growing, the demand ever rising. Even manufacturer no longer sufficed. Thereupon, steam and machinery revolutionised industrial production. The place of manufacture was taken by the giant, Modern Industry; the place of the industrial middle class by industrial millionaires, the leaders of the whole industrial armies, the modern bourgeois.

Modern industry has established the world market, for which the discovery of America paved the way. This market has given an immense development to commerce, to navigation, to communication by land. This development has, in its turn, reacted on the extension of industry; and in proportion as industry, commerce, navigation, railways extended, in the same proportion the bourgeoisie developed, increased its capital, and pushed into the background every class handed down from the Middle Ages.

We see, therefore, how the modern bourgeoisie is itself the product of a long course of development, of a series of revolutions in the modes of production and of exchange.

Each step in the development of the bourgeoisie was accompanied by a corresponding political advance of that class. An oppressed class under the sway of the feudal nobility, an armed and self-governing association in the medieval commune[5]: here independent urban republic (as in

---

[5]   This was the name given their urban communities by the townsmen of Italy and France, after they had purchased or conquered their initial rights of self-government from their feudal lords. [Engels, 1890 German edition] "Commune" was the name taken in France by the nascent towns even before they had conquered from their feudal lords and masters local self-government and political rights as the "Third Estate". Generally speaking, for the economical development of the bourgeoisie, England is here taken as the typical country, for its political development, France. [Engels, 1888 English Edition]

Italy and Germany); there taxable "third estate" of the monarchy (as in France); afterwards, in the period of manufacturing proper, serving either the semi-feudal or the absolute monarchy as a counterpoise against the nobility, and, in fact, cornerstone of the great monarchies in general, the bourgeoisie has at last, since the establishment of Modern Industry and of the world market, conquered for itself, in the modern representative State, exclusive political sway. The executive of the modern state is but a committee for managing the common affairs of the whole bourgeoisie.

The bourgeoisie, historically, has played a most revolutionary part.

The bourgeoisie, wherever it has got the upper hand, has put an end to all feudal, patriarchal, idyllic relations. It has pitilessly torn asunder the motley feudal ties that bound man to his "natural superiors", and has left remaining no other nexus between man and man than naked self-interest, than callous "cash payment". It has drowned the most heavenly ecstasies of religious fervour, of chivalrous enthusiasm, of philistine sentimentalism, in the icy water of egotistical calculation. It has resolved personal worth into exchange value, and in place of the numberless indefeasible chartered freedoms, has set up that single, unconscionable freedom—Free Trade. In one word, for exploitation, veiled by religious and political illusions, it has substituted naked, shameless, direct, brutal exploitation.

The bourgeoisie has stripped of its halo every occupation hitherto honoured and looked up to with reverent awe. It has converted the physician, the lawyer, the priest, the poet, the man of science, into its paid wage labourers.

The bourgeoisie has torn away from the family its sentimental veil, and has reduced the family relation to a mere money relation.

The bourgeoisie has disclosed how it came to pass that the brutal display of vigour in the Middle Ages, which reactionaries so much admire, found its fitting complement in the most slothful indolence. It has been the first to show what man's activity can bring about. It has accomplished wonders far surpassing Egyptian pyramids, Roman aqueducts, and Gothic cathedrals; it has conducted expeditions that put in the shade all former Exoduses of nations and crusades.

The bourgeoisie cannot exist without constantly revolutionising the instruments of production, and thereby the relations of production, and with them the whole relations of society. Conservation of the old modes of production in unaltered form, was, on the contrary, the first condition of existence for all earlier industrial classes. Constant revolutionising of production, uninterrupted disturbance of all social conditions, everlasting uncertainty and agitation distinguish the bourgeois epoch from all earlier ones. All fixed, fast-frozen relations, with their train of ancient and venerable prejudices and opinions, are swept away, all new-formed ones become antiquated before they can ossify. All that is solid melts into air, all that is holy is profaned, and man is at last compelled to face with sober senses his, real conditions of life, and his relations with his kind.

The need of a constantly expanding market for its products chases the bourgeoisie over the entire surface of the globe. It must nestle everywhere, settle everywhere, establish connexions everywhere.

The bourgeoisie has through its exploitation of the world market given a cosmopolitan character to production and consumption in every country. To the great chagrin of Reactionists, it has drawn from under the feet of industry the national ground on which it stood. All old-established national industries have been destroyed or are daily being destroyed. They are dislodged by new industries, whose introduction becomes a life and death question for all civilised nations, by industries that no longer work up indigenous raw material, but raw material drawn from the remotest zones; industries whose products are consumed, not only at home, but in every quarter of the globe. In place of the old wants, satisfied by the production of the country, we find new wants, requiring for their satisfaction the products of distant lands and climes. In place of the old local and national seclusion and self-sufficiency, we have intercourse in every direction, universal inter-dependence of nations. And as in material, so also in intellectual production. The intellectual creations of individual nations become common property. National one-sidedness and narrow-mindedness become more and more impossible, and from the numerous national and local literatures, there arises a world literature.

The bourgeoisie, by the rapid improvement of all instruments of production, by the immensely facilitated means of communication, draws all, even the most barbarian, nations into civilisation. The cheap prices of commodities are the heavy artillery with which it batters down all Chinese walls, with which it forces the barbarians' intensely obstinate hatred of foreigners to capitulate. It compels all nations, on pain of extinction, to adopt the bourgeois mode of production; it compels them to introduce what it calls civilisation into their midst, i.e., to become bourgeois themselves. In one word, it creates a world after its own image.

The bourgeoisie has subjected the country to the rule of the towns. It has created enormous cities, has greatly increased the urban population as compared with the rural, and has thus rescued a considerable part of the population from the idiocy of rural life. Just as it has made the country dependent on the towns, so it has made barbarian and semi-barbarian countries dependent on the civilised ones, nations of peasants on nations of bourgeois, the East on the West.

The bourgeoisie keeps more and more doing away with the scattered state of the population, of the means of production, and of property. It has agglomerated population, centralised the means of production, and has concentrated property in a few hands. The necessary consequence of this was political centralisation. Independent, or but loosely connected provinces, with separate interests, laws, governments, and systems of taxation, became lumped together into one nation, with one government, one code of laws, one national class-interest, one frontier, and one customs-tariff.

The bourgeoisie, during its rule of scarce one hundred years, has created more massive and more colossal productive forces than have all preceding generations together. Subjection of Nature's forces to man, machinery, application of chemistry to industry and agriculture, steam-navigation, railways, electric telegraphs, clearing of whole continents for cultivation, canalisation or rivers, whole populations conjured out of the ground—what earlier century had even a presentiment that such productive forces slumbered in the lap of social labour?

We see then: the means of production and of exchange, on whose foundation the bourgeoisie built itself up, were generated in feudal society. At a certain stage in the development of these means of production and of exchange, the conditions under which feudal society produced and exchanged, the feudal organisation of agriculture and manufacturing industry, in one word, the feudal relations of property became no longer compatible with the already developed productive forces; they became so many fetters. They had to be burst asunder; they were burst asunder.

Into their place stepped free competition, accompanied by a social and political constitution adapted in it, and the economic and political sway of the bourgeois class.

A similar movement is going on before our own eyes. Modern bourgeois society, with its relations of production, of exchange and of property, a society that has conjured up such gigantic means of production and of exchange, is like the sorcerer who is no longer able to control the powers of the nether world whom he has called up by his spells. For many a decade past the history of industry and commerce is but the history of the revolt of modern productive forces against modern conditions of production, against the property relations that are the conditions for the existence of the bourgeois and of its rule. It is enough to mention the commercial crises that by their periodical return put the existence of the entire bourgeois society on its trial, each time more threateningly. In these crises, a great part not only of the existing products, but also of the previously created productive forces, are periodically destroyed. In these crises, there breaks out an epidemic that, in all earlier epochs, would have seemed an absurdity—the epidemic of over-production. Society suddenly finds itself put back into a state of momentary barbarism; it appears as if a famine, a universal war of devastation, had cut off the supply of every means of subsistence; industry and commerce seem to be destroyed; and why? Because there is too much civilisation, too much means of subsistence, too much industry, too much commerce. The productive forces at the disposal of society no longer tend to further the development of the conditions of bourgeois property; on the contrary, they have become too powerful for these conditions, by which they are fettered, and so soon as they overcome these fetters, they bring disorder into the whole of bourgeois society, endanger the existence of bourgeois property. The conditions of bourgeois society are too narrow to comprise the wealth created by them. And how does the bourgeoisie get over these crises? On the one hand by enforced destruction of a mass of productive forces; on the other, by the conquest of new markets, and by the more thorough exploitation of the old ones. That is to say, by paving the way for more extensive and more destructive crises, and by diminishing the means whereby crises are prevented.

The weapons with which the bourgeoisie felled feudalism to the ground are now turned against the bourgeoisie itself.

But not only has the bourgeoisie forged the weapons that bring death to itself; it has also called into existence the men who are to wield those weapons—the modern working class—the proletarians.

In proportion as the bourgeoisie, i.e., capital, is developed, in the same proportion is the proletariat, the modern working class, developed—a class of labourers, who live only so long as they find work, and who find work only so long as their labour increases capital. These labourers, who must sell themselves piecemeal, are a commodity, like every other article of commerce, and are consequently exposed to all the vicissitudes of competition, to all the fluctuations of the market.

Owing to the extensive use of machinery, and to the division of labour, the work of the proletarians has lost all individual character, and, consequently, all charm for the workman. He becomes an appendage of the machine, and it is only the most simple, most monotonous, and most easily acquired knack, that is required of him. Hence, the cost of production of a workman is restricted, almost entirely, to the means of subsistence that he requires for maintenance, and for the propagation of his race. But the price of a commodity, and therefore also of labour, is equal to its cost of production. In proportion, therefore, as the repulsiveness of the work increases, the wage decreases. Nay more, in proportion as the use of machinery and division of labour increases, in the same proportion the burden of toil also increases, whether by prolongation of the working hours, by the increase of the work exacted in a given time or by increased speed of machinery, etc.

Modern Industry has converted the little workshop of the patriarchal master into the great factory of the industrial capitalist. Masses of labourers, crowded into the factory, are organised like soldiers. As privates of the industrial army they are placed under the command of a perfect hierarchy of officers and sergeants. Not only are they slaves of the bourgeois class, and of the bourgeois State; they are daily and hourly enslaved by the machine, by the overlooker, and, above all, by the individual bourgeois manufacturer himself. The more openly this despotism proclaims gain to be its end and aim, the more petty, the more hateful and the more embittering it is.

The less the skill and exertion of strength implied in manual labour, in other words, the more modern industry becomes developed, the more is the labour of men superseded by that of women. Differences of age and sex have no longer any distinctive social validity for the working class. All are instruments of labour, more or less expensive to use, according to their age and sex.

No sooner is the exploitation of the labourer by the manufacturer, so far, at an end, that he receives his wages in cash, than he is set upon by the other portions of the bourgeoisie, the landlord, the shopkeeper, the pawnbroker, etc.

The lower strata of the middle class—the small tradespeople, shopkeepers, and retired tradesmen generally, the handicraftsmen and peasants—all these sink gradually into the proletariat, partly because their diminutive capital does not suffice for the scale on which Modern Industry is carried on, and is swamped in the competition with the large capitalists, partly because their specialised skill is rendered worthless by new methods of production. Thus the proletariat is recruited from all classes of the population.

The proletariat goes through various stages of development. With its birth begins its struggle with the bourgeoisie. At first the contest is carried on by individual labourers, then by the workpeople of a factory, then by the operative of one trade, in one locality, against the individual bourgeois who directly exploits them. They direct their attacks not against the bourgeois conditions of production, but against the instruments of production themselves; they destroy imported wares that compete with their labour, they smash to pieces machinery, they set factories ablaze, they seek to restore by force the vanished status of the workman of the Middle Ages.

At this stage, the labourers still form an incoherent mass scattered over the whole country, and broken up by their mutual competition. If anywhere they unite to form more compact bodies, this is not yet the consequence of their own active union, but of the union of the bourgeoisie, which class, in order to attain its own political ends, is compelled to set the whole proletariat in motion, and is moreover yet, for a time, able to do so. At this stage, therefore, the proletarians do not fight their enemies, but the enemies of their enemies, the remnants of absolute monarchy, the landowners, the non-industrial bourgeois, the petty bourgeois. Thus, the whole historical movement is concentrated in the hands of the bourgeoisie; every victory so obtained is a victory for the bourgeoisie.

But with the development of industry, the proletariat not only increases in number; it becomes concentrated in greater masses, its strength grows, and it feels that strength more. The various interests and conditions of life within the ranks of the proletariat are more and more equalised, in proportion as machinery obliterates all distinctions of labour, and nearly everywhere reduces wages to the same low level. The growing competition among the bourgeois, and the resulting commercial crises, make the wages of the workers ever more fluctuating. The increasing improvement of machinery, ever more rapidly developing, makes their livelihood more and more precarious; the collisions between individual workmen and individual bourgeois take more and more the character of collisions between two classes. Thereupon, the workers begin to form combinations (Trades' Unions) against the bourgeois; they club together in order to keep up the rate of wages; they found permanent associations in order to make provision beforehand for these occasional revolts. Here and there, the contest breaks out into riots.

Now and then the workers are victorious, but only for a time. The real fruit of their battles lies, not in the immediate result, but in the ever expanding union of the workers. This union is helped on by the improved means of communication that are created by modern industry, and that place the workers of different localities in contact with one another. It was just this contact that was needed to centralise the numerous local struggles, all of the same character, into one national struggle between classes. But every class struggle is a political struggle. And that union, to attain which the burghers of the Middle Ages, with their miserable highways, required centuries, the modern proletarian, thanks to railways, achieve in a few years.

This organisation of the proletarians into a class, and, consequently into a political party, is continually being upset again by the competition between the workers themselves. But it ever rises up again, stronger, firmer, mightier. It compels legislative recognition of particular interests of the workers, by taking advantage of the divisions among the bourgeoisie itself. Thus, the ten-hours' bill in England was carried.

Altogether collisions between the classes of the old society further, in many ways, the course of development of the proletariat. The bourgeoisie finds itself involved in a constant battle. At first with the aristocracy; later on, with those portions of the bourgeoisie itself, whose interests have become antagonistic to the progress of industry; at all time with the bourgeoisie of foreign countries. In all these battles, it sees itself compelled to appeal to the proletariat, to ask for help, and thus, to drag it into the political arena. The bourgeoisie itself, therefore, supplies the proletariat with its own elements of political and general education, in other words, it furnishes the proletariat with weapons for fighting the bourgeoisie.

Further, as we have already seen, entire sections of the ruling class are, by the advance of industry, precipitated into the proletariat, or are at least threatened in their conditions of existence. These also supply the proletariat with fresh elements of enlightenment and progress.

Finally, in times when the class struggle nears the decisive hour, the progress of dissolution going on within the ruling class, in fact within the whole range of old society, assumes such a violent, glaring character, that a small section of the ruling class cuts itself adrift, and joins the revolutionary class, the class that holds the future in its hands. Just as, therefore, at an earlier period, a section of the nobility went over to the bourgeoisie, so now a portion of the bourgeoisie goes over to the proletariat, and in particular, a portion of the bourgeois ideologists, who have raised themselves to the level of comprehending theoretically the historical movement as a whole.

Of all the classes that stand face to face with the bourgeoisie today, the proletariat alone is a really revolutionary class. The other classes decay and finally disappear in the face of Modern Industry; the proletariat is its special and essential product.

The lower middle class, the small manufacturer, the shopkeeper, the artisan, the peasant, all these fight against the bourgeoisie, to save from extinction their existence as fractions of the middle class. They are therefore not revolutionary, but conservative. Nay more, they are reactionary, for they try to roll back the wheel of history. If by chance, they are revolutionary, they are only so in view of their impending transfer into the proletariat; they thus defend not their present, but their future interests, they desert their own standpoint to place themselves at that of the proletariat.

The "dangerous class", [lumpenproletariat] the social scum, that passively rotting mass thrown off by the lowest layers of the old society, may, here and there, be swept into the movement by a proletarian revolution; its conditions of life, however, prepare it far more for the part of a bribed tool of reactionary intrigue.

In the condition of the proletariat, those of old society at large are already virtually swamped. The proletarian is without property; his relation to his wife and children has no longer anything in common with the bourgeois family relations; modern industry labour, modern subjection to capital, the same in England as in France, in America as in Germany, has stripped him of every trace of national character. Law, morality, religion, are to him so many bourgeois prejudices, behind which lurk in ambush just as many bourgeois interests.

All the preceding classes that got the upper hand sought to fortify their already acquired status by subjecting society at large to their conditions of appropriation. The proletarians cannot become masters of the productive forces of society, except by abolishing their own previous mode of appropriation, and thereby also every other previous mode of appropriation. They have nothing of their own to secure and to fortify; their mission is to destroy all previous securities for, and insurances of, individual property.

All previous historical movements were movements of minorities, or in the interest of minorities. The proletarian movement is the self-conscious, independent movement of the immense majority, in the interest of the immense majority. The proletariat, the lowest stratum of our present society, cannot stir, cannot raise itself up, without the whole superincumbent strata of official society being sprung into the air.

Though not in substance, yet in form, the struggle of the proletariat with the bourgeoisie is at first a national struggle. The proletariat of each country must, of course, first of all settle matters with its own bourgeoisie.

In depicting the most general phases of the development of the proletariat, we traced the more or less veiled civil war, raging within existing society, up to the point where that war breaks out into open revolution, and where the violent overthrow of the bourgeoisie lays the foundation for the sway of the proletariat.

Hitherto, every form of society has been based, as we have already seen, on the antagonism of oppressing and oppressed classes. But in order to oppress a class, certain conditions must be assured to it under which it can, at least, continue its slavish existence. The serf, in the period of serfdom, raised himself to membership in the commune, just as the petty bourgeois, under the yoke of the feudal absolutism, managed to develop into a bourgeois. The modern labourer, on the contrary, instead of rising with the process of industry, sinks deeper and deeper below the conditions of existence of his own class. He becomes a pauper, and pauperism develops more rapidly than population and wealth. And here it becomes evident, that the bourgeoisie is unfit any longer to be the ruling class in society, and to impose its conditions of existence upon society as an over-riding law. It is unfit to rule because it is incompetent to assure an existence to its slave within his slavery, because it cannot help letting him sink into such a state, that it has to feed him, instead of being fed by him. Society can no longer live under this bourgeoisie, in other words, its existence is no longer compatible with society.

The essential conditions for the existence and for the sway of the bourgeois class is the formation and augmentation of capital; the condition for capital is wage-labour. Wage-labour rests exclusively on competition between the labourers. The advance of industry, whose involuntary promoter is the bourgeoisie, replaces the isolation of the labourers, due to competition, by the revolutionary combination, due to association. The development of Modern Industry, therefore, cuts from under its feet the very foundation on which the bourgeoisie produces and appropriates products. What the bourgeoisie therefore produces, above all, are its own grave-diggers. Its fall and the victory of the proletariat are equally inevitable.

PROLETARIANS AND COMMUNISTS

In what relation do the Communists stand to the proletarians as a whole? The Communists do not form a separate party opposed to the other working-class parties.

They have no interests separate and apart from those of the proletariat as a whole.

They do not set up any sectarian principles of their own, by which to shape and mould the proletarian movement.

The Communists are distinguished from the other working-class parties by this only:

(1) In the national struggles of the proletarians of the different countries, they point out and bring to the front the common interests of the entire proletariat, independently of all nationality.
(2) In the various stages of development which the struggle of the working class against the bourgeoisie has to pass through, they always and everywhere represent the interests of the movement as a whole.

The Communists, therefore, are on the one hand, practically, the most advanced and resolute section of the working-class parties of every country, that section which pushes forward all others; on the other hand, theoretically, they have over the great mass of the proletariat the advantage of clearly understanding the lines of march, the conditions, and the ultimate general results of the proletarian movement.

The immediate aim of the Communists is the same as that of all other proletarian parties: formation of the proletariat into a class, overthrow of the bourgeois supremacy, conquest of political power by the proletariat.

The theoretical conclusions of the Communists are in no way based on ideas or principles that have been invented, or discovered, by this or that would-be universal reformer.

They merely express, in general terms, actual relations springing from an existing class struggle, from a historical movement going on under our very eyes. The abolition of existing property relations is not at all a distinctive feature of communism.

All property relations in the past have continually been subject to historical change consequent upon the change in historical conditions.

The French Revolution, for example, abolished feudal property in favour of bourgeois property.

The distinguishing feature of Communism is not the abolition of property generally, but the abolition of bourgeois property. But modern bourgeois private property is the final and most complete expression of the system of producing and appropriating products, that is based on class antagonisms, on the exploitation of the many by the few.

In this sense, the theory of the Communists may be summed up in the single sentence: Abolition of private property.

We Communists have been reproached with the desire of abolishing the right of personally acquiring property as the fruit of a man's own labour, which property is alleged to be the groundwork of all personal freedom, activity and independence.

Hard-won, self-acquired, self-earned property! Do you mean the property of petty artisan and of the small peasant, a form of property that preceded the bourgeois form? There is no need to abolish that; the development of industry has to a great extent already destroyed it, and is still destroying it daily.

Or do you mean the modern bourgeois private property?

But does wage-labour create any property for the labourer? Not a bit. It creates capital, i.e., that kind of property which exploits wage-labour, and which cannot increase except upon condition of begetting a new supply of wage-labour for fresh exploitation. Property, in its present form, is based on the antagonism of capital and wage labour. Let us examine both sides of this antagonism.

To be a capitalist, is to have not only a purely personal, but a social status in production. Capital is a collective product, and only by the united action of many members, nay, in the last resort, only by the united action of all members of society, can it be set in motion.

Capital is therefore not only personal; it is a social power.

When, therefore, capital is converted into common property, into the property of all members of society, personal property is not thereby transformed into social property. It is only the social character of the property that is changed. It loses its class character.

Let us now take wage-labour.

The average price of wage-labour is the minimum wage, i.e., that quantum of the means of subsistence which is absolutely requisite to keep the labourer in bare existence as a labourer. What, therefore, the wage-labourer appropriates by means of his labour, merely suffices to prolong and reproduce a bare existence. We by no means intend to abolish this personal appropriation of the products of labour, an appropriation that is made for the maintenance and reproduction of human life, and that leaves no surplus wherewith to command the labour of others. All that we want to do away with is the miserable character of this appropriation, under which the labourer lives merely to increase capital, and is allowed to live only in so far as the interest of the ruling class requires it.

In bourgeois society, living labour is but a means to increase accumulated labour. In Communist society, accumulated labour is but a means to widen, to enrich, to promote the existence of the labourer.

In bourgeois society, therefore, the past dominates the present; in Communist society, the present dominates the past. In bourgeois society capital is independent and has individuality, while the living person is dependent and has no individuality.

And the abolition of this state of things is called by the bourgeois, abolition of individuality and freedom! And rightly so. The abolition of bourgeois individuality, bourgeois independence, and bourgeois freedom is undoubtedly aimed at.

By freedom is meant, under the present bourgeois conditions of production, free trade, free selling and buying.

But if selling and buying disappears, free selling and buying disappears also. This talk about free selling and buying, and all the other "brave words" of our bourgeois about freedom in general, have a meaning, if any, only in contrast with restricted selling and buying, with the fettered traders of the Middle Ages, but have no meaning when opposed to the Communistic abolition of buying and selling, of the bourgeois conditions of production, and of the bourgeoisie itself.

You are horrified at our intending to do away with private property. But in your existing society, private property is already done away with for nine-tenths of the population; its existence for the few is solely due to its non-existence in the hands of those nine-tenths. You reproach us, therefore, with intending to do away with a form of property, the necessary condition for whose existence is the non-existence of any property for the immense majority of society.

In one word, you reproach us with intending to do away with your property. Precisely so; that is just what we intend.

From the moment when labour can no longer be converted into capital, money, or rent, into a social power capable of being monopolised, i.e., from the moment when individual property can no longer be transformed into bourgeois property, into capital, from that moment, you say, individuality vanishes.

You must, therefore, confess that by "individual" you mean no other person than the bourgeois, than the middle-class owner of property. This person must, indeed, be swept out of the way, and made impossible.

Communism deprives no man of the power to appropriate the products of society; all that it does is to deprive him of the power to subjugate the labour of others by means of such appropriations.

It has been objected that upon the abolition of private property, all work will cease, and universal laziness will overtake us.

According to this, bourgeois society ought long ago to have gone to the dogs through sheer idleness; for those of its members who work, acquire nothing, and those who acquire anything do not work. The whole of this objection is but another expression of the tautology: that there can no longer be any wage-labour when there is no longer any capital.

All objections urged against the Communistic mode of producing and appropriating material products, have, in the same way, been urged against the Communistic mode of producing and appropriating intellectual products. Just as, to the bourgeois, the disappearance of class property is the disappearance of production itself, so the disappearance of class culture is to him identical with the disappearance of all culture.

That culture, the loss of which he laments, is, for the enormous majority, a mere training to act as a machine.

But don't wrangle with us so long as you apply, to our intended abolition of bourgeois property, the standard of your bourgeois notions of freedom, culture, law, &c. Your very ideas are but the outgrowth of the conditions of your bourgeois production and bourgeois property, just as your jurisprudence is but the will of your class made into a law for all, a will whose essential character and direction are determined by the economical conditions of existence of your class.

The selfish misconception that induces you to transform into eternal laws of nature and of reason, the social forms springing from your present mode of production and form of property—historical relations that rise and disappear in the progress of production—this misconception you share with every ruling class that has preceded you. What you see clearly in the case of ancient property, what you admit in the case of feudal property, you are of course forbidden to admit in the case of your own bourgeois form of property.

Abolition [Aufhebung] of the family! Even the most radical flare up at this infamous proposal of the Communists.

On what foundation is the present family, the bourgeois family, based? On capital, on private gain. In its completely developed form, this family exists only among the bourgeoisie. But this state of things finds its complement in the practical absence of the family among the proletarians, and in public prostitution.

The bourgeois family will vanish as a matter of course when its complement vanishes, and both will vanish with the vanishing of capital.

Do you charge us with wanting to stop the exploitation of children by their parents? To this crime we plead guilty.

But, you say, we destroy the most hallowed of relations, when we replace home education by social.

And your education! Is not that also social, and determined by the social conditions under which you educate, by the intervention direct or indirect, of society, by means of schools, &c.? The Communists have not invented the intervention of society in education; they do but seek to alter the character of that intervention, and to rescue education from the influence of the ruling class.

The bourgeois clap-trap about the family and education, about the hallowed co-relation of parents and child, becomes all the more disgusting, the more, by the action of Modern Industry, all the family ties among the proletarians are torn asunder, and their children transformed into simple articles of commerce and instruments of labour.

But you Communists would introduce community of women, screams the bourgeoisie in chorus.

The bourgeois sees his wife a mere instrument of production. He hears that the instruments of production are to be exploited in common, and, naturally, can come to no other conclusion that the lot of being common to all will likewise fall to the women.

He has not even a suspicion that the real point aimed at is to do away with the status of women as mere instruments of production.

For the rest, nothing is more ridiculous than the virtuous indignation of our bourgeois at the community of women which, they pretend, is to be openly and officially established by the Communists. The Communists have no need to introduce community of women; it has existed almost from time immemorial.

Our bourgeois, not content with having wives and daughters of their proletarians at their disposal, not to speak of common prostitutes, take the greatest pleasure in seducing each other's wives.

Bourgeois marriage is, in reality, a system of wives in common and thus, at the most, what the Communists might possibly be reproached with is that they desire to introduce, in substitution for a hypocritically concealed, an openly legalised community of women. For the rest, it is self-evident that the abolition of the present system of production must bring with it the abolition of the community of women springing from that system, i.e., of prostitution both public and private.

The Communists are further reproached with desiring to abolish countries and nationality.

The working men have no country. We cannot take from them what they have not got. Since the proletariat must first of all acquire political supremacy, must rise to be the leading class of the nation, must constitute itself the nation, it is so far, itself national, though not in the bourgeois sense of the word.

National differences and antagonism between peoples are daily more and more vanishing, owing to the development of the bourgeoisie, to freedom of commerce, to the world market, to uniformity in the mode of production and in the conditions of life corresponding thereto.

The supremacy of the proletariat will cause them to vanish still faster. United action, of the leading civilised countries at least, is one of the first conditions for the emancipation of the proletariat.

In proportion as the exploitation of one individual by another will also be put an end to, the exploitation of one nation by another will also be put an end to. In proportion as the antagonism between classes within the nation vanishes, the hostility of one nation to another will come to an end.

The charges against Communism made from a religious, a philosophical and, generally, from an ideological standpoint, are not deserving of serious examination.

Does it require deep intuition to comprehend that man's ideas, views, and conception, in one word, man's consciousness, changes with every change in the conditions of his material existence, in his social relations and in his social life?

What else does the history of ideas prove, than that intellectual production changes its character in proportion as material production is changed? The ruling ideas of each age have ever been the ideas of its ruling class.

When people speak of the ideas that revolutionise society, they do but express that fact that within the old society the elements of a new one have been created, and that the dissolution of the old ideas keeps even pace with the dissolution of the old conditions of existence.

When the ancient world was in its last throes, the ancient religions were overcome by Christianity. When Christian ideas succumbed in the 18th century to rationalist ideas, feudal society fought its death battle with the then revolutionary bourgeoisie. The ideas of religious liberty and freedom of conscience merely gave expression to the sway of free competition within the domain of knowledge.

"Undoubtedly," it will be said, "religious, moral, philosophical, and juridical ideas have been modified in the course of historical development. But religion, morality, philosophy, political science, and law, constantly survived this change."

"There are, besides, eternal truths, such as Freedom, Justice, etc., that are common to all states of society. But Communism abolishes eternal truths, it abolishes all religion, and all morality, instead of constituting them on a new basis; it therefore acts in contradiction to all past historical experience."

What does this accusation reduce itself to? The history of all past society has consisted in the development of class antagonisms, antagonisms that assumed different forms at different epochs.

But whatever form they may have taken, one fact is common to all past ages, viz., the exploitation of one part of society by the other. No wonder, then, that the social consciousness of past ages, despite all the multiplicity and variety it displays, moves within certain common forms, or general ideas, which cannot completely vanish except with the total disappearance of class antagonisms.

The Communist revolution is the most radical rupture with traditional relations; no wonder that its development involved the most radical rupture with traditional ideas.

But let us have done with the bourgeois objections to Communism.

We have seen above, that the first step in the revolution by the working class is to raise the proletariat to the position of ruling class to win the battle of democracy.

The proletariat will use its political supremacy to wrest, by degree, all capital from the bourgeoisie, to centralise all instruments of production in the hands of the State, i.e., of the proletariat organised as the ruling class; and to increase the total productive forces as rapidly as possible.

Of course, in the beginning, this cannot be effected except by means of despotic inroads on the rights of property, and on the conditions of bourgeois production; by means of measures, therefore, which appear economically insufficient and untenable, but which, in the course of the movement, outstrip themselves, necessitate further inroads upon the old social order, and are unavoidable as a means of entirely revolutionising the mode of production.

These measures will, of course, be different in different countries.

Nevertheless, in most advanced countries, the following will be pretty generally applicable:

1. Abolition of property in land and application of all rents of land to public purposes.
2. A heavy progressive or graduated income tax.
3. Abolition of all rights of inheritance.

4. Confiscation of the property of all emigrants and rebels.
5. Centralisation of credit in the banks of the state, by means of a national bank with State capital and an exclusive monopoly.
6. Centralisation of the means of communication and transport in the hands of the State.
7. Extension of factories and instruments of production owned by the State; the bringing into cultivation of waste-lands, and the improvement of the soil generally in accordance with a common plan.
8. Equal liability of all to work. Establishment of industrial armies, especially for agriculture.
9. Combination of agriculture with manufacturing industries; gradual abolition of all the distinction between town and country by a more equable distribution of the populace over the country.
10. Free education for all children in public schools. Abolition of children's factory labour in its present form. Combination of education with industrial production, &c, &c.

When, in the course of development, class distinctions have disappeared, and all production has been concentrated in the hands of a vast association of the whole nation, the public power will lose its political character. Political power, properly so called, is merely the organised power of one class for oppressing another. If the proletariat during its contest with the bourgeoisie is compelled, by the force of circumstances, to organise itself as a class, if, by means of a revolution, it makes itself the ruling class, and, as such, sweeps away by force the old conditions of production, then it will, along with these conditions, have swept away the conditions for the existence of class antagonisms and of classes generally, and will thereby have abolished its own supremacy as a class.

In place of the old bourgeois society, with its classes and class antagonisms, we shall have an association, in which the free development of each is the condition for the free development of all.

POSITION OF THE COMMUNISTS IN RELATION TO THE VARIOUS EXISTING OPPOSITION PARTIES

The Communists fight for the attainment of the immediate aims, for the enforcement of the momentary interests of the working class; but in the movement of the present, they also represent and take care of the future of that movement. In France, the Communists ally with the Social-Democrats[6] against the conservative and radical bourgeoisie, reserving, however, the right to take up a critical position in regard to phases and illusions traditionally handed down from the great Revolution.

In Switzerland, they support the Radicals, without losing sight of the fact that this party consists of antagonistic elements, partly of Democratic Socialists, in the French sense, partly of radical bourgeois.

In Poland, they support the party that insists on an agrarian revolution as the prime condition for national emancipation, that party which fomented the insurrection of Cracow in 1846.

In Germany, they fight with the bourgeoisie whenever it acts in a revolutionary way, against the absolute monarchy, the feudal squirearchy, and the petty bourgeoisie.

But they never cease, for a single instant, to instill into the working class the clearest possible recognition of the hostile antagonism between bourgeoisie and proletariat, in order that the German workers may straightway use, as so many weapons against the bourgeoisie, the social and political conditions that the bourgeoisie must necessarily introduce along with its supremacy, and in order that, after the fall of the reactionary classes in Germany, the fight against the bourgeoisie itself may immediately begin.

The Communists turn their attention chiefly to Germany, because that country is on the eve of a bourgeois revolution that is bound to be carried out under more advanced conditions of European civilisation and with a much more developed proletariat than that of England was in the seventeenth, and France in the eighteenth century, and because the bourgeois revolution in Germany will be but the prelude to an immediately following proletarian revolution.

In short, the Communists everywhere support every revolutionary movement against the existing social and political order of things.

In all these movements, they bring to the front, as the leading question in each, the property question, no matter what its degree of development at the time.

---

6   The party then represented in Parliament by Ledru-Rollin, in literature by Louis Blanc, in the daily press by the Réforme. The name of Social-Democracy signifies, with these its inventors, a section of the Democratic or Republican Party more or less tinged with socialism. [Engels, English Edition 1888]

Finally, they labour everywhere for the union and agreement of the democratic parties of all countries.

The Communists disdain to conceal their views and aims. They openly declare that their ends can be attained only by the forcible overthrow of all existing social conditions. Let the ruling classes tremble at a Communistic revolution. The proletarians have nothing to lose but their chains. They have a world to win.

WORKING MEN OF ALL COUNTRIES, UNITE!

D. STANLEY EITZEN

1944-

"THE FRAGMENTATION OF SOCIAL LIFE: SOME CRITICAL SOCIETAL CONCERNS FOR THE NEW MILLENNIUM"

2000

David Stanley Eitzen is an American sociologist specializing in the study of social stratification, the sociology of sports, social problems, and social welfare policies. A professor emeritus of sociology at Colorado State University, his scholarly output is prodigious: 11 books, 13 edited volumes of readings, 105 articles (many of which have been reprinted in numerous collections), and 49 book chapters.

Eitzen studied history as an undergraduate at Bethel College in North Newton, Kansas, and then went on to pursue a Master's degree in social science at Emporia State University. He earned a doctorate in sociology at the University of Kansas in 1968, having received a Master's in sociology from the same institution two years earlier.

Editor of *The Social Science Journal* from 1978 to 1984, Eitzen currently serves as associate editor or as a member of the editorial board for eleven scholarly journals. A former president of the North American Society for the Sociology of Sport and a 1996 Sports Ethics Fellow of the Institute for International Sport, he was inducted into the Council of Fellows of the Text and Academic Authors Association in 2001 and received the Bethel College Distinguished Achievement Award in 1992.

Among Eitzen's impressive list of books may be found the following titles: *Where the Welfare State Works, They Are Still Among Us: the*

Normalization of Homelessness in America, Fair and Foul: Beyond the Myths and Paradoxes of Sport, Diversity in Families, Social Problems, Criminology: Crime and Criminal Justice, Social Inequality: Social Class and Its Consequences, Globalization: The Transformation of Social Worlds, Experiencing Poverty: Voices from the Bottom, and *Sport in Contemporary Society.*

For much of his work, Eitzen adopts a structural functionalist approach to the study of social phenomena, arguing that social problems and structures are products of, and influenced by, the ebb and flow of larger societal forces. This perspective suggests, for example, that poverty, school violence and even changes in family structure are a function of, say, cultural values, technology and economic circumstances. In his own words (Eitzen, 1990, 477)

> [A]s a social scientist I embrace a theoretical perspective that focuses on the system as the source of social problems. However, I do recognize that while human actors are subject to powerful social forces, they make choices and must be held accountable for those choices. But I also believe that it is imperative that we understand the social factors that influence behavior and propel a disproportionate number of children in certain social categories to act in deviant ways.

As you read this selection, think about the long-term consequences of increasing social fragmentation and evaluate the concerns raised by the author. To what degree are the trends described in this essay consistent with the predictions made by Marx? Using Eitzen's theoretical perspective (as outlined above), compare the plight of the Rudkus family in Sinclair's *The Jungle* with the experience of blacks as chronicled by Du Bois. Finally, ask yourself whether Eitzen's approach is compatible with the economic theory of human behavior, and consider the extent to which the two approaches, taken together, provide a richer explanation of social phenomena than either is capable of doing by itself.

SELECTION FROM:

Eitzen, D. (2000). The fragmentation of social life: Some critical societal concerns for the new millennium [Electronic version]. *Vital Speeches of the Day,* 66(18), 563-566.

The Fragmentation of Social Life: Some Critical Societal Concerns for the New Millennium

Vital Speeches of the Day
New York
July 1, 2000

Abstract:

For many observers of American society this is the best of times. The current economic expansion is the longest in US history. The US is the dominant player in the world both militarily and economically. But every silver lining has a cloud. While basking in unprecedented wealth and economic growth, the US has serious domestic problems. The US has the highest poverty rate and the highest child poverty rate in the Western world. I want to address another crucial problem that our society faces—the fragmentation of social life. While there are many indicators of reduced societal cohesion, I will limit my discussion to four: 1. excessive individualism 2. heightened personal isolation 3. the widening income and wealth gap; and 4. the deepening racial /ethnic/religious/sexuality divide. The challenge facing US society as we enter the new millennium is to shift from building walls to building bridges. (*Copyright City News Publishing Company Jul 1, 2000*)

Full Text:

For many observers of American society this is the best of times. The current economic expansion is the longest in U. S. history. Unemployment is the lowest in three decades. Inflation is low and under control. The stock market has risen from 3500 to over 11,000 in eight years. The number of millionaires has more than doubled in the past five years to 7.1 million. The Cold War is over. The United States is the dominant player in the world both militarily and economically. Our society, obviously, is in good shape.

But every silver lining has a cloud. While basking in unprecedented wealth and economic growth, the U.S. has serious domestic problems. Personal bankruptcies are at a record level. The U.S. has the highest poverty rate and the highest child poverty rate in the Western world. We do not have a proper safety net for the disadvantaged that other countries take for granted. Hunger and homelessness are on the rise. Among the Western nations, the U.S. has the highest murder rate as well as the highest incarceration rate. Also, we are the only Western nation without a universal health care system, leaving 44 million Americans without health insurance.

I want to address another crucial problem that our society faces—the fragmentation of social life. Throughout U.S. history, despite a civil war, and actions separating people by religion, class, and race, the nation has somehow held together. Will society continue to cohere or will new crises pull us apart? That is the question of the morning. While there are many indicators of reduced societal cohesion, I will limit my discussion to four: (1) excessive individualism; (2) heightened personal isolation; (3) the widening income and wealth gap; and (4) the deepening racial/ethnic/religious/ sexuality divide.

EXCESSIVE INDIVIDUALISM

We Americans celebrate individualism. It fits with our economic system of capitalism. We are self-reliant and responsible for our actions. We value individual freedom, including the right to choose our vocations, our mates, when and where to travel, and how to spend our money. At its extreme, the individualistic credo says that it is our duty to be selfish and in doing so, according to Adam Smith's notion of an "invisible hand," society benefits. Conservative radio commentator Rush Limbaugh said as much in his response to an initiative by President Clinton to encourage citizen volunteerism: "Citizen service is a repudiation of the principles upon which our country was based. We are here for ourselves."

While Rush Limbaugh may view rugged individualism as virtuous, I do not. It promotes inequality; it promotes the tolerance of inferior housing, schools, and services for "others"; and it encourages public policies that are punitive to the disadvantaged. For example, this emphasis on the individual has meant that, as a society, the United States has the lowest federal income tax rates in the Western world. Our politicians, especially Republicans, want to lower the rates even more so that individuals will have more and governments, with their presumed interest in the common good, will have less. As a result, the United States devotes relatively few resources to help the disadvantaged and this minimal redistribution system is shrinking.

In effect, our emphasis on individualism keeps us from feeling obligated to others.

Consider the way that we finance schools. Schools are financed primarily by the states through income taxes and local school districts through property taxes. This means that wealthy states and wealthy districts have more money to educate their children than the less advantaged states and districts. The prevailing view is that if my community or state is well-off, why should my taxes go to help children from other communities and other states?

The flaw in the individualistic credo is that we cannot go it alone—our fate depends on others. Paradoxically, it is in our individual interest to have a collective interest. We deny this at our peril for if we disregard those unlike ourselves, in fact doing violence to them, then we invite their hostility and violence, and, ultimately, a fractured society.

HEIGHTENED PERSONAL ISOLATION

There are some disturbing trends that indicate a growing isolation as individuals become increasingly isolated from their neighbors, their co-workers, and even their family members. To begin, because of computers and telecommunications there is a growing trend for workers to work at home. While home-based work allows flexibility and independence not found in most jobs, these workers are separated from social networks. Aside from not realizing the social benefits of personal interaction with colleagues, working from home means being cut off from pooled information and the collective power that might result in higher pay and better fringe benefits.

Our neighborhoods, too, are changing in ways that promote isolation. A recent study indicates that one in three Americans has never spent an evening with a neighbor. This isolation from neighbors is exacerbated in the suburbs. Not only do some people live in gated communities to physically wall themselves off from "others" but they wall themselves off from their neighbors behaviorally and symbolically within gated and non-gated neighborhoods alike. Some people exercise on motorized treadmills and other home exercise equipment instead of running through their neighborhoods. Rather than walking to the corner grocery or nearby shop and visiting with the clerks and neighbors, suburbanites have to drive somewhere away from their immediate neighborhood to shop among strangers. Or they may not leave their home at all, shopping and banking by computer. Sociologist Philip Slater says that "a community life exists when one can go daily to a given location at a given time and see many of the people one knows." Suburban neighborhoods in particular are devoid of such meeting places for adults and children. For suburban teenagers almost everything is away—practice fields, music lessons, friends, jobs, school, and the malls. Thus, a disconnect from those nearby. For adults many go through their routines without sharing stories, gossip, and analyses of events with friends on a regular basis at a coffee shop, neighborhood tavern, or at the local grain elevator.

Technology also encourages isolation. There was a major shift toward isolation with the advent of television as people spent more and more time within their homes rather than socializing with friends and neighbors. Now, we are undergoing a communications revolution that creates the illusion of intimacy but the reality is much different. Curt Suplee, science and technology writer for the Washington Post, says that we have seen "tenfold increases in 'communication' by electronic means, and tenfold reductions in person-to-person contact." In effect, as we are increasingly isolated before a computer screen, we risk what Warren Christopher has called "social malnutrition." John L. Locke, a professor communications argues in The De-Voicing of Society that e-mail, voice mail, fax machines, beepers, and Internet chat rooms are robbing us of ordinary social talking. Talking, he says, like the grooming of apes and monkeys, is the way we build and maintain social relationships. In his view, it is only through intimate conversation that we can know others well enough to trust them and work with them harmoniously. In effect, Locke argues that we are becoming an autistic society, communicating messages electronically but without really connecting. Paradoxically, then, these incredible communication devices that combine to connect us in so many dazzling ways also separate us increasingly from intimate relationships.

Fragmentation is also occurring within many families, where the members are increasingly disconnected from each other. Many parents are either absent altogether or too self-absorbed to pay very much attention to their children or each other. On average, parents today spend 22 fewer hours a week with their children than parents did in the 1960s. Although living in the same house, parents or children may tune out each other by engaging in solitary activities. A survey by the Kaiser Family Foundation found that the average child between 2 and 18, spends 5 and one-half hours a day alone watching television, at a computer, playing video games, on the Internet, or reading. Many families rarely eat together in an actual sit-down meal. All too often material things are substituted for love and attention. Some children even have their own rooms equipped with a telephone, television, VCR, microwave, refrigerator, and computer, which while convenient, isolates them from other family members. Such homes may be full of people but they are really empty.

The consequences of this accelerating isolation of individuals are dire. More and more individuals are lonely, bitter, alienated, gnomic, and disconnected. This situation is conducive to alcohol and drug abuse, depression, anxiety, and violence. The lonely and disaffected are ripe candidates for membership in cults, gangs, and militias where they find a sense of belonging and a cause to believe in but in the process they may become more paranoid and, perhaps, even become willing terrorists. At a less extreme level, the alienated will disengage from society by shunning voluntary associations, by home schooling their children, and by not participating in elections. In short, they will become increasingly individualistic, which compounds their problem and society's problem with unity.

THE WIDENING INEQUALITY GAP

There is an increasing gap between the rich and, the rest of us, especially between the rich and the poor. Data from 1998 show that there were at least 268 billionaires in the United States, while 35 million were below the government's official poverty line.

Timothy Koogle, CEO of Yahoo made $4.7 million a day in 1999, while the median household income in that year was $110 a day. Bill Gates, CEO of Microsoft is richer than Koogle by far. He is worth, depending on stock market on a given day, around $90 billion or so. Together, eight Americans—Microsoft billionaires Bill Gates, Paul Allen, and Steve Ballmer plus the five Wal-Mart heirs—have a net worth of $233 billion, which is more than the gross domestic product of the very prosperous nation of Sweden. The Congressional Budget Office reports that in 1999, the richest 2.7 million Americans, the top 1 percent of the population, had as many after tax dollars to spend as the bottom 100 million put together.

Compared to the other developed nations, the chasm between the rich and the poor in the U.S. is the widest and it is increasing. In 1979, average family income in the top 5 percent of the earnings distribution was 10 times that in the bottom 20 percent. Ten years later it had increased to 16:1, and in 1999 it was 19:1, the biggest gap since the Census Bureau began keeping track in 1947.

The average salary of a CEO in 1999 was 419 times the pay of a typical factory worker. In 1980 the difference was only 42 times as much. This inequality gap in the United States, as measured by the difference in pay between CEOs and workers, is by far the highest in the industrialized world. While ours stands at 419 to 1, the ratio in Japan is 25 to 1, and in France and Germany it is 35 to 1.

At the bottom end of wealth and income, about 35 million Americans live below the government's official poverty line. One out of four of those in poverty are children under the age of 18. Poor Americans are worse off than the poor in other western democracies. The safety net here is weak and getting weaker. We do not have universal health insurance. Funds for Head Start are so inadequate that only one in three poor children who are eligible actually are enrolled in the program. Welfare for single mothers is being abolished, resulting in many impoverished but working mothers being less well-off because their low-wage work is not enough to pay for child care, health care, housing costs, and other living expenses. Although the economy is soaring, a survey of 26 cities released by the U.S. Conference on Mayors shows that the numbers of homeless and hungry in the cities have risen for 15 consecutive years. The demand for emergency food is the highest since 1992 and the demand for emergency shelter is the largest since 1994. According to the U.S. Department of Agriculture, there were about 36 million, including 14 million children living in households afflicted with what they call "food insecurity," which is a euphemism for hunger.

Of the many reasons for the increase in homelessness and hunger amidst increasing affluence, three are crucial. First, the government's welfare system has been shrinking since the Reagan administration with the support of both Republicans and Democrats. Second, the cost of housing has risen dramatically causing many of the poor to spend over 50 percent of their meager incomes for rent. And, third, charitable giving has not filled the void, with less than 10 percent of contributions actually going to programs that help the poor. In effect, 90 percent of philanthropy is funneled to support the institutions of the already advantaged—churches (some of which trickles down to the poor), hospitals, colleges, museums, libraries, orchestras, and the arts.

The data on inequality show clearly, I believe, that we are moving toward a two-tiered society. Rather than "a rising tide lifting all boats," the justification for capitalism as postulated by President John Kennedy, the evidence is that "a rising tide lifts only the yachts." The increasing gap between the haves and the have-nots has crucial implications for our society. First, it divides people in the "deserving" and the "undeserving." If people are undeserving, then we are justified in not providing them with a safety net. As economist James K. Galbraith says: "A high degree of inequality causes the comfortable to disavow the needy. It increases the psychological distance separating these groups, making it easier to imagine that defects of character or differences of culture, rather than an unpleasant turn in the larger schemes of economic history, lie behind the separation." Since politicians represent the monied interests, the wealthy get their way as seen in the continuing decline in welfare programs for the poor and the demise of affirmative action. Most telling, the inequality gap is not part of the political debate in this, or any other, election cycle.

A second implication is that the larger the gap, the more destabilized society becomes.

In this regard economist Lester Thurow asks: "How much inequality can a democracy take? The income gap in America is eroding the social contract. If the promise of a higher standard of living is limited to a few at the top, the rest of the citizenry, as history shows, is likely to grow disaffected, or worse." Former Secretary of Labor, Robert Reich, has put it this way: "At some point, if the trends are not reversed, we cease being a society at all. The stability of the country eventually is threatened. No country can endure a massive gap between people at the top and people at the bottom." (Or, as economist Galbraith puts it: "[Equality] is now so wide it threatens, as it did in the Great Depression, the social stability of the country. It has come to undermine our sense of ourselves as a nation of equals. Economic inequality, in this way, challenges the essential unifying myth of American national life."

THE DEEPENING RACIAL/ETHNIC/ RELIGIOUS/ SEXUALITY DIVIDE

The United States has always struggled with diversity. American history is stained by the enslavement of Africans and later the segregated and unequal "Jim Crow" south, the aggression toward native peoples based on the belief in "Manifest Destiny," the internment of Japanese Americans during World War II, episodes of intolerance against religious minorities, gays and lesbians, and immigrants. In each instance, the majority was not only intolerant of those labeled as "others," but they also used the law, religious doctrine, and other institutional forms of discrimination to keep minorities separate and unequal. Despite these ongoing societal wrongs against minorities, there has been progress culminating in the civil rights battles and victories of the 1950s, 1960s, and early 1970s.

But the civil rights gains of the previous generation are in jeopardy as U.S. society becomes more diverse. Currently, the racial composition of the U.S. is 72 percent white and 28 percent nonwhite. In 50 years it will be 50 percent nonwhite. The racial landscape is being transformed as approximately 1 million immigrants annually set up permanent residence in the United States and another 300,000 enter illegally and stay. These new residents are primarily Latino and Asian, not European as was the case of earlier waves of immigration. This "browning of America" has important implications including increased division.

An indicator of fragmentation along racial lines is the "White flight" from high immigration areas, which may lead to what demographer William Frey as called the "Balkanization of America." The trends toward gated neighborhoods, the rise of private schools and home schooling are manifestations of exclusiveness rather than inclusiveness and perhaps they are precursors to this "Balkanization."

Recent state and federal legislation has been aimed at reducing or limiting the civil rights gains of the 1970s. For example, In 1994 California passed Proposition 187 by a 3—to 2—popular vote margin, thereby denying public welfare to undocumented immigrants. Congress in 1996 voted to deny most federal benefits to legal immigrants who were not citizens. A number of states have made English the official state language. In 1997 California passed Proposition 209, which eliminated affirmative action (a policy aimed at leveling the playing field so that minorities would have a fair chance to succeed). Across the nation, Congress and various state legislatures, most recently Florida, have taken measures to weaken or eliminate affirmative action programs.

Without question racial and ethnic minorities in the U. S. are the targets of personal prejudicial acts as well as pervasive institutional racism. What will the situation be like by 2050 when the numbers of Latinos triple from their present population of 31.4 million, and the Asian population more than triples from the current 10.9 million, and the African-American population increases 70 percent from their base of 34.9 million now?

Along with increasing racial and ethnic diversity, there is a greater variety of religious belief. Although Christians are the clear majority in the United States, there are also about 7 million Jews, 6 million Muslims (there are more Muslims than Presbyterians), and millions of other non-Christians, including Buddhists, and Hindus, as well as atheists.

While religion often promotes group integration, it also divides. Religious groups tend to emphasize separateness and superiority, thereby defining "others" as infidels, heathens, heretics, or nonbelievers. Strongly held religious ideas sometimes split groups within a denomination or congregation. Progressives and fundamentalists within the same religious tradition have difficulty finding common ground on various issues, resulting in division. This has always been the case to some degree, but this tendency seems to be accelerating now. Not only are there clashes within local congregations and denominational conferences but they spill out into political debates in legislatures and in local elections, most notably school board elections, as religious factions often push their narrow, divisive sectarian policies. These challenges to religious pluralism are increasing, thus promoting fragmentation rather than unity.

There is also widespread intolerance of and discrimination toward those whose sexual orientation differs from the majority. The behaviors of gay men and lesbian women are defined and stigmatized by many members of society as sinful; their activities are judged by the courts as illegal; and their jobs and advancement within those jobs are often restricted because of their being different sexually. As more and more homosexuals become public with their sexuality, their presence and their political agenda are viewed as ever more threatening and must be stopped.

My point is this: diversity and ever increasing diversity are facts of life in our society. If we do not find ways to accept the differences among us, we will fragment into class, race, ethnic, and sexual enclaves.

Two social scientists, John A. Hall and Charles Lindholm, in a recent book entitled *Is America Breaking Apart?* argue that throughout American history there has been remarkable societal unity because of its historically conditioned institutional patterns and shared cultural values. Columnist George Will picked up on this theme in a Newsweek essay, postulating that while the U. S. has pockets of problems, "American society is an amazing machine for homogenizing people." That has been the case but will this machine continue to pull us together? I believe, to the contrary, that while the U.S. historically has overcome great obstacles, a number of trends in contemporary society have enormous potential for pulling us apart. Our society is moving toward a two-tiered society with the gap between the haves and the have-nots, a withering bond among those of different social classes, and a growing racial, ethnic, and sexuality divide. The critical question is whether the integrative societal mechanisms that have served us well in the past will save us again or whether we will continue to fragment?

The challenge facing U. S. society as we enter the new millennium is to shift from building walls to building bridges. As our society is becoming more and more diverse, will Americans feel empathy for, and make sacrifices on behalf of, a wide variety of people who they define as different? The answer to this crucial question is negative at the present time. Social justice seems to be an outmoded concept in our individualistic society.

I shall close with a moral argument posed by one of the greatest social thinkers and social activists of the 20th century, the late Michael Harrington. Harrington, borrowing from philosopher John Rawls, provides an intuitive definition of a justice. A just society is when I describe it to you and you accept it even if you do not know your place in it. Harrington then asks (I'm paraphrasing here): would you accept a society of 275 million where 44 million people do not have health insurance, where 35 million live in poverty including one-fifth of all children? Would you accept a society as just where discrimination against minorities is commonplace, even by the normal way society works? Would you accept a society where a sizable number of people live blighted lives in neighborhoods with a high concentration of poverty, with inferior schools, with too few good jobs? You'd be crazy to accept such a society but that is what we have. Harrington concludes: "If in your mind you could not accept a society in which we do unto you as we do unto them, then isn't it time for us to change the way we are acting towards them who are a part of us?" If, however, we accept an unjust society, then our society will move inexorably toward a divided and fortress society.

SOURCES

Abrams, F. W. (1951, May). Management's Responsibilities in a Complex World, *Harvard Business Review*, Vol. XXIX, 3, 29-34.

Biography of Kingsley Davis and Obituary. (2005, January 08). *American Sociological Association*, Retrieved 1/2008 http://www2.asanet.org/governance/davis.html.

Biography of Wilbert Ellis Moore and Obituary. (2005, January 08). *American Sociological Association.* Retrieved January 2008 from http://www2.asanet.org/governance/moore.html.

Biography of Milton Friedman. (2008). *The Concise Encyclopedia of Economics.* Library of Economics and Liberty. Retrieved January 2008 from http://www.econlib.org/library/Enc/bios/Friedman.html.

Bluestone, B. (1995). *The Polarization of American Society: Victims, Suspects, and Mysteries to Unravel,* New York: Twentieth Century Fund Press.

Breit, W. and Ransom, R. L. (1971). *The Academic Scribblers: American Economists in Collision,* Austin, Texas: Holt, Rinehart and Winston, Inc.

Breit, W. and Spencer, G. W. (1990). *Lives of the Laureates: Ten Nobel Economists,* 2nd edition. Cambridge, MA: The MIT Press.

Buchholz, T. G. (2007). *New Ideas from Dead Economists: An Introduction to Modern Economic Thought,* New York: Plume.

Cohen, J. M. "Introduction," in Rousseau, Jean-Jacques. The Confessions. 1953. J. M. Cohen, Translation. Penguin Books, Ltd., Middlesex, England.

Compa, L. (2004). *Blood, Sweat, and Fear: Workers' Rights in U.S. Meat and Poultry Plants,* New York, N.Y.: Human Rights Watch.

Delaney, J. J. Jean-Jacques Rousseau. (2006). *Internet Encyclopedia of Philosophy,* Accessed at http://www.iep.utm.edu/r/rousseau.htm.

Den, U., Rasmussen, D. J. and Rasmussen, D. B. (Eds). (1986). *The Philosophic Thought of Ayn Rand*. Chicago, IL: University of Illinois Press.

Donaldson, T. and Preston, L. E. (1995). The Stakeholder Theory of the Corporation: Concepts, Evidence, and Implications. *Academy of Management Review*, Vol. 20, No. 1, 65-91.

Engels, F. Letters of Marx and Engels, (1845, March 17); Engels to Marx in Brussels; Barmen. Accessed June 30, 2007 at http://www.marxists. org/archive/marx/works/1845/letters/45_03_17.htm.

Eitzen, D. S. (2003, December 15). Avoiding Trends that Deprive Us of Humanity. *Vital Speeches of the Day, 70*, Issue 5. 42-46.

Eitzen, D. S. (1996, June 15). Dismantling the Welfare State. *Vital Speeches of the Day, 62*, Issue 17. 532-536.

Eitzen, D. S. (1993, March 1). National Security. *Vital Speeches of the Day, 59*, Issue 10. 315-316.

Eitzen, D. S. (1990, May 15). Problem Students. *Vital Speeches of the Day. 56*, Issue 15. 476-480.

Freeman, R. E. (1984). *Strategic Management: A stakeholder approach*. Boston: Pitman.

Furtak, R. A. (2005). Henry David Thoreau. *Stanford Encyclopedia of Philosophy*, Accessed January 5, 2008 at http://plato.stanford. edu/entries/thoreau/.

Gates, H. L., Jr. (1989). Introduction, *The Souls of Black Folk*. New York: Bantam Books.

Greenspan, A. (2007, January 29). On Milton Friedman. Letter. Milton Friedman Memorial Service, accessed 12/11/07 at http://www.cme. com/files/greenspan_on_friedman.pdf.

Haakonssen, K. (Ed). (2006). *The Cambridge Companion to Adam Smith*. New York, New York: Cambridge University Press.

Hacker, A. (1992). *Two Nations: Black and White, Separate, Hostile, Unequal*. New York: Charles Scribner's Sons.

Hare, N. (1969). W. E. Burghardt Du Bois: An Appreciation. *The Souls of Black Folk*. New York: New American Library.

Harris, F. R. and Curtis, L. A. (1998). *The Millennium Breach: The American Dilemma, Richer and Poorer*, 2nd Ed. The Milton S. Eisenhower Foundation. Retrieved December 2, 2007 at http://www. eisenhowerfoundation.org/frames/main_frameMB.html.

Hauhart, R. C. (2003, December). The Davis-Moore Theory of Stratification: The Life Course of a Socially Constructed Classic. *The American Sociologist, 34*, No. 4, 5-24.

Heer, D. M. (2005). *Kingsley Davis: A Biography and Selections from His Writings*. Edison, N. J.: Transaction Publishers.

Heilbroner, R. L. (1980). *Marxism: For and Against*. New York: Norton.

Heilbroner, R. L. (1992). *The Worldly Philosophers: The Lives, Times and Ideas of the Great Economic Thinkers*. 6th Ed. New York, N.Y.: Simon & Schuster, Inc.

Heilbroner, R. L. (1996). *Teachings from the Worldly Philosophy*. NY: Norton.

Henderson, D. R. (2002). Biography of Jeremy Bentham. *The Concise Encyclopedia of Economics*, Accessed November 19, 2007 at http://www.econlib.org/library/Enc/bios/Bentham.html.

Heydt, C. (2006). "John Stuart Mill: Overview," *The Internet Encyclopedia of Philosophy*. Accessed December 28, 2007 from http://www.iep.utm.edu/.

Hynes, G. C. (2004). A Biographical Sketch of W.E.B. DuBois. W.E.B. DuBois Learning Center, Accessed June 6, 2007 at http://www.duboislc.org/html/DuBoisBio.html.

Jacoby, R. (1951). Afterward. *White Collar: The American Middle Classes*, New York: Oxford University Press.

MacDonald, J. M., Ollinger, M. E. Nelson, K. E., and Handy, C. R. (1999, March). *Consolidation in U.S. Meatpacking*, Agricultural Economics Report No. 785, Economic Research Service, Washington, D.C.: U. S. Department of Agriculture.

McLaughlin, M. (2007, January). Signs of the Times: The US Catholic Bishops' Pastoral Letter on the Economy—An Unfinished Agenda? *Center Focus*, Issue 172. Retrieved November 4, 2007 at http://coc.org/index.fpl/1090/article/10604.html.

Merton, R. K. (1957). *Social Theory and Social Structure*. Glencoe, IL: Free Press.

Mills, C. W. (1953). Introduction. *The Theory of the Leisure Class*. New York: New American Library.

Mill, John Stuart. (1909). Autobiography. In *The Harvard Classics*, C.W. Eliot (Ed.). New York: P.F. Collier & Son, *25*, 7-192.

Milton Friedman's Bio. (nd). Milton and Rose D. Friedman Foundation, accessed 12/11/07 at http://www.friedmanfoundation.org/friedman/friedmans/friedmansbio.jsp.

Moore, J. B. (1932). Thoreau Rejects Emerson. *American Literature*, *4*, No. 3, 241-256. Accessed January 5, 2008 at http://links.jstor.org/.

Muller, J. Z. (1995). *Adam Smith in His Times and Ours: Designing the Decent Society*. Princeton, N.J.: Princeton University Press.

Nicoll, I. (2007, November 6). Jeremy Bentham. Bentham Project, University College London. Accessed November 18, 07 at http://www.ucl.ac.uk/Bentham-Project/info/jb.htm.

Nocera, J. (1986, January). Making capitalism moral—Catholic bishops' pastoral letter. *Washington Monthly.* Accessed May 24, 2007 at http://findarticles.com/p/articles/mi_m1316/is_v17/ai_3916864.

Office for Social Justice, Archdiocese of St. Paul/Minneapolis. Answers to 25 Questions About Catholic Social Teaching. Accessed June 15, 2007 at http://www.osjspm.org/25questons.aspx.

Pampel, F. C. (2007). *Sociological Lives and Ideas: An Introduction to the Classical Theorists,* 2nd edition, New York: Worth Publishers.

Peikoff, L. (1993). *Objectivism: The Philosophy of Ayn Rand.* New York, NY: Meridian.

Pizzigati, S. (2004). *Greed and Good: Understanding and Overcoming the Inequality that Limits Our Lives,* New York, New York: The Apex Press.

Porter, M. E. and Kramer, M. R. (2006, December). Strategy and Society: The Link Between Competitive Advantage and Corporate Social Responsibility, *Harvard Business Review*, 78-92.

Poussaint, A. F. (1969). The Souls of Black Folk: A Critique. In *The Souls of Black Folk.* New York: New American Library.

Rand, A. (1961). *For the New Intellectual: The Philosophy of Ayn Rand.* New York: Random House.

Rand, A. (1947, October 20). Testimony before the House Un-American Activities Committee. Accessed May 10, 2007 at www.cnn.com/SPECIALS/cold.war/episodes/06/documents/huac/rand.html.

Rawls, J. (1971). *A Theory of Justice*, Cambridge, MA: Harvard University Press.

Reddy, S. (2006, November 21). Processing Plants' Dangers Don't Scare Off Migrants. *The Dallas Morning News.* Dallas, Texas. The Dallas Morning News, Inc.

Reich, R. (1996). Pink Slips, Profits, and Paychecks: Corporate Citizenship in an Era of Smaller Government. Accessed December 16, 2007 at http://www.dol.gov/oasam/programs/history/reich/speeches/sp960206.htm.

Report of the National Advisory Commission on Civil Disorders. (1968). New York: Bantam Books.

Ritter, A. and Bondanella, J.C., (Eds). (1988). *Rousseau's Political Writings.* New York: W. W. Norton & Company.

Ritzer, G. (1992). *Classical Sociological Theory.* New York, NY: McGraw-Hill.

Rousseau, J. J. *The Confessions.* (1953). J. M. Cohen, Translation. Middlesex, England: Penguin Books, Ltd.

Rousseau, J.J. *Discourse on the Arts and Sciences.* (1750). Ian Johnston, Translation. Accessed January 2007 at http://www.mala. bc.ca/~johnstoi/rousseau/firstdiscourse.htm.

Schlosser, E. (2002). *Fast Food Nation: The Dark Side of the All-American Meal,* New York, N.Y.: Harper Collins.

Schneider, R. J. (2006). Thoreau's Life. Accessed January 9, 2008 at http://209.200.116.65/_news_abouthdt.htm.

Silk, L. (1976). *The Economists.* New York: Basic Books.

Silk, L. (1984). *Economics in the Real World: How Political Decisions Affect the Economy,* New York, N.Y.: Simon and Schuster.

Smith, A. (2004). *The Theory of Moral Sentiments.* New York, N.Y.: Barnes & Noble Publishing, Inc.

Smith, M. K. (1999). C. Wright Mills: Private Troubles and Public Issues. Accessed on February 18, 2008 at http://www.infed. org/thinkers/wright_mills.htm.

Sweet, W. (2006). Jeremy Bentham (1748-1832). The Internet Encyclopedia of Philosophy. Accessed December 30, 2007 at http://www.iep.utm.edu/b/bentham.htm.

The American Academy of Achievement. (1976). Biography of Milton Friedman. Accessed December 11, 07 at http://www.achievement. org/autodoc/page/fri0int-1.

The Economist (1992, September 11). Corporate Governance Special Section, 52-62.

Thernstrom, S., Siegel, F., and Woodson, R., Sr. (1998, June 24). The Kerner Commission Report and the Failed Legacy of Liberal Social Policy. Heritage Lecture #619, The Heritage Foundation, Accessed June 13, 2007 at http://www.heritage.org/Research/ PoliticalPhilosophy/hl619.cfm.

Thoreau, H. D. (1929). *A Week on the Concord and Merrimack Rivers and Walden.* Boston and New York: Houghton Mifflin Company, The Riverside Press.

Toffler, A. (1964, March). *Playboy's Interview with Ayn Rand. Playboy,* No. 123. Accessed June 3 2007 at http://ellensplace.net/ar_pboy.html.

Weiss, A. R (1995). Cracks in the foundation of stakeholder theory. *Electronic Journal of Radical Organization Theory, 1* No.1.

Witherell, E. and Dubrulle, E. (1995). Reflections on Walden. Accessed January 5, 2008 at http://www.library.ucsb.edu/thoreau/ thoreau_walden.html.

Wogaman, J. P. (1986). *Economics and Ethics: A Christian Inquiry.* Philadelphia, PA: Fortress Press.

Zimmer, B. (2007, January 29). Comments at the Milton Friedman Memorial Service. Accessed May 20, 2008 at http://www-news.uchicago.edu/releases/07/video/070129.friedman.memorial-512k.mov.

INDEX

A

agriculture, 62, 79, 126, 176, 203, 204, 266, 339, 353, 363

American Revolution, 162

approbation, 25, 27, 32, 35, 40, 46, 192

Athens, 11

B

Banfield, Edward, 17

barter, 50, 51, 52, 56

beggar, 51, 156

Bentham, Jeremy, 5, 16, 19, 21, 22, 23, 36, 37, 170, 219, 371, 372, 373

Benthamite, 36, 38

Bill of Rights, 85

Black Belt, 259, 260, 262, 264, 265, 266, 267, 268, 273

Blacks, 87, 104, 113, 114, 173, 236, 247, 255, 256, 257, 258, 259, 260, 261, 262, 263, 264, 265, 266, 267, 268, 269, 270, 271, 273, 277, 278, 279, 280, 281, 282, 283, 284, 285, 286, 287, 288, 289, 290, 292, 293, 294, 295, 296, 297, 298, 299, 300, 301, 302, 303, 306, 307, 309, 312, 313, 314, 315, 318, 319, 320, 321, 324, 325, 326, 327, 328, 329

Blackstone, William, 21

blue-collar jobs, 325, 328

Boileau, Donald, 11

bourgeoisie, 333, 334, 335, 336, 337, 338, 339, 340, 341, 342, 343, 344, 345, 346, 348, 349, 350, 351, 352, 353, 354

Brookings Institution, 81, 95

business, 16, 18, 30, 33, 48, 51, 66, 74, 86, 111, 119, 158, 159, 160, 161, 164, 166, 167, 168, 172, 177, 178, 189, 211, 261, 268, 312, 322, 328, 331

C

Canada, 170

capital, 58, 59, 60, 61, 62, 83, 84, 108, 111, 178, 227, 228, 259, 270, 271, 272, 332, 333, 336, 340, 341, 344, 345, 347, 348, 349, 352, 353

capitalism, 5, 19, 66, 67, 68, 86, 87, 92, 96, 97, 110, 145, 146, 165, 167, 233, 235, 257, 359, 363, 372